Beginning Windows Store Application Development–HTML and JavaScript Edition

Scott Isaacs
Kyle Burns

Apress®

Beginning Windows Store Application Development—HTML and JavaScript Edition

ISBN-13 (pbk): 978-1-4302-5779-0

ISBN-13 (electronic): 978-1-4302-5780-6

President and Publisher: Paul Manning
Lead Editor: Jonathan Hassell
Technical Reviewer: Gerry Heidenreich
Editorial Board: Steve Anglin, Ewan Buckingham, Gary Cornell, Louise Corrigan, Morgan Ertel, Jonathan Gennick, Jonathan Hassell, Robert Hutchinson, Michelle Lowman, James Markham, Matthew Moodie, Jeff Olson, Jeffrey Pepper, Douglas Pundick, Ben Renow-Clarke, Dominic Shakeshaft, Gwenan Spearing, Matt Wade, Tom Welsh
Coordinating Editor: Kevin Shea
Copy Editor: Michael G. Laraque
Compositor: SPi Global
Indexer: SPi Global
Artist: SPi Global
Cover Designer: Anna Ishchenko

Distributed to the book trade worldwide by Springer Science+Business Media New York, 233 Spring Street, 6th Floor, New York, NY 10013. Phone 1-800-SPRINGER, fax (201) 348-4505, e-mail orders-ny@springer-sbm.com, or visit www.springeronline.com.

For information on translations, please e-mail rights@apress.com, or visit www.apress.com.

Apress and friends of ED books may be purchased in bulk for academic, corporate, or promotional use. eBook versions and licenses are also available for most titles. For more information, reference our Special Bulk Sales–eBook Licensing web page at www.apress.com/bulk-sales.

Any source code or other supplementary materials referenced by the author in this text is available to readers at www.apress.com. For detailed information about how to locate your book's source code, go to www.apress.com/source-code.

This book is dedicated to Kelly, who has been an amazing support while I was writing this book, picking up the pieces that I dropped, and to my kids, Charlize and Brytan, who think that the coffee shop is my office. Thanks for everything. I couldn't have done this without you.

I love you guys more than anything.

—Scott

Contents at a Glance

Contents

About the Authors

Scott Isaacs is a Solutions Director with SafeNet Consulting, in the Milwaukee, Wisconsin, area. Although introduced to computers and programming in the early '80s, it wasn't until the mid-'90s that Scott realized he would rather be writing software for a living, instead of pursuing a career as a physicist or mathematician. He's worked in a number of industries, including government, news, finance, marketing, and product development, holding early positions at three successful start-ups. Additionally, Scott runs the WI .NET Users Group and plays bass guitar in his church band.

Originally from California, Scott moved to Wisconsin in 1999. Two days after his arrival, he met a girl. Kelly and Scott have been happily married since 2001 and have two amazing children, Charlize and Brytan.

You can connect with Scott at www.scottisaacs.com or www.twitter.com/daughtkom.

Kyle Burns is a technical architect with Perficient, living in Indianapolis, Indiana. He first discovered a love for writing computer applications when his father brought home their first Apple II computer and he would spend hours transcribing programs from *BASIC* magazine to see what they would do. After serving as a tuba and euphonium player in the Marine Corps Band, Kyle realized that people were writing software for pay, and he started his professional career. During his career, Kyle has worked in companies ranging from a six-person start-up to a Fortune 100 company and is constantly looking for new ways to explore solving problems with people, process, and technology.

About the Technical Reviewer

Gerry Heidenreich is a Lead Business Analyst in the legal industry with more than 15 years of wide-ranging technical experience, from collaborating directly with clients and customers to design and implementation of enterprise solutions and integration architectures. He is obsessed with the process of building simple solutions for complex problems, and software engineering has always been as much a calling as it has been a career. He is happily married to his wife and best friend, Jeanne. They are blessed with two amazing daughters, Natalie and Cora.

Acknowledgments

First, thank you. To anyone that is reading this book, thank you for taking the time and for putting your trust in me to introduce this topic to you.

I would like to thank the entire editorial staff at Apress, especially Kevin Shea and Chris Nelson, for keeping things moving and being patient with me while I learn about the book-writing process. In addition to fixing my mistakes, my technical reviewer, Gerry Heidenreich, has provided thoughtful feedback and suggestions throughout the writing process, as well as while planning the content before writing ever began. I'd also like to thank Jonathan Hassell for giving me this opportunity in the first place.

Thanks to the many family members, friends, and coworkers who have encouraged and supported me through this project. All of the baristas at my local Caribou Coffee shop have been great; they have my favorite drink ready for me by the time I reach the register.

Finally, I'd like to thank my wife, Kelly, and my kids, Charlize and Brytan. They endured months on their own, while I hid myself away to finish this book. I love them more than anything and am looking forward to hanging out with them again, now that this project is over.

—Scott Isaacs

Introduction

When I was asked a few months ago about writing a book on building applications for Windows 8 with JavaScript, my first thought was, "What can I bring to the table by writing this book?" Other authors have covered this topic, but as I reviewed a number of other books, I realized that there was a hole that I could fill by taking on this project.

I wanted to see a book that not only covered the basic technical concepts but one that would also walk a beginner through the process of building a commercial-quality, real-world application from start to finish. I wanted a book that not only presented snippets of code but one that also offered tips to improve the user experience of the reader's applications. I wanted a book that was more of a tutorial than a reference, introducing concepts that might be new to the reader, more than digging deeper into familiar topics you might find in another book. I wanted a book that you could pick up one day and be building real applications a few days later.

Beginning Windows Store Application Development—HTML and JavaScript Edition is my attempt at providing a book that I would want to read. I've learned a lot while writing this book, and I hope you learn a lot by reading it.

Who This Book Is For

This book is intended for developers who have experience building web applications with HTML, CSS, and JavaScript and are interested in using their existing skills to build applications for Windows 8. It is also a good beginner's guide for those with experience building applications for earlier versions of Windows using other technologies, such as .NET. Some coverage of HTML, CSS, and JavaScript topics is included for those with less experience, but the focus of the book is not on those technologies themselves but, instead, using those technologies to build Windows Store applications.

Throughout this book, I'll remind you that, just like building a web application, you have the freedom to follow whatever HTML, CSS, and JavaScript practices you prefer. For example, when creating page controls, which will be first illustrated in Chapter 5 but used heavily throughout the book, I've opted to keep the CSS and JavaScript file created by Visual Studio in the same directory as the HTML file. Because much of my background is as a .NET developer, this is familiar, as, by default, Visual Studio keeps ASPX and ASCX files in the same directory as the C# or VB code behind files. However, you could choose to move all JavaScript files to a js folder and all CSS files to a css folder. Additionally, you might notice that the JavaScript code that I've written isn't idiomatic JavaScript. Feel free to modify the code samples to match your coding style.

How This Book Is Structured

While you could certainly skip directly to the topics that interest you, this book was written to be read from beginning to end, with each chapter building upon the previous. In Chapters 1 through 3, you'll find an overview of Windows 8 concepts, such as the touch interface and gestures, and the Microsoft design language. In Chapters 4 through 8, I'll introduce you to working with Visual Studio, covering the various project templates available, as well as the different controls you might use in the user interface (UI) of your application.

Between Chapters 9 and 22, you'll build a fully functional, real-world application. Each chapter will cover a core concept of Windows Store application development, implemented with HTML and JavaScript. The topic of each chapter is not necessarily a prerequisite for the following chapter, but the sample application has been carefully designed such that the code samples in each of these chapters build upon those in previous chapters.

Finally, in Chapter 23, I'll cover some steps you should take to brand your application and publish it in the Windows Store.

Downloading the Code

The code for the examples shown in this book is available on the Apress web site, www.apress.com. A link can be found on the book's information page under the Source Code/Downloads tab. This tab is located under the Related Titles section of the page.

Additionally, the source code for the sample application built in Chapters 9 through 23 is available on GitHub, at www.github.com/daughtkom/Clok.

Contacting the Author

Should you have any questions or comments—or even spot a mistake you think I should know about—you can contact me through my personal web site, at www.scottisaacs.com, or on Twitter, at www.twitter.com/daughtkom.

■ ■ ■

CHAPTER 1

Welcome to a Touch-First World

In April 2010, I first heard the phrase that defined Microsoft's new strategy: "three screens and the cloud." This referred to a targeted approach to ensure that Microsoft's products were ubiquitous on mobile phones, desktop computers, and television screens and that these platforms provided a seamless experience by being held together with data in the cloud. The products represented on the three screens were Windows Phone 7, Windows 7, and Xbox 360. Microsoft still dominates the television screen, with its Xbox line accounting for approximately half of all game consoles sold worldwide and a continued focus to move that platform beyond gaming, but to me, Windows 8 brings a different meaning to three screens and the cloud—one where the three screens include phones, tablets, and PCs, all running on the Windows 8 core and tied with cloud services, as shown in Figure 1-1.

Figure 1-1. *Windows 8 vision of three screens and the cloud*

This book is about developing applications in this new environment, but before you start any development, you must understand the environment and how it will be used. In this chapter, I will provide some background on the user interface of Windows 8 and how users will interact with applications running on this platform. I will focus primarily on touch, but because Windows 8 is a touch-first environment and not a touch-only environment, I will also discuss when touch is not appropriate and cover alternative input methods.

Moving to More Natural Interaction

In 1985, users interacted with PCs primarily by using a keyboard, but the first Macintosh was increasing the popularity of the mouse, and Microsoft introduced Windows 1.0, which was essentially a shell that allowed people to point and click to open programs and documents instead of requiring them to remember appropriate commands to type. These mouse-based environments were successful in both the business and consumer markets and made computing accessible to the masses: by the time Windows 95 was released, PCs were not uncommon in people's homes.

Over the years, computer and software makers have flirted with the idea of a computer that could be carried anywhere in a pocket or attached to a belt. Apple attempted to realize this vision as early as 1992, but it wasn't until the mid-2000s that technology really caught up and hardware manufacturers could create small, lightweight computing devices capable of running software comparable to what would be found on the desktop. By the time hardware was ready for prime-time mobile computing by consumers, the Windows brand was firmly entrenched in the market, and Microsoft made several attempts with Windows CE, Pocket PC, and various flavors of Windows Mobile to create a mobile experience that was simply a scaled-down version of Windows. This approach yielded screens that required a lot of precision to interact with, and computers running the mobile version of Windows were largely looked at as specialized devices and not accepted by the average consumer.

The introduction of Windows Phone 7 in 2010, likely driven by the successes of Apple's iPhone three years before and the subsequent popularity of Android, discarded the notion of a tiny version of Windows and went with an entirely new user-interface concept dubbed Microsoft design language. The Microsoft design language is based on a set of core design principles focused around the user, and the finger became the primary tool for interacting with the computer. Unlike with previous versions of Microsoft's mobile operating systems, Windows Phone devices no longer shipped with the stylus being a standard component.

■ **Note**   You may be familiar with the term *Metro*. Metro is a code name that Microsoft and others have previously used in a few different contexts. The Microsoft design language has been extensively referred to as the Metro design language. Additionally, the Windows Start screen has often been called the Metro interface. Applications formerly called Metro apps are officially called Windows Store applications.

With Windows 8, Microsoft has taken the opportunity to hit the "reset" button on user-interface expectations and reversed its previous strategy by bringing the interactions that are natural by necessity in the mobile world to the desktop environment, instead of taking desktop concepts to the mobile world.

Windows 8 Touch Language

With the full incorporation of touch as a first-class citizen in Windows 8, it is important to understand the language of touch gestures recognized by the operating system. This is important not only as a user of Windows 8 but even more so as a developer who wants to make sure users can learn applications as quickly as possible and have a consistent experience. The Windows touch language consists primarily of eight gestures, which I will discuss in this section.

Press and Hold

The *press-and-hold* gesture, illustrated in Figure 1-2, is analogous to the right-click gesture with a mouse. The gesture is intended to allow the user to learn something about the target or be presented with additional options, such as a context menu. This gesture is accomplished by touching a single finger to the screen and pausing until the system acknowledges the hold, often by outlining the user-interface element held.

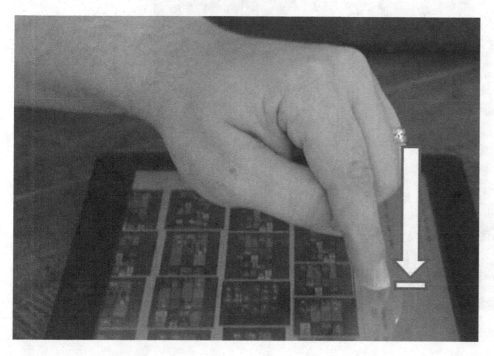

Figure 1-2. *Press and hold*

Tap

While the press-and-hold gesture can easily be equated to a single mouse gesture, the same cannot be said for the *tap* gesture. The tap gesture, illustrated in Figure 1-3, is intended to invoke the primary action on a user-interface element. Often, this will be an action such as activating a button or following a link. The mouse gesture most closely resembling the tap gesture is the left-click, but the left-click is also used for other tasks that have their own gestures in the touch language, such as selection. This gesture is accomplished by placing a finger on the user-interface element and then immediately lifting the finger straight up.

Figure 1-3. *Tap*

Slide

The *slide* gesture in the Windows touch language, shown in Figure 1-4, is used for panning or scrolling content that extends beyond the bounds of the screen or a screen section. In a mouse-driven environment, this is accomplished using scrollbars, but with touch, the slide gesture is more natural, and the scrollbar would either have to grow to the point of taking up too much real estate on the screen or be a difficult touch target. To accomplish the slide gesture, a finger is placed on the screen and then pulled up and down or side to side, depending on the orientation of the content.

Figure 1-4. *Slide*

Swipe

The *swipe* gesture is used to communicate selection, much as left-click, Ctrl+left-click, and Shift+left-click are used when interacting with the computer using a mouse and keyboard. To achieve this gesture, shown in Figure 1-5, the finger is placed on the screen either on top of or adjacent to the item selected and then drawn through the item. The direction of the gesture depends on the orientation of the content, with horizontally oriented content being swiped vertically and vertically oriented content being swiped horizontally. The gesture going against what would be used to slide sometimes causes it to be referred to as a *cross swipe*. Use of this gesture, as opposed to a tap, eliminates the confusion that could arise when trying to accomplish multiselect scenarios with no keyboard modifier keys, such as Ctrl and Shift, that aid in mouse selection.

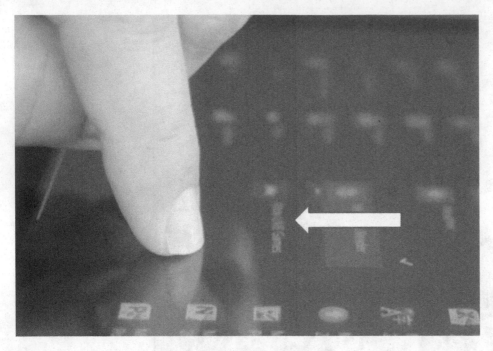

Figure 1-5. *Swipe*

Pinch

The *pinch* gesture, illustrated in Figure 1-6, does not have a direct equivalent in most mice and is considered a "zoom" gesture. The pinch zooms out from a narrow view with a high level of detail to a broader view with less detail. You will see in later chapters that in addition to the optical zoom, applications can take advantage of this gesture at a semantical level as well and use it to navigate summary and detail data. To accomplish the pinch gesture, two fingers are placed separated and roughly equidistant from the center of the element that is the target of the gesture, and then the fingers are slid together until either the desired zoom is met or the fingers meet.

Figure 1-6. *Pinch*

■ **Note** In many cases on mice with scroll wheels, pressing the Ctrl key while scrolling performs the same action as the pinch or stretch gestures.

Stretch

The *stretch* gesture, shown in Figure 1-7, is the opposite of the pinch gesture, both in its execution and in the results. The stretch gesture is used to zoom in from a broader, less-detailed view to a narrower view with more detail. As with pinch, you will find that applications can be designed to allow the gesture to be either an optical zoom or a semantical one. To accomplish the gesture, fingers are placed together, centered on the element to be zoomed, and then are moved in opposite directions along the screen until either the desired zoom level is achieved or one of the fingers reaches the edge of the screen.

Figure 1-7. Stretch

Swipe from Edge

As you learn more about Windows 8 and the Microsoft design language, you will find that content is king and anything that distracts from the content is to be left off the screen. You will also find that users must be able to perform actions with the least effort possible. Windows Store applications balance these needs by placing less frequently accessed commands off the edge of the screen in what are called *app bars* and *charm bars*. The *swipe-from-edge* gesture, illustrated in Figure 1-8, is used to access these commands. To achieve the gesture, a finger is placed beyond the edge of the screen and then pulled onto the screen.

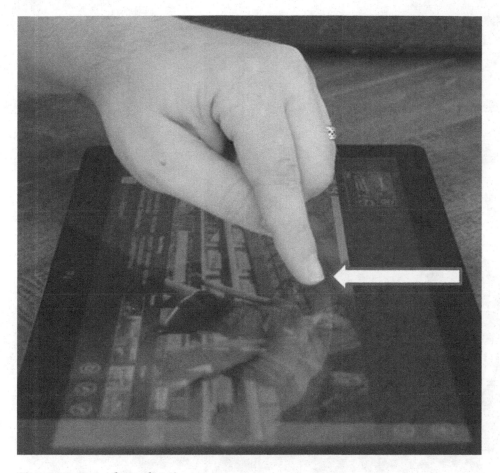

Figure 1-8. *Swipe from edge*

Turn

The *turn* gesture, illustrated in Figure 1-9, is used for rotating either the view or the content within the view. One example of where this type of gesture could be used would be in a touch version of the classic videogame Tetris, where falling blocks can be rotated to fit together. To accomplish this gesture, two fingers are placed on the screen, then either both fingers are pulled around the circumference of a circle or one is rotated around the other, which remains stationary.

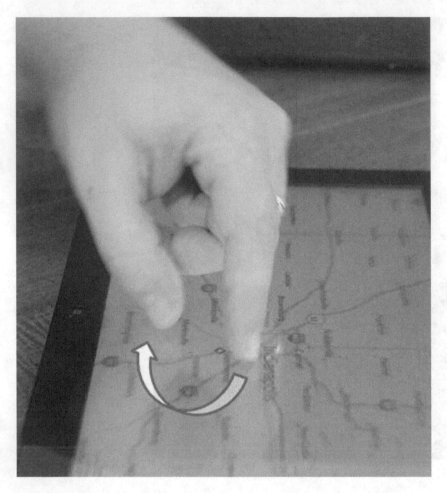

Figure 1-9. Turn

Keys to a Successful Touch Interface

Building a successful touch interface requires careful thought and consideration on the part of the designer and developer. Many of these considerations are embedded in the design principles governing the Microsoft design language, which I will discuss in Chapter 2, but in this section, I will discuss a few concepts that are critical to touch interfaces, whether or not they use these principles.

Responsiveness

Although responsiveness is important to any application, it is especially important for users of a touch application to never be left looking at an unresponsive screen. Users are aware, even if only at a subconscious level, that a mouse pointer is a much more precise tool than the end of a finger, so if it is not readily apparent that the user's last command was accepted and is being carried out, the user is likely to feel like he or she did not hit the target and issue the command again. Responsiveness can be achieved with actions such as giving a visual clue that a long-running process has begun or ensuring that content follows the user's finger as it is dragged across the screen.

Touch Targets

As mentioned in the previous section, the mouse pointer is a far more precise tool than the human fingertip. While nothing can eliminate the possibility of the user missing targets within certain applications, using large touch targets spaced well apart is an important way to minimize missed targets. When at all possible, targets should be no smaller than 7mm square, with at least 2mm between them. As a general rule, when hitting the wrong target has severe consequences or is hard to correct, the target should be larger in proportion and should also have more space between it and other targets.

Intuitive Interface

To the end user, the best applications "just work." Usually, this is because the application makes it easy for the user to do what needs to be done, rather than figure out how to do what needs to be done. Many desktop applications today make up for a lack of intuitiveness by providing detailed instructions in tooltips that appear as the user explores the application with a mouse pointer. Touch interfaces can still use tooltips, and the touch language defines the press-and-hold gesture for this type of learning, but it takes more effort than with a mouse, so more effort should be put into a design that clearly communicates what the user should do.

■ **Note** For additional guidance on implementing a high-quality touch-based user experience, please refer to these two MSDN articles: http://msdn.microsoft.com/en-us/library/windows/apps/xaml/hh465415.aspx and http://msdn.microsoft.com/en-us/library/windows/desktop/cc872774.aspx.

Beyond Touch

As Windows 8 does, this chapter has placed a lot of importance on the user interacting with the computer through the use of touch gestures. It should be noted, however, that the Windows 8 user interface is referred to as *touch-first* and not as *touch-only*. Windows 8 boasts the ability to run on much of the hardware that ran on Windows XP and Windows 7 and, in many cases, will perform better because of optimizations that have been made to accommodate mobile devices. This means that even though vendors are rushing to market with innovative touch hardware, for the foreseeable future, application developers must acknowledge that many of their users will approach the application equipped only with a keyboard and mouse.

In addition to the volume of older hardware that will remain in use, it's also important to understand that some usage scenarios simply do not translate as well to a touch environment. Users sitting for hours doing data entry are going to be much more comfortable and suffer less fatigue and injury using a keyboard and mouse than users performing the same tasks with their arm outstretched to reach a touch-screen monitor set up like most monitors today. Hardware vendors will meet this new need by continuing to innovate, and you will likely see changes such as multitouch trackpads replacing the traditional mouse and monitors that adjust to lie flat or at least angled on the desk. Additionally, expect to see devices similar to Microsoft's Kinect device evolve and be used in even more innovative ways than seen today.

Conclusion

In this chapter, you looked at Windows 8 as the touch-first world in which your applications will live. You learned about the basic gestures that have been defined in the Windows touch language and how end users will expect applications to react to them. You also learned that regardless of what the computer of tomorrow looks like, the computer of today often looks remarkably like computers sold the day before or even five years before Windows 8 released to market and that your applications must take the users of today's computers into account. Regardless of whether the user is interacting with hands or a mouse, Windows Store applications should be fluid, intuitive, and responsive.

CHAPTER 2

■ ■ ■

The Microsoft Design Language

Beyond the basic touch principles discussed in the previous chapter, the design teams at Microsoft developed the Microsoft design language, previously referred to as Metro, which is used to guide the user-interface development for Windows Phone 7, Windows Phone 7.5, and now for Windows 8 and Windows Phone 8. The Microsoft design language was inspired by the simple, easily understood language seen in street signs in metropolitan areas and in mass transit and strives to bring this simplicity and intuitive flavor to computing. In this chapter, I will cover the elements of the Microsoft design language, show examples, and explain how Windows 8 incorporates them. Before jumping into the Microsoft design language itself, I will cover the Swiss design style, whose influence can be clearly seen in elements of the Microsoft design language.

Swiss Design Style

The Microsoft design language is influenced most by a design style known as the Swiss design style, or international typographic style, which was developed in Switzerland in the 1950s and really started coming into its own in the 1960s and 1970s.

Influence of Bauhaus

The Swiss design style was heavily influenced by the Bauhaus movement, which Walter Gropius founded in 1919 with the establishment of the art school Staatliches Bauhaus in Weimar, Germany. The guiding principle of the Bauhaus movement was that of function over form, thus favoring concise communication and stark contrast over abstract ideas and gradient transition. It promoted art and architecture designed for an industrialized society and for which it could be mass-produced. The Bauhaus movement had a significant influence on the development of modern design and architecture. Today, the web site `http://Bauhaus-online.de` is maintained by the Bauhaus Archive Berlin/Museum for Design, the Weimar Classic Foundation, and the Bauhaus Dessau Foundation (see Figure 2-1) as an effort to preserve and disseminate information about the school and educate people about the impact of the institution.

Figure 2-1. *Bauhaus building in Dessau, Germany*

Elements of Swiss Design Style

The Swiss design style is characterized by a number of elements, which I will discuss in this chapter. These elements include typography, photography, iconography, generous use of whitespace, and strict organization. Brought together, the elements produce the distinct look and feel of a work designed in the Swiss style.

Typography

Front and center among the arts influenced by Swiss design style principles is typography. The developers of the Swiss style, and those who design with it today, hold steadily that text should be clear and simple and that unnecessary adornment not only occludes the message being conveyed in the text but also actively distracts from the message. In keeping with the idea that text should be clear, concise, and simple, Swiss designs will typically feature sans-serif fonts with text left-justified and jagged (ragged) on the right. Figures 2-2 and 2-3 are examples of a newsletter designed with justified columns and a serif font (Times New Roman) followed by the same newsletter designed using a sans-serif font (Helvetica) and left-justified to align with Swiss design style principles. Note the marked difference, specifically in the typeface, between the two examples and how the sans-serif typeface produces a cleaner look. The headlines are especially good examples of this.

LEAD STORY HEADLINE

Lorem ipsum dolor sit amet, consectetur adipiscing elit. Integer nec odio. Praesent libero. Sed cursus ante dapibus diam. Sed nisi. Nulla quis sem at nibh elementum imperdiet. Duis sagittis ipsum. Praesent mauris. Fusce nec tellus sed augue semper porta. Mauris massa. Vestibulum lacinia arcu eget nulla. Class aptent taciti sociosqu ad litora torquent per conubia nostra, per inceptos himenaeos. Curabitur sodales ligula in libero. Sed dignissim lacinia nunc.

Curabitur tortor. Pellentesque nibh. Aenean quam. In scelerisque sem at dolor. Maecenas mattis. Sed convallis tristique sem. Proin ut ligula

vel nunc egestas porttitor. Morbi lectus risus, iaculis vel, suscipit quis, luctus non, massa. Fusce ac turpis quis ligula lacinia aliquet. Mauris ipsum. Nulla metus metus, ullamcorper vel, tincidunt sed, euismod in, nibh. Quisque volutpat condimentum velit. Class aptent taciti sociosqu ad litora torquent per conubia nostra, per inceptos himenaeos. Nam nec ante.

Sed lacinia, urna non tincidunt mattis, tortor neque adipiscing diam, a cursus ipsum ante quis turpis. Nulla facilisi. Ut fringilla. Suspendisse potenti. Nunc feugiat mi a tellus consequat imperdiet. Vestibulum sapi-

en. Proin quam. Etiam ultrices. Suspendisse in justo eu magna luctus suscipit. Sed lectus. Integer euismod lacus luctus magna. Quisque cursus, metus vitae pharetra auctor, sem massa mattis sem, at interdum magna augue eget diam. Vestibulum ante ipsum primis in faucibus orci luctus et ultrices posuere cubilia Curae; Morbi lacinia molestie dui. Praesent blandit dolor.

Sed non quam. In vel mi sit amet augue congue elementum. Morbi in ipsum sit amet pede facilisis laoreet. Donec lacus nunc, viverra nec, blandit vel, egestas et, augue. Vestibulum tincidunt malesuada tellus. Ut ultrices

Figure 2-2. *Mock newsletter in non–Swiss style*

LEAD STORY HEADLINE

Lorem ipsum dolor sit amet, consectetur adipiscing elit. Integer nec odio. Praesent libero. Sed cursus ante dapibus diam. Sed nisi. Nulla quis sem at nibh elementum imperdiet. Duis sagittis ipsum. Praesent mauris. Fusce nec tellus sed augue semper porta. Mauris massa. Vestibulum lacinia arcu eget nulla. Class aptent taciti sociosqu ad litora torquent per conubia nostra, per inceptos himenaeos. Curabitur sodales ligula in libero. Sed dignissim lacinia nunc.

Curabitur tortor. Pellentesque nibh. Aenean quam. In scelerisque sem

at dolor. Maecenas mattis. Sed convallis tristique sem. Proin ut ligula vel nunc egestas porttitor. Morbi lectus risus, iaculis vel, suscipit quis, luctus non, massa. Fusce ac turpis quis ligula lacinia aliquet. Mauris ipsum. Nulla metus metus, ullamcorper vel, tincidunt sed, euismod in, nibh. Quisque volutpat condimentum velit. Class aptent taciti sociosqu ad litora torquent per conubia nostra, per inceptos himenaeos. Nam nec ante.

Sed lacinia, urna non tincidunt mattis, tortor neque adipiscing diam, a cursus

ipsum ante quis turpis. Nulla facilisi. Ut fringilla. Suspendisse potenti. Nunc feugiat mi a tellus consequat imperdiet. Vestibulum sapien. Proin quam. Etiam ultrices. Suspendisse in justo eu magna luctus suscipit. Sed lectus. Integer euismod lacus luctus magna. Quisque cursus, metus vitae pharetra auctor, sem massa mattis sem, at interdum magna augue eget diam. Vestibulum ante ipsum primis in faucibus orci luctus et ultrices posuere cubilia Curae; Morbi lacinia molestie dui. Praesent blandit dolor.

Sed non quam. In vel mi sit amet augue congue

Figure 2-3. *Mock newsletter using Swiss-style typography*

In addition to its focus on simple, sans-serif typefaces, another key element of Swiss design with regard to typography is the use of contrasting font sizes and weights to draw attention to certain points in the text or to create emphasis. This calls for stark differences in font sizes when different font sizes are used, so while some design schools may advocate 12-point headlines and 10-point body text, Swiss design may call for 18-point headlines and 10-point body text, to ensure that there is no question regarding the difference between the two text elements.

Photography

Swiss design style is also marked by the idea that the design should convey a sense of reality and that visual elements will be perceived as "more real" when photographs are used in place of drawn illustrations.

Figure 2-4 shows the sunset over a body of water. The photograph captures the ripples in the water and the effect of the sun's light on the water in a way that feels very real to the viewer.

Figure 2-4. *Photograph of sunset over water*

Figure 2-5 also depicts a sunset over a body of water. Many of the same elements that are featured in the photograph are present, such as the sun's reflection over ripples in the water and silhouetted figures, but the theories driving Swiss design hold that viewers are not left feeling as though what they are viewing is real when illustration is used instead of photography. Both the photograph and the painting are pleasing to the eye, but the photograph is more in line with the Swiss style.

Figure 2-5. *Painting of sunset over water*

Iconography

While photographs are preferred to drawings or other illustrations, in many cases, works created using Swiss design often feature the extensive use of icons, either to augment or replace text. This is particularly the case when Swiss design is used in a setting where information must be conveyed to an international audience or in one where you cannot be sure that the viewer in need of the information being conveyed can understand the printed words, regardless of the language in which they are written. Rich iconography used in conjunction with other elements of Swiss design made a big show on the international stage during the 1972 Summer Olympics in Munich, Germany. Otl Aicher designed the brochures and leaflets for the Olympic Games in the Swiss style and used what is now a familiar system of figure icons to represent individuals participating in various events for the games. This facilitated communication with the international audience present for the games. Additional places where you see prominent examples of Swiss design and iconography are bus and train stations, public restrooms (Figure 2-6), and warning labels on many consumer goods.

Figure 2-6. *Familiar Swiss-style design helps to avoid an embarrassing mistake*

Generous Use of Whitespace

In Swiss design, content is king. Too much of anything packed haphazardly into a space is considered excessively cluttered or noisy and a distraction from the information being conveyed. This leads to a design goal that includes plenty of whitespace, to ensure that anything appearing within that expanse will immediately become the focus of attention.

Figure 2-7 shows a dog that appears to be standing watch in a snowy country setting. "The Sentinel" is a descriptive caption, but no particular attention is drawn to either the dog or the caption because the contents are all allowed to run together without any separation and because the trees produce "noise" that detracts from the message of the caption. While this figure is visually appealing, it lacks the stark contrast favored by Swiss design principles. I'll use the natural whitespace present in the expanse of snow to highlight both the portion of the photo where I want attention focused and the caption, as shown in Figure 2-8.

Figure 2-7. *Photo and caption with no whitespace*

Figure 2-8. *Photo and caption with whitespace for contrast*

In Figure 2-8, the only change that I made was to move the text out of the noise produced by the trees, allowing the caption to sit by itself within uninterrupted whitespace. This narrows the focus of the photograph to exclude what is not directly related to the subject and really makes the caption stand out. More of the photograph could have been cropped from the top and bottom to bring even more focus to the subject, but in this case, enough was left to ensure the winter scene did not escape the viewer. Neither the first nor the second version should be considered better or worse, because there are instances when the intent would be to focus on the entire setting and where adhering to the principles of Swiss design is not the goal, in which case, the first treatment illustrated may be preferred.

Strict Organization

In keeping with the overarching theme of clean simplicity and avoidance of anything that distracts from the content, Swiss design is typically marked by strict organization. This is observed in the uniformity of geometric figures as well as in the use of font size to communicate informational hierarchy within text and in the adherence to a grid system to lay out both text and other visual elements in a structured manner. The use of grids is definitely not limited to the Swiss style and has been used in typography design for centuries. With a grid-based design, the design surface is divided into one or more grids, which are used to position text and elements with cells. This provides for an organized and aligned look. At times, the use of grid layout may not be quite as pronounced, because the grid lines need not be perpendicular and parallel with the edges of the design surface, making it possible for a design to follow a grid layout while the content appears angled to the viewer.

Figure 2-9 shows the structural organization achieved by using a grid layout, but it also demonstrates the way that typography is used to achieve organization within the Swiss design style by using a stark difference in font size to delineate different levels within the informational hierarchy. At the highest level of the informational hierarchy, the page header is presented in a 56-point font size. At the next level, group headers are given around one-half the font size of the page header. At the lowest level of the hierarchy for this page, the item title is about half the size of the group header.

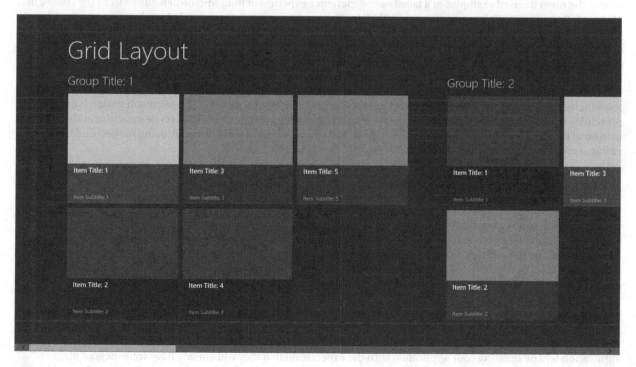

Figure 2-9. *Windows Store application demonstrating grid layout and hierarchy*

Microsoft Design Language

Rooted heavily in the Swiss design style that I've just covered, the Microsoft design language guides user-experience design for the Windows Phone 7/7.5/8 and Windows 8 operating systems as well as for current incarnations of the Zune and Xbox 360 user interfaces, striving to give a consistent look and feel regardless of the device with which you are interacting.

Microsoft Design Language Principles

Microsoft's earliest guidance on the Microsoft design language characterized it as a confluence of five guiding principles rather than a book of rules or recipes. In this section, I'll cover the principles that you should weigh when making design choices.

Show Pride in Craftsmanship

Not even the smallest detail should be left to chance in your user interface. Everything the user sees and experiences should be part of the plan and work according to that plan. Additionally, information should be presented according to a carefully thought out visual hierarchy and should be laid out using a grid-based design.

Be Fast and Fluid

Applications should allow users to interact directly with the content and should remain constantly responsive by using motion to provide feedback to interactions. Applications should typically be designed with "touch-first" in mind.

Be Authentically Digital

One of the most flagrant examples of a failed user-experience experiment from Microsoft resulted from the release of Microsoft Bob in 1995. This application was a shell for the operating system that intended to abstract away the whole "computerness" of the computer by providing real-world analogies for different operations. If you wanted to retrieve documents, you clicked the file cabinet. Need to write a letter? Click the pen on the desk! Bob's failure was driven ultimately by two factors. The first was that it was perceived as childish and patronizing (many shells similar to Bob do find favor in preschool classrooms). The second was that it simply was not an effective way for people to interact with the computer, and introducing abstractions intended to hide the computer tended to make interactions much less efficient, especially for people who have to use a computer for most of the day. The Microsoft design language principles acknowledge that people know they are interacting with a computer and call on designers to embrace the medium. This includes using the cloud to keep users and apps connected and effectively using motion and bold, vibrant colors to communicate with the user.

Do More with Less

Windows 8 provides rich functionality to allow applications running both on your device and in the cloud to interact with each other. This enables applications to focus on doing a very narrowly defined set of things and to do one thing in an extraordinary manner rather than do several things poorly. In keeping with the Bauhaus and Swiss design influences, the content should be the primary focus of attention, and very little else should be present to distract from this content. The full-screen nature of Windows Store apps even removes the need for window chrome, allowing a completely immersive experience, so that when the user is in your application, your application receives all of his or her attention.

Win As One

One of the keys to working in a Windows Store application is that the style has been set. Users of a Windows Store application will be opening your application with the expectation that they will already have some degree of familiarity with it, because they are familiar with the look and feel of other Windows Store applications. Some things that can really be harmful to individual applications and, eventually, to the ecosystem in which the applications reside are design decisions that radically change the design paradigm of the application to give users something "new" and "better" than what they are used to having. You should strive to impress your users with how well your application does the things it is meant to be good at, but trying to surprise those users by changing user-interface and navigation paradigms will only confuse them and make them lose trust in your application. Microsoft has provided guidance, tools, templates, and style sheets to make it easy for developers to create Windows Store applications with a consistent look and feel, and you should make full use of these resources.

User-Experience Guidelines for Windows Store Apps

In addition to the more generalized principles that Microsoft has published for Windows Store applications, a comprehensive set of guidelines has also been made available in order to provide detailed prescriptive guidance in regard to the look, feel, and behavior of applications designed to run in this new ecosystem. Although not a comprehensive treatment of these guidelines, which are freely available in their entirety on the MSDN Library web site at http://dev.windows.com, this section covers a few of the aspects that are most applicable to designers/developers getting a feel for the Windows 8 experience.

Application Layout

Applications should be designed using a grid layout, organized using either a hierarchical navigation scheme or a flat view, as dictated by the content.

When a hierarchical approach is taken, the top of the hierarchy represents the lowest level of detail, and each subsequent level in the navigation hierarchy zooms in with increasing detail. Typically, the highest level, sometimes referred to as the *Hub*, is the entry point of the application and reveals one or more groups that the user can drill into (see Figure 2-10).

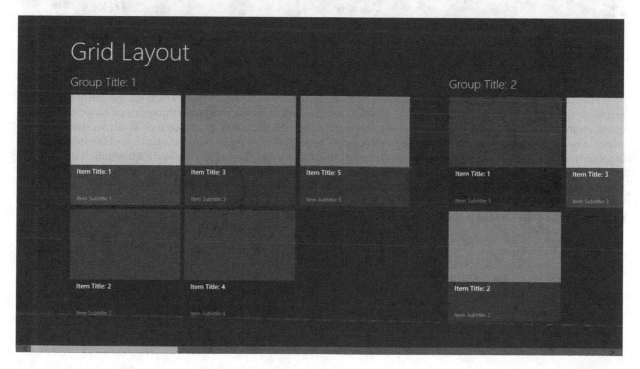

Figure 2-10. *Hierarchical navigation at highest level (the Hub)*

By selecting a group from the main Hub, the next level of navigation (commonly referred to as a *Section*) is revealed. The Section page is arranged to provide some context about the Section itself and lists the individual items that are the lowest level of navigation and highest level of detail (see Figure 2-11).

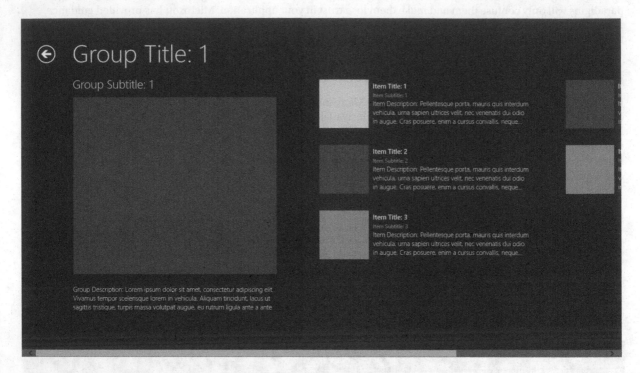

Figure 2-11. *Hierarchical navigation at Section level*

From the Section page, the user is offered a way to navigate back up a level, typically through the use of a back arrow, as shown in Figure 2-11, to the Hub, a means to navigate to sibling Section pages through a swipe gesture (if touch enabled) or through the use of arrows at the left and right edge of the screen centered vertically, or items to select in order to continue to the Detail page. At the Detail page level of navigation, a granular view of the item data is presented (see Figure 2-12). As with the Section page, the back arrow is presented to allow for navigation up the hierarchy to the Section page in which the item is organized. As with Section pages, users can choose to navigate between Detail pages within the same section through the use of a swipe gesture on touch-enabled systems or through interaction with arrows at the left and right edge of the screen. The hierarchical navigation is especially well suited for browsing and interacting with information that can be fit into master-detail categorization.

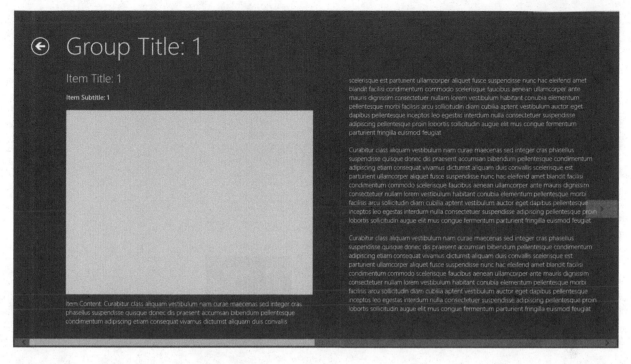

Figure 2-12. *Hierarchical navigation at Detail page*

Many applications do not fit into the master-detail categorization that works well with a hierarchical navigation structure and focus more on the document-based style familiar with Microsoft Word, Excel, or Internet Explorer. For this type of application, a flat navigation system works much better. At the core of the flat navigation is that content is separated into pages with information that is either unrelated or at the same hierarchical level (see Figure 2-13). The navigation bar is presented when activated by the user and is employed to switch between active documents, often presenting a command that the user can access to add a document to the session (see Figure 2-14).

Figure 2-13. *Internet Explorer's design presents a flat view with a single document using an entire viewport*

Figure 2-14. *Internet Explorer with navigation bar activated to switch active document*

Typography

With its heavy emphasis on typography and text-centered content, no coverage of the user-experience guidelines for Windows Store applications would be complete without providing advice for the formatting and use of text. Following in the tradition of Swiss design, consistent fonts should be used when building applications. Which specific font should be used varies according to the purpose of the text. Text that is intended to be used for buttons or labels on UI elements should favor the Segoe UI font, which is used throughout Windows 8 user-interface elements (see Figure 2-15).

Product Search

Figure 2-15. *Segoe UI is used for labels and other UI elements*

Blocks of text that are to be presented to the reader in a read-only fashion, such as news articles, should favor the serif Cambria font, because readers are accustomed to extended blocks of text being presented in a serif font (see Figure 2-16). This font should be presented in 9 points, 11 points, or 20 points, depending on the need to draw focus or show emphasis. This is a departure from the Swiss style's preference for sans-serif fonts in all things, because the Microsoft design team found serif fonts to be easier on the eyes for extended reading.

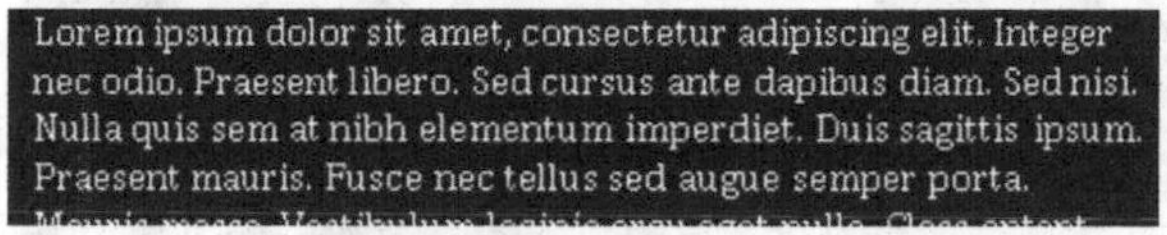

Lorem ipsum dolor sit amet, consectetur adipiscing elit. Integer
nec odio. Praesent libero. Sed cursus ante dapibus diam. Sed nisi.
Nulla quis sem at nibh elementum imperdiet. Duis sagittis ipsum.
Praesent mauris. Fusce nec tellus sed augue semper porta.

Figure 2-16. *Cambria for read-only text blocks*

Continuous blocks that are intended for the user to both read and edit should favor the sans-serif font Calibri (see Figure 2-17). The recommended size for this font is 13 points, which shares the same height as 11-point Segoe UI, so the two will maintain a consistent appearance when used together on the same line.

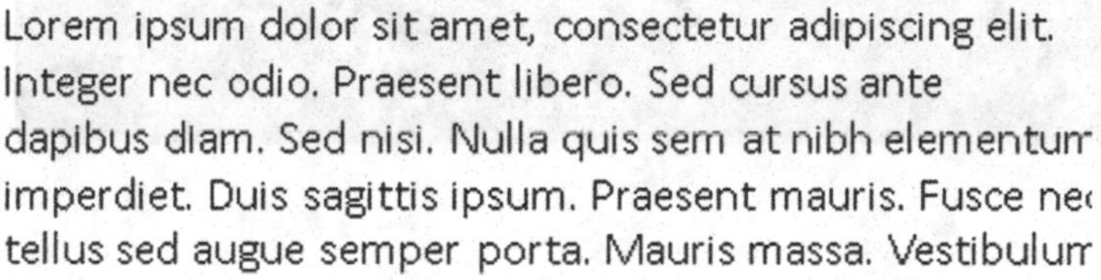

Lorem ipsum dolor sit amet, consectetur adipiscing elit.
Integer nec odio. Praesent libero. Sed cursus ante
dapibus diam. Sed nisi. Nulla quis sem at nibh elementum
imperdiet. Duis sagittis ipsum. Praesent mauris. Fusce nec
tellus sed augue semper porta. Mauris massa. Vestibulum

Figure 2-17. *Calibri for read-edit text blocks*

Regardless of the font face, when emphasis is needed on certain pieces of text, the appropriate way to produce emphasis is through the use of stark contrast with the font size or the font weight. At the same level within the information hierarchy, weight is used for emphasis, while size draws the distinction between levels. Using text decorations such as underline or italics reduces clarity and should not be used for emphasis in a Windows Store application.

Other Windows Store App User-Experience Guidelines

In this section, I have touched on some of the user-experience guidelines but have intentionally focused on those that deal with the visual look of the application, leaving more of the behavioral aspects to topics that will be covered elsewhere in this book when I discuss the tools available to developers for building great Windows Store applications. If you want to see these guidelines all in one place or don't want to wait, I encourage you to take a deeper look at the Windows Store apps section of the MSDN web site (http://msdn.microsoft.com/en-US/windows/default.aspx).

Microsoft Design Language in the Windows 8 User Interface

With the exception of Desktop mode, the Windows 8 user interface is largely based on the Microsoft design language guidelines and principles. Let's start by looking at the Start screen (see Figure 2-18).

Figure 2-18. *Start screen with charms activated*

The Start screen features a full-screen grid displaying the applications that are most important to the user (indicated by the user selecting the app for inclusion in the Start screen) and from which the user selects the application he or she wants to run. This assumes that the first thing the user wants to do is run one of the applications he or she normally uses, and the grid is very much laid out to accomplish this very specific task in as efficient a manner as possible. By activating the app bar (not shown), the user can request that all applications be presented instead of their narrower list of favorites, allowing the user to run any application that is installed on the machine through an additional step. If the user intends not to run an application but to perform some other task, such as changing system settings or searching for a file, the user activates the charm bar on the right side of the screen, presenting a list of additional commands.

Earlier in this chapter, you saw how Internet Explorer running in Windows UI mode is a good example of the flat navigational style. For an example of the hierarchical navigational style, you can look to the Windows Store, where apps are available for purchase or free download. When you enter the application, the Hub is displayed, showing the different categories for which applications are available (see Figure 2-19).

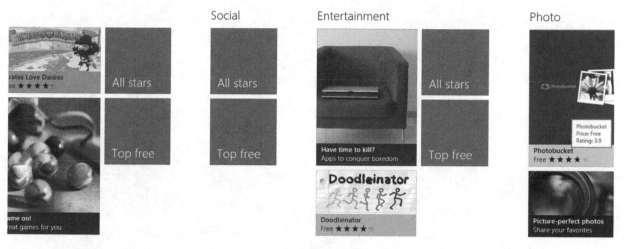

Figure 2-19. *Windows Store Hub page*

From this Hub, users can either select certain Detail items directly or choose to drill down through Section pages. Throughout the Windows 8 interface, and the applications supplied with it, you can see a recurring theme of clean typographic-based interfaces, vibrant colors, and animation to ensure that the user perceives the applications as being responsive and providing connectivity to information in other apps and the cloud.

Conclusion

In this chapter, you learned about the Microsoft design language, which is the basis for the Windows 8 user interface and Windows Store applications, and you learned about some of the earlier styles and design paradigms that influenced the development of the Microsoft design language. These concepts will remain in either the background or the foreground whenever you are building Windows Store applications and should influence every design decision you make. Although simple enough in nature that a developer with little design skill can effectively create these user interfaces, the guidelines also provide for much more sophisticated designs created by people skilled in the art and craft of visual design. These skilled designers are encouraged to delve more deeply into Bauhaus, the Swiss style, and Microsoft's user-experience design guidelines.

CHAPTER 3

■ ■ ■

Designing Windows Store Applications

In a perfect world, application developers are handed clear, concise packets of paper that lay out exactly how their application should look and everything that it should do. They work from that paper, which, from their perspective, may have spontaneously generated itself, and produce a working and useful application. While many developers have managed to find such a world, to the majority of people who make their living writing code, this arrangement seems as unattainable as reaching Shangri-La.

Developers who are not handed a completed design have to become more than those who translate requirements to code and, instead, must take on what I view as the much more difficult and interesting task of designing software. This chapter is for developers who, either by choice or necessity, will take part in the design of Windows Store applications, and it is intended to provide an overview of important steps in this process. In it, I will introduce important concepts related to deciding what an application should do and how it should be presented to the user. My primary focus in this chapter is gathering requirements that serve as the input to the design, because a novice designer who fully understands the problems that need to be solved by an application can produce a more useful application than a skilled designer who does not.

■ **Note** There are many different methodologies for gathering requirements and for designing and building software. While some of the terminology I use in this chapter may lean toward one methodology or another, my intent is to capture concepts that are important and relevant, regardless of the methodology (if any) you use to build your software.

Communication Is Key

A colleague once told me that in the development of applications, no truth should be considered self-evident. Years later, this was reinforced by a conversation I had with a relative. This relative began a conversation by saying, "I have a friend who is doing court reporting and needs software to help. How long would something like that take to build?" I started to reply, "You just asked how long it would take to build. . .," and my relative quickly interjected, "But I didn't tell you what the darn thing needs to do!" Often, a conversation such as this reveals the disconnect between what the client has in mind and what the person building the software hears, but in an atypical twist, my relative picked up on something that many business partners do not—namely, that if you want something built, you must clearly communicate your requirements. Figure 3-1 illustrates this disconnect, often referred to as *impedance mismatch*.

Figure 3-1. Impedance mismatch

The primary cause of the impedance mismatch that often causes developers to build what is asked for instead of what is needed is that everyone involved in the process sees his or her own view very clearly and cannot imagine how others could see things any differently. The impedance mismatch can be reduced, if not avoided altogether, by starting the design process by acknowledging that people's understanding of different topics will vary and by committing to an environment where nothing is taken for granted.

■ **Note** Developers not participating in building software as part of a team should still separate the roles of developer and user in their minds, to force themselves to look at things from the vantage point of the user. Here, forcing yourself to mentally "explain" everything as if trying to avoid impedance mismatch will help uncover hidden requirements.

What Should the Application Be Good At?

It may seem like an obvious point, but the first thing to determine when beginning the task of designing your application is to determine the purpose that it serves. At this point, specifics are not necessary; just create a general statement or description of the application that clearly states the use or purpose of the application. A well-designed application will have one thing that it is really good at, especially Windows Store applications, which, as you will learn in Chapter 19, can work together to solve problems larger than what each individual application's developers envisioned. It's good to use a template statement such as "This application will _____ so that _____" to help focus your thoughts not only on *what* the application will do but also on *why* the application will do it or the benefit that it provides. If I am building an application to track the gas mileage of a vehicle, the statement may be something such as "This application will calculate the fuel economy of a vehicle so that I can better anticipate my fuel costs."

■ **Note**   Be sure to document the high-level purpose of your application in a manner that will be very visible throughout the design and development. This forms the backbone of your application, and you will often refer to it as you decide whether a piece of functionality belongs in the application. If it isn't required for some sort of legal or regulatory means and does not contribute to the application's stated purpose, then it does not belong in the application.

Identify Functional Requirements

Once the primary purpose of the application has been identified as a sort of guiding principle, the work of identifying the requirements necessary to support the primary purpose, known as *functional requirements*, begins. Depending on the type of application you are building and the availability of others to participate in the requirements process, several techniques exist to discover or elicit requirements. Some of the more regularly practiced techniques include the following:

- *Interviewing*: Stakeholders, or people who have some sort of interest either in the software being produced or in the output or benefit produced by the software, are consulted to learn what they expect and need from the application. During the interview, stakeholders should feel that they can freely express their wants and needs without being told they can't have something, in order to ensure they don't neglect to mention critical requirements.

- *Brainstorming*: Stakeholders and members of the design team work together to come up with ideas for requirements. This session begins in an "anything goes" atmosphere, as in the interviewing technique, for the same reason of not discouraging stakeholders from voicing wants and needs. Brainstorming sessions are often most effective when all participants can be in the same room at the same time, with tools such as whiteboards and sticky notes available, but a disciplined team can achieve similar effectiveness remotely, by using teleconferencing tools. The key is to get everybody focused and actively participating at the same time.

- *Process mapping*: Existing processes are walked through and thoroughly documented to capture all of the steps that are carried out to meet the goal. This technique requires an existing process and works best when each step can be subjected to scrutiny. It's not enough to know what is currently done, but the motivations behind each step and how it contributes to meeting the end goal are also critical to understand.

■ **Note**   "We've always" and "we've never" are two phrases that can prevent an organization from improving, unless the organization is willing to add "until now" to them when it becomes necessary to begin a beneficial activity or end one that adds no value. This brings to mind the old tale of a woman who was taught by her mother to begin preparing a roast by cutting off 1 inch from each end, just as was done by the woman's grandmother. When the grandmother came for dinner, she noticed her granddaughter cutting the ends off the roast and asked why she was doing that. "Grandma, that's the way you always made yours," the granddaughter replied. The grandmother just laughed and responded, "But my pan was 2 inches too short." Software projects present an excellent opportunity to ask "why" and ensure that similar situations don't exist in your organization.

Evaluate Identified Requirements

The techniques for identifying requirements all specify that care be taken not to discourage communication of any requirement that seems important or valid to any stakeholder or member of the team. This doesn't mean that every identified requirement can or should be implemented in the finished product, just that they should all be available to evaluate. Once the realm of potential requirements has been identified, the next step is to review each requirement for appropriateness. The determining factor for appropriateness is simple and straightforward. If you can directly (and honestly) communicate how fulfilling the requirement is necessary to allow the application to meet its goal, the requirement is appropriate. The exception to this rule is that some requirements are driven by outside forces, such as contractual obligations and regulatory requirements, and these must be met regardless of whether they contribute to meeting the application's higher-level goal. Figure 3-2 illustrates the decision process used to decide whether to promote a potential requirement to a requirement that will be implemented.

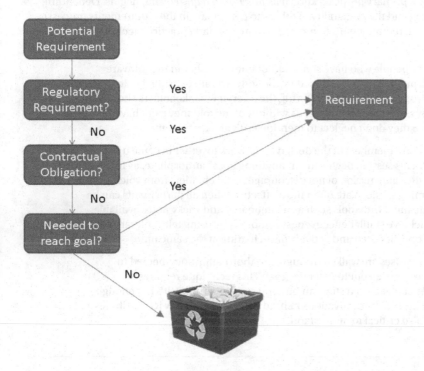

Figure 3-2. *Potential requirement to requirement decision*

Another measurement that is often used to determine whether a potential requirement should become promoted to an actual requirement is to categorize the items as either "must have," "nice to have," or "don't need." The idea is that "must have" items become requirements; "don't need" items are excluded from consideration; and "nice to have" items get considered if additional resources are available after the "must have" items are accounted for. The danger with this ranking pattern is that too much focus can easily be given to "nice to have" items, causing more time, effort, and, ultimately, dollars to be spent on items that are not actually required to make a successful application. On a project without an experienced project manager to keep it on track, the more rigid requirements definition process described in Figure 3-2 is recommended.

■ **Tip** Practitioners of Agile methodologies tend to express requirements in what is called a *user story*. The user story often takes some form of the statement "As a _____, I need the system to _____ so that _____." While the term *user story* is specific to certain methodologies, the idea of identifying the key stakeholder and purpose for each requirement is a valuable practice for any methodology.

The act of measuring requirements against the purpose of the application is not just an exercise in keeping the application true to purpose, but it is also intended to help maintain balance between the three key factors that drive any project, whether it is building software or a skyscraper.

- *Time*: When must the project be completed in order to meet organizational goals?

- *Money*: How much can be spent?

- *Scope*: What is the body of work to be completed?

These three factors are often part of what is known as the *project management triangle*, as illustrated in Figure 3-3. The triangle is a great way to depict the relationship between these factors, because, as with the sides of the triangle, one factor cannot be changed without affecting the other two. For example, if more money is available, additional developers may be hired, and the time required to complete the project will be shortened. Often, the easiest way to rein in a software development project is to keep firm control over the scope.

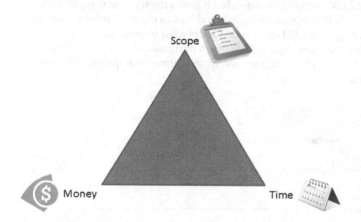

Figure 3-3. Project management triangle

In some projects, the "must have" items can't all fit into the scope, because the project is constrained on time, money, or both. In these cases, the project must be evaluated to determine whether there are items that have to be implemented but can wait until later. This prioritization process provides time to really think critically about needs and can make the difference between being able to produce something of value or having to scrap the project because of the requirements process stalling.

Decompose Requirements

Once the requirements necessary for the application to meet its goals have been identified, an iterative process called *decomposition* begins. Decomposition in software development is when a large problem is broken into individual steps. With iterative decomposition, the steps are then themselves broken into smaller pieces, and this continues either until there is nothing left to break down or until you're "done." *Done* is a bit of a subjective term, but I view it as having reached the point where a developer familiar with the project should have every expectation of being able to sit down and use the requirement as a blueprint for building the application. In organizations where the developers are very familiar with the problems that they are solving, "done" will not be decomposed to nearly as granular a level as when the development work will be performed by developers who are not as familiar with those problems.

■ **Note**   Decomposition is an important way to turn daunting problems into a set of little problems that are easily resolved. Remember the advice about how to eat an elephant: one bite at a time.

Build Interaction Flows

Up until this point, the focus has been entirely on what needs to be accomplished by the application as a whole, and you should have a good idea of what information needs to come into and out of the application to meet those requirements. Once those needs are established, you can turn your attention to determining how the user can most effectively get that information into and out of the application. Here, for the first time, you begin to think about the idea of a screen, but it is still a bit of an amorphous concept, because you are trying to determine what goes where. At this point in the design process, I typically prefer to avoid language that suggests decisions have been made about how the screen will be laid out and with what kind of controls. I favor phrases such as "and then the user selects the save action" over "and then the user clicks the save button." It's a subtle difference, but it leaves the focus at this point on determining the sequence of steps needed to accomplish the application's goals and how to organize information into screens for users' interactions. Coming out of this step, you should have a good idea of what screens the application will have and what will trigger movement between these screens. Figure 3-4 shows a navigation diagram, which is a useful means to help define and document these flows. In it, you clearly see the views that are anticipated within the application and how the user will move between them.

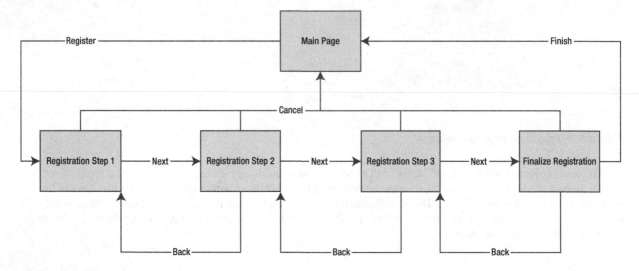

Figure 3-4. Navigation diagram

Wireframes

Once the team has settled on the flow of the application, it's time to work on wireframes. Wireframes are low-fidelity sketches of the application screen that focus on what information and commands the screens will hold, rather than worrying about making them pretty and getting bogged down in aesthetic details. Wireframes may be captured on the back of a napkin, a whiteboard (be sure to take a picture), or via tools such as Visio, PowerPoint, Balsamic, or SketchFlow in Expression Blend. This is the step where you decide what type of controls the user will interact with the application most effectively with. In a Windows 8 application, the wireframes should reflect full-screen experiences, where the user can focus on content. Figure 3-5 illustrates a sample wireframe. Notice how no effort was expended in making it look like a Windows application; instead, it focuses on the information and what will result from different interactions.

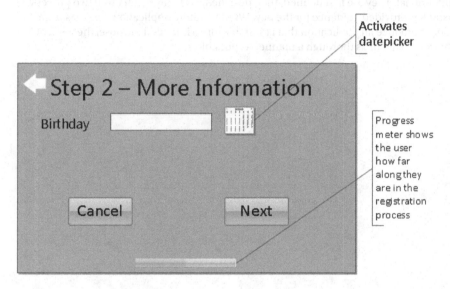

Figure 3-5. *Wireframe*

Visual Design

After the wireframes for the application are agreed upon, some project teams will pass the wireframes to a visual designer, who will use a tool such as Microsoft's Blend for Visual Studio 2012 to turn the ideas in the wireframes into a visually appealing interface. Ideally, the designer will follow the guidelines in the Microsoft design language and the Swiss design style to produce an application that has a consistent look and feel with other Windows 8 applications. Blend for Visual Studio can produce HTML-based projects, which are compatible with Visual Studio, so the designer's work can become the base on which the developer adds code to create a finished application.

■ **Note**   Microsoft has multiple editions of their Blend software. Expression Blend can be used for prototyping with SketchFlow and building WPF and Silverlight applications. Blend for Visual Studio 2012 is installed with Visual Studio and can be used for designing Windows Store applications.

More often than not, teams will not have a dedicated visual designer. They may have a developer who has a better eye for design than the other developers on the team, or the visual design may just be left up to chance. Unlike with some design paradigms, using the new Windows design guidelines actually gives a developer who is not artistically inclined a chance to create an appealing user interface. Additionally, Microsoft includes built-in styles in the project templates that can be used to help ensure that the application has the new Windows look and feel.

Conclusion

In this chapter, I briefly introduced many of the concepts and steps that go into designing an application. While the focus has been on what this looks like when the process is executed by a team, all the steps are worth considering when you are creating your applications as a team of one. The important thing to remember is that, with rare exception, great applications are intentional. They are first defined, then designed, and only when these two processes are complete are they built. Microsoft has provided guidance for the new Windows Store applications that eases the task of the visual design, but in order to produce an application that is suitable for its intended purpose, the work of requirement definition still must be completed in as thorough a manner as possible.

■ ■ ■

CHAPTER 4

Visual Studio 2012 and Windows Store Application Types

In application development, the integrated development environment (IDE) can make the difference between feeling like you can work easily and focus on the problem your application is supposed to solve and feeling like you are so distracted trying to figure out how to maneuver within the IDE that you cannot focus on the real task of producing software. With the last several versions of Visual Studio, Microsoft has increasingly built upon a reputation of having one of the best development IDEs available. Even many developers who don't care to develop for the Microsoft platform will say (if grudgingly) that one is hard-pressed to find a better development environment. In this chapter, you will learn about Visual Studio 2012, which is the latest release in this lineup. As complete coverage of the tools and features would require a book of its own, I will cover in this chapter the topics that I consider to be most important to finding your way around the environment well enough to complete the exercises in this book. In addition to learning about Visual Studio in general, you will also learn about the project templates that are used for Windows Store application development.

Visual Studio Editions

Visual Studio is often used generically to describe the IDE for developing applications built on Microsoft platforms, but rather than a single product, it designates an entire line of products. In addition to the freely available Express editions, the Visual Studio 2012 lineup includes the following:

- Visual Studio Express 2012 for Windows 8
- Visual Studio Express 2012 for Web
- Visual Studio Express 2012 for Windows Desktop
- Visual Studio Express 2012 for Windows Phone 8
- Visual Studio Test Professional 2012
- Visual Studio Professional 2012
- Visual Studio Premium 2012
- Visual Studio Ultimate 2012

The Visual Studio Express 2012 editions each provide an environment for developing applications targeting different portions of the Microsoft stack and can be used without having to invest in one of the full Visual Studio 2012 products. Visual Studio Express 2012 for Windows 8 is focused on providing the necessary tools to build and test Windows Store applications as well as providing support for sharing and selling your Windows Store applications in the Windows Store. Visual Studio Express 2012 for Windows 8 is sufficient for completing the exercises in this book, and features available in this edition will be the focus of discussion in this chapter. The following are key features of Visual Studio Express 2012 for Windows 8:

- Basic analysis of code for errors or practices that could prevent Windows Store certification

- Integrated debugger

- Simulator for running Windows Store applications

- Profiler to help identify code that requires tuning

- Unit testing support

With the exception of Visual Studio Test Professional 2012, which is designed for people assigned to the testing role in an application development organization, the non-Express editions of Visual Studio 2012 are designed for professional developers. Visual Studio Professional 2012, Visual Studio Premium 2012, and Visual Studio Ultimate 2012 each progressively add features to assist in the following areas of application development:

- Design

- Construction

- Testing

- Analysis

- Troubleshooting

You can find a full comparison of the features that come with each Visual Studio 2012 edition at www.microsoft.com/visualstudio. You can also find Visual Studio Express 2012 for Windows 8 at this site. If you do not already have a Visual Studio 2012 edition installed, I encourage you to install Visual Studio Express 2012 for Windows 8 before reading further.

Getting Started with Visual Studio

When you first open Visual Studio 2012 Express, the default view appears, as shown in Figure 4-1. The most important features in the user interface at this point are the menu bar (labeled A in the figure) and the Start Page (labeled B). The menu bar provides access to many commands, but when first opening Visual Studio, you are most likely going to head for the File menu (shown in Figure 4-2), where you will select either New Project or Open Project. The Start Page offers links to items of interest to developers, such as articles on how to be more productive in Visual Studio or perform certain development tasks.

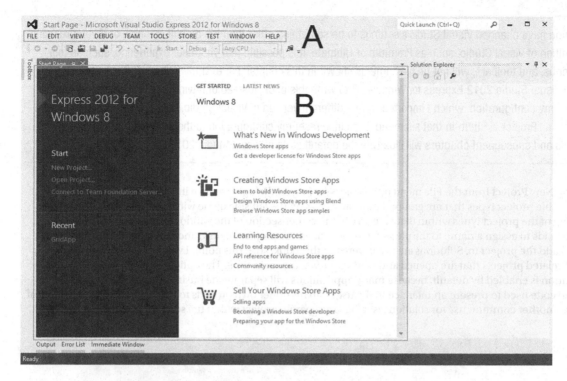

Figure 4-1. *Visual Studio initial user interface*

Figure 4-2. *File menu*

■ **Note** If you have changed Visual Studio's settings to be something other than the default settings, or if you are using a different edition of Visual Studio, such as Premium or Ultimate, it is possible that your user experience, such as tool windows, menus, and toolbars, will not be the same as shown in this chapter. For example, when I initially started working with Visual Studio 2012 Express for Windows 8 to write this book, instead of having a "New Project…" item in the File menu, my configuration, which I imported from a different version of Visual Studio, had a "New" submenu in the File menu, and a "Project…" item in that submenu. I've since reset my configuration to the default for the Express edition, so this and subsequent chapters will illustrate the default state of Visual Studio 2012 Express for Windows 8.

Selecting New Project from the File menu opens the New Project dialog, as shown in Figure 4-3. This dialog presents available project types that are grouped into categories on the left side of the window. Selecting a category shows a listing of the project types within that category in the center section of the window. At the bottom of the windows are fields to assign a name to the project, the location of the project on disk, and the name for a solution to create and add the project to. Solutions are not covered in this book, so at this point, I will just describe them as a collection of related projects that are opened and worked with at the same time. The option to create new projects within a solution is enabled by default, because many applications will separate the business logic, the data access code, and the code used to present an interface to the user into his or her own projects to help create a clean division of these duties. Another common use for solutions is to have a separate project within the solution to test the application.

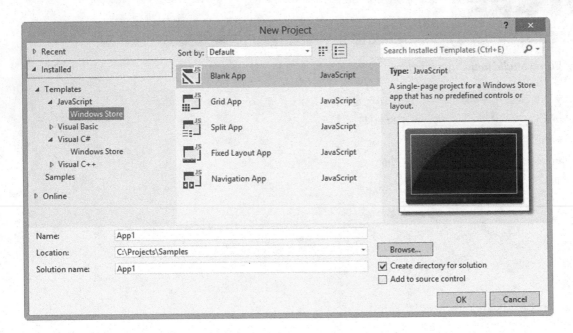

Figure 4-3. *New Project dialog*

Once a project has been created or opened, additional functionality is revealed. At the right side of the screen, the Solution Explorer window (shown in Figure 4-4) is populated with the file/folder structure of your project, allowing you to navigate to any file within the project and double-click to open a code editor. Figure 4-5 shows `default.js` open in the code editor.

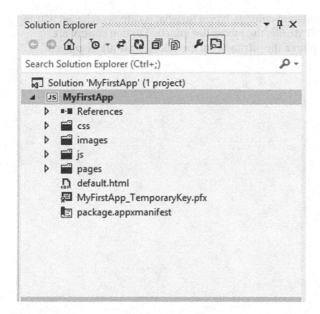

Figure 4-4. *Solution Explorer window*

```
1   // For an introduction to the Grid template, see the following documentation:
2   // http://go.microsoft.com/fwlink/?LinkID=232446
3   (function () {
4       "use strict";
5
6       WinJS.Binding.optimizeBindingReferences = true;
7
8       var app = WinJS.Application;
9       var activation = Windows.ApplicationModel.Activation;
10      var nav = WinJS.Navigation;
11
12      app.addEventListener("activated", function (args) {
13          if (args.detail.kind === activation.ActivationKind.launch) {
14              if (args.detail.previousExecutionState !== activation.ApplicationExecutionState
15                  // TODO: This application has been newly launched. Initialize
16                  // your application here.
17              } else {
18                  // TODO: This application has been reactivated from suspension.
19                  // Restore application state here.
20              }
21
22              if (app.sessionState.history) {
23                  nav.history = app.sessionState.history;
24              }
25              args.setPromise(WinJS.UI.processAll().then(function () {
26                  if (nav.location) {
27                      nav.history.current.initialPlaceholder = true;
28                      return nav.navigate(nav.location, nav.state);
29                  } else {
30                      return nav.navigate(Application.navigator.home);
31                  }
32              }));
```

Figure 4-5. *Code editor*

The Properties window, shown in Figure 4-6, contains different content, based on what is actively selected within Visual Studio. If the actively selected item is a control in an HTML file, the properties attached to that control are displayed. If the selected item is a file within the Solution Explorer, the attributes of the selected file are displayed.

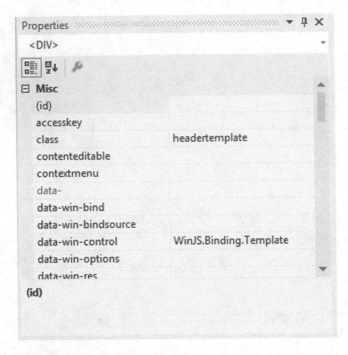

Figure 4-6. *Properties window*

The final user interface element I will discuss in this chapter is the Debug button on the toolbar, which is shown in Figure 4-7. This button is used to initiate a build and debugging session of your application within either your local machine, the built-in Windows 8 simulator, or a remote machine on your network. By activating the drop-down in this button, you can change the default runtime environment for your application.

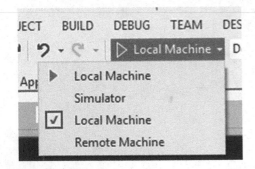

Figure 4-7. *Debug button*

I often run my applications on my local machine during development, but the simulator is handy because it provides the ability to test at different resolutions, change orientations, simulate touch events on a display that isn't touch enabled, and capture screenshots, which will come in handy when you prepare to submit your application to the Windows Store in Chapter 23. If you have a tablet, or any other machine for that matter, that you'd like to use for debugging your applications, using the Remote Machine option is pretty seamless once you configure both the remote machine and the Visual Studio project. You can find a good walkthrough of this process on MSDN at http://msdn.microsoft.com/en-us/library/windows/apps/hh441469.aspx. I followed these instructions to configure my Windows RT tablet for debugging in a matter of minutes.

I have just guided you through a whirlwind tour of the Visual Studio interface, stopping only to show you those features that you will need to work successfully with this book. I strongly encourage you to explore the different windows, menus, and options that are available within Visual Studio and learn how each can help with your development tasks.

Windows Store Application Types

In this section, I will cover the different application types that you can create using the project templates that ship with Visual Studio 2012. You can find these templates in the New Project dialog categorized under Installed ➤ Templates ➤ JavaScript ➤ Windows Store. I will cover only these application types here:

- Blank App
- Fixed Layout App
- Grid App
- Split App
- Navigation App

I will introduce the Windows Runtime Components project type, using the C# language, in Chapter 18.

Blank App

Blank App is the most basic of all the available Windows Store application project templates. The project it creates includes a starting set of images to be replaced with your own custom images for the application's logo and splash screen as well as a standard style sheet and a blank page. This project type works well when you have a single-page app that does not require the layout provided by the other templates.

Fixed Layout App

The Fixed Layout App project template, like the Blank App, provides a very basic starting point for your Windows Store application. In fact, the only difference between the Blank App and the Fixed Layout App templates is that the Fixed Layout App template is meant for applications that require a fixed aspect ratio. The contents of your application are contained in a ViewBox control, which scales its contents to fit.

This is recommended for games, because you can design your scene at, for example, a 1366 x 768 resolution, which is common for today's tablet computers. If the device has a different resolution, your game will be scaled accordingly, so that it appears the same for users on all devices.

Grid App

The Grid App template gives everything provided by the Blank App template, but it also provides the screens and application code for an application that drills down through varying levels of detail to browse hierarchical data. The application consists of three pages: a high-level view that shows all groups with a summarized view of the items within each group (illustrated in Figure 4-8), a group detail page that provides additional information about the group and a listing of the items that it contains (illustrated in Figure 4-9), and an item detail page that gives the finest level of detail on a single item within the group (illustrated in Figure 4-10). As you can see in the figures, this project template provides an application that has been practically prebuilt for you, requiring only that you modify it to fit your data.

Figure 4-8. *Default Grid App grouped items view*

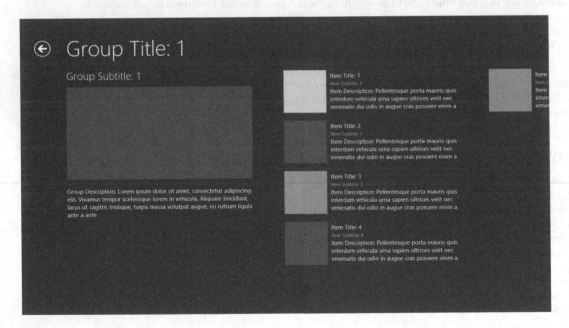

Figure 4-9. *Default Grid App group details view*

Figure 4-10. *Default Grid App item details view*

Split App

The Split App project template, as with the Grid App template, provides a ready-made application designed to browse hierarchical data. The main difference between Grid App and Split App is that Split App uses only two views to display the information. The first view, which is shown in Figure 4-11, displays a list of the groups into which items are categorized. Unlike Grid App, this view contains information only about the groups and does not display any item information. Selecting any group navigates to that group's item screen (shown in Figure 4-12), which provides a listing of the items in the group on the left side of the screen and shows the details of the selected item on the right side of the screen.

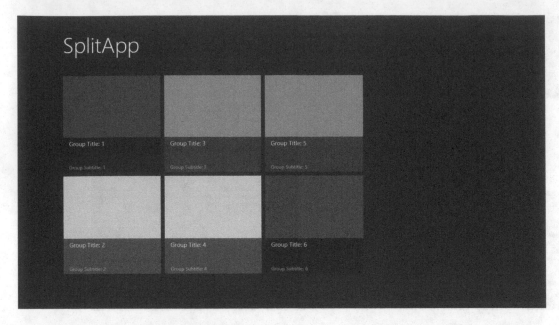

Figure 4-11. *Default Split App group view*

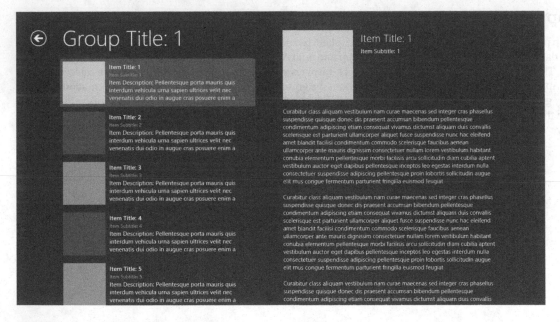

Figure 4-12. *Default Split App items view*

Navigation App

The Navigation App project template is my personal favorite. It includes the necessary components to support the navigation style common to Windows Store application without populating your solution with a number of files that are unnecessary or too niche. This project type will be the basis for an application that you will start building in Chapter 9 and continue to build across several chapters as you learn more concepts that can be applied to the application. New screens are added to your application by creating page controls, a process I will introduce in Chapter 5 and continue to do throughout most of the rest of this book.

If the Blank App template were a sheet of white printer paper, the Navigation App template would be a sheet of graph paper—both are essentially empty, but one provides some helpful structure. By contrast, the Grid App or Split App templates might be pages from a coloring book, where the outline of your application is provided and only the details must be filled in.

Conclusion

In this chapter, you were introduced to Visual Studio 2012 and to the Windows Store application types that can be built using the built-in project templates. For further learning, examine some existing Windows Store applications with the Grid App and Split App templates in mind. You may be surprised at how often you see components of these two approaches. For example, the News and Store apps installed with Windows 8 both take the Grid App approach, while the Mail app was designed based on the Split App template.

■ ■ ■

HTML Controls

As is the case with many new technologies, many people don't know exactly what HTML5 is. To some, it's all about video. To some, it's about semantic tags, such as the new header and nav tags. To some, it's a kind of new magic that makes web sites work on mobile devices. To others, it's simply the next version of the HTML we've known and loved for the last few decades. Regardless of what you may have heard, it's pretty safe to say that HTML5 isn't a single thing. In fact, much of what is considered HTML5 is a combination of three things: HTML, JavaScript, and CSS. There is no shortage of information on the Internet about HTML5 and its capabilities. A great resource is the HTML5 Rocks web site (www.html5rocks.com).

If you're not yet familiar with HTML5, this chapter is for you. In it, I will provide an overview of some of its more common elements. Because I am in the "HTML5 is simply the next version of HTML" camp, I'll generally refer to it simply as HTML. Also, I will often refer to HTML elements as controls, specifically when referring to an interface element that the user interacts with.

Fortunately, if you are familiar with HTML and the controls it offers, you'll be happy to know that all of that knowledge now applies to Windows 8 application development. The HTML and JavaScript that we will use to develop Windows 8 applications are the same HTML and JavaScript we would use to develop web sites. That said, you should still skim this chapter, as it does cover a few concepts that are particular to Windows Store application development.

Before diving in, you need to create a Visual Studio project to work with the samples.

Visual Studio Projects

As I mentioned in Chapter 4, Visual Studio is available in a number of different editions. Of the eight editions currently available, four can be used to create Windows Store applications. Those four are

- Visual Studio Express 2012 for Windows 8

- Visual Studio Professional 2012

- Visual Studio Premium 2012

- Visual Studio Ultimate 2012

Throughout this book, I will be using the free Express edition for all examples discussed. While the other editions provide some extra benefit for professional developers, you will see that it is very feasible to build a real-world application using free developer tools.

■ **Note** If you have access to the Professional, Premium, or Ultimate editions, by all means, take advantage of the extra features that they include. Just be aware that some default settings—such as menu items, keyboard shortcuts, and toolbars—may be different in these editions from screenshots and instructions in this book.

Over the next few pages, we're going to prepare our environment for the work we will be doing in this chapter and Chapters 6, 7, and 8. I'll walk through

- Creating a project
- Reviewing default project contents
- Adding a new page
- Navigating to the new page

Let's get started!

Creating a Project

As described in Chapter 4, there are many project templates available in Visual Studio for building Windows 8 applications with HTML and JavaScript. I've found that, for my tastes, the Navigation App template strikes the right balance of including enough of a framework to get started on an application, without including too much "new project bloat." So, let's start by creating a project from that template.

■ **Note** The source code that accompanies this book includes a completed project named WinJSControlsSample, which includes the sample code used in Chapters 5, 6, 7, and 8. You can find the code samples for this chapter on the Source Code/Downloads tab of the book's Apress product page (www.apress.com/9781430257790).

---

1. Open Visual Studio.
2. Select File ➤ New Project. This will open the New Project dialog (see Figure 5-1).

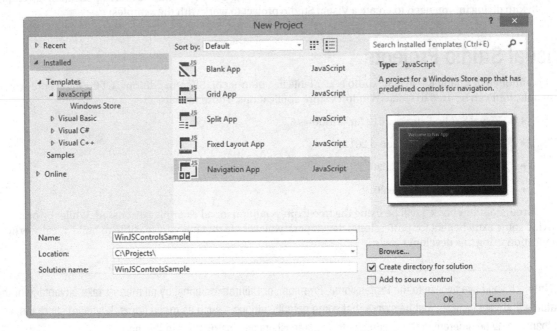

Figure 5-1. *New Project dialog*

3. In the left pane of the New Project dialog, select Templates ➤ JavaScript ➤ Windows Store.

4. Select the Navigation App project template.

5. Give the project a name: WinJSControlsSample.

6. Click "OK" to create your project.

At this point, you have a new project. Now, build it and run it by pressing Ctrl+F5. You should see something similar to Figure 5-2.

Figure 5-2. *The Navigation App, out of the box*

■ **Note** There are a few methods to stop the application from running. You can swipe down from the top of your touch screen or use your mouse to "grab" the top of the application and then drag it to the bottom of the screen. Alternatively, you can press Alt+F4 on your keyboard. Finally, if you are debugging (i.e., you pressed F5 instead of Ctrl+F5), you can use Alt+Tab to return to Visual Studio and stop the debugger.

Great! It's not very exciting, but it's a start. Now let's prepare the project for use in the samples over the next few chapters.

Reviewing Default Project Contents

A number of files are included when you create a project using the Navigation App template. A file named default.html is the starting point for your application. Visual Studio also created corresponding default.css and default.js files, as well as a navigator.js file, which contains the logic for our Navigation App. Some placeholder logo images were added, as well as a PageControl named home.html. You'll see most of these files as you work through the rest of the book, so I won't cover them in depth here.

Let's start by switching your application in order to use the light theme. Open default.html and find the code in Listing 5-1. This step isn't required, but it does make the screenshots in the next few chapters easier to read. You'll use a customized dark theme in the application you'll begin to build in Chapter 9.

Listing 5-1. Changing the Theme

```
<title>WinJSControlsSample</title>

<!-- WinJS references -->
<link href="//Microsoft.WinJS.1.0/css/ui-dark.css" rel="stylesheet" />
<script src="//Microsoft.WinJS.1.0/js/base.js"></script>
<script src="//Microsoft.WinJS.1.0/js/ui.js"></script>
```

Change the CSS reference from ui-dark.css to ui-light.css, then make the same change in home.html. Now, look through default.html and find the code in Listing 5-2. The PageControlNavigator will be the host to all of the page controls that you will add to this application. Notice that there is a reference to /pages/home/home.html. This is the home page of your app, and it will be loaded into default.html when the application launches. As you navigate through the completed application, default.html will always be visible, and the other pages will be loaded into this PageControlNavigator dynamically.

Listing 5-2. The PageControlNavigator

```
<div id="contenthost"
    data-win-control="Application.PageControlNavigator"
    data-win-options="{home: '/pages/home/home.html'}"></div>
```

Adding a New Page

Now let's add a new page to the application for the samples you'll be viewing in this chapter.

1. Right-click the pages folder and select Add ➤ New Folder. Name the new folder htmlcontrols (see Figure 5-3).

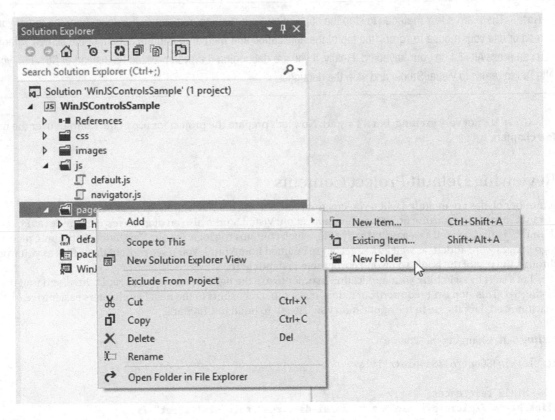

Figure 5-3. *Adding a new folder*

2. Right-click the htmlcontrols folder and select Add ➤ New Item.... This will open the Add New Item dialog.

3. Select the Page Control item.

4. Give the page control a name: htmlcontrols.

Visual Studio now creates three files, which, together, make up the page control: htmlcontrols.css, htmlcontrols.html, and htmlcontrols.js. In this chapter, most of your code will go into the htmlcontrols.html file. Open htmlcontrols.html and add the form element as shown in Listing 5-3.

Listing 5-3. Adding a Form

```
<body>
    <form id="myForm">
    <!-- SNIPPED -->
    </form>
</body>
```

While not required for your application, the form will allow you later in this chapter to take advantage of some built-in validation and button functionality. By default, however, when HTML forms are submitted, the data in the form is sent to the server in a request for a new page.

Because you don't wish to navigate to a new page when your form is submitted, you modify the ready function of htmlcontrols.js, as shown in Listing 5-4. This prevents the application from navigating away from your page.

Listing 5-4. Preventing the Default Form Submit

```
ready: function (element, options) {
    document.getElementById("myForm").addEventListener("submit", function (e) {
        e.preventDefault();
    });
},
```

Now, there's one last thing to do to prepare your sample application: let the user navigate to this new page.

Navigating to the New Page

As discussed above, right now the application will load home.html when the application launches. However, you're going to be adding your code to htmlcontrols.html. You need to provide some way to navigate from the one page to the other. Open home.html and find the main section element. Replace the placeholder content with code for a button, as I've done in Listing 5-5.

Listing 5-5. The New Main Content Section of home.html

```
<section aria-label="Main content" role="main">
    <p><button id="htmlButton">Chapter 5 - HTML Controls</button></p>
</section>
```

Now, open home.js and make the highlighted code changes in Listing 5-6.

Listing 5-6. Changes to home.js

```
"use strict";

var nav = WinJS.Navigation;

WinJS.UI.Pages.define("/pages/home/home.html", {
    // This function is called whenever a user navigates to this page. It
    // populates the page elements with the app's data.
    ready: function (element, options) {
        htmlButton.addEventListener("click", function (e) {
            nav.navigate("/pages/htmlcontrols/htmlcontrols.html")
        }, false);
    }
});
```

That's it. Save all your changes and run the application. When the application launches, you should see a page similar to Figure 5-4.

Welcome to WinJSControlsSample!

Chapter 5 - HTML Controls

Figure 5-4. *The home page of the application*

Clicking the button should take you to a page similar to Figure 5-5. Because you are using the Navigation App template and page controls for your pages, the back button is automatically wired up. Clicking it will return you to the application home page.

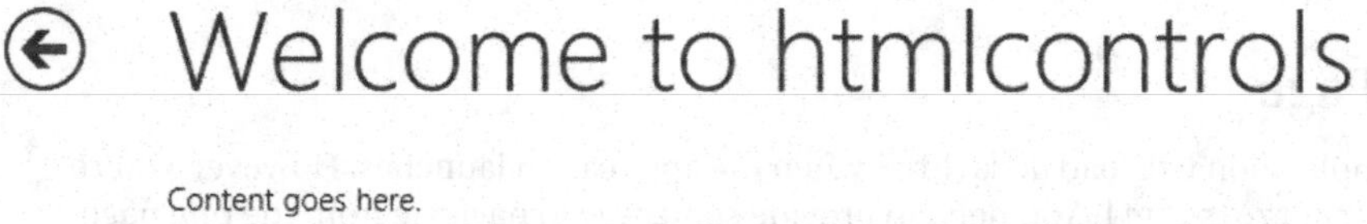

(←) Welcome to htmlcontrols

Content goes here.

Figure 5-5. *The current contents of htmlcontrols.html*

The Controls

HTML has been used to build web applications for many years now. Building a Windows 8 application with HTML and JavaScript is similar in many ways to building web applications. Many controls are provided by HTML for building applications. In this chapter, I'll quickly cover many of the most common controls. This chapter is not meant to be an exhaustive reference on these HTML controls, but a brief description and sample usage will be provided for each.

■ **Note** If you're following along, implementing all of the examples in this chapter, be sure to put all of your sample code between the `<section aria-label="Main content" role="main">` and `</section>` elements of htmlcontrols.html.

Labels

The label is perhaps the simplest of all the HTML controls I'll cover. By default, it doesn't change the appearance of its content in any way, although it can be styled with CSS. A label is typically used to associate some text with an input field using the `for` attribute. When the `for` attribute of a label control matches the `id` attribute of an input control, clicking or touching that label selects or toggles the input control. This is great for usability, especially when using touch, as it gives the user a bigger, contextual target for selecting an input field.

Adding a label to a page is straightforward. In Listing 5-7, you can see the single line that is required to place a label on the page. By setting the `id` attribute to `"myLabel"`, you can refer to this label in your JavaScript code, as well as style the label with CSS.

Listing 5-7. Adding a Label

```
<label id="myLabel" for="myTextbox">This is text in a label</label>
```

Setting the `for` attribute to `"myTextbox"` associates this label with another control defined somewhere on this page. When a user clicks `myLabel`, the `myTextbox` control will be brought into focus. The result of this code can be seen in Figure 5-6.

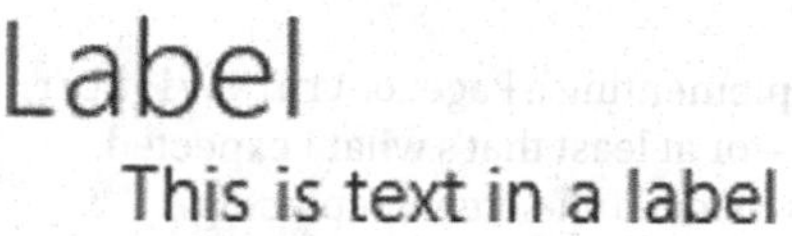

Label
This is text in a label

Figure 5-6. *Label*

In addition to associating text with an input field, one might consider using a label for other text, such as error messages and other dynamic user feedback, or even as a simple way to make text stylable. While this is functionally possible, it is considered by many to be semantically incorrect. For cases such as these, you should consider using the HTML `span` or `div` elements, or other elements that make more sense semantically. An example of this can be seen in Chapter 6 in the discussion of the `MessageDialog`, where a `span` element is used to dynamically display the user's choice in the `MessageDialog`.

Links

An application with only one screen can certainly be useful, but more often than not, your application will require multiple screens. There are a few ways to navigate from one screen to another, but one of the simplest uses the HTML link.

HTML Link

Listing 5-8 shows that code you can add to `htmlcontrols.html` to place a link on the page. Add this code, then add another page control named `otherpage`, following the same steps you used to create the `htmlcontrols` page control. This is the page that your link will navigate to.

Listing 5-8. Adding a Link

```
<a id="myLink" href="/pages/otherpage/otherpage.html">Link to another page</a>
```

Now run the application. Things look pretty good, and you should see a link on the page similar to that illustrated in Figure 5-7. Clicking the link will navigate to `otherpage.html`; so, give that a try.

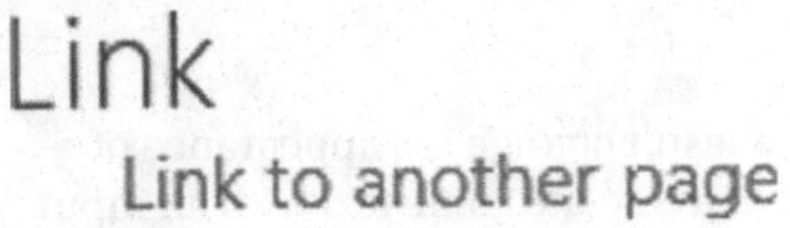

Link
Link to another page

Figure 5-7. Link

Did the other page look how you expected it to? Probably not. I know that the first time I clicked a link in an application I was building, the result was a little jarring. I saw the content I expected from `otherpage.html`, but I had expected the application's formatting to be retained on the new page. Instead, the margins and other styling had disappeared, as seen in Figure 5-8.

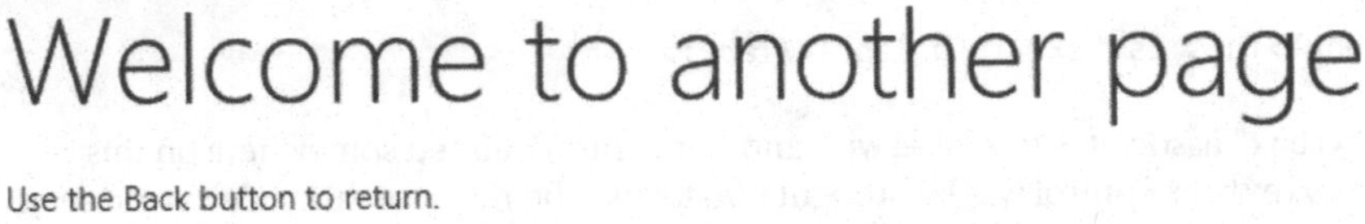

Welcome to another page

Use the Back button to return.

Figure 5-8. Another page, but not quite what was expected

So what happened? Earlier, in Listing 5-2, you saw code in `default.html` implementing a `PageControlNavigator`. All of your pages, such as `otherpage.html`, were to be loaded into that container—or at least that's what I expected. Instead, clicking the link caused a top-level navigation, and `otherpage.html` was loaded full-screen, replacing `default.html` and the navigation container. As it turns out, using the `PageControlNavigator` requires navigation to be handled differently.

The Navigate Method

When you created this application from the Navigation App project template, you implicitly made the decision to trade ability to use simple links for the convenience of an application that handles navigation between pages and provides a consistent user experience. In order to have the navigation happen as you expect, you need a special method for navigating between pages. Windows 8 provides the `WinJS.Navigation.navigate` method for this purpose. You were already introduced to this method in Listing 5-6. You added a button to `home.html`, and in `home.js` you added an event handler to the button's `click` event. Then as you viewed `home.html` and `htmlcontrols.html`, the navigation "just worked." To get this link to work as expected, you have only to use that same method here. Let's remove the `href` attribute from the link in `htmlcontrols.html` (see Listing 5-9), and let's add a handler for the link's `click` event to the **ready** function in `htmlcontrols.js` (see Listing 5-10).

Listing 5-9. Changing the Link

```
<a id="myLink">Link to another page</a>
```

Listing 5-10. Handling the Links Click Event

```
ready: function (element, options) {
    myLink.addEventListener("click", function (e) {
        nav.navigate("/pages/otherpage/otherpage.html")
    }, false);
},
```

Now if you run the application and click the link, you see what was expected (see Figure 5-9). The margins and back button appear to be correct for otherpage.html. In fact, the back button is already wired up to navigate back to htmlcontrols.html when it is clicked.

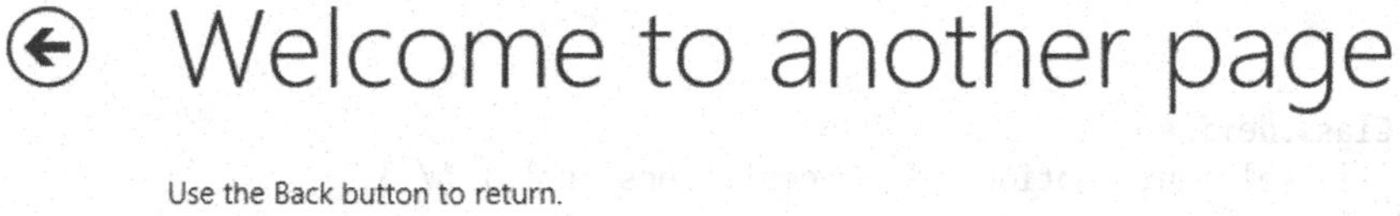

← Welcome to another page

Use the Back button to return.

Figure 5-9. *This is what was expected*

Mission accomplished! Right? Well, technically, yes, but what if you have five links on a page? What if you have twenty-five links in your application? What if you have a list of links dynamically generated from a data source? Updating each link and adding a click event handler to each, while possible, is not very efficient. Fortunately, there is an alternative.

Using Queries to Convert HTML Links to Use the Navigate Method

Windows 8 provides the WinJS.Utilities.query method, which allows you to grab a collection of elements matching a query selector and then do something with each element in that collection. In your case, you will add click event handlers to each element that matches a query for links (see Listing 5-11).

Listing 5-11. Adding Event Handlers to a Collection of Links

```
WinJS.Utilities.query("a").listen("click", function (e) {
    e.preventDefault();
    nav.navigate(e.target.href);
});
```

I'll walk you through this to explain what each statement is doing. The function call WinJS.Utilities. query("a") finds all links—all the a elements—on the current page. For each link that is found, the listen method is called to handle the click event, and an anonymous function is provided as the event handler. Calling e.preventDefault prevents the default behavior, a top-level navigation to the address specified in the link's href attribute, from happening. Then, the call to navigate performs the navigation as expected.

■ **Note** If you're familiar with jQuery, WinJS.Utilities.query behaves very similarly to the jQuery $ function. Both take a selector (www.w3.org/TR/css3-selectors/) and return a collection of matching DOM elements. If you prefer jQuery, you will be happy to know that you can use it in your Windows 8 applications, along with WinJS functionality.

Now you have a few options on where you can place the code from Listing 5-11. One choice would be to place it in the ready function of each page control, similar to what you did with the button click handler in home.js (Listing 5-6). That would be perfectly valid, but it would potentially lead to several files with duplicated code. When you selected the Navigation App template for your project, Visual Studio added a file named navigator.js to the js folder, which is where the PageControlNavigator control is defined. This seems like a good place to add your click event handler. In Listing 5-12, I'll define a class named NavigationUtilities and add a static method named HandleLinkClickWithNavigate to that class. I'll add the code from Listing 5-11 as the body of the HandleLinkClickWithNavigate method.

Listing 5-12. Defining the NavigationUtilities Class

```
WinJS.Namespace.define("Application", {
    PageControlNavigator: WinJS.Class.define(
        // SNIPPED
    ),

    NavigationUtilities: WinJS.Class.define(
        function NavigationUtilities(element, options) { /* empty constructor */ },
        { /* no instance methods */ },
        { /* static methods */
            // change all links to use navigation methods instead
            HandleLinkClickWithNavigate: function () {
                WinJS.Utilities.query("a").listen("click", function (e) {
                    e.preventDefault();
                    nav.navigate(e.target.href);
                });
            }
        }
    )
});
```

Now, you must make sure this method is called after the page has loaded. As in Listing 5-13, you do that by calling the HandleLinkClickWithNavigate in the ready function of htmlcontrols.js.

Listing 5-13. The Modified Ready Function in htmlcontrols.js

```
ready: function (element, options) {
    Application.NavigationUtilities.HandleLinkClickWithNavigate();
    document.getElementById("myForm").addEventListener("submit", function (e) {
        e.preventDefault();
    });
},
```

The last thing you must do is to add the link's href attribute again, which you removed earlier, making it look similar to Listing 5-8 again. Now when you run the application and click the link, the navigation happens as expected, but you have the added benefit that any other links you add to your application will also work as expected.

One thing to keep in mind, though, is that this approach will cause *all* links to behave this way. If you have any links that you want to behave differently, you will have to modify the HandleLinkClickWithNavigate method. One possibility would be to change the query from WinJS.Utilities.query("a") to WinJS.Utilities.query ("a:not(.defaultClick)"), then adding a CSS class of defaultClick to any link for which you wish to preserve the default behavior. There are many ways around this, and this is only one option.

Text Input Controls

Most applications accept text input from users in one form or another. It may be a search field, a login screen, or a data entry form, but it's rare than an application does not accept text input. HTML provides a few choices for text input: a single-line text input, password input, and multiline text input.

Single-Line Text Input

Adding basic text input to a page of your application is done with the HTML `input` element. As you'll see throughout this chapter, the `input` element is used for many different types of input, which are specified by the `type` attribute. Perhaps the most widely used is the text input, commonly called a text box. Add the code from Listing 5-14 to `htmlcontrols.html` and run your application and you'll see a simple text input, similar to that shown in Figure 5-10.

Listing 5-14. Adding a Text Input Control

```
<input type="text" id="myTextbox" />
```

Text input

Figure 5-10. *Text input*

This control also has a few other attributes that can be set to change the behavior of the text input control. Some of the more common attributes are

- `placeholder`: This attribute allows you to provide some text that is used to provide some instruction to the user, often a sample of valid input. The text is visible when the field is empty, but disappears when the field is in focus.

- `maxlength`: This attribute allows you to specify the maximum number of characters allowed in a text input control. It is a simple, first level of data validation and is especially useful when user input will ultimately be saved to a database field that has a specified maximum length.

- `required`: This attribute indicates that the user must enter something into the text input control in order to be valid. This is a validation attribute that is part of the validation functionality provided by HTML.

- `pattern`: This attribute allows you to specify a regular expression that will be used to validate the text the user enters into the text input control. This is a validation attribute that is part of the validation functionality provided by HTML.

- `title`: This attribute allows you to specify text to be used as a tooltip for the control. Additionally, if the pattern attribute is specified and the user enters invalid text, the content of this attribute is also included as part of the error message shown to the user.

Listing 5-15 shows the simple syntax for using these attributes.

Listing 5-15. Adding Placeholder Text to Your Text Input

```
<input type="text" id="myTextbox"
    placeholder="Enter your name"
    maxlength="15"
    required
    pattern="^[A-Za-z]*$"
    title="Only characters, A-Z or a-z" />
```

When you run the application, you will see a control with placeholder text, as in Figure 5-11, and you will not be able to enter more than 15 characters into this field. Additionally, when the user attempts to submit the form, validation will occur to make sure the user entered something (because of the `required` attribute) and that only alpha characters were entered (because the `pattern` attribute only allows letters). Submitting the form with invalid text, or failing to enter any text at all, will result in an error message being shown to the user (see Figure 5-12).

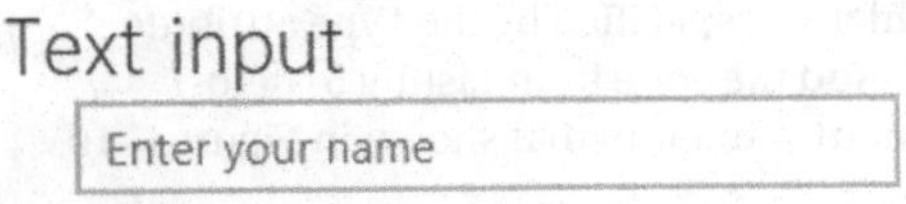

Text input

Enter your name

Figure 5-11. Text input, with placeholder text

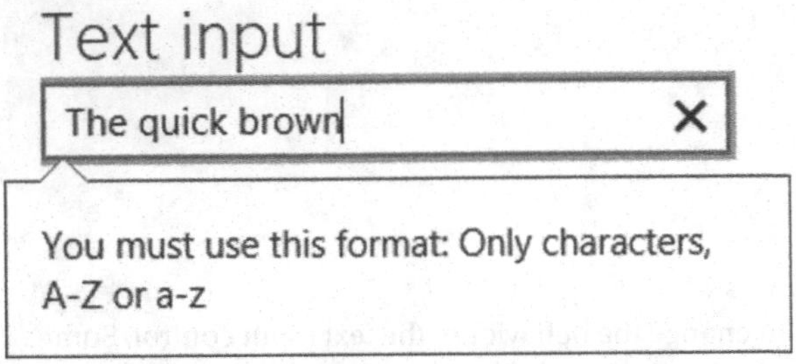

Text input

The quick brown ✕

You must use this format: Only characters, A-Z or a-z

Figure 5-12. Text input, with invalid text containing spaces

■ **Note** While the `maxlength` attribute is always enforced, the HTML validation does not get triggered until the form is submitted. I will discuss submitting forms later in this chapter when I get to the "Buttons" section. A great tutorial about the new form validation functionality provided by HTML5 can be found at `www.html5rocks.com/en/tutorials/forms/constraintvalidation/`.

As long as the user enters valid text, no error messages are displayed. One feature of text input controls new to Windows 8 applications (and Microsoft's Internet Explorer 10 web browser) can be seen in Figure 5-13. As the user is entering text, an × button appears in the text input control. Clicking this button clears the text input control so the user can enter new text.

Text input

Scott ✕

Figure 5-13. Text input with text, in focus

If you have a reason to hide this clear button, you can use the CSS to style the `-ms-clear` pseudo-element. The code in Listing 5-16 can be added to `default.css` to remove the clear button from all text input controls in your application.

Listing 5-16. Removing the Clear Button from Text Input Controls

```
::-ms-clear {
    display: none;
}
```

Password Input

Passwords are another type of text commonly typed into an application, and HTML provides a password input control. These controls behave very much like the single-line text input controls I just covered, but with the added security benefit of masking the user input so that prying eyes cannot see what is being typed. To add a password input control, add the code from Listing 5-17 to `htmlcontrols.html`.

Listing 5-17. Adding a Password Input Control

```
<input type="password" id="myPassword" />
```

Run the application, and you will see a password field that looks very much like a text input control (Figure 5-14). Typing in the field, however, does not show your text by default. Instead, it shows the familiar black dots seen in Figure 5-15.

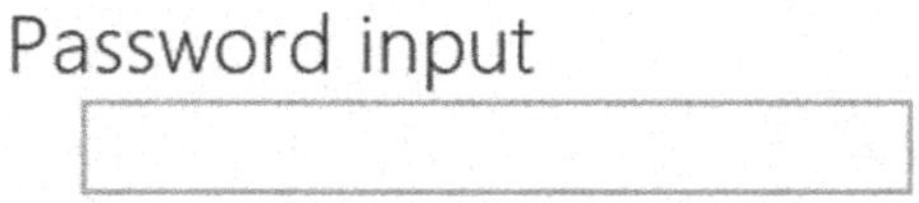

Password input

Figure 5-14. *Password input*

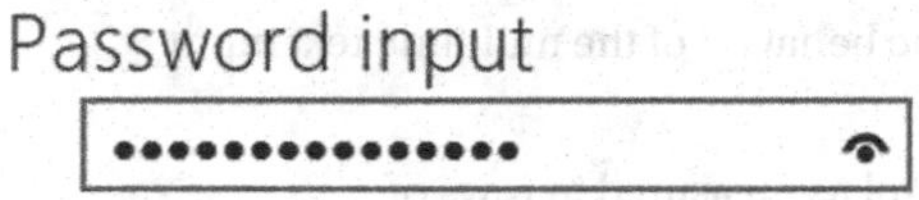

Password input

•••••••••••••   ⌃

Figure 5-15. *Password input, with text (masked with dots)*

Most of the optional attributes that can be applied to text input controls can also be applied to password input controls. Specifically, the `placeholder`, `maxlength`, `required`, `pattern`, and `title` attributes all create the behavior for password controls, as they do for regular text controls.

I mentioned that the password input control doesn't show the user's text by default. However, similar to the × button that clears text on text input controls, password input controls have a button that will reveal the text that has been entered. While the button is clicked and held the password is revealed, and when the button is released, the password is again masked with dots (see Figure 5-16). Similar to removing the × button on text input controls with CSS, this button can be removed by styling the `-ms-reveal` pseudo-element.

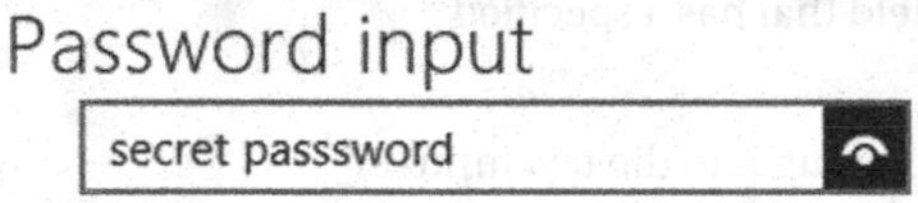

Password input

secret passsword   ⊙

Figure 5-16. *Password input, with password revealed*

Multiline Text Input

Sometimes you need more text than a single-line text input control can provide. Using HTML's `textarea` element, you can create a multiline text input control, which allows for long text and text with carriage returns. Add the code from Listing 5-18 to `htmlcontrols.html`.

Listing 5-18. Adding a Multiline Text Input Control

```
<textarea id="myTextarea"></textarea>
```

This will create the most basic multiline text input control, as seen in Figure 5-17. Scrollbars appear if the content is too big to fit into the control (see Figure 5-18).

Multiline text input

Figure 5-17. *Multiline text input*

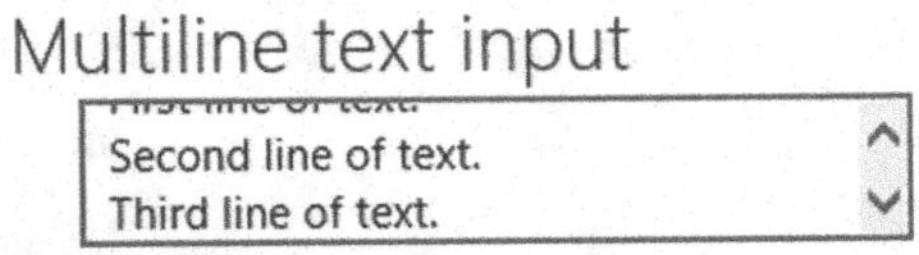

Multiline text input

First line of text.	
Second line of text.	∧
Third line of text.	∨

Figure 5-18. *Multiline text input, with text and scrollbar*

This control also has a few other attributes that can be set to change the behavior of the multiline text input control. Some of the more common ones are

- `rows`: This attribute allows you to specify the height of the control as measured in rows of text. For example, setting `rows="5"` will increase the height of your above control to make five lines of text visible. The height of a multiline text input control can also be set in CSS with the `height` property.

- `cols`: This attribute allows you to specify the width of the control as measured by the approximate number of characters that will fit on a line. For example, setting `cols="50"` will increase the width of your above control so that approximately 50 characters fit on each line. Because character width is not constant in most fonts, some characters take up more space than others, and you may have more or fewer characters per line, depending on the content. The width of a multiline text input control can also be set in CSS with the `width` property.

- `maxlength`: This attribute allows you to specify the maximum number of characters allowed in a multiline text input control. It is a simple, first level of data validation and is especially useful when user input will ultimately be saved to a database field that has a specified maximum length.

- `required`: This attribute indicates that the user must enter something into the text input control in order to be valid. This is a validation attribute that is part of the validation functionality provided by HTML.

- `title`: This attribute allows you to specify text to be used as a tooltip for the control.

Choice Controls

What size pizza do you want? Which toppings do you want on your pizza? Do you want to dine in, carry out, or have it delivered? As with placing a pizza order, applications can present a multitude of choices to users. HTML provides a few controls for making choices: a drop-down list, a check box, and a radio button.

Drop-Down List

Drop-down lists can offer a large number of options to the user in a small space. Let's add one and experiment with it a bit. Add the code in Listing 5-19 to `htmlcontrols.html`.

Listing 5-19. Adding a Drop-Down List Control

```
<select id="mySelect">
    <option value="option1">Option 1</option>
    <option value="option2">Option 2</option>
    <option value="option3">Option 3</option>
    <option selected="selected" value="option4">Option 4</option>
    <option value="option5">Option 5</option>
    <option value="option6">Option 6</option>
    <option value="option7">Option 7</option>
    <option value="option8">Option 8</option>
    <option value="option9">Option 9</option>
    <option value="option10">Option 10</option>
</select>
```

This code does a number of things. It adds a drop-down list to the page; it adds ten options to that drop-down list for the user to choose between; and it makes the fourth option the default, selected option when the page loads (see Figure 5-19). The default behavior of the drop-down list is to allow only one selection and to show only the option that is selected. Clicking or touching the drop-down list expands the control to show all of the options to the user (see Figure 5-20). If the list were too long, scrollbars would be automatically added.

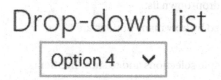

Figure 5-19. *Drop-down list control*

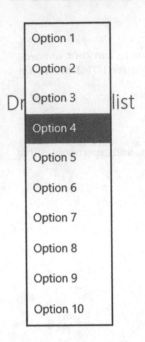

Drop-down list

Figure 5-20. *Drop-down list control, expanded*

This control also has a few attributes that can be set to change the behavior of the drop-down list. Some of the more common ones are

- selected: This is an attribute of the option element, seen in Listing 5-19, that allows you to specify which options are selected by default. If the multiple attribute is used, then the selected attribute can be added to more than one option element.

- multiple: This attribute allows you to specify that the user can select multiple options from the list. This is done by pressing the Ctrl key while selecting each of the desired options. When this attribute is set, the list is displayed as a list box, instead of as a drop-down list.

- size: This attribute allows you to specify the size of the list measured by how many options are visible to the user without scrolling.

In Listing 5-20, you can modify your previous drop-down list to allow multiple selections and to show five items at a time.

Listing 5-20. Adding a Drop-Down List Control That Allows Multiple Selections

```
<select id="mySelect" multiple size="5">
    <option value="option1">Option 1</option>
    <option value="option2">Option 2</option>
    <option value="option3">Option 3</option>
    <option selected="selected" value="option4">Option 4</option>
    <option value="option5">Option 5</option>
    <option value="option6">Option 6</option>
```

```
        <option value="option7">Option 7</option>
        <option value="option8">Option 8</option>
        <option value="option9">Option 9</option>
        <option value="option10">Option 10</option>
</select>
```

When you run the application, you will see a list, similar to Figure 5-21. You'll be able to select multiple items (because of the `multiple` attribute) by holding down Ctrl while selecting options.

Drop-down list

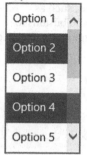

Figure 5-21. *Drop-down list, resized and allowing multiple selections*

Check Box

A check box is a great choice when you need to ask the user a "yes or no" question, or when there are a number of options and the user is allowed to select multiple. In Listing 5-21, you can add a single check box to `htmlcontrols.html`.

Listing 5-21. Adding a Check Box Control

```
<input type="checkbox" id="myCheckbox" />
<label for="myCheckbox">Check the box</label>
```

Check box

☐ Check the box

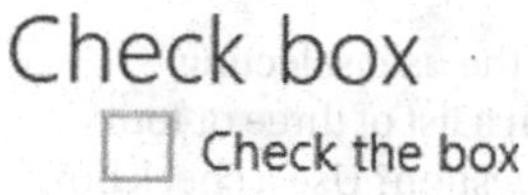

Figure 5-22. *Check box, unchecked*

Note the use of a label, which toggles the check box when its contents are clicked or touched. By default, the check box is unchecked, as seen in Figure 5-22.

This control has a few attributes that can be set to change the behavior of the check box control. The most common is the checked attribute (see Listing 5-22).

Listing 5-22. Adding a Check Box Control

```
<input type="checkbox" id="myCheckbox" checked />
<label for="myCheckbox">Check the box</label>
```

65

This attribute allows you to specify which, if the check box is checked by default (see Figure 5-23).

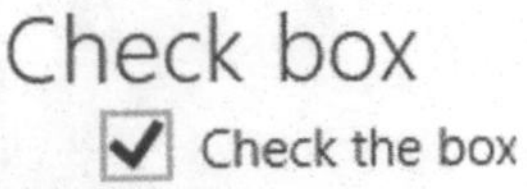

Check box

☑ Check the box

Figure 5-23. *Check box, checked*

Radio Button

Radio buttons are useful when the user needs to select one option from a short list of possible options, such as answering questions on multiple-choice tests or responding to a survey. In Listing 5-23, I add two radio buttons to `htmlcontrols.html`. Each radio button is represented by an HTML `input` element with the `type` attribute set to `radio`. I have again added a label control for each radio button for better usability.

Listing 5-23. Adding Radio Buttons

```
<input type="radio" id="myRadio1" name="myRadioButtonGroup" value="radio1" />
<label for="myRadio1">Option 1</label>
<input type="radio" id="myRadio2" name="myRadioButtonGroup" value="radio2" checked />
<label for="myRadio2">Option 2</label>
```

When you run your application, you will see two radio buttons (see Figure 5-24). Option 2 is initially selected, owing to the checked attribute, and you should be able to toggle between the two options. Each radio button has a unique `id` attribute, but the `name` attribute is the same. The `name` attribute is used to group related radio buttons together, and each group of radio buttons on your page will require a different `name` attribute.

Radio buttons

○ Option 1 ● Option 2

Figure 5-24. *Radio buttons*

Choosing a Choice Control

A number of factors should be considered when deciding which type of choice control to use. Is the user selecting one option from a long list of options? Use a drop-down list. Is the user selecting one option from a list of three or four options? Perhaps a series of radio buttons would be better. Is the user answering a "yes or no" question? Use a check box.

Clearly, there is more to making this decision than exemplified in these three simple scenarios. Microsoft has provided guidance on how to determine if a control is the right one to use in a number of situations.

- *Drop-down list*: http://msdn.microsoft.com/en-us/library/windows/desktop/aa511458.aspx

- *Check box*: http://msdn.microsoft.com/en-us/library/windows/desktop/aa511452.aspx

- *Radio button*: http://msdn.microsoft.com/en-us/library/windows/desktop/aa511488.aspx

Buttons

When a user has to initiate some sort of action, such as saving data or performing a search, you should provide a button control. HTML provides three different types of button control, two of which are designed to meet very specific needs: a reset button, used to reset all the fields in a form to their default values; a submit button, to trigger a form's submit event; and a standard button, for any other use. Add the code from Listing 5-24 to htmlcontrols.html.

Listing 5-24. Adding Button Controls

```
<button type="button" id="myButton">Button</button>
<button type="reset" id="myReset">Reset</button>
<button type="submit" id="mySubmit">Submit</button>
```

Run the application to see the buttons, as seen in Figure 5-25.

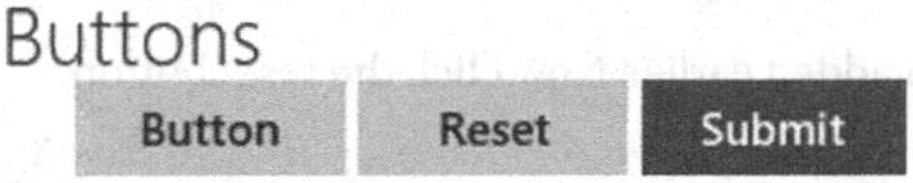

Buttons

Button   Reset   Submit

Figure 5-25. *Buttons*

While your button will typically contain only plain text, buttons are allowed to contain other, richer types of content as well, such as images or formatted text. For example, in Listing 5-25, you can create a button that contains an image of a squirrel and some formatted text.

Listing 5-25. Adding a Richer Button

```
<button type="button" id="myButton">
    <img src="/images/60/Squirrel.png" /><br />
    Click the <em>squirrel</em>!
</button>
```

Your squirrel button can be seen in Figure 5-26.

Buttons

Click the *squirrel*!

Figure 5-26. *Rich button*

■ **Note** The squirrel image can be found in the WinJSControlsSample project, which is included in source code that accompanies this book. You can find the code samples for this chapter on the Source Code/Downloads tab of the book's Apress product page (www.apress.com/9781430257790).

Reset Button

The reset button is the simplest, so I'll start with that. When a button control's `type` attribute is set to `reset`, the button is assigned default functionality that will change the value of all other fields in a form to their initial value. Because this behavior is assigned automatically, you do not need to handle the `click` event of a reset button; however, a reset button must be within the form for this default behavior to work. At the beginning of this chapter, in Listing 5-3 (repeated here in Listing 5-26), I added a `form` to `htmlcontrols.html` to allow this example to work.

Listing 5-26. *Adding a Form*

```
<body>
    <form id="myForm">
    <!-- SNIPPED -->
    </form>
</body>
```

Run the application and enter some text into the text input control you added earlier. Now click the reset button, and the text should be cleared.

Submit Button

Another instance when a button control has default behavior assigned to it is when its `type` attribute is set to `submit`. In this case, clicking or touching the button will submit the form by triggering the form's `submit` event. Submit buttons also receive different styling by default, as seen in Figure 5-25. Additionally, submit buttons are the default button on a page, so if the Enter key is pressed while the cursor is in a single-line text input field, for example, the form is submitted. As with the reset button, the submit button must be within a form for the default behavior to work, and you do not need to handle its `click` event; however, you can choose to handle the form's `submit` event.

Actually, this is exactly what you did earlier in Listing 5-4 (repeated here in Listing 5-27). In that case, you just canceled the form submission by calling the `preventDefault` function. Later in this book, I'll add more functionality to the `submit` event to do more interesting things when a form is submitted.

Listing 5-27. *Preventing the Default Form Submit*

```
ready: function (element, options) {
    document.getElementById("myForm").addEventListener("submit", function (e) {
        e.preventDefault();
    });
},
```

Standard Button

The standard button is what HTML provides when you set the `type` attribute of the button control to `button`, and it is used to initiate some action. While the reset button and submit button each have a very specific purpose, the standard button is for everything else. In fact, you can use a standard button to submit or reset a form as well. However, you would lose the benefits of having the default behavior that comes with using these specialized buttons. When using a standard button on your page, you will add your functionality to the button's `click` event. This is what you see in Listing 5-6, where I added a `click` event handler to the button on `home.html`.

Progress Indicators

A progress indicator control provides visual feedback to your user about the status of some action or process. It could be used to indicate that the user is on the third of five steps in a wizard, or to provide feedback on a multifile download. Windows 8 applications can display progress indicators in three different ways: a determinate bar, an indeterminate bar, and an indeterminate ring.

Determinate Bar

A determinate bar is used when the amount of remaining work or time is known. This indicator lets the user see how much progress your application has made. It is displayed as a bar, and as work is completed, the color changes from left to right until the work is complete and the bar is filled. To add a determinate progress bar, add the code from Listing 5-28 to `htmlcontrols.html`.

Listing 5-28. Adding a Determinate Progress Bar Control

```
<progress id="myProgressDeterminate" value="75" max="100" />
```

Specifying the `value` and `max` attributes adds a progress bar that is 75 percent filled. You can see this in Figure 5-27.

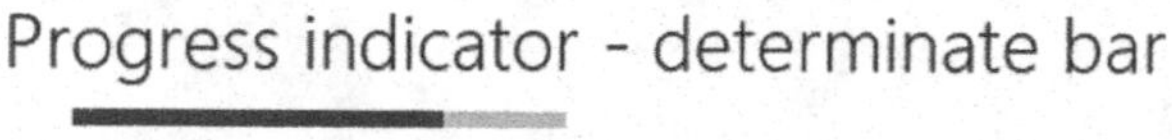

Progress indicator - determinate bar

Figure 5-27. *Progress indicator, determinate bar*

Indeterminate Bar

An indeterminate bar is used when the amount of remaining work or time is not known. This indicator is displayed as a repeating animation of dots scrolling from left to right. This indicator is typically used when the user can still interact with your application while the action or process is in progress. To add an indeterminate progress bar, add the code from Listing 5-29 to `htmlcontrols.html`.

Listing 5-29. Adding an Indeterminate Progress Bar Control

```
<progress id="myProgressIndeterminateBar" />
```

Because no `value` or `max` attributes are specified, this adds the animated progress bar seen in Figure 5-28.

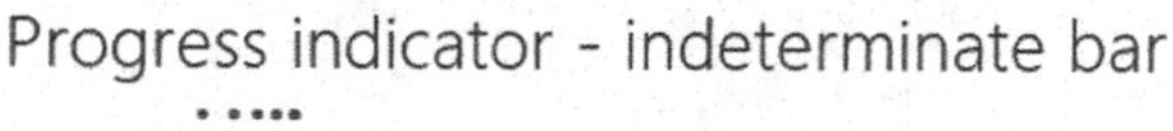

Progress indicator - indeterminate bar

• •••••

Figure 5-28. *Progress indicator, indeterminate bar*

Indeterminate Ring

An indeterminate ring is used when the amount of remaining work or time is not known. This indicator is displayed as a repeating animation of dots spinning in a circle. This indicator is typically used when the user is not allowed to interact with your application while the action or process in progress. To add an indeterminate progress ring, add the code from Listing 5-30 to `htmlcontrols.html`.

Listing 5-30. Adding an Indeterminate Progress Ring Control

```
<progress id="myProgressIndeterminateRing" class="win-ring" />
```

Just as with the indeterminate bar, no value or max attributes are specified. In this case, the special "win-ring" CSS class provided by Windows 8 is added, and this adds the animated progress ring seen in Figure 5-29.

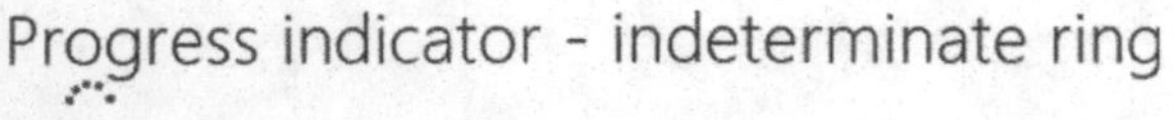

Progress indicator - indeterminate ring

Figure 5-29. *Progress indicator, indeterminate ring*

Conclusion

In this chapter, you learned about some of the more common controls provided by HTML. If you are a web developer, then you have probably already seen all of these controls in web applications. The controls have been used to build web applications for years, and many useful Windows 8 applications can be built using only these controls. In Chapters 6 and 7, I will discuss additional controls provided by Windows 8 to make your applications look and feel like Windows 8 applications.

CHAPTER 6

■ ■ ■

WinJS Controls

In Chapter 5, I covered some common HTML controls available for use in your Windows 8 applications built with HTML and JavaScript. If you have a background in web development, you are probably familiar with the material I covered in Chapter 5. Over the course of the next few chapters, I'll cover the various controls included with WinJS.

In this chapter, I'll introduce most of the common WinJS controls that you are likely to use in any applications you might build. The controls in this chapter will allow you to build things such as navigation, user input, and user feedback mechanisms in a manner consistent with the rest of Windows 8.

In Chapter 7, I'll introduce the ListView, FlipView, and SemanticZoom controls, which are built to work with collections of objects. These controls allow you to define a template that is used to display each item in your collection. If you have a piece of complicated UI that you'd like to use more than once in your application, then Chapter 8 is for you. You'll discover how you can use WinJS to build your own custom controls.

But before I dig into WinJS and all of the options it has created for controls, I'll cover first what WinJS actually is.

WinJS, WinRT, Windows RT, and Windows 8

In 2012, Microsoft released a new operating system named Windows 8. You, of course, know that, or you wouldn't be reading this book. Simultaneous with the release of Windows 8, Microsoft released another new operating system, named Windows RT. Windows RT is designed to run specifically on ARM-based devices, such as tablets.

Windows 8 and Windows RT have a few key differences, the two most notable are

- Windows RT cannot run applications built for earlier versions of Windows.

- Windows RT runs on devices with ARM processors, whereas Windows 8 runs on the same familiar hardware architecture that supported Windows 7.

Differences aside, Windows 8 and Windows RT do have a lot in common. Some of the shared features of Windows 8 and Windows RT include

- The Start screen with the tile layout

- The use of "live tiles" to present the user with a wealth of personalized information

- The use of the Microsoft design language, discussed in Chapter 2

- The ability to run Windows Store applications

Because this book is about creating Windows Store applications, you'll be happy to know that any application you build using these concepts will work on both Windows 8 and Windows RT devices. In fact, all of the code that I'm presenting has been tested on both operating systems: Windows 8, on my laptop, and Windows RT, on my Surface tablet. So, unless specifically called out otherwise, whenever I refer to the Windows operating system in this book, I am referring to both Windows 8 and Windows RT.

Windows provides two different libraries for building Windows Store applications with HTML and JavaScript. The first is the Windows Runtime, frequently referred to as WinRT. The Windows Runtime is common to both Windows 8 and Windows RT, and it can be used to build Windows Store applications in many languages. For example, the Windows Runtime supports building applications in C#, VB.NET, and C++, in addition to HTML and JavaScript. WinRT provides all of the core functionality to build Windows Store applications, such as the application model, access to the device and sensors on the device, networking, security, and storage.

The second library Windows provides for building Windows Store applications in HTML and JavaScript is the Windows Library for JavaScript, or WinJS. WinJS is a collection of JavaScript and CSS code to simplify Windows Store application development. The provided CSS ensures that, by default, your applications will look and feel like a Windows Store application rather than a web site. The JavaScript provides a number of UI controls, which I will discuss later in this chapter, as well as animation and navigation classes, DOM manipulation, events, and the ability to create custom classes and controls.

Unfortunately, naming products isn't one of Microsoft's strengths, in my opinion. As I will through the course of this book, the Windows Runtime is often referred to as WinRT, a name remarkably similar to that of the Windows RT operating system. To further confuse matters, the classes and functionality provided by WinRT are in the Windows namespace, although the functionality provided by WinJS is conveniently in the WinJS namespace. While this may appear to be potentially frustrating and confusing to less familiar users, in practice, it isn't really an issue.

The Controls

WinJS provides a number of controls for displaying and editing information in your Windows 8 applications. Similar to the HTML controls discussed in Chapter 5, WinJS controls are typically created by adding some markup to your HTML file, and the control is able to be manipulated in JavaScript after being added in HTML. Because WinJS controls are not part of HTML, they do not have corresponding HTML elements that can be added to your HTML file. Instead, you use the data-win-control attribute of a div element to specify the type of WinJS control you'd like to create. Additionally, because WinJS controls do not have dedicated HTML elements, they do not have dedicated attributes for setting properties in your HTML file. Instead, you use the data-win-options attribute if certain properties require an initial value. You'll see how this all works over the next several pages, as I discuss the different WinJS controls.

Before getting started, you need a place to put your code from this chapter. Open the WinJSControlsSample project from Chapter 5. Create a new folder named windowscontrols in the pages folder, and then add another page control named windowscontrols.html, following the steps used in Chapter 5 when you added the htmlcontrols.html page control. When you're done, your Solution Explorer should look like Figure 6-1.

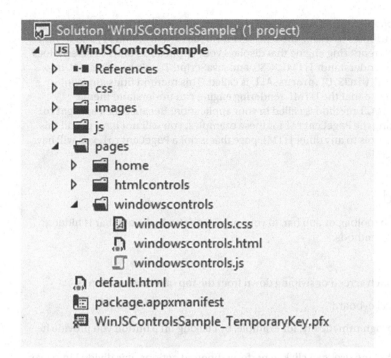

Figure 6-1. *Add a new page control named windowscontrols.html*

Be sure to change the CSS reference in windowscontrols.html from ui-dark.css to ui-light.css and to add a button and corresponding click event handler to home.html to navigate to this new page. When you're done, run the application to make sure everything looks and works as expected so far (see Figure 6-2).

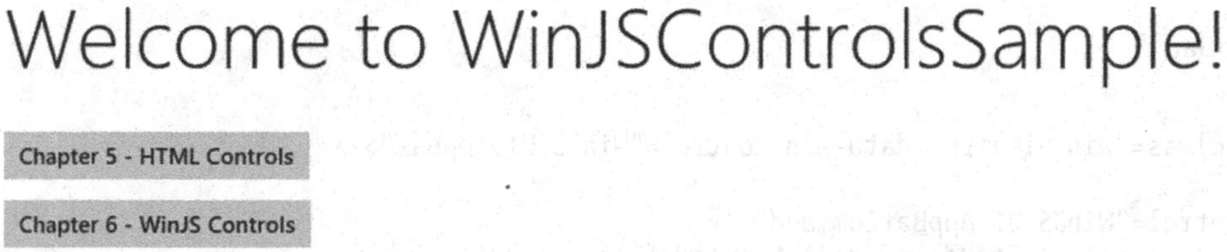

Welcome to WinJSControlsSample!

Chapter 5 - HTML Controls

Chapter 6 - WinJS Controls

Figure 6-2. *The home page with the new button*

■ **Note** If you're following along, implementing all of the examples in this chapter, be sure to put all of your sample code between the <section aria-label="Main content" role="main"> and </section> elements of windowscontrols.html, unless a different location is specifically identified. A rule of thumb is that if the control is always visible on the screen, such as a DatePicker, you'll add it to the main section. If it only shows when the user performs an action, such as swiping from the edge of the screen to see an AppBar or SettingsFlyout, it probably needs to be defined as a top-level element inside the body element of your page or possibly in an entirely separate file.

As you work through the exercises in this chapter, you'll see that WinJS controls are added to the page using HTML elements, usually a div element, with attributes to define the type of control (data-win-control) and its initial state (data-win-options). By default, the HTML rendering engine that displays your application on your screen does not know anything about WinJS controls. It only understands HTML, CSS, and JavaScript. Turning your HTML into WinJS controls only occurs when a WinJS method, WinJS.UI.processAll, is called. This method finds any WinJS controls in your HTML file and instantiates them so that the HTML rendering engine can understand them.

You must ensure that the WinJS.UI.processAll method is called in your application. Because the PageControl automatically calls processAll, and you are using the PageControl for these examples, you will not have to add this method call manually. If you add any WinJS controls to any other HTML page that is not a PageControl, you will have to call the method explicitly in your JavaScript code.

AppBar and AppBarCommand

The AppBar control is used to add an application toolbar, or app bar, to your page. By default, the app bar is hidden until the user activates it by one of the following methods:

- Right-clicking with a mouse

- Swiping up from the bottom of a touch screen or swiping down from the top of a touch screen

- Pressing Windows Logo Key+Z on a keyboard

The AppBar control can also be activated programmatically, for example, by clicking on a button you provide in your application.

The app bar contains command buttons that the user can click to perform different actions. It is divided into two sections: the "global" section and the "selection" section. Commands in the selection section apply to an item, or a group of items, that is currently selected or active, such as checked items in a list, while the global section applies to the current page. For languages read from left to right, such as English, the global section is on the right side of the app bar, and the selection section is on the left. This is reversed for languages read from right to left. Let's add an AppBar control to your new page. The code to add this control must be directly contained by the body element of the page, so add the code from Listing 6-1 immediately after the beginning body element in windowscontrols.html.

Listing 6-1. Adding an AppBar

```
<body>
    <div id="myAppBar" class="win-ui-dark" data-win-control="WinJS.UI.AppBar">
        <button
            data-win-control="WinJS.UI.AppBarCommand"
            data-win-options="{id:'myAddCommand',label:'Add',icon:'add',
                section:'global',tooltip:'Add item'}">
        </button>
        <button
            data-win-control="WinJS.UI.AppBarCommand"
            data-win-options="{id:'myRemoveCommand',label:'Done',icon:'accept',
                section:'selection',tooltip:'Mark item done'}">
        </button>
        <hr
            data-win-control="WinJS.UI.AppBarCommand"
            data-win-options="{type:'separator',section:'selection'}" />
```

```
    <button
        data-win-control="WinJS.UI.AppBarCommand"
        data-win-options="{id:'myDeleteCommand',label:'Delete',icon:'delete',
            section:'selection',tooltip:'Delete item'}">
    </button>
  </div>
  <!-- SNIPPED -->
</body>
```

Let's dig into what's going on here. The WinJS library identified the div element as an AppBar control because of the data-win-control attribute, and setting the class attribute to win-ui-dark will display the AppBar in a dark color, black by default, making it stand out nicely against the light background of your application. I'll illustrate how you can style your application with colors in Chapter 9.

Next, you add a few buttons and a separator to the AppBar, setting the data-win-control attribute to WinJS.UI.AppBarCommand. Additionally, because there is no AppBarCommand element in HTML, and consequently no standard HTML attributes corresponding to it, I use the data-win-options attribute to set initial properties for our buttons. In the first button, I set the icon property to add, which displays a plus symbol (see Figure 6-3), and I set the section property to global, causing it to display on the right side of the AppBar. Imagine a task list application. In this case, the first button would add a new task to the list. I added the second and third buttons to the selection section. In the task list application, these buttons would apply to the currently selected task.

Figure 6-3. *An app bar with two selection commands and one global command*

■ **Note** While nothing prevents you from adding a global command to the selection section, and vice versa, as your users gain expertise with Windows 8 applications, they will come to expect the buttons to be organized this way.

You may be wondering where the icons for the AppBarCommand are defined. By default, the available icons are different characters displayed using the Segoe UI Symbol font. WinJS provides a list of available icons in the WinJS.UI.AppBarIcon enumeration. By specifying one of these as the value of the icon property, you can show the icon of your choice. There are close to 200 icons in that enumeration, and the full list can be seen on Microsoft's MSDN site (http://msdn.microsoft.com/en-us/library/windows/apps/hh770557.aspx). With so many icons available, it is very likely that you can find an icon on that list to meet your need. Sometimes, however, you need something different. In these cases, it is possible to provide a custom image to be used instead of a font-based image. We'll take a look at how to do this in Chapter 12.

The AppBar and AppBarCommand classes have a number of different properties available. Some of the more common ones are

- layout: This AppBar attribute allows you to specify that you are providing a custom layout of the app bar and that WinJS should not expect to show a series of AppBarCommand objects.

- placement: This AppBar attribute allows you to specify whether it should be placed at the top or bottom of the page. Placing an app bar with a custom layout at the top of the screen is a common way to provide navigation options in your application.

- **sticky**: This AppBar attribute can be used to indicate that the app bar remain visible when the user clicks or touches elsewhere in your application. The user can still hide the app bar using one of the same methods that would typically activate it, such as swiping from the top of the screen or right-clicking with a mouse.

- **disabled**: This AppBarCommand attribute can be used to make a command unavailable to a user. For example, if no items in your previous task list example are selected, a Delete command should be disabled.

- **type**: This AppBarCommand attribute is used to change the type of command the user will see. You briefly saw this in your code example, where you set the type property of one of your commands to separator. Valid choices for this property are button (the default if not specified), separator, toggle, and flyout. A toggle command is a command button that alternates between two states as the user repeatedly selects it, such as a "Mark Read" / "Mark Unread" button in an e-mail application. A flyout command is used to show a Flyout control, which I will be covering later in this chapter.

A full list of available properties can be found on MSDN for both the AppBar (http://msdn.microsoft.com/en-us/library/windows/apps/br229670.aspx) and AppBarCommand (http://msdn.microsoft.com/en-us/library/windows/apps/hh700497.aspx).

Tooltip

I briefly mentioned tooltips in Chapter 5. If you aren't familiar with tooltips, they are small boxes of text shown when you hover over another control on your page. They usually contain a description of the item your mouse is hovering over or instructions on what to do with that item. For most HTML controls, you can add a simple tooltip by setting the value of the title attribute to the text you'd like to display in the tooltip. Add the code from Listing 6-2 to windowscontrols.html. This code will produce a simple, plain text tooltip, as seen in Figure 6-4.

Listing 6-2. Adding a Simple Tooltip to a Label

```
<label title="This is a simple, text only tooltip">This label has a simple tooltip.</label>
```

← WinJS Controls

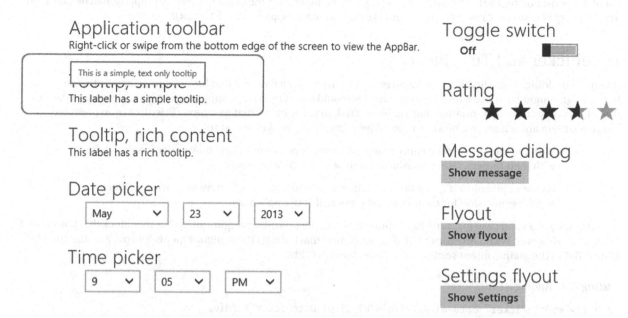

Figure 6-4. Your sample application (as it will look at the end of the chapter), highlighting a label with a simple tooltip

Simple tooltips like this go pretty far in improving users' experience, as they get to know your application. However, if you'd like to provide something a little richer, WinJS provides a Tooltip control that can contain formatted content. Add the code in Listing 6-3 to windowscontrols.html and run the application again.

Listing 6-3. Adding a Tooltip with Rich Content to a Label

```
<label id="myRichTooltip" data-win-control="WinJS.UI.Tooltip"
    data-win-options="{infotip: true,
        innerHTML: 'Here is a <strong>richer</strong> <em>tooltip</em>.'}">
    This label has a rich tooltip.
</label>
```

Notice that the tooltip (see Figure 6-5) actually contains formatted HTML content. Also, the infotip property is used to indicate that this Tooltip, which may contain a lot of information, should be displayed for a longer period of time than a regular Tooltip.

Tooltip,
This label has a rich tooltip.

Figure 6-5. A label with a rich tooltip

If you need an even richer tooltip, containing images or other controls, you can create one by taking advantage of the contentElement property to use the contents of a separate HTML element as the content of your Tooltip. A full list of properties of the Tooltip control, including documentation for the contentElement property, can be found on MSDN (http://msdn.microsoft.com/en-us/library/windows/apps/br229763.aspx).

DatePicker and TimePicker

If you are building an application that requires the user to supply a date, such as for scheduling appointments, your first thought might be to use a text-input control. You could certainly do this, supplying a regular expression pattern that allows only correctly formatted dates to be entered. In many cases, that may be sufficient, or even preferred. However, there are at least two reasons to consider using a dedicated date control.

- With the increasing prevalence of touch-screen devices, your users may prefer to select a date with their fingers, rather than having to type a date on a keyboard.

- If your application is going to be used internationally, you would have to provide a different regular expression for each localized version of your application.

If you have a good case for using text-input, neither of the preceding requirements is a roadblock that you cannot overcome. However, WinJS provides a DatePicker control that handles these requirements for you. Add the code in Listing 6-4 to the main content section of windowscontrols.html.

Listing 6-4. Adding a DatePicker

```
<div id="myDatePicker" data-win-control="WinJS.UI.DatePicker"></div>
```

If your users have to enter the times of their appointments in addition to the dates, you probably won't be surprised to find that WinJS also provides a TimePicker control for just these purposes, and it is just as simple to add. Add the code from Listing 6-5 to windowscontrols.html.

Listing 6-5. Adding a TimePicker

```
<div id="myTimePicker" data-win-control="WinJS.UI.TimePicker"></div>
```

Now, when you run your application, you should see the controls displayed as in Figure 6-6.

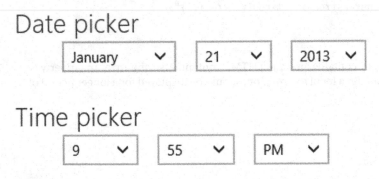

Figure 6-6. *A DatePicker control and TimePicker control*

The `DatePicker` and `TimePicker` classes have a number of different properties available. Some of the more common `DatePicker` properties are

- `current`: This attribute allows you to specify the default date that is displayed when the `DatePicker` control initially loads. If you do not specify a value for this property, the default date will be the current date.

- `minYear`, `maxYear`: These attributes allow you to specify the earliest and latest years that a user can specify when selecting a date. The default value of `minYear` is 100 years before the current year, and the default value of `maxYear` is 100 years after the current year.

- `yearPattern`, `monthPattern`, `datePattern`: These attributes allow you to control how the different parts of the date are formatted. For example, setting the `datePattern` property to `"{day.integer(2)} - {dayofweek.full}"` will cause the date drop-down list to display each date as a two-digit date, with leading zero, followed by the day of the week.

A full list of properties of the `DatePicker` control, including the list of options for the `yearPattern`, `monthPattern`, and `datePattern` properties, can be found on MSDN (`http://msdn.microsoft.com/en-us/library/windows/apps/br211681.aspx`).

Some of the more common `TimePicker` properties are

- `current`: This attribute allows you to specify the default time that is displayed when the `TimePicker` control initially loads. If you do not specify a value for this property, the default time will be the current time.

- `clock`: This attribute allows you to specify that the time be displayed in a 12-hour format (`12HourClock`) or a 24-hour format (`24HourClock`). If you use a 24-hour format, the drop-down list for choosing the period, AM or PM, is not shown.

- `minuteIncrement`: This attribute allows you to limit the choices for the minute portion of the time. For example, if you are writing an application for scheduling dental appointments, you might set this value to 15, causing the minute drop-down list to offer only 00, 15, 30, and 45 as choices.

- `hourPattern`, `minutePattern`, `periodPattern`: These attributes allow you to control how the different parts of the time are formatted. For example, setting the `hourPattern` property to `"{hour.integer(2)}"` will cause the hour to be formatted as two digits, with a leading zero, if needed.

A full list of properties of the `TimePicker` control can be found on MSDN (`http://msdn.microsoft.com/en-us/library/windows/apps/br229736.aspx`).

ToggleSwitch

If you've used Windows 8 for any length of time, you've probably seen a `ToggleSwitch` (see Figure 6-7).

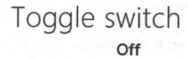

Figure 6-7. A basic ToggleSwitch

Much like a check box, it is used to alternate between two possible states, allowing your user to make such selections as "on and off," "yes or no," "true or false," "Love it or Hate it," etc. The simplest usage of a ToggleSwitch can be seen in Listing 6-6.

Listing 6-6. Adding a ToggleSwitch

```
<div id="myToggle" data-win-control="WinJS.UI.ToggleSwitch"></div>
```

The ToggleSwitch class has a number of different properties available. Some of the more common ones are

- title: This attribute allows you to specify the text prompt that is displayed above the ToggleSwitch. No prompt is displayed if title is not specified.

- labelOn, labelOff: This attribute allows you to specify the text that is displayed when the user toggles the control on and off. By default, labelOn is set to On, and labelOff is set to Off.

- checked: This attribute allows you to specify the initial state of the ToggleSwitch when the page is loaded. By default, checked is false, and the ToggleSwitch is off.

A full list of properties of the ToggleSwitch control can be found on MSDN (http://msdn.microsoft.com/en-us/library/windows/apps/hh701411.aspx). To see how these properties affect the ToggleSwitch, let's replace the code from Listing 6-6 with the following code in Listing 6-7.

Listing 6-7. Adding a More Valuable ToggleSwitch

```
<div id="myToggle" data-win-control="WinJS.UI.ToggleSwitch"
    data-win-options="{title:'What do you think about pizza?',
        labelOn:'Love it',
        labelOff:'Hate it',
        checked:true}"></div>
```

After looking at the code, you probably won't be surprised to see that your application now looks like Figure 6-8.

Toggle switch
What do you think about pizza?

Love it

Figure 6-8. *Your customized ToggleSwitch*

As I mentioned, a ToggleSwitch behaves very much like a check box. Both allow you to turn something on or off. Microsoft has provided guidance on ToggleSwitch usage (http://msdn.microsoft.com/en-us/library/windows/apps/hh465475.aspx), including the following advice for choosing between a ToggleSwitch and check box:

- Use a ToggleSwitch when the change will take effect immediately, such as in a SettingsFlyout.

- Use a check box when the change will not take effect until the user performs an additional action, such as clicking a Submit button.

- Use a check box when the user can select multiple items from a list.

Based on this guidance, while it illustrates the usage of some of the different properties, the example in Figure 6-8 is probably not the best usage of a ToggleSwitch control. Users would be better served by the Rating control.

Rating

With the Rating control, you can provide a familiar mechanism for, well, rating things. Displayed as the familiar series of stars, the Rating control is an intuitive way for gathering feedback on something's quality. Add the code from Listing 6-8 to windowscontrols.html, then run your application.

Listing 6-8. Adding a Rating Control

```
<div id="myRating" data-win-control="WinJS.UI.Rating"></div>
```

When the page first loads, you'll see a series of five stars similar to Figure 6-9. In addition to this view, two other views of the Rating controls are provided out of the box: the tentative rating view and the user rating view. As you hover your mouse over each rating star, the tentative rating view is displayed. The color of the stars will dynamically change as you hover over each one, and a tooltip will display the value that would be set if you were to select that option (see Figure 6-10). When you finally select one of the stars, the color change is set, and the tooltip is hidden (see Figure 6-11).

Figure 6-9. *A standard Rating control*

Figure 6-10. *The tentative rating while the user's mouse is hovering over the fourth star*

Figure 6-11. *The user's selected rating*

The Rating class has a number of different properties available. Some of the more common ones are

- maxRating: This attribute allows you to specify the maximum possible rating a user can choose. By default, maxRating is set to 5.

- averageRating: This attribute allows you to specify the average rating this item has received by your users. The method of determining this average is up to you and is not provided by the Rating control.

- tooltipStrings: This attribute allows you to specify the tooltip that is displayed when the user hovers over each option in the Rating control. This property takes an array of strings, and the number of items in that array must match the value of the maxRating property. By default, tooltipStrings is null, and numbers are displayed in the tooltip for each option.

- disabled: This attribute allows you to specify that the Rating control is in a read-only state. The user cannot add or change a rating when the disabled property is set to true.

A full list of properties of the Rating control can be found on MSDN (http://msdn.microsoft.com/en-us/library/windows/apps/br211895.aspx). To see how some of these properties affect the Rating, let's replace the code from Listing 6-8 with the following code in Listing 6-9.

Listing 6-9. A Better Pizza Rating Interface

```
<div id="myRating" data-win-control="WinJS.UI.Rating"
    data-win-options="{averageRating:3.6,
        tooltipStrings:['Hate it','Dislike it','It\'s Ok','Like it','Love it']}"></div>
```

Now, when you run the application, you'll see a control more appropriate for measuring people's fondness for pizza. The same five stars are there, but they will be highlighted to indicate the current value of the averageRating property. In this example, 3.6 of the stars are highlighted (see Figure 6-12).

Figure 6-12. *A Rating control with an average rating*

When you hover your mouse over the different stars, you can see the different values specified for the tooltipStrings property (see Figure 6-13). Additionally, while you are hovering your mouse over the stars, they are highlighted in a different color, blue by default.

Figure 6-13. *Customized tooltips for each option*

MessageDialog

If you've been writing, or using, software for any length of time, you are undoubtedly familiar with message boxes. Usually displayed as a modal window—a window in front of the application, which prevents use of the application until addressed—message boxes are used to display urgent information to the user, or to request information the application needs in order to continue being useful. For Windows Store applications, you use the MessageDialog control for this purpose.

■ **Note**   The `MessageDialog` control is actually provided by the Windows Runtime, WinRT, and is not part of WinJS.

Adding a dialog box is a little more involved than some of the controls I've discussed previously, but is still pretty straightforward. For your example, you'll add a button to your page that will be used to open the `MessageDialog` control, although in practice, you could create the `MessageDialog` based on any number of criteria. Start by adding the code in Listing 6-10 to `windowscontrols.html`.

Listing 6-10. Adding a Button to Display a MessageDialog and a Placeholder to Display the Result

```
<button id="myShowDialogButton">Show message</button>
<span id="myDialogResult"></span>
```

Now, you need to make the button do something when the user clicks it. Add the highlighted code in Listing 6-11 to the ready function in `windowscontrols.js`. This code will cause a function named `myShowDialogButton_Click`, which you will create in a moment, to be executed when someone clicks the button.

Listing 6-11. Wiring Up the Event Handler for the Button Click

```
ready: function (element, options) {
    // message dialog event binding
    document.getElementById("myShowDialogButton")
        .addEventListener("click", myShowDialogButton_Click, false);
},
```

Now let's create the function that will actually handle the button click and show the `MessageDialog` to the user. Listing 6-12 contains the function definition of the `myShowDialogButton_Click` function previously mentioned. It is important to note where this code is placed in `windowscontrols.js`. The function should be defined after the `PageControl` is defined. To help clarify this, Listing 6-12 also includes the definition of the `PageControl`, but with the contents removed for simplicity.

Listing 6-12. Adding the Event Handler After the PageControl Definition

```
"use strict";

WinJS.UI.Pages.define("/pages/windowscontrols/windowscontrols.html", {
    // SNIPPED
});

function myShowDialogButton_Click() {
    // Create the message dialog and set its content
    var msg = new Windows.UI.Popups.MessageDialog("Some irreversible process is about to "
        + "begin. Do you wish to continue?", "Message dialog sample");

    // Add commands and set their command handlers
    msg.commands.append(new Windows.UI.Popups.UICommand("Continue", function (command) {
        myDialogResult.textContent = "You chose 'Continue'";
    }));
```

```
    msg.commands.append(new Windows.UI.Popups.UICommand("Cancel", function (command) {
        myDialogResult.textContent = "You chose 'Cancel'";
    }));

    // Set the command that will be invoked by default
    msg.defaultCommandIndex = 0;
    msg.cancelCommandIndex = 1;

    // Show the message dialog
    msg.showAsync();
}
```

The event handler defined in Listing 6-12 creates a MessageDialog object. Before it is displayed to the user, you create two UICommand objects and add them to your MessageDialog. These commands are the buttons that the user will be able to choose between when the MessageDialog is displayed. In this case, you handle the click of each of these buttons by setting the textContent property of your placeholder from Listing 6-10.

■ **Note**   If your event handler is short, you can eliminate the need for a separate event handler function. Instead, you can use an anonymous function to declare the click event handler right in the call to addEventListener. You can see this technique within Listing 6-12, where I define the MessageDialog object's command buttons. While an anonymous function would also work in this example, a long handler would make the code more difficult to read.

A MessageDialog can have a default command and a cancel command defined. The default command is the button that will be clicked if the user presses the ENTER key. The cancel command is the button that will be clicked if the user presses the ESC key. Set the defaultCommandIndex property of the MessageDialog to 0, indicating that your first button, the Continue button, will be the default button. Likewise, use the cancelCommandIndex to indicate that the other button will be the Cancel button. Finally, call the MessageDialog object's showAsync function to show the dialog to the user and require him or her to take some action before continuing to use the application.

Run the application and click the "Show message" button. The contents of your application will be dimmed and your dialog will be displayed, as in Figure 6-14. When you click the Continue or Cancel button, the result of your choice will be displayed, as in Figure 6-15.

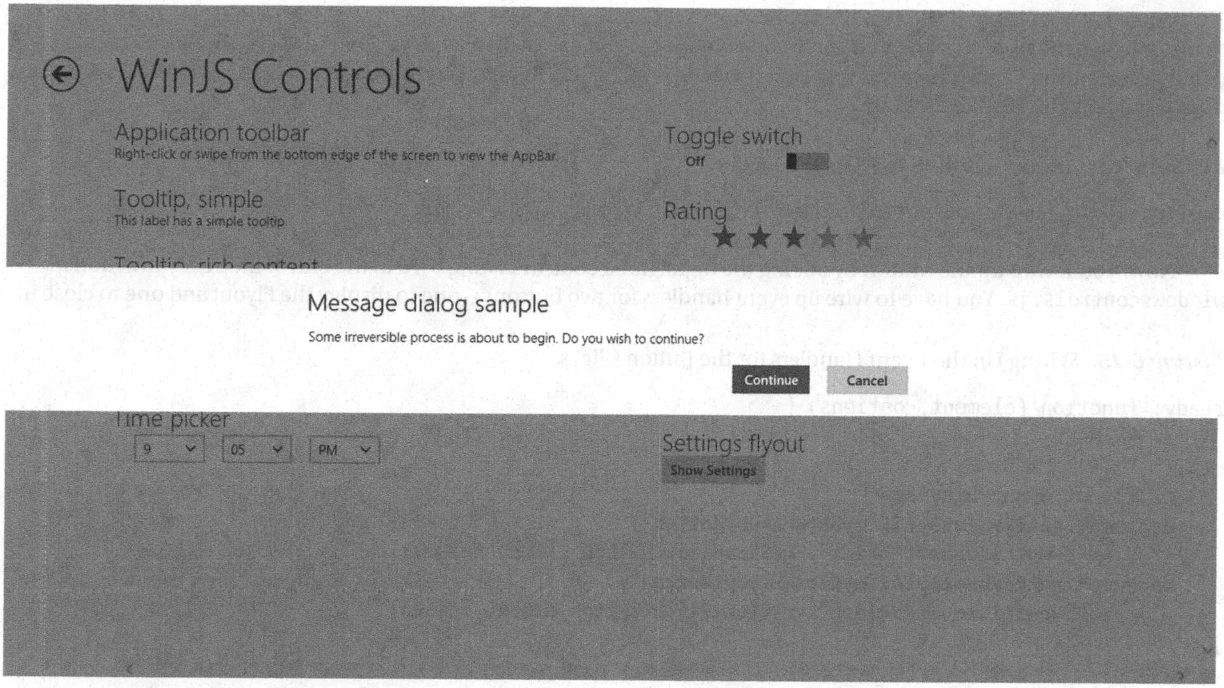

Figure 6-14. *Page displaying a MessageDialog to the user*

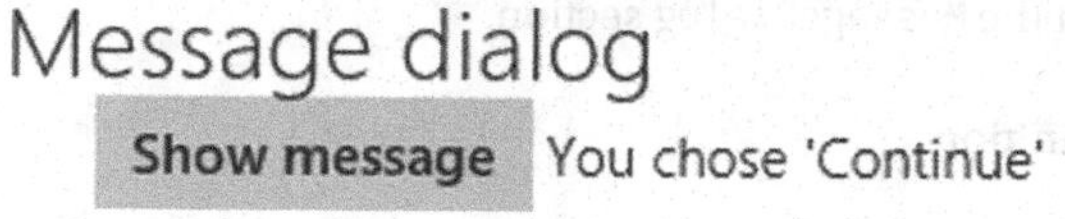

Message dialog

| Show message | You chose 'Continue'

Figure 6-15. *The result of the MessageDialog*

Flyout

Falling somewhere between tooltips and message dialogs, WinJS provides a Flyout control that is used to show contextual content and other controls to the user. With this content appearing in a box floating above the main page of your application, it is visually similar to a tooltip; however, where a tooltip appears to provide a description or instruction when the user's mouse hovers over some trigger, the Flyout control is usually displayed when the user takes more deliberate action, such as clicking something. For example, you might use a flyout to have your users confirm that they want to delete some data.

Similar to adding a message dialog box, adding a flyout to your application involves a number of steps. As was the case with the AppBar example, the code for a Flyout control must be directly contained by the body element of the page, so add the code from Listing 6-13 immediately after our app bar declaration in windowscontrols.html.

Listing 6-13. Adding a Flyout

```
<div id="myFlyout" data-win-control="WinJS.UI.Flyout">
    <div>This is a flyout.</div>
    <button id="myCloseFlyoutButton">Close flyout</button>
</div>
```

While it's not visible if you run the application right now, you have created a Flyout with some text and a button. In order to see the Flyout, you need some control the user can use to display it. As you did for the MessageDialog, you'll add a button to your page for this. Add the code from Listing 6-14 to windowscontrols.html after the button you used to display the MessageDialog.

Listing 6-14. Adding a Button to Display a Flyout

```
<button id="myShowFlyoutButton">Show flyout</button>
```

Now, you'll wire up the button by adding the highlighted code in Listing 6-15 to the end of the ready function in windowscontrols.js. You have to wire up event handlers for two buttons—one to display the Flyout and one to close it.

Listing 6-15. Wiring Up the Event Handlers for the Button Clicks

```
ready: function (element, options) {
    // SNIPPED

    // flyout event binding
    document.getElementById("myShowFlyoutButton")
        .addEventListener("click", myShowFlyoutButton_Click, false);
    document.getElementById("myCloseFlyoutButton")
        .addEventListener("click", myCloseFlyoutButton_Click, false);
},
```

The final step is to define the two event handlers you wired up in Listing 6-15. Listing 6-16 contains the two function definitions referenced in your ready function. As with your event handler in Listing 6-12, note that I have defined these functions outside the PageControl definition. Add the code from Listing 6-16 to windowscontrols.js after the definition of the myShowDialogButton_Click function from the MessageDialog section.

Listing 6-16. Adding the Event Handlers After the PageControl Definition

```
function myShowFlyoutButton_Click() {
    myFlyout.winControl.show(myShowFlyoutButton, "top");
}

function myCloseFlyoutButton_Click() {
    myFlyout.winControl.hide();
}
```

Now that you have all of your code in place, run your application and click the "Show flyout" button. Because you specified top as the value for the placement parameter when you called the show function, the flyout you created in Listing 6-13 is displayed above myShowFlyoutButton (see Figure 6-16). Other valid options are "bottom", "left", or "right".

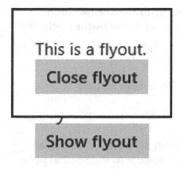

Figure 6-16. *Your Flyout is visible*

Any time a flyout is visible, the user can dismiss it by pressing ESC or by clicking off of it, a type of interaction referred to as *light dismissing*. In addition, clicking a button in the flyout should hide it. Changes caused by using any other controls you might add, such as a ToggleSwitch or Rating control, should take effect immediately, but not hide the Flyout control.

SettingsFlyout

The SettingsFlyout control is used to add a small window to your application that contains settings for some aspect of your application. Your application can have several SettingsFlyout controls, and, for consistency with other Windows applications, each of these should be listed on the Settings pane. Figure 6-17 shows the Bing Finance application with its About settings flyout open.

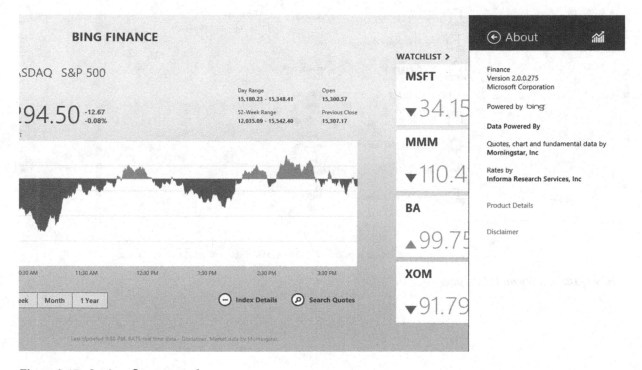

Figure 6-17. *Settings flyout opened*

By default, the Settings pane is hidden until the user activates it. Once activated, the Settings pane lists each SettingsFlyout that is available to the user. The user can activate the Settings pane by any of the following methods:

- Opening the Windows charms bar by moving the mouse to the upper-right corner of the screen, then clicking the Settings button;

- Opening the Windows charms bar by swiping in from the right of a touch screen, then tapping the Settings button;

- Pressing Windows Logo Key+I on a keyboard.

The Settings pane, or even a specific SettingsFlyout, can also be activated programmatically, for example, by clicking a button you provide in your application. You'll add a button to your application that opens the Settings pane where you can then choose a SettingsFlyout to open. Add the code from Listing 6-17 to windowscontrols.html.

Listing 6-17. Adding a Button to Display a SettingsFlyout

```
<button id="myShowSettingsButton">Show Settings</button>
```

Defining the SettingsFlyout is different from any of the other controls I've discussed so far. That's because it is defined in its own HTML file. In Visual Studio's Solution Explorer, add a new folder named settingsflyout to the pages folder. Right-click this new folder and select the option to add a new item. Visual Studio's Add New Item dialog opens (see Figure 6-18). Instead of selecting the Page Control item, this time select the HTML Page item and name the page settingsflyout.html.

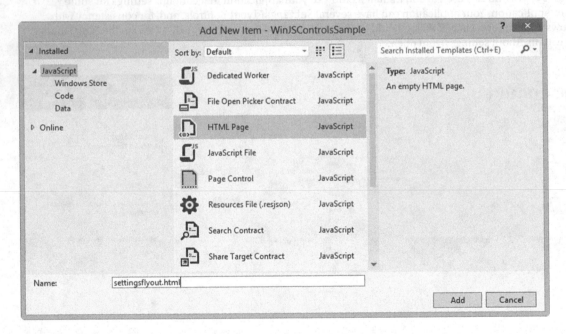

Figure 6-18. *Adding an HTML page*

Then open the settingsflyout.html file and replace its contents with the code from Listing 6-18.

Listing 6-18. The SettingsFlyout Page

```
<!DOCTYPE html>
<html>
<head>
    <title>Settings Flyout Sample</title>
    <script src="//Microsoft.WinJS.1.0/js/ui.js"></script>
</head>
<body>
    <div id="settingsDiv" data-win-control="WinJS.UI.SettingsFlyout"
        aria-label="Settings flyout sample"
        data-win-options="{settingsCommandId:'settingsflyout',width:'wide'}">

        <div class="win-ui-dark win-header" style="background-color: #464646">
            <button type="button" class="win-backbutton"
                onclick="WinJS.UI.SettingsFlyout.show()"></button>
            <div class="win-label">Settings Flyout Sample</div>
        </div>
        <div class="win-content">
            Put your settings here.
        </div>
    </div>
</body>
</html>
```

Notice the first div element with an id of settingsDiv. You've indicated that it is a WinJS SettingsFlyout control using the data-win-control attribute. You've also set the settingsCommandId property, which you will use later when adding the settings flyout to the Settings pane. You also set the width property to wide instead of the default, which is narrow. Within the SettingsFlyout control, you have a div element for your header and another to contain the actual contents you wish to see when it is visible.

Now that you've created the page you will use for your SettingsFlyout, you have to wire up a few events. Add the highlighted code in Listing 6-19 to the end of the ready function in windowscontrols.js.

Listing 6-19. Wiring Up the Event Handler for the Button Click

```
ready: function (element, options) {
    // SNIPPED

    // show the Settings pane when our button is clicked
    document.getElementById("myShowSettingsButton").addEventListener("click", function () {
        WinJS.UI.SettingsFlyout.show();
    }, false);
},
```

This code is the event handler code for your button, and it shows the Settings pane with the call to WinJS.UI.SettingsFlyout.show. If you had wanted to instead jump right to your SettingsFlyout instead of showing the Settings pane, you would have used the WinJS.UI.SettingsFlyout.showSettings method.

The last step is to have your application let Windows know what settings you want to be displayed in the Settings pane. The highlighted code in Listing 6-20 should be added before the call to processAll in the default.js file located in the js folder. This code defines a command associated with the SettingsFlyout control and adds it to the Settings pane. Name this command settingsflyout, to match the settingsCommandId property you set in settingsflyout.html. The title property determines the text shown in the Settings pane for this command.

Listing 6-20. Wiring Up the Event Handler to Populate the List of Settings Commands

```
app.addEventListener("activated", function (args) {
    if (args.detail.kind === activation.ActivationKind.launch) {

        // SNIPPED

        // add our SettingsFlyout to the list when the Settings pane is shown
        WinJS.Application.onsettings = function (e) {
            e.detail.applicationcommands = {
                "settingsflyout": {
                    title: "Settings Flyout Sample",
                    href: "/pages/settingsflyout/settingsflyout.html"
                }
            };
            WinJS.UI.SettingsFlyout.populateSettings(e);
        };

        args.setPromise(WinJS.UI.processAll().then(function () {
            // SNIPPED
        }));
    }
});
```

■ **Note** Adding this code in default.js allows the settings flyout to be available from any PageControl your application loads into default.html. It is possible to have different settings be available from each page of the application by moving this code to the ready function of each PageControl. However, Microsoft's guidance suggests showing the same list of settings throughout your application, disabling any that are not applicable in a certain situation.

Now, if you run your application and open the Settings pane by clicking the Show Settings button (or by any other method), you now have a button to open your SettingsFlyout, as seen in Figure 6-19.

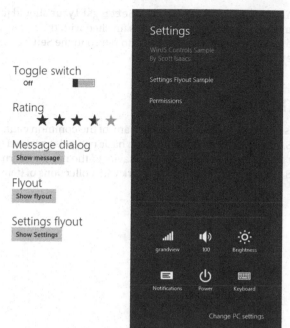

Figure 6-19. *The Settings pane for your application*

Clicking this button opens your wide-formatted SettingsFlyout, as seen in Figure 6-20.

Figure 6-20. *The settings flyout*

Any setting changes made in a SettingsFlyout should take effect immediately, and the user shouldn't have to click a Save button. When the user is finished with the settings flyout, whether or not any changes were made, he or she can either click the Back button to return to the Settings pane or light dismiss it by clicking somewhere outside of the SettingsFlyout.

Conclusion

In this chapter, you learned about many of the common controls provided by the Windows Library for JavaScript, or WinJS. These controls go beyond the basic controls provided by HTML and allow you to interact with your users in a way that matches the look and behavior of the new, modern interface of Windows 8. In Chapter 7, I will discuss the WinJS controls that were built to work with collections of items: the ListView, FlipView, and SemanticZoom.

CHAPTER 7

∎ ∎ ∎

WinJS Collection Controls

In the last two chapters, I introduced a number of controls that you can use to build your Windows Store applications. With the exception of the DropDownList control, all of the controls I've presented so far were designed to deal with a single value. Each text input control is associated with a single string; each button control is associated with a single action; and each tooltip displays a description or instructions for a single item. In fact, even though the DropDownList control contains many items to choose from, it is logically associated with the choices associated with a single setting.

In this chapter, I'll cover the collection-based controls provided by WinJS. You can use these controls when you have a list of items that you want to display using a template. If you've used Windows 8, then the most obvious example of this is the Windows Start screen, seen in Figure 7-1. This Start screen shows a list of applications that I have installed. For each one, there is a title; a tile image, either small or large; and, optionally, some live content displayed on the tile. As you can see, I'm currently in the middle of a heat wave.

Figure 7-1. *A Windows 8 Start screen*

Although I'm not going to demonstrate how to replicate the Windows Start screen in this chapter, you will see how you can build similar functionality by binding a collection control to a list of data. But before binding to a list of data, you need to understand what it means to have a list of data in the first place.

Collections

If you've been programming for any amount of time, you are undoubtedly already familiar with collections of items. Arrays are a common type of collection, as are the results of a database query, a list of files on your drive, or the items in the RSS feed of your favorite blog. WinJS provides the WinJS.UI.IListDataSource interface for working with these types of collections in your Windows Store applications. This interface can be used to add new items to your collection, edit or remove existing items in your collection, or bind your collection to a control for display in your application. The WinJS collection controls you will look at in this chapter, the ListView and the FlipView, are both commonly used to display data from an IListDataSource.

In some cases, you will have to create your own JavaScript class that implements IListDataSource, such as when you want to bind a ListView control directly to the results of a web service call. However, in many cases, you can take advantage of the WinJS.Binding.List class to create an IListDataSource from an array of data. That is what I will explain in this chapter. In fact, for most cases, I recommend this approach, even when working with data from a web service. Loading web service data into an array, and then wrapping them in a List object provides a nice separation of your UI from the underlying data source and gives you more flexibility and control. I'll cover data binding in more detail in Chapters 11. For now, I'll keep it pretty simple, because the main focus of this chapter is the controls utilized to display this data.

Let's start by making some changes to your WinJSControlsSample project, from Chapters 5 and 6, which will allow you to work with the ListView and FlipView controls later in this chapter.

Project Setup

All of the examples you will look at in this chapter will use the same collection of items. In this case, it's an array of types of animals. Each animal definition has the name of the animal, the scientific classification, and an image in both a small and large size. Let's add that data to your project.

1. Open your WinJSControlsSample project.

2. Right-click on the js folder in the Solution Explorer and add a new item (see Figure 7-2).

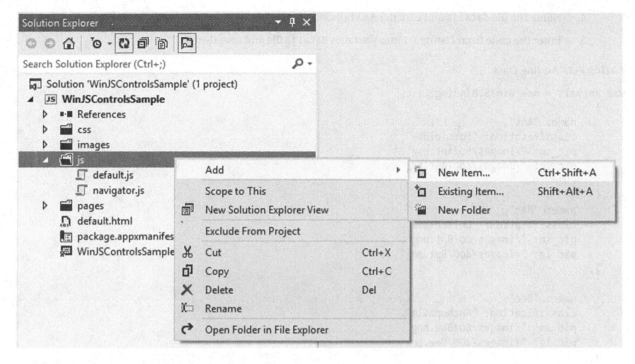

Figure 7-2. Adding a new item to the js folder

3. Select the JavaScript File item (see Figure 7-3).

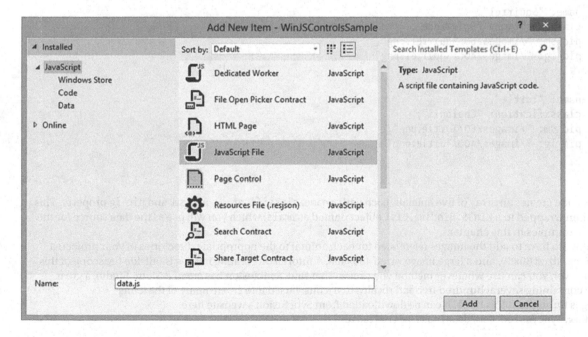

Figure 7-3. Creating a JavaScript file

4. Name the file data.js and click the Add button.

5. Enter the code from Listing 7-1 into your new data.js file and save the file.

Listing 7-1. Adding Data

```
var animals = new WinJS.Binding.List([
    {
        name: "Ant",
        classification: "Formicidae",
        pic_sm: "/images/60/Ant.png",
        pic_lg: "/images/400/Ant.png"
    },
    {
        name: "Bat",
        classification: "Chiroptera",
        pic_sm: "/images/60/Bat.png",
        pic_lg: "/images/400/Bat.png"
    },
    {
        name: "Bee",
        classification: "Anthophila",
        pic_sm: "/images/60/Bee.png",
        pic_lg: "/images/400/Bee.png"
    },

    // SNIPPED

    {
        name: "Squirrel",
        classification: "Sciuridae",
        pic_sm: "/images/60/Squirrel.png",
        pic_lg: "/images/400/Squirrel.png"
    },
    {
        name: "Turtle",
        classification: "Chelonii",
        pic_sm: "/images/60/Turtle.png",
        pic_lg: "/images/400/Turtle.png"
    }
]);
```

This code creates an array of five animals, each with a name, classification, pic_sm, and pic_lg property. This array is then wrapped in a WinJS.Binding.List object named animals, which you will use as the data source for the rest of the examples in this chapter.

You'll also have to add the images referenced for each animal to the appropriate directories in your project: a small image, sized 60×60, and a large image, sized 400×400. A tutorial on creating images is outside the scope of this book; however, you can use whatever method you prefer. That said, Syncfusion has created Metro Studio, a great resource containing several hundred free and royalty-free icons. I used it to create many of the icons and images throughout this book. It can be downloaded from Syncfusion's website here: http://www.syncfusion.com/downloads/metrostudio.

■ **Note** The source code that accompanies this book includes a completed project named WinJSControlsSample, which includes the sample code used in Chapters 5, 6, 7, and 8. It includes all the image files used in these examples, as well as a longer list of animals in the data.js file. You can find the code samples for this chapter on the Source Code/Downloads tab of the book's Apress product page (www.apress.com/9781430257790).

Now that you have the data you need, let's take a look at the different controls available to display collections of items.

The Controls

WinJS provides two controls for displaying a collection of items in your Windows Store applications: the ListView control and the FlipView control. As you'll see, they are similar in many ways, but they have one significant difference. The ListView control can display multiple items at a time, filling the available space with your items. The FlipView control, on the other hand, highlights one item at a time, and the user scrolls through your collection similar to turning pages in a book.

WinJS also provides a few other classes that are meant to be used with the ListView or FlipView. Both support using a WinJS.Binding.Template object for formatting the individual items of your collection. The ListView also supports two layout modes, WinJS.UI.GridLayout and WinJS.UI.ListLayout, which determine where each of your items is displayed. Finally, you can use the WinJS.UI.SemanticZoom class with two ListView controls to allow your user to choose the resolution of the data he or she is viewing, either summary or group-level information while zoomed out, or item-level information while zoomed in. You'll take a look at each of these controls and classes below, starting in the next section with some basics of the ListView control.

As you work through the examples in this chapter, they should be added to the WinJSControlsSample project from the previous chapters. For each of the following sections, you will have to add another page control to the project, following the steps used in Chapter 5, when you added the htmlcontrols page control. Be sure to put all of your sample code between the <section aria-label="Main content" role="main"> and </section> elements of the page control. You must also add a navigation button for each page control to home.html. Finally, each of these page controls will have to reference the data.js file you created earlier in this chapter. You can add this reference in the head section of each of the page controls you create throughout the rest of this chapter (see Listing 7-2).

Listing 7-2. Referencing Your Animal Data on Each Page Control

```
<head>
    <!-- SNIPPED -->
    <script src="/js/data.js"></script>
</head>
```

ListView Basics

In almost every application, you will be required to display a list of items, and using the ListView control is the most common way of doing this. In the current example, you will display the list of animal data defined in Listing 7-1. Start by creating a new page control named listViewBasics.html, then add the code from Listing 7-3 into the main section, which adds a ListView to your page and binds it to the animals list you created earlier in data.js. Don't forget to reference data.js as seen in Listing 7-2.

Listing 7-3. Adding a ListView

```
<div id="listView"
    class="win-selectionstylefilled"
    data-win-control="WinJS.UI.ListView"
    data-win-options="{
        itemDataSource: animals.dataSource,
        selectionMode: 'none',
        tapBehavior: 'none',
        swipeBehavior: 'none'
    }">
</div>
```

■ **Note**   To display a ListView, or any other WinJS control, that you add in HTML, you must add a call to WinJS.UI.processAll in your JavaScript code for the page. However, because our examples are using page controls, this is taken care of for you under the covers. This is important to remember, though, if you are ever building your pages in a different manner.

I've set a few other options as well. By setting the class attribute to win-selectionstylefilled, the ListView will highlight items with a solid background color. If this class is not added, the default is to instead draw a rectangle around the item. Additionally, I've set the selectionMode, tapBehavior, and swipeBehavior properties to none, which essentially puts your list into a read-only mode where no items can be selected and nothing happens when you click on one. Now run the application. You should see something similar to Figure 7-4.

⊙ List View - Basics

```
{"name":"Ant","classification":"Formicidae","pic_sm":"/images/60/Ant.png","pic_lg":"/images/400/Ant.png"}    {"name":"Elephant","classification":"Elephantidae","pic_sm":"/images/60/Elephant.p

{"name":"Bat","classification":"Chiroptera","pic_sm":"/images/60/Bat.png","pic_lg":"/images/400/Bat.png"}    {"name":"Fish","classification":"Salvelinus","pic_sm":"/images/60/Fish.png","pic_lg":"

{"name":"Bee","classification":"Anthophila","pic_sm":"/images/60/Bee.png","pic_lg":"/images/400/Bee.png"}    {"name":"Fly","classification":"Diptera","pic_sm":"/images/60/Fly.png","pic_lg":"/ima

{"name":"Bird","classification":"Aves","pic_sm":"/images/60/Bird.png","pic_lg":"/images/400/Bird.png"}    {"name":"Giraffe","classification":"Giraffa

{"name":"Bug","classification":"Insecta","pic_sm":"/images/60/Bug.png","pic_lg":"/images/400/Bug.png"}    {"name":"Goat","classification":"Capra aegagrus

{"name":"Butterfly","classification":"Lepidoptera","pic_sm":"/images/60/Butterfly.png","pic_lg":"/images/400/    {"name":"Hen","classification":"Gallus gallus

{"name":"Cat","classification":"Felis","pic_sm":"/images/60/Cat.png","pic_lg":"/images/400/Cat.png"}    {"name":"Horse","classification":"Equus ferus

{"name":"Crab","classification":"Brachyura","pic_sm":"/images/60/Crab.png","pic_lg":"/images/400/Crab.png"    {"name":"Jelly Fish","classification":"Cyanea capillata","pic_sm":"/images/60/Jelly

{"name":"Crocodile","classification":"Crocodylidae","pic_sm":"/images/60/Crocodile.png","pic_lg":"/images/4    {"name":"Lion","classification":"Panthera

{"name":"Dog","classification":"Canis    {"name":"Monkey","classification":"Macaca","pic_sm":"/images/60/Monkey.png","pi

{"name":"Dolphin","classification":"Delphinidae","pic_sm":"/images/60/Dolphin.png","pic_lg":"/images/400/D    {"name":"Octopus","classification":"Octopoda","pic_sm":"/images/60/Octopus.png"

{"name":"Dove","classification":"Columbidae","pic_sm":"/images/60/Dove.png","pic_lg":"/images/400/Dove.p    {"name":"Owl","classification":"Strigiformes","pic_sm":"/images/60/Owl.png","pic_lg

{"name":"Duck","classification":"Anatidae","pic_sm":"/images/60/Duck.png","pic_lg":"/images/400/Duck.png"    {"name":"Peacock","classification":"Pavo","pic_sm":"/images/60/Peacock.png","pic_l
```

Figure 7-4. *An unhelpful ListView*

All of your data is there, but that's not a very helpful view of it. In fact, it's pretty confusing and, frankly, kind of ugly. I'll explain how to make it more practical, using templates, in the next section. Documentation for selectionMode, tapBehavior, swipeBehavior, and other ListView properties is available on MSDN at http://msdn.microsoft.com/en-us/library/windows/apps/br211837.aspx. I encourage you to take a few minutes to explore some other combinations of values for these properties before continuing. For example, setting selectionMode to multi and swipeBehavior to select, you can see how you might start to create an interface that behaves similarly to the list of your e-mail messages in the Mail application that comes with Windows.

Templates

You probably noticed in Listing 7-1 that the items in your collection can be more complex than a single value, such as a string, for example. In the current case, each item has four different properties: name, classification, pic_sm, and pic_lg. Without further instructions, the ListView simply displays a text representation of each item in the collection, as seen in Figure 7-4. Using a Template, you can specify how each of the properties of your items should be displayed. Modify the code you added to listViewBasics.html to match Listing 7-4 by adding the highlighted lines to your code.

Listing 7-4. Adding a Template to Your ListView

```
<div id="listViewTemplate" data-win-control="WinJS.Binding.Template" style="display: none">
    <div class="listViewItem">
        <img src="#" class="listViewItemImage" data-win-bind="src: pic_sm" />
        <div class="listViewItemText">
            <h4 data-win-bind="innerText: name"></h4>
            <h6 data-win-bind="innerText: classification"></h6>
        </div>
    </div>
</div>

<div id="listView"
    class="win-selectionstylefilled"
    data-win-control="WinJS.UI.ListView"
    data-win-options="{
        itemDataSource: animals.dataSource,
        itemTemplate: select('#listViewTemplate'),
        selectionMode: 'none',
        tapBehavior: 'none',
        swipeBehavior: 'none'
    }">
</div>
```

This code creates a Template control, which defines how the individual properties of each item in your data source should be displayed. You will use the data-win-bind attribute throughout the Template to set up the bindings that will be used to assign your item's values to the correct HTML attributes. By assigning a value to the id attribute, you are then able to set the itemTemplate property of your ListView so that it uses this Template when displayed. I'll cover data binding in more detail in Chapter 11 When you run the application, you can see, as in Figure 7-5, you're getting closer, but still not quite there.

⊙ List View - Basics

Figure 7-5. *Your ListView is almost there*

You have to add some CSS to your page control to polish things up a bit. Visual Studio added a file named listViewBasics.css when you created the page control. Open that file and add the CSS code from Listing 7-5. This code sets appropriate widths, height, margins, and other style attributes needed to make your page display as expected.

Listing 7-5. CSS for Your Basic ListView Example

```css
.listViewItem {
    width: 250px;
    height: 75px;
    padding: 5px;
    overflow: hidden;
    display: -ms-grid;
}

    .listViewItem img.listViewItemImage {
        width: 60px;
        height: 60px;
        margin: 5px;
        -ms-grid-column: 1;
    }

    .listViewItem .listViewItemText {
        margin: 5px;
        -ms-grid-column: 2;
    }
```

```
#listView {
    height: 400px;
    width: 100%;
    -ms-grid-column-span: 2;
}
```

Now that all of your code has been added, you can run the application again. This time, you finally see what you're expecting to see: a nicely formatted grid containing the data from your `animals` data source (see Figure 7-6). Each item displays the colorful icon, the name of the animal, and its classification, which you defined in `data.js` earlier in this chapter.

Figure 7-6. *A nicely styled ListView*

Layouts

You probably noticed that the default display of items in a `ListView` control is in a grid pattern. Starting at the top left (in left-to-right languages, such as English), items are loaded from top to bottom in a column. When the bottom of the `ListView` is reached, a new column is begun to the right of the first. If the visual size of each item being displayed is small in comparison to the space occupied by the ListView control, this is usually preferred display. However, if the item template requires more space, or if the ListView is being displayed in a narrow space, such as when your application is in snapped mode, a more compact, vertical layout may be preferred. This can be accomplished using the layout property of the `ListView`.

Add a new page control named `listViewLayouts.html` and reference `data.js`. Then add the code from Listing 7-6 into the main section. This code is very similar to what you added in the previous sections. There is a `Template` control and two `ListView` controls. Both `ListView` controls are bound to the same data source and reference the same `Template` control. The only difference is that the first `ListView` has its layout property set to `WinJS.UI.GridLayout`, while the second `ListView` has its layout property set to `WinJS.UI.ListLayout`.

■ **Note**   I've intentionally glossed over some of the HTML and CSS used to lay out the screens of your sample application. I will cover all of the code relevant to the functionality described, but because some supporting code snippets were not included in code listings, your application may look slightly different from the figures included here. You can see all of the code I've used by referencing the completed project named WinJSControlsSample, which is included in the source code that accompanies this book. You can find the code samples for this chapter on the Source Code/Downloads tab of the book's Apress product page (www.apress.com/9781430257790).

Listing 7-6. Adding ListView Controls with Different Layouts

```
<div id="listViewTemplate" data-win-control="WinJS.Binding.Template" style="display: none">
    <div class="listViewItem">
        <img src="#" class="listViewItemImage" data-win-bind="src: pic_sm" />
        <div class="listViewItemText">
            <h4 data-win-bind="innerText: name"></h4>
            <h6 data-win-bind="innerText: classification"></h6>
        </div>
    </div>
</div>


<div id="col1">
    <div id="listViewGridLayout"
        class="win-selectionstylefilled"
        data-win-control="WinJS.UI.ListView"
        data-win-options="{
            itemDataSource: animals.dataSource,
            itemTemplate: select('#listViewTemplate'),
            selectionMode: 'none',
            tapBehavior: 'none',
            swipeBehavior: 'none',
            layout: { type: WinJS.UI.GridLayout }
        }">
    </div>
</div>


<div id="col2">
    <div id="listViewListLayout"
        class="win-selectionstylefilled"
        data-win-control="WinJS.UI.ListView"
        data-win-options="{
            itemDataSource: animals.dataSource,
            itemTemplate: select('#listViewTemplate'),
            selectionMode: 'none',
            tapBehavior: 'none',
            swipeBehavior: 'none',
            layout: { type: WinJS.UI.ListLayout }
        }">
    </div>
</div>
```

Next, add the code from Listing 7-7 to listViewLayouts.css and then run the application. You should see two ListView controls, as in Figure 7-7. Aside from being narrower to allow both ListView controls to fit on the screen, the first is identical to the ListView from the previous section. The second ListView displays its items in a vertical list. Each individual item is displayed the same in both controls, illustrating that a Template can be reused across many controls and multiple controls can be bound to the same data source.

Listing 7-7. CSS for Your ListView Layouts Example

```
.listViewItem {
    width: 250px;
    height: 75px;
```

```
    padding: 5px;
    overflow: hidden;
    display: -ms-grid;
}

    .listViewItem img.listViewItemImage {
        width: 60px;
        height: 60px;
        margin: 5px;
        -ms-grid-column: 1;
    }

    .listViewItem .listViewItemText {
        margin: 5px;
        -ms-grid-column: 2;
    }

#listViewGridLayout {
    height: 400px;
    width: calc(100% - 50px);
    border: 1px solid #464646; /* make it easier to distinguish  */
}

#listViewListLayout {
    height: 400px;
    width: 300px;
    border: 1px solid #464646; /* make it easier to distinguish  */
}
```

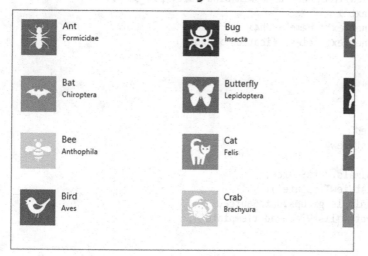

Figure 7-7. *Two ListView controls using different layouts*

WinJS includes only these two layout options: `GridLayout` and `ListLayout`. If you require a different layout, such as a grid layout that positions data in rows instead of columns, you have the option of implementing a new layout option on your own by implementing the `WinJS.UI.ILayout` interface. This is outside the scope of this book, but more information about this interface is available on MSDN at `http://msdn.microsoft.com/en-us/library/windows/apps/jj712247.aspx`.

Grouping and Semantic Zoom

Often, long lists of items make perfect sense. Sometimes, however, especially when the list is long, the user experience can be improved by grouping the data. For example, a list of cities might be grouped by country, a list of e-mail messages might be grouped by the e-mail address of the sender, or, as you will do in our example, a list of animals could be grouped alphabetically.

Add a new page control named `listViewGrouping.html` and reference `data.js`. Then add the code from Listing 7-8 into the main section. This code is similar to our first `ListView` example, except in this example, I have added another `Template` control that will be used for the heading of each group. I've also set some properties on the `ListView` control to indicate what text should be displayed in the group heading and that the heading should use our new `Template`.

Listing 7-8. Adding a ListView with Grouping

```
<div id="listViewHeaderTemplate"
    data-win-control="WinJS.Binding.Template"
    style="display: none">
    <div class="listViewHeader">
        <h1 data-win-bind="innerText: name"></h1>
    </div>
</div>

<div id="listViewTemplate"
    data-win-control="WinJS.Binding.Template"
    style="display: none">
    <div class="listViewItem">
        <img src="#" class="listViewItemImage" data-win-bind="src: pic_sm" />
        <div class="listViewItemText">
            <h4 data-win-bind="innerText: name"></h4>
            <h6 data-win-bind="innerText: classification"></h6>
        </div>
    </div>
</div>

<div id="listView"
    class="win-selectionstylefilled"
    data-win-control="WinJS.UI.ListView"
    data-win-options="{
        itemDataSource: groupedAnimals.dataSource,
        itemTemplate: select('#listViewTemplate'),
        groupDataSource: groupedAnimals.groups.dataSource,
        groupHeaderTemplate: select('#listViewHeaderTemplate'),
        selectionMode: 'none',
        tapBehavior: 'none',
        swipeBehavior: 'none'
    }">
</div>
```

In Listing 7-8, I set the itemDataSource property of the ListView to groupedAnimals.dataSource and the groupDataSource property of the ListView to groupedAnimals.groups.dataSource, but groupedAnimals doesn't exist yet. You can define it by adding the code in Listing 7-9 to the end of the data.js JavaScript file created earlier. This code defines a function (compareGroups) used for sorting groups, a function (getGroupKey) indicating which items in your collection should be grouped together, and a function (getGroupData) indicating what data should be used to populate the Template specified in the groupHeaderTemplate property. The code then uses these three functions to create a new WinJS.Binding.List based on your animals collection. More information about creating a grouped list is available on MSDN at http://msdn.microsoft.com/en-us/library/windows/apps/hh700742.aspx.

Listing 7-9. Grouping Your Data

```
function compareGroups(left, right) {
    return left.toUpperCase().charCodeAt(0) - right.toUpperCase().charCodeAt(0);
}

function getGroupKey(dataItem) {
    return dataItem.name.toUpperCase().charAt(0);
}

function getGroupData(dataItem) {
    return {
        name: dataItem.name.toUpperCase().charAt(0)
    };
}

var groupedAnimals = animals.createGrouped(getGroupKey, getGroupData, compareGroups);
```

In this example, I've used the first letter of the name of the animal as your grouping key as well as your group heading. In a more complex example, where you might group cities by country, the getGroupKey function could return the ISO country code of the country. Likewise, because the template specified in the groupHeaderTemplate property is not limited to simple text, the getGroupData could return an object with the name of the country, its continent, and an image of the country's flag. In this case, you might also change the compareGroups function to sort by country name, continent, or even the size of the country in square miles.

Now all that's left to make this work is to style this ListView, so let's do that by adding the code in Listing 7-10 to the listViewGrouping.ccs file that was created with your page control. Again, this is similar to the CSS code added in Listing 7-5, except that this one includes a style for your group heading. Run the application to see a grouped ListView similar to Figure 7-8.

Listing 7-10. Styles Used for ListView Grouping

```
.listViewHeader
{
    width: 50px;
    height: 50px;
    padding: 8px;
}

.listViewItem {
    width: 250px;
    height: 75px;
    padding: 5px;
    overflow: hidden;
    display: -ms-grid;
}
```

```
.listViewItem img.listViewItemImage {
    width: 60px;
    height: 60px;
    margin: 5px;
    -ms-grid-column: 1;
}

.listViewItem .listViewItemText {
    margin: 5px;
    -ms-grid-column: 2;
}

#listView {
    height: 400px;
    width: 100%;
    -ms-grid-column-span: 2;
}
```

← List View - Grouping and Semantic Zoom

Figure 7-8. *A ListView with its items grouped alphabetically*

Not bad, but imagine a ListView containing data for hundreds of animals. It would be nice to be able to see a list of your animal groups as an index, and then be able to use that index to find the animal you are looking for. WinJS provides the SemanticZoom control for just this purpose. If you aren't familiar with the concept of semantic zooming and how it differs from optical zooming, I'll attempt to describe them. Optical zooming is viewing the same item at different levels of magnification, while semantic zooming allows you to see a smaller amount of data for each item in exchange for seeing data about more items. Let's look at a few analogies.

Optical zooming is a common function of photo-editing software. You can zoom in on a single blade of grass in a photo, or you can zoom out to see the entire lawn. In both cases, you are looking at the same photo, just at different magnification levels. Semantic zooming, on the other hand, is a common function of online mapping software. You can zoom in to see the street where you live, but as you zoom out, your street disappears, and you see cities. Keep zooming out, and you see states, then countries, then continents. Unlike the photo where the detail of the blade of grass is still part of the photo, zooming out on a map causes the detail of your street to be replaced with details of something else.

Another common-use case for semantic zooming is a calendar. At the lowest level, you can see all of the meetings you have on a particular day, with details concerning the time, location, and other meeting attendees. As you zoom out, you might see the entire week, with only the meeting titles and times listed. Zooming farther out, you might not see any information at all about your meetings but only years and months.

■ **Note** The SemanticZoom control only supports one zoom level. If your application has a deeper hierarchy, I encourage you to follow the lead of the Grid App project template introduced in Chapter 4, navigating to a new page for each level of the hierarchy.

The SemanticZoom control allows you to specify different views of your data, with differing amounts of detail. If you had hundreds of animals in your list, it would be helpful to be able to zoom out to see only the group headings. Then you could select one to jump directly to that part of your list of animals. You can add these features with a few additional steps. First, add the highlighted code from Listing 7-11 to listViewGrouping.html. I've added another Template control and ListView control that will be used when you have zoomed out. I've also added the SemanticZoom control, which contains, first, the ListView the user sees when he or she has zoomed in to the greatest level of detail, and, second, the ListView seen when the user has zoomed out to see fewer details about a greater number of items. Note that the order of these controls is important, and the more detailed, zoomed-in view must be placed before the less detailed, zoomed-out view.

Listing 7-11. Adding the SemanticZoom and Related Controls

```
<div id="listViewHeaderTemplate" data-win-control="WinJS.Binding.Template" style="display: none">
    <div class="listViewHeader">
        <h1 data-win-bind="innerText: name"></h1>
    </div>
</div>


<div id="listViewTemplate" data-win-control="WinJS.Binding.Template" style="display: none">
    <div class="listViewItem">
        <img src="#" class="listViewItemImage" data-win-bind="src: pic_sm" />
        <div class="listViewItemText">
            <h4 data-win-bind="innerText: name"></h4>
            <h6 data-win-bind="innerText: classification"></h6>
        </div>
    </div>
</div>


<div id="semanticZoomTemplate" data-win-control="WinJS.Binding.Template" style="display: none">
    <div class="semanticZoomItem">
        <h2 class="semanticZoomItemText" data-win-bind="innerText: name"></h2>
    </div>
</div>


<div id="semanticZoom" data-win-control="WinJS.UI.SemanticZoom">

    <!-- zoomed in view -->
    <div id="listView"
        class="win-selectionstylefilled"
        data-win-control="WinJS.UI.ListView"
        data-win-options="{
```

```
        itemDataSource: groupedAnimals.dataSource,
        itemTemplate: select('#listViewTemplate'),
        groupDataSource: groupedAnimals.groups.dataSource,
        groupHeaderTemplate: select('#listViewHeaderTemplate'),
        selectionMode: 'none',
        tapBehavior: 'none',
        swipeBehavior: 'none'
    }">
    </div>

    <!-- zoomed out view -->
    <div id="zoomedOutListView"
        data-win-control="WinJS.UI.ListView"
        data-win-options="{
            itemDataSource: groupedAnimals.groups.dataSource,
            itemTemplate: select('#semanticZoomTemplate'),
            selectionMode: 'none',
            tapBehavior: 'invoke',
            swipeBehavior: 'none'
    }">
    </div>

</div>
```

You could stop there and have a working SemanticZoom example, but with a bit of styling you can have a working example that is also nice-looking. Add the code from Listing 7-12 to listViewGrouping.css and run the application.

Listing 7-12. Additional Styles for SemanticZoom

```
#zoomedOutListView {
    height: 400px;
    width: 100%;
    -ms-grid-column-span: 2;
}

#semanticZoom {
    height: 400px;
    width: 100%;
    -ms-grid-column-span: 2;
}

.semanticZoomItem
{
    color: #ffffff;
    background-color: #464646;
    width: 150px;
    height: 40px;
    padding: 5px 15px;
}
```

At first, the ListView looks pretty much how it did when you added grouping, showing the full list of all animals with details (see Figure 7-9). One difference you will notice, however, is the addition of a small minus ("-") button in the lower right corner of the ListView. This button is one of a few ways to activate the SemanticZoom and zoom out.

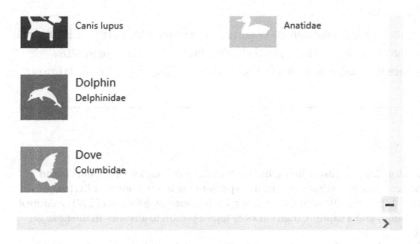

Canis lupus

Dolphin
Delphinidae

Dove
Columbidae

Anatidae

Figure 7-9. *A ListView with SemanticZoom added*

To zoom out and view Figure 7-10, users can

- Click the minus button.
- Press and hold down the Ctrl button on their keyboard and scroll down using the scroll wheel on their mouse.
- Use the pinch gesture described in Chapter 1. This, of course, only works on a touch screen.

⊙ List View - Grouping and Semantic Zoom

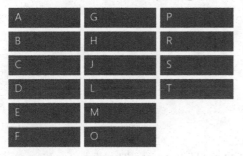

Figure 7-10. *A zoomed-out ListView*

After identifying the desired position in the ListView, the user can perform one of the following actions to zoom in:

- Select the group by clicking or tapping directly on it.
- Hover over the desired group and Ctrl-scroll up on the scroll wheel of their mouse.
- Use the stretch gesture described in Chapter 1. Again, this requires a touch screen.

■ **Note** Out of the box, the only WinJS control that will work with the `SemanticZoom` control is the `ListView`. However, it is possible to create your own control, or modify another control, by implementing the `WinJS.UI.IZoomableView` interface. More information about this interface is available on `MSDN` at `http://msdn.microsoft.com/en-us/library/windows/apps/br229794.aspx`.

FlipView

So far you've seen a number of techniques for viewing a list of items, but each of them displays several items to the user at once. While this is a very common scenario, sometimes, you want to present the items from your list to the user one at a time, and WinJS provides the `FlipView` control for this task. A common-use case for the `FlipView` control is a photo album where the user sees one photo and a caption, then clicks or taps a button to advance to the next. So let's build an example that does just that.

Add a new page control named `flipView.html` and reference `data.js`. Then add the code from Listing 7-13 into the main section. Once again, you'll notice that this code is very similar to previous `ListView` examples. In fact, if you changed the `data-win-control` attribute from `WinJS.UI.FlipView` to `WinJS.UI.ListView`, you would still have a working application. That's because the `FlipView` and the `ListView` both bind to the same types of data sources and both display their items with the same type of templates.

Listing 7-13. Adding a FlipView

```
<div id="flipViewTemplate" data-win-control="WinJS.Binding.Template" style="display: none">
    <div class="imageWithOverlay">
        <img class="image" data-win-bind="src: pic_lg; alt: name" />
        <div class="overlay">
            <h2 class="title" data-win-bind="innerText: name"></h2>
        </div>
    </div>
</div>
<div id="flipView"
    data-win-control="WinJS.UI.FlipView"
    data-win-options="{
        itemDataSource: animals.dataSource,
        itemTemplate: select('#flipViewTemplate')
    }">
</div>
```

Let's style the `FlipView` by adding the CSS code from Listing 7-14 to `flipView.css`. There's quite a bit more CSS code in this example, but that is mostly due to the fact that I wanted the image caption to display in a semi-transparent block overlaid at the bottom of the image. You can see the result in Figure 7-11. The user can scroll from one image to the next by clicking the arrows or by swiping on a touch screen.

Listing 7-14. Styling Your FlipView

```
#flipView
{
    width: 400px;
    height: 400px;
    border: solid 1px black;
}


.flipViewContent
{
    width: 400px;
    height: 400px;
}


.imageWithOverlay
{
    display: -ms-grid;
    -ms-grid-columns: 1fr;
    -ms-grid-rows: 1fr;
    width: 400px;
    height: 400px;
}


    .imageWithOverlay img
    {
        width: 100%;
        height: 100%;
    }

    .imageWithOverlay .overlay
    {
        position: relative;
        -ms-grid-row-align: end;
        background-color: rgba(0,0,0,0.65);
        height: 40px;
        padding: 20px 15px;
        overflow: hidden;
    }

        .imageWithOverlay .overlay .title
        {
            color: rgba(255, 255, 255, 0.8);
        }
```

⊛ Flip View

Figure 7-11. A FlipView of your animals

A common improvement on this would be to provide thumbnails of images in a ListView beneath your FlipView, with both controls bound to the same data source. However, a FlipView isn't limited to displaying images with captions. If you were building a custom document reading application, for example, you could use a FlipView to display each page of the document.

Conclusion

In this chapter, you saw a few different techniques for displaying collections of items to your user. The controls covered here—the ListView and its layout options, the Template, the SemanticZoom, and the FlipView—will undoubtedly find their way into your Windows Store applications. While I only scratched the surface of these controls, they offer a wealth of functionality, and numerous customizations are available. I'll explore some of this functionality in later chapters.

CHAPTER 8

■ ■ ■

WinJS Custom Controls

Using the controls I've covered in the last three chapters, you can build an application to meet pretty much any requirements, and as you'll see as we dig into more of the details of these controls and other concepts, that is exactly what you will be doing starting in Chapter 9. That said, sometimes you might find yourself wishing for some additional controls that aren't provided out of the box, and custom controls could just be what you need.

In this chapter I will examine the case in which some clock functionality is needed in your application. While it wouldn't be difficult to use some basic HTML and JavaScript to build a clock, your fictitious application requirements state that you have clocks in multiple places throughout the application. One of the great benefits of using controls, whether out-of-the-box controls or custom controls, is that they are easily reusable. If you build a control to represent a clock, you can use it multiple times, just as you can add multiple text input boxes to your application.

Custom Controls

In a nutshell, a control can be thought of as any piece of a user interface that is bundled together in some manner that allows you to add it to your application. A custom control, at least for the purposes of this chapter, is any such control that is not provided out of the box when developing Windows Store applications. Often, when developers refer to custom controls, they are referring to controls written by the developers of the application for which they are used. That certainly isn't incorrect, but the term could also refer to controls purchased from a third-party control vendor. There is no shortage of third-party controls that can be used, for example, to display charts or graphs, and you can find many of these with the help of your favorite web search engine.

That said, the focus of this chapter is not those third-party controls. Instead, I'm going to cover the steps to build your own controls, specifically WinJS controls, to meet your own specific needs. I'll discuss two common methods for building custom controls.

- I'll spend the majority of this chapter discussing how to build custom WinJS controls with JavaScript.

- I'll briefly cover building custom WinJS controls using the PageControl, which you have already seen in the last few chapters, provided by WinJS.

You can certainly create custom controls without using the WinJS libraries. If you are an experienced JavaScript developer, that is a perfectly valid choice, although it is outside the scope of this book. Because the Windows Store applications are built with HTML and JavaScript, you can use many popular JavaScript libraries and nearly all common JavaScript techniques in your application. However, there are benefits to using functionality from WinJS to build your custom controls. The WinJS libraries provide a pattern that helps you maintain code consistency and avoid common pitfalls related to the JavaScript language, allowing you instead to focus more on your business need than the inner workings of control building. Like any software abstraction, it's not always the right choice, but I've found that nearly always, I prefer building custom WinJS controls over building controls purely in JavaScript.

Custom WinJS Controls with JavaScript

As I mentioned above, we're going to spend the majority of this chapter building a custom clock control with JavaScript and the WinJS libraries. Let's start by identifying some requirements of this control.

- The clock can display the current local time in 12-hour or 24-hour formats.

- When used to display current time, the seconds can be optionally shown or hidden from the user.

- The clock can be used as a countdown timer or a "count-up" timer, to measure elapsed time.

- When used as a countdown or count-up timer, an initial time can be specified.

- When used as a countdown or count-up timer, the timer can be started automatically when created.

- The clock can be programmatically started, stopped, or reset.

- The page that contains the clock control can be notified by events such as when the clock was started, stopped, or reset, as well as when a countdown timer has completed.

■ **Note**   The source code that accompanies this book includes a completed project named WinJSControlsSample, which includes the sample code used in Chapters 5, 6, 7, and 8. You can find the code samples for this chapter on the Source Code/Downloads tab of the book's Apress product page (www.apress.com/9781430257790).

You'll build this functionality into your existing WinJSControlsSample project from the last few chapters. Before I get into the details of building this control, you'll have to do some project setup. After you've opened the project in Visual Studio, add a page control named `customcontrols.html` following the steps used in Chapter 5. Be sure to put all of your sample code between the `<section aria-label="Main content" role="main">` and `</section>` elements of the page control. You must also add a navigation button for this page control to `home.html`.

Next, add a new folder named `controls` to the root of your project, and within that add another folder named `js` (see Figure 8-1). This is where you are going to create your custom control, so right-click on this folder and select the option to add a new item to the project. Add a new JavaScript file named `clockControl.js` (see Figure 8-2).

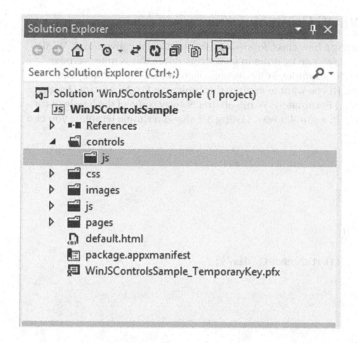

Figure 8-1. *The home for your JavaScript control*

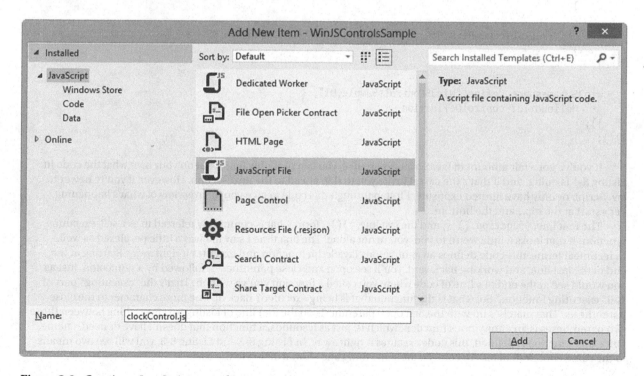

Figure 8-2. *Creating a JavaScript control in your project*

Anatomy of a JavaScript Custom WinJS Control

A WinJS JavaScript control is produced simply by creating a new class, following a few particular conventions. While object-oriented development tasks, such as creating classes, can be done in JavaScript, doing this is more verbose, as opposed to using many other languages, such as C#, for example. Full coverage of object-oriented concepts, let alone in JavaScript, is outside the scope of this book. (If you want to explore this topic, see *Pro JavaScript Design Patterns* by Ross Harmes and Dustin Diaz [Apress 2008].) Fortunately, WinJS abstracts away some of the hassle of this verbosity and allows you to create classes, and controls, in a simpler way. Listing 8-1 shows a simple template you can use when defining controls in your application.

Listing 8-1. A Template for Defining Controls

```
(function () {
    "use strict";

    var controlDefinition = WinJS.Class.define(
        function Control_ctor(element, options) {
            this.element = element || document.createElement("div");
            this.element.winControl = this;

            // control initialization
        },
        {
            // instance members
        },
        {
            // static members
        }
    );

    WinJS.Namespace.define("WinJSControlsSample.UI", {
        HelloWorld: controlDefinition
    });
})();
```

If you've got a fair amount of JavaScript experience, you can probably figure out on your own what the code in Listing 8-1 is doing, and if that's the case, I invite you to skip ahead to the next section. However, if you're newer to JavaScript, or only have limited exposure, I'll step through this code to give you an overview of what's happening. Let's start at the top...and the bottom.

The first line, (function () {, and the last line, })();, form what is commonly referred to as a self-executing function. If that looks a little weird to you, you're not alone. The first time I saw it, I was a little perplexed as well. In technical terms, this code defines an anonymous JavaScript function and executes it right away. Starting at the end of the last line, and working backward, you'll see open and close parentheses, followed by a semicolon, just as you would see at the end of a line of code where you called a function you've written. That's the "executing" part of "self-executing function." So, what is the function that is being executed? Back up one more character to the close parenthesis. That matches up with the first open parenthesis on the first line of Listing 8-1. Everything between those two parentheses is an anonymous function, which is, just as it sounds, a function that doesn't have or need a name. Once that function is defined, this code executes it right away. In Listing 8-2 and Listing 8-3, you will see two means to the same end. Both blocks of code do the same thing and show a dialog to the user.

Listing 8-2. Sample Function Definition and Function Call

```
function myFunction() {
    alert("foo");
}

myFunction();
```

Listing 8-3. Sample Self-Executing Function

```
(function() {
    alert("foo");
})();
```

Why would we do this? There are a few reasons, and plenty of detailed articles to read online about the topic, but in a nutshell, we do it for scoping purposes. Variables that are defined within a function are not available to any code outside that function. This means that we can safely create our own members—variables, properties, and functions—without worrying about conflicting with another member with the same name. In Listing 8-1, the variable named controlDefinition will not have any effect on, or be affected by, any other variable in our application named controlDefinition. With our functions members protected in this manner, we can selectively expose them in a way that makes sense. If you are familiar with a language such as C#, this is a concept parallel to defining private variables and functions that are not available outside of the class where they are defined and providing public members, so that other code can still work with the class in a meaningful way. You'll see more of this throughout the book. If it's a little foggy now, don't worry. By the time you've seen it a few times, it will become clearer. For now, the important point is to remember to define your controls within a self-executing function.

■ **Note**   Different people have different opinions on what self-executing functions should be called. Other common names include *immediately invoked function expression (IIFE)*, *immediately executed function*, or *self-executing anonymous function*. As long as you are aware of the different names and have an understanding of the concept, any name will do. For consistency, I'll refer to them as *self-executing functions* throughout the rest of the book.

The next line of the code in Listing 8-1 is the string literal "use strict";. This declares that the code in this scope is in strict mode, which allows for better error checking. In strict mode, certain practices are not permitted, usually those that can cause ambiguity or other unexpected behavior. This allows you to find potential errors in your code much sooner, rather than deploying an application that seems to work in your testing only to later cause issues. It helps reduce the "it works on my machine" bugs.

So far in this section, I've talked about self-executing functions and the "use strict" directive. Both of these concepts are common modern JavaScript development practices, and page upon page has been written about them. Next up in Listing 8-1, though, is something specific to WinJS development. We are defining a class using the WinJS.Class.define method and assigning that class definition to a private variable named controlDefinition.

■ **Note**   Assigning function and class definitions to a variable might seem strange if your background is with a statically typed language such as C#, although it is becoming increasingly common to see similar patterns in C#. It's important to notice here that classes and functions in JavaScript are treated just like any other value and can be assigned as the value of a variable. The common phrase to describe this is to say that functions are *first-class objects* in JavaScript.

The `WinJS.Class.define` method is called with three parameters. The first is a constructor function, in this case named `Control_ctor`. This function is called every time a new instance of this class is created. When you are defining a control, this constructor expects two parameters. Our example, and common convention, names these parameters `element` and `options`. The first is a reference to the HTML element that is used to place the control on your page. The second is used, as you saw in Chapter 6, to provide specific options to your control using the `data-win-options` attribute in your HTML markup.

The second parameter is an object describing the instance members of the class, and the third is an object defining the static members of the class. An example scenario is probably the easiest way to describe instance and static members.

Assume for a moment that you are creating a `Person` class. In that case, you might have an instance property named `firstName`. It's called an instance property because `firstName` is something that describes an individual instance of a `Person`. Your `Person` class might also have a static method named `search`, which you could call to find a single `Person`, or collection of `Person` objects, that match some criteria. Listing 8-4 shows an example of how you might reference these properties. Note that the `firstName` property requires an instance of a `Person` class, for which the `search` function is available directly from the `Person` class without any specific instance of that class. As this chapter progresses, you'll see examples of how to construct the object being passed to the `WinJS.Class.define` method for the instance members. Our example in this chapter does not require any static members, but specifying those is done in the same manner.

Listing 8-4. Properties and Methods of Your Fictitious Person Class

```
var myPerson = new Person();
myPerson.firstName = "Scott";

var searchResults = Person.search("Scott");
```

The remaining code from Listing 8-1 is used to define a namespace, which includes your class definition. This is how you expose your private `controlDefinition` class to other code in your application that would need to reference it. Your code calls the `WinJS.Namespace.define` method, which takes two parameters. The first is the name of the namespace itself, which is used to group related functionality and prevent naming collisions (two classes can each have a property with the same name). The second parameter is an object that describes the different things you are exposing to other code. In this case, you are exposing your private `controlDefinition` class to the rest of your application and giving it the public name of `HelloWorld` in the `WinJSControlsSample.UI` namespace. With this, your basic control definition is complete, and you can use it elsewhere in your application by either adding the control to your HTM page declaratively, which you will see in the next section, or in JavaScript, using code similar to Listing 8-5.

Listing 8-5. Creating an Instance of Your Control Class

```
var myControl = new WinJSControlsSample.UI.HelloWorld();
```

Version 1: A Simple 12-Hour Clock

Okay, so you've made a control in the previous section, but it doesn't actually do anything. Let's build on that example and create some real functionality. Open the `clockControl.js` JavaScript file and add the code from Listing 8-6. You'll recognize the pattern I described in Listing 8-1, with a few differences. First, instead of exposing your class as `HelloWorld`, I've changed the name to `Clock,` to represent the functionality this control will provide. Second, and most notable, I've supplied quite a bit of definition for the instance members parameter of `WinJS.Class.define`.

Listing 8-6. Your First "Real" Custom Control

```
(function () {
    "use strict";

    var controlDefinition = WinJS.Class.define(
        function Control_ctor(element, options) {
            this.element = element || document.createElement("div");
            this.element.winControl = this;

            this._init();
        },
        {
        // instance members

        _init: function () {
            this.start();
        },

        start: function () {
            setInterval(this._refreshTime.bind(this), 500);
        },

        _refreshTime: function () {
            var dt = new Date();

            var hr = dt.getHours();
            var min = dt.getMinutes();
            var sec = dt.getSeconds();
            var ampm = (hr >= 12) ? " PM" : " AM";

            hr = hr % 12;
            hr = (hr === 0) ? 12 : hr;

            min = ((min < 10) ? "0" : "") + min;
            sec = ((sec < 10) ? "0" : "") + sec;

            var formattedTime = new String();
            formattedTime = hr + ":" + min + ":" + sec + ampm;

            this.element.textContent = formattedTime;
        },
        }
    );

    WinJS.Namespace.define("WinJSControlsSample.UI", {
        Clock: controlDefinition,
    });

})();
```

This instance member object is defined using JavaScript object notation (JSON) syntax. JSON allows you to specify an object literally, defining it in place, rather than creating a class definition and then setting a number of properties. It is also a widely used format for transmitting data between applications, because it is easily converted to and from a text representation readable by any programming language. In JSON, an object's members are separated by commas, and each member is defined using the pattern memberName: memberDefinition. You can see this in our example, where the object for your class's instance members has three members of its own: the _init function, the start function, and the _refreshTime function.

■ **Note**　The convention used when defining classes with the WinJS utilities is that the names of private members—variables and functions only available within your class itself—begin with an underscore character (_), while public members—variables and functions available from the code that uses your class—names begin with a letter.

The _init function, which I call as the last line of our constructor, is very simple: it just calls the start function. The start function, in turn, creates an interval, which is a JavaScript feature to allow code to be executed repeatedly after a certain amount of time has passed, in this case 500 milliseconds. The _refreshTime function gets the current time, formats it, and then displays it on the page by setting the textElement property of the HTML element used to add this control to the page.

Speaking of that element, it's time to see how to do this. The first step is to add a reference for your custom control JavaScript file to your HTML page. Add the code from Listing 8-7 to the end of the head section of customcontrols.html. Then add the code from Listing 8-8 to the main section.

Listing 8-7. Add Script Reference to HTML File

```
<head>
    <!-- SNIPPED -->
    <script src="/controls/js/clockControl.js"></script>
</head>
```

Listing 8-8. Adding Your Custom Control

```
<div id="myClock12" data-win-control="WinJSControlsSample.UI.Clock"></div>
```

If you look carefully at what you just did in customcontrols.html, you'll see that, once a custom control has been defined, adding it to a page is just like adding the WinJS controls you saw in Chapters 6 and 7. You add a reference to the script file where the control is defined—clockControl.js in this example and base.js or ui.js in previous chapters—then you add a div element and set the data-win-control attribute to the full name of your control. When you run the application, you should see a clock displaying the current local time (see Figure 8-3), and it will be updating as the seconds pass.

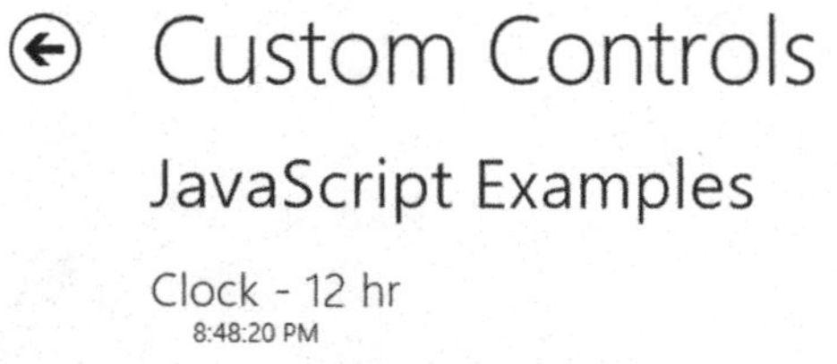

⊖ Custom Controls

JavaScript Examples

Clock - 12 hr
8:48:20 PM

Figure 8-3. *A custom clock control*

Version 2: Adding a 24-Hour Clock Option

So far, you've completed half of one of the requirements I defined for your custom control at the beginning of this chapter. You made a clock that displays local time in a 12-hour format, but not in a 24-hour format. In this section, you'll complete the rest of that requirement, as well as adding the ability to optionally show or hide the seconds of the current time.

Let's start by describing what modes your clock control can use. The highlighted code in Listing 8-9 defines a variable containing the two different clock modes that are part of your current development task. You will use the Object.freeze JavaScript function to prevent the clockModes variable from being changed. This, along with exposing clockModes in your namespace, effectively allows you to use WinJSControlsSample.UI.ClockModes as an enumeration of values. This will allow you to specify later a mode by its variable name, instead of using a number or string, which could more easily be mistyped by a developer adding your control to a page.

Listing 8-9. Defining Options for Different Clock Modes

```
(function () {
    "use strict";

    var controlDefinition = WinJS.Class.define(
        // SNIPPED
    );

    // clockModes is an enum(eration) of the different ways our clock control can behave
    var clockModes = Object.freeze({
        CurrentTime12: "currenttime12",
        CurrentTime24: "currenttime24",
    });

    WinJS.Namespace.define("WinJSControlsSample.UI", {
        Clock: controlDefinition,
        ClockModes: clockModes,
    });

})();
```

Now that you've defined the different modes that you can choose for your clock to use, you need a way to set the individual mode you'll need for each instance of your clock. While you're at it, let's add a way to show or hide the seconds of the current time. There are three steps to doing this, as seen in Listing 8-10.

- *Adding instance property definitions for mode and showClockSeconds:* In our example, the mode property has both a get and set function defined, so it is both readable and writable by the code that is using the control. However, the showClockSeconds property is only writable, because it has only a set function defined. Later in this chapter, you'll create a property that has only a get function, making it a read-only property.

- *Setting default values for those properties in our constructor:* By default, your clock will be in 12-hour mode and will show the seconds of the current time.

- *Calling the WinJS.UI.setOptions method that takes the options passed into our constructor and sets the mode, showClockSeconds and any other properties:* You'll see how this works later in this section.

Listing 8-10. Adding a Mode Property to Your Clock Control

```
var controlDefinition = WinJS.Class.define(
    function Control_ctor(element, options) {
        this.element = element || document.createElement("div");
        this.element.winControl = this;

        // Set option defaults
        this._mode = clockModes.CurrentTime12;
        this._showClockSeconds = true;

        // Set user-defined options
        WinJS.UI.setOptions(this, options);

        this._init();
    },
    {
        // instance members

        mode: {
            get: function () {
                return this._mode;
            },
            set: function (value) {
                this._mode = value;
            }
        },

        showClockSeconds: {
            set: function (value) {
                this._showClockSeconds = value;
            }
        },

        _init: function () {
            this.start();
        },

        // SNIPPED

    }
);
```

Now let's add another clock control to your page. Add the code from Listing 8-11 to customcontrols.html. Note that I am setting the mode to show the current time, 24-hour format, and that I have decided to hide the seconds from this clock.

Listing 8-11. Adding a 24-Hour Clock

```
<div id="myClock24"
    data-win-control="WinJSControlsSample.UI.Clock"
```

```
        data-win-options="{
            mode: WinJSControlsSample.UI.ClockModes.CurrentTime24,
            showClockSeconds: false
        }">
</div>
```

Go ahead and run the application. Not what you expected? So far, you've described what modes your clock can use, and you set properties on your new clock control to choose the 24-hour clock mode and hide the seconds. However, you haven't yet changed the code that actually renders the time. After updating the _refreshTime function with the highlighted code in Listing 8-12, run the application again. This time, you should see a new 24-hour clock without the seconds (see Figure 8-4). Although I didn't specify a value for mode or showClockSeconds for your original clock control, it still behaves the same, because of the default values I set in our constructor in Listing 8-10.

Listing 8-12. Rendering Different Clocks Based on Values of Properties

```
_refreshTime: function () {
    var dt = new Date();

    var hr = dt.getHours();
    var min = dt.getMinutes();
    var sec = dt.getSeconds();
    var ampm = (hr >= 12) ? " PM" : " AM";

    if (this._mode === clockModes.CurrentTime12) {
        hr = hr % 12;
        hr = (hr === 0) ? 12 : hr;
    } else {
        ampm = "";
    }

    min = ((min < 10) ? "0" : "") + min;
    sec = ((sec < 10) ? "0" : "") + sec;

    var formattedTime = new String();
    formattedTime = hr + ":" + min
        + ((this._showClockSeconds) ? ":" + sec : "") + ampm;

    this.element.textContent = formattedTime;
},
```

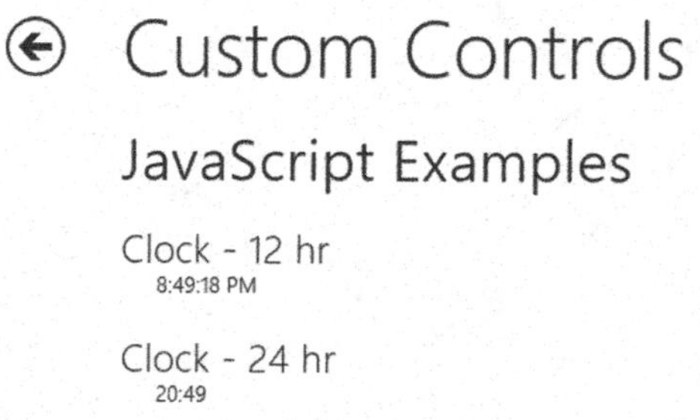

⊙ Custom Controls

JavaScript Examples

Clock - 12 hr
8:49:18 PM

Clock - 24 hr
20:49

Figure 8-4. *Two instances of your custom clock control*

Version 3: Adding Timer Options and Raising Events

Two requirements down, five to go. You have a perfectly working control to show the current time. The remaining requirements will give you the option to use this control as a timer as well. More important for the purpose of this tutorial is that you'll be adding support for calling methods on your control and raising events from your control that can be handled on the page where the control is displayed.

Let's first add the code from Listing 8-13 to clockControl.js. This listing includes the full source of that file, highlighting the parts that are different. I'll be covering the changes throughout the remainder of this section. It is a few pages long, but I suggest you read through it before you continue. As you read through it, you'll notice the changes that add new modes to your control to allow it to be used as a timer and provide the ability to set an initial value for the timer. Additionally, you'll see the new code that will enable you to start, stop, and reset the timer and raise events based on the status of the control.

Listing 8-13. Full Source of clockControl.js

```javascript
(function () {
    "use strict";

    var controlDefinition = WinJS.Class.define(
        function Control_ctor(element, options) {
            this.element = element || document.createElement("div");
            this.element.winControl = this;

            // Set option defaults
            this._mode = clockModes.CurrentTime12;
            this._showClockSeconds = true;
            this._initialCounterValue = [0, 0, 0];
            this._autoStartCounter = false;

            // Set user-defined options
            WinJS.UI.setOptions(this, options);

            this._init();
        },
        {
            // instance members

            _intervalId: 0,
            _counterValue: 0,

            isRunning: {
                get: function () {
                    return (this._intervalId != 0);
                }
            },

            mode: {
                get: function () {
                    return this._mode;
                },
```

```
            set: function (value) {
                this._mode = value;
            }
        },

        autoStartCounter: {
            get: function () {
                return this._autoStartCounter;
            },
            set: function (value) {
                this._autoStartCounter = value;
            }
        },

        initialCounterValue: {
            set: function (value) {
                if (isNaN(value)) {
                    // if not a number, value is an array of hours minutes and seconds
                    this._counterValue = (value[0] * 3600) + (value[1] * 60) + (value[2]);
                    this._initialCounterValue = value;
                } else {
                    this._counterValue = value;
                    this._initialCounterValue = [0, 0, value];
                }
            }
        },

        showClockSeconds: {
            set: function (value) {
                this._showClockSeconds = value;
            }
        },

        _init: function () {
            if (this._mode === clockModes.CurrentTime12
                    || this._mode === clockModes.CurrentTime24) {
                this.start();
            } else {
                this._updateCounter();
                if (this._autoStartCounter) {
                    this.start();
                }
            }
        },

        start: function () {
            if (!this.isRunning) {
                if (this._mode === clockModes.CurrentTime12
                        || this._mode === clockModes.CurrentTime24) {
                    this._intervalId =
                        setInterval(this._refreshTime.bind(this), 500);
                } else {
```

```
            this._intervalId =
                setInterval(this._refreshCounterValue.bind(this), 1000);
        }
        this.dispatchEvent("start", {});
    }
},

stop: function () {
    if (this.isRunning) {
        clearInterval(this._intervalId);
        this._intervalId = 0;
        this.dispatchEvent("stop", {});
    }
},

reset: function () {
    this.initialCounterValue = this._initialCounterValue;
    this._updateCounter();
    this.dispatchEvent("reset", {});
},

_refreshTime: function () {
    var dt = new Date();

    var hr = dt.getHours();
    var min = dt.getMinutes();
    var sec = dt.getSeconds();
    var ampm = (hr >= 12) ? " PM" : " AM";

    if (this._mode === clockModes.CurrentTime12) {
        hr = hr % 12;
        hr = (hr === 0) ? 12 : hr;
    } else {
        ampm = "";
    }

    min = ((min < 10) ? "0" : "") + min;
    sec = ((sec < 10) ? "0" : "") + sec;

    var formattedTime = new String();
    formattedTime = hr + ":" + min
        + ((this._showClockSeconds) ? ":" + sec : "") + ampm;

    this.element.textContent = formattedTime;
},

_refreshCounterValue: function () {
    if (this._mode === clockModes.CountDown) {
        this._counterValue--;
        if (this._counterValue <= 0) {
            this._counterValue = 0;
```

```
                                this.stop();
                                this.dispatchEvent("countdownComplete", {});
                            }
                        } else {
                            this._counterValue++;
                        }

                        this._updateCounter();

                        this.dispatchEvent("counterTick", {
                            value: this._counterValue
                        });
                    },

                    _updateCounter: function () {
                        var sec = this._counterValue % 60;
                        var min = ((this._counterValue - sec) / 60) % 60;
                        var hr = ((this._counterValue - sec - (60 * min)) / 3600);

                        min = ((min < 10) ? "0" : "") + min;
                        sec = ((sec < 10) ? "0" : "") + sec;

                        var formattedTime = new String();
                        formattedTime = hr + ":" + min + ":" + sec;

                        this.element.textContent = formattedTime;
                    },
                }
            );

// clockModes is an enum(eration) of the different ways our clock control can behave
var clockModes = Object.freeze({
    CurrentTime12: "currenttime12",
    CurrentTime24: "currenttime24",
    CountDown: "countdown",
    CountUp: "countup",
});

WinJS.Namespace.define("WinJSControlsSample.UI", {
    Clock: controlDefinition,
    ClockModes: clockModes,
});

WinJS.Class.mix(WinJSControlsSample.UI.Clock,
    WinJS.Utilities.createEventProperties("counterTick"),
    WinJS.Utilities.createEventProperties("countdownComplete"),
    WinJS.Utilities.createEventProperties("start"),
    WinJS.Utilities.createEventProperties("stop"),
    WinJS.Utilities.createEventProperties("reset"),
    WinJS.UI.DOMEventMixin);

})();
```

Did you get all that? From a technical point of view, much of Listing 8-13 is similar to the previous section, setting default values and adding instance members. Let's quickly run through those changes here.

- We set default values for two private properties, _initialCounterValue and _autoStartCounter, in the constructor. We then exposed these as instance properties, named initialCounterValue and autoStartCounter, respectively.

- We took advantage of the fact that JavaScript is a dynamically typed language in our definition of initialCounterValue by allowing values to set as either an integer number of seconds or as an array of three numbers representing the number of hours, minutes, and seconds.

- We added a private property named _counterValue to keep track of the current value of the counter, measured in seconds. A new method named reset was used to (surprise) reset _counterValue to _initialCounterValue.

- We added the property named _intervalId to keep track of the JavaScript interval that makes the counter tick. The isRunning property indicates whether or not the counter is currently running, based on whether or not the _intervalId property is set. The _intervalId property gets set in our modified start method and gets cleared in a new stop method.

- We modified the start and _init methods so that their behavior is unchanged when the control is in one of our existing clock modes, but they behave differently when the control is in one of the newly added counter modes, CountDown and CountUp.

- We added a new _updateCounter method to format and display the current value of the counter. Also, every 1000ms, the start function calls the _refreshCounterValue method to increment or decrement the counter value.

While all of those changes do add quite a bit of new functionality to your control, the process of implementing them is very similar to that which I discussed in the previous section. There are a few new concepts in Listing 8-13, however, that I want to cover in a little more detail. Near the end of the file, I've defined five new event mixins and attached, or merged, them to your control with the WinJS.Class.mix method: counterTick, countdownComplete, start, stop, and reset. Listing 8-14 is an example, excerpted from Listing 8-13, that creates the events and attaches them to your control. The WinJS.Class.mix method takes your control as the first parameter, followed by a list of the mixin objects we want to attach.

Listing 8-14. Defining an Event, Excerpted from Listing 8-13

```
WinJS.Class.mix(WinJSControlsSample.UI.Clock,
    WinJS.Utilities.createEventProperties("counterTick"),
    WinJS.Utilities.createEventProperties("countdownComplete"),
    WinJS.Utilities.createEventProperties("start"),
    WinJS.Utilities.createEventProperties("stop"),
    WinJS.Utilities.createEventProperties("reset"),
    WinJS.UI.DOMEventMixin);
```

■ **Note** Mixins are objects that define reusable functionality, in this case, defining events. These mixins can then be attached to other classes to add this reusable functionality. If you are familiar with object-oriented programming, this is somewhat similar to implementing an interface in your class. The primary difference is that a mixin includes the implementation of the reusable functionality, and an interface describes the functionality that your class must then implement.

These events give you the ability to notify the calling code when certain things occur in your class. Simply having these events defined, though, doesn't do anything. You have to decide where to raise these events in your control. You could, theoretically, raise the countdownComplete event in the _init method, but, of course, that doesn't make sense. Instead, you use the dispatchEvent method, which was added to your class from the WinJS.UI.DOMEventMixin mixin, to raise the start event in the start method (see Listing 8-15) and the stop event in the stop method, for example.

Listing 8-15. Raising the Start Event

```
this.dispatchEvent("start", {});
```

Both the countdownComplete event and the counterTick events are raised in the _refreshCounterValue method. Look in particular at counterTick for a moment. The call to dispatchEvent takes two parameters: the name of the event to raise and an object of event-specific data argument to pass to the event handler. With all of the other events, there wasn't any data to pass to the event handler, but in the case of counterTick, it could be useful for the event handler to know the current value of the private _counterValue property (see Listing 8-16). You'll see how to take advantage of that argument later in this section.

Listing 8-16. Raising the counterTick Event with a Data Argument

```
this.dispatchEvent("counterTick", {
    value: this._counterValue
});
```

With your control finally complete, let's see how to take advantage of some of this new functionality. Add the code from Listing 8-17 and Listing 8-18 to customcontrols.html. Notice that in Listing 8-17, the counter will count down from an initial value of 10 seconds, and in Listing 8-18, the counter will automatically start counting up, measuring elapsed time, starting at 10 hours, 59 minutes, and 50 seconds. Run the application and take a look at what's happening (see Figure 8-5).

Listing 8-17. Adding a "Countdown" Timer

```
<div id="myCountDown"
    data-win-control="WinJSControlsSample.UI.Clock"
    data-win-options="{
        mode: WinJSControlsSample.UI.ClockModes.CountDown,
        initialCounterValue: 10 }">
</div>
<button id="downStart">Start</button>
<button id="downStop" disabled>Stop</button>
<button id="downReset" disabled>Reset</button>
<span id="downEventStatus"></span>
```

Listing 8-18. Adding a "Count-Up" Timer

```
<div id="myCountUp"
    data-win-control="WinJSControlsSample.UI.Clock"
    data-win-options="{
        mode: WinJSControlsSample.UI.ClockModes.CountUp,
        initialCounterValue: [10, 59, 50],
        autoStartCounter: true }">
</div>
<div id="upEventStatus">10 second ticks: </div>
```

⊙ Custom Controls

JavaScript Examples

Clock - 12 hr
12:14:02 PM

Clock - 24 hr
12:14

Count Down
0:00:10
[Start] [Stop] [Reset]

Count Up (Elapsed Time)
10:59:56
10 second ticks:

Figure 8-5. *Timers have been added*

At this point, your 12-hour clock, 24-hour clock, and "countup" timer are all updating. The countdown timer is not counting, because it hasn't been started yet. You have buttons, but they don't do anything yet, so let's add the highlighted code from Listing 8-19 to the ready function in customcontrols.js. Because myCountDown is the id of the div element we added in Listing 8-17, we use the winControl property to reference the control represented by that element. With that reference, we can call your control's start, stop, and reset methods.

Listing 8-19. Adding Button-Click Handlers

```
ready: function (element, options) {
    downStart.addEventListener("click", function (e) {
        myCountDown.winControl.start();
    }, false);
    downStop.addEventListener("click", function (e) {
        myCountDown.winControl.stop();
    }, false);
    downReset.addEventListener("click", function (e) {
        myCountDown.winControl.reset();
        downReset.disabled=true;
    }, false);
},
```

Now that you can control the "countdown" timer, the last thing I'll cover is handling the events that your control raises. You'll notice in Listing 8-17 and Listing 8-18 placeholders named downEventStatus and upEventStatus, respectively. You'll use those as a place to display the results from each event your controls raise. Examining your updated ready function in Listing 8-20, the first change you'll notice is a function named handleCountDownEvent. In a real application, you would handle each event with its own logic, but I wanted to keep things simple at the moment. So, the handleCountDownEvent function takes the name of an event as a parameter and displays it in the downEventStatus placeholder, then toggles the state of the buttons based on which event is being handled. Each of the four events being handled on myCountDown simply call handleCountDownEvent, passing in the event type as a parameter. Finally, when we handle the counterTick event of the myCountUp control, we examine the value data argument, which we set in Listing 8-16, and append a "tick" character to the upEventStatus placeholder each time another 10 seconds has passed.

Listing 8-20. Adding Event Handlers for Your Timer Events

```
ready: function (element, options) {
    downStart.addEventListener("click", function (e) {
        myCountDown.winControl.start()
    }, false);
    downStop.addEventListener("click", function (e) {
        myCountDown.winControl.stop()
    }, false);
    downReset.addEventListener("click", function (e) {
        myCountDown.winControl.reset()
    }, false);


    var handleCountDownEvent = function (eventName) {
        downEventStatus.textContent = eventName;
        var enableStart = (eventName === "start") ? false : true;
        downStart.disabled = !enableStart;
        downStop.disabled = enableStart;
        downReset.disabled = !enableStart;
    };

    myCountDown.addEventListener("countdownComplete", function (e) {
        handleCountDownEvent(e.type);
    }, false);
    myCountDown.addEventListener("start", function (e) {
        handleCountDownEvent(e.type);
    }, false);
    myCountDown.addEventListener("stop", function (e) {
        handleCountDownEvent(e.type);
    }, false);
    myCountDown.addEventListener("reset", function (e) {
        handleCountDownEvent(e.type);
    }, false);

    myCountUp.addEventListener("counterTick", function (e) {
        if (e.value % 10 === 0) upEventStatus.textContent += "'";
    }, false);
},
```

With that, all four instances of your Clock control are now completely functional. You can set properties, call methods, and handle events for each control. Run the application again to see how it all came together (see Figure 8-6).

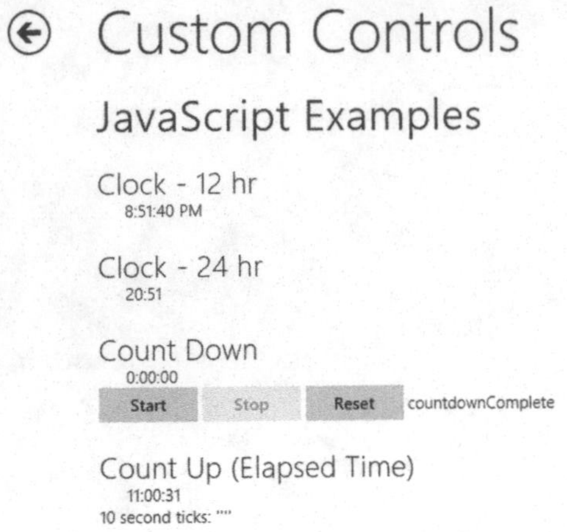

⊖ Custom Controls

JavaScript Examples

Clock - 12 hr
8:51:40 PM

Clock - 24 hr
20:51

Count Down
0:00:00

| Start | Stop | Reset | countdownComplete |

Count Up (Elapsed Time)
11:00:31
10 second ticks: ""

Figure 8-6. *Your Fully Functional Clock Control*

Custom WinJS Controls Using the PageControl

The previous method of creating WinJS controls with JavaScript can be pretty powerful. In fact, it is essentially the process used to create all of the controls I discussed in Chapter 6. As I mentioned at the start of this chapter, however, there are other ways to create custom controls in JavaScript. The other method I will briefly cover here is to create controls using the PageControl. You've already used the PageControl throughout the last few chapters to add new screens to your application, but here you'll see an example of how to create a simple Contact control that you can display on a page in your application, nesting one PageControl inside another. Our Contact control doesn't do much. The only requirements for this version of this control are to display a person's first name, last name, and birthday, but this could be extended to include more data about the person, or even to include controls to edit a person's contact information.

You'll follow the same steps you've been using in the last few chapters to add a PageControl, but before you do that, let's create a more logical home for the control. In practice, you can add the control pretty much anywhere in your Visual Studio project, but like any project, organizing files into appropriate folders helps keep things organized, especially as your projects grow in size and have many files. Let's start by creating a folder named pages within your existing controls folder. Then, within that folder, create a contactControl folder and add a new PageControl named contactControl.html within that folder. When you're done, your Solution Explorer should look like Figure 8-7. Now, replace the contents of contactControl.js with the code from Listing 8-21.

Listing 8-21. *The Code-Behind File of Your New PageControl*

```
(function () {
    "use strict";

    var controlDefinition = WinJS.UI.Pages.define(
        "/controls/pages/contactControl/contactControl.html",
        {
            // This function is called whenever a user navigates to this page. It
            // populates the page elements with the app's data.
            ready: function (element, options) {
                options = options || {};
                this._first = "";
                this._last = "";
                this._birthday = "";

                // Set user-defined options
                WinJS.UI.setOptions(this, options);

                firstContent.textContent = this.first;
                lastContent.textContent = this.last;
                birthdayContent.textContent = this.birthday;
            },

            first: {
                get: function () { return this._first; },
                set: function (value) {
                    this._first = value;
                }
            },

            last: {
                get: function () { return this._last; },
                set: function (value) { this._last = value; }
            },

            birthday: {
                get: function () { return this._birthday; },
                set: function (value) { this._birthday = value; }
            },

            unload: function () {
                // TODO: Respond to navigations away from this page.
            },

            updateLayout: function (element, viewState, lastViewState) {
                /// <param name="element" domElement="true" />

                // TODO: Respond to changes in viewState.
            }
        }
    );
```

```
    WinJS.Namespace.define("WinJSControlsSample.UI", {
        Contact: controlDefinition,
    });
})();
```

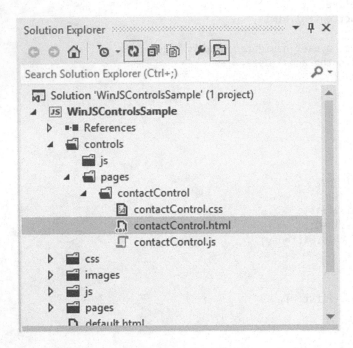

Figure 8-7. *Your new PageControl*

Looking through this file, you'll see some differences from the JavaScript control we created in Listing 8-13, but there are some similar concepts. The first difference to notice is that instead of defining a class, we use the WinJS.UI.Pages.define method to define a PageControl. We still, however, expose that control publicly as part of our WinJSControlsSample.UI namespace. Another difference is that the PageControl does not have a constructor function; however, it does have a ready function, which is used to initialize your control properties. Finally, while there is no object for instance members, your first, last, and birthday properties are declared alongside the ready function.

The noticeable difference between a JavaScript control and a PageControl is that the PageControl also includes an HTML (and CSS) file, allowing you to define more of the layout and design of your control in markup. Listing 8-22 contains the code you need to add to contactControl.html for your PageControl. If you're familiar with using ASP.NET for web development, a JavaScript control is similar in concept to an ASP.NET server control, while a PageControl is similar in concept to an ASP.NET user control. Like the ASP.NET server control, the JavaScript control can be, and often is, defined within a single code file. This makes reusability between projects very simple. The definition of a PageControl, on the other hand, is spread across multiple files of multiple types, usually a file to contain the presentation logic—HTML for a PageControl and ASCX for an ASP.NET user control—and another file to contain the behavior logic—JavaScript for a PageControl and a .NET language, such as C# or VB.NET, for an ASP.NET user control. While this offers a simpler way to control the presentation of your control, it does make reusability between projects slightly less convenient.

Listing 8-22. The Markup for Your PageControl

```
<script src="/controls/pages/contactControl/contactControl.js"></script>

<body>
    <div class="contactControl">
        <p class="contactControl-first">
            <strong>First name:</strong>
            <span id="firstContent">First name goes here</span>
        </p>
        <p class="contactControl-last">
            <strong>Last name:</strong>
            <span id="lastContent">Last name goes here</span>
        </p>
        <p class="contactControl-birthday">
            <strong>Birthday:</strong>
            <span id="birthdayContent">Birthday goes here</span>
        </p>
    </div>
</body>
```

Once your page control has been created, the process of adding one to your page, and setting options, is not any different from adding your custom JavaScript control or the controls that WinJS provides out of the box. Add the code from Listing 8-23 to customcontrols.html. In this example, you are setting the first, last, and birthday properties declaratively here, in your markup. In practice, you would likely set these values in JavaScript, possibly in the course of data binding, a topic I will cover more fully in Chapter 11.

Listing 8-23. Adding Your PageControl to customcontrols.html

```
<div id="myContact"
    data-win-control="WinJSControlsSample.UI.Contact"
    data-win-options="{
        first: 'Scott',
        last: 'Isaacs',
        birthday: 'December 1' }">
</div>
```

Granted, this PageControl example was pretty simple, but you can see how similar developing a PageControl is to developing a custom JavaScript control. This can be especially useful when you need a reusable control that is a composite control—a control that contains multiple controls itself. If you think about it for a moment, this is exactly what we have been doing with thePageControl since the beginning of Chapter 5. You've been using it as a way to contain the contents of an entire screen of your sample application, with several child controls. You have treated the controls as autonomous units, each independent of the other. However, with a few extra properties defined, you can see how your PageControl from Listing 8-21 and Listing 8-22 can be used to display data that is provided from outside its own definition (see Figure 8-8).

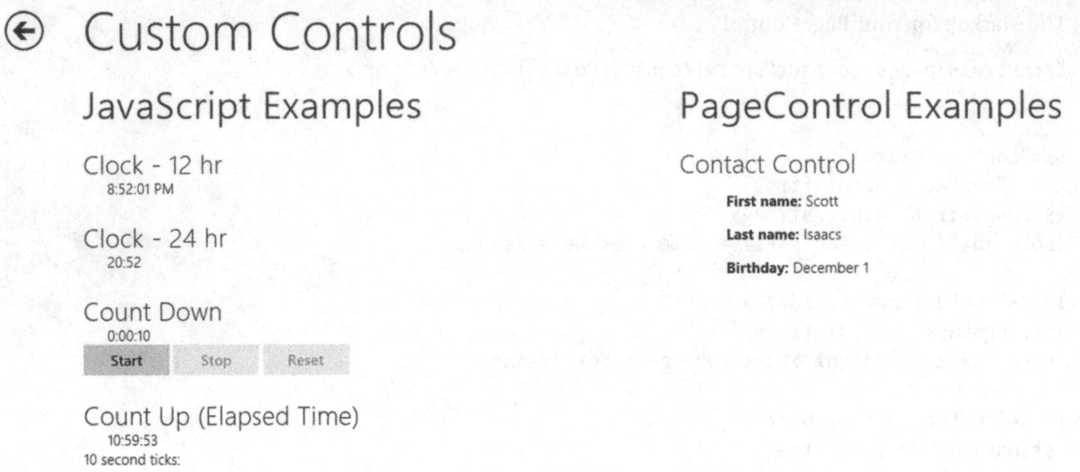

⊖ Custom Controls

JavaScript Examples

Clock - 12 hr
8:52:01 PM

Clock - 24 hr
20:52

Count Down
0:00:10

| Start | Stop | Reset |

Count Up (Elapsed Time)
10:59:53
10 second ticks:

PageControl Examples

Contact Control

First name: Scott

Last name: Isaacs

Birthday: December 1

Figure 8-8. *Your PageControl displayed with your custom JavaScript control*

Conclusion

In this chapter, I introduced two techniques for creating reusable controls in your application. Custom controls provide convenient reusability, both within your project and in other projects you may develop in the future, by encapsulating some user interface and behavior into a bundle. Custom controls should be considered whenever you find yourself building the same interface multiple times. I spent most of the chapter building a custom JavaScript WinJS control, which you will use again later in this book, and briefly covered the PageControl, which you have already been using for a few chapters.

■ ■ ■

CHAPTER 9

Building the User Interface

Now that I've covered touch concepts, the principles of the Microsoft design style, creating Visual Studio projects, and working with the many controls that are available for your Windows Store applications, it's time to do something a little more interesting. In this chapter, you will start building a real-world application that you'll continue to build upon throughout the remainder of the book. We'll be building a time-keeping application geared to software consultants, designers, freelancers, and any others that perform project-based work.

When I'm not writing books, I spend my time as a software-development consultant. Like many consulting firms, the firm I work with uses a third-party time-and-expense tracking system to support all of the consultants it has working with various clients. It's accessible from anywhere using a web browser, and it is a pretty complete system, with bells and whistles and configurability options at every turn. Unfortunately, it is not the easiest system to use. All of the bells and whistles and configurability options require that a fair amount of clicking and navigating be done to enter my billable time for each day. As a result, like many who must keep track of time spent on projects, I've found myself keeping track of all of my time using the poor man's all-purpose database: Microsoft Excel. Once per month, I open our time-and-expense system in one window and Excel in another and copy hours from one to the other. It's not so bad, but every now and then I have billings for multiple clients on the same day. I could address this by making an adjustment to the way I record my time in Excel, or I could write an app. Since I just happen to be writing a book about building Windows Store applications, I chose the latter, so we could build it together.

Introducing Clok

Over the course of the remaining chapters in this book, we are going to build Clok, a time sheet application for the Windows Store. To prevent this book from running to 1,500 pages, I'll keep the feature set pretty basic. Following are the high-level functions a consultant can perform with Clok:

- Track time for a project by starting and stopping a timer

- Add photos and documents to a project

- Manage a list of projects

- Manage previously tracked time entries

That might not sound like much, but as you'll discover, there are many techniques useful for building Windows Store applications with HTML and JavaScript that can be woven together to build a real-world, but simple, application. In Figure 9-1, you can see how the main screen of our application will look when you finish this chapter.

Figure 9-1. The completed Clok dashboard

There is a button for each of the four high-level functions I defined. The biggest button is used to turn the timer on and off. In Figure 9-1, the timer is currently running, and I have indicated which project I'm working on and added a few notes. Additionally, a logo and the current time have been added. Over the next several pages, you'll see how this screen was created.

■ **Note** The source code that accompanies this book includes a completed project containing all source code and image files used in this chapter. You can find the code samples for this chapter on the Source Code/Downloads tab of the book's Apress product page (www.apress.com/9781430257790).

Creating the Project Shell

So let's roll up our sleeves and get started by creating a new Visual Studio project using the Navigation App template. If Figure 9-2 is not enough of a refresher, you can refer to Chapter 5 and follow those same steps. Name your new project Clok. I'll spend the remainder of this book building out all of the functionality of the application in this project.

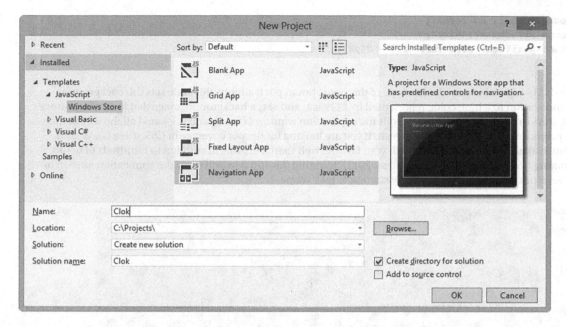

Figure 9-2. *The New Project dialog*

As you saw in Chapter 5, the Navigation App project template creates a number of files for us. In this chapter, we edit most of these files, as well as create a few new files, to implement the application design shown in Figure 9-1. In addition to the main screen that we are developing in this chapter, we will use this design throughout the application as we add more screens in later chapters.

Implementing the Design

When we created our project in Chapter 5, we configured the application to use the theme defined in `ui-light.css` instead of the default theme defined in `ui-dark.css`. For Clok, however, we'll keep the default dark theme in place. It is not required to use either of these two themes; however, they provide a simple way to ensure that your application looks and behaves like many other applications your users will have already installed and used.

The theme defined in `ui-dark.css` has a dark-colored background and light-colored text. The default background is a very dark gray, and the text is white. Conversely, the theme defined in `ui-light.css` has a light-colored background and dark-colored text, with default of black text on white background. While we do want to use the dark theme, we want a blue background with a faint version of our application logo in the lower right corner of the screen. Add the highlighted code from Listing 9-1 to `default.css`. Be sure you also add `background.png`, which can be found in the source code that accompanies this book, to the `images` folder.

Listing 9-1. Changing the Background of Our Application

```
#contenthost {
    height: 100%;
    width: 100%;

    background-color: #3399aa;
    background-image: url('/images/background.png');
```

```
    background-repeat: no-repeat;
    background-attachment: fixed;
    background-position: 100% calc(100% - 85px);
}
```

A detailed CSS tutorial is outside the scope of this book, but to put it simply, this code sets the background color of the application to a blue color, represented by #3399aa, and sets a background image that is displayed once (no-repeat), stays in place when the user scrolls the application window (fixed), and is located all the way to the right and 85 pixels from the bottom of the screen. If you are looking for deeper coverage of CSS, there is a wealth of information available that you can find with your favorite web search engine, in addition to hundreds of books, such as *Beginning CSS3* by David Powers (Apress, 2012). Running the app now will show the application as seen in Figure 9-3. We're not there yet, but it's already starting to take shape.

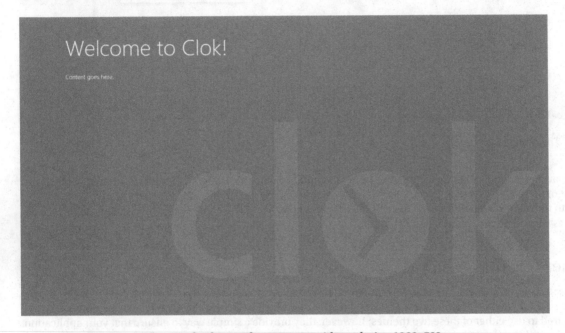

Figure 9-3. *Our new application background on a screen with resolution 1366×768*

It looks mostly good, but the Clok logo is quite a bit larger than in Figure 9-1. Depending on your screen resolution, it may take up more of your screen than you want. For example, many Windows RT tablets have a screen resolution of 1366×768; however, my laptop screen has a screen resolution of 1920×1080. Figure 9-4 shows how the same application looks on this larger screen.

Figure 9-4. *Our same new application background displayed on a larger screen with resolution 1920×1080*

We don't really want our time-entry form to cover our application logo. We want the logo to be visible to the user, especially on the main screen of the Clok application. We could make the logo smaller, so that it would not be hidden by our form on smaller screens such as tablets, but then at larger screen resolutions, the logo might appear too small. The solution is to use CSS media queries to define CSS rules that are only applied if certain conditions are met. Add the code from Listing 9-2 at the end of `default.css`. This will cause the background logo to be resized when the application window is fewer than 1400 pixels in width. In the next section, I'll cover a technique for testing this behavior.

Listing 9-2. Changing the Size of Our Background Image on Smaller Screens

```
@media screen and (max-width: 1400px) {
    #contenthost {
        background-size: 40%;
    }
}
```

The next step in implementing our design for Clok is to add the current time to the bottom of the screen. We'll use a modified version of the clock control we built in Chapter 8. The modifications include a couple of simple helper functions that will come in handy later, as well as changing the namespace. The modified version is included in the source control for this chapter. Listing 9-3 highlights the modifications to make to `default.html` to add the control.

Listing 9-3. Adding the Current Time

```
<!DOCTYPE html>
<html>
<head>
    <title>Clok</title>
```

```
<!-- WinJS references -->
<link href="//Microsoft.WinJS.1.0/css/ui-dark.css" rel="stylesheet" />
<script src="//Microsoft.WinJS.1.0/js/base.js"></script>
<script src="//Microsoft.WinJS.1.0/js/ui.js"></script>

<!-- Clok references -->
<link href="/css/default.css" rel="stylesheet" />
<script src="/js/default.js"></script>
<script src="/js/navigator.js"></script>
<script src="/controls/js/clockControl.js"></script>
</head>
<body>
    <div id="contenthost"
        data-win-control="Application.PageControlNavigator"
        data-win-options="{home: '/pages/home/home.html'}"></div>
    <div id="currentTime" data-win-control="Clok.UI.Clock"></div>
</body>
</html>
```

The default configuration of the control is to show the current time, including seconds. You'll remember from Chapter 8 that you can use data-win-options to set showClockSeconds to false. You can also set that same value in JavaScript by adding the highlighted code from Listing 9-4 to default.js.

Listing 9-4. Setting Control Options in JavaScript

```
args.setPromise(WinJS.UI.processAll().then(function () {
    currentTime.winControl.showClockSeconds = false;

    if (nav.location) {
        nav.history.current.initialPlaceholder = true;
        return nav.navigate(nav.location, nav.state);
    } else {
        return nav.navigate(Application.navigator.home);
    }
}));
```

Finally, add the CSS rule in Listing 9-5 to default.css. This rule sets the font size and weight, sets the color to a semitransparent white, and positions the time in the bottom left corner of the screen.

Listing 9-5. Styling the Current Time

```
#currentTime {
    font-size: 60pt;
    font-weight: 200;
    letter-spacing: 0;
    line-height: 1.15;
    color: rgba(255, 255, 255, 0.2);
    position: fixed;
    top: calc(100% - 85px);
    left: 10px;
}
```

The final step we'll take in implementing our design is to add some incremental CSS rules to override the colors of various controls, so that they match our intended design. Microsoft has provided a wealth of sample applications to illustrate different aspects of building Windows Store applications. You can download many of the samples individually, but I suggest downloading the entire sample app pack from MSDN: http://msdn.microsoft.com/en-US/windows/apps/br229516. While all of the samples in this pack are helpful references for trying to understand how different features can be implemented in your code, the Theme Roller sample is actually a useful piece of software for developers. It allows you to select a light or dark theme and specify a handful of different colors you intend to use in your application. Then it generates and previews a number of CSS rules to add to the code of your own application (see Figure 9-5).

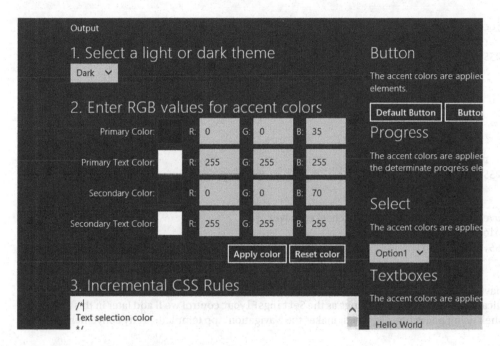

Figure 9-5. *The Theme Roller sample application*

■ **Note**   The Theme Roller application is included in the sample app pack, or it can be downloaded individually: http://code.msdn.microsoft.com/windowsapps/Theme-roller-sample-64b679f2.

The sample code that accompanies this chapter includes a file named themeroller.css, which contains the incremental CSS rules generated by the Theme Roller sample application. You can copy this file into your Visual Studio project, or you can generate the CSS rules yourself with the Theme Roller sample application. You'll have to add a reference to this CSS file to default.html (see Listing 9-6).

Listing 9-6. Referencing the New CSS File

```
<!-- SNIPPED -->
<link href="/css/default.css" rel="stylesheet" />
<link href="/css/themeroller.css" rel="stylesheet" />
<!-- SNIPPED -->
```

Because Clok is currently fairly empty, you won't actually see any changes in our application yet, but the generated styles override some of default styles in ui-light.css and ui-dark.css, so that controls we add later match the theme we have defined. For example, Listing 9-7 contains a snippet from themeroller.js that will change the color of any drop-down list controls you add, such as the one used to select a project in Figure 9-1.

Listing 9-7. Overriding Default CSS Rules with Incremental CSS Rules

```
/*
Text selection color
*/
::selection, select:focus::-ms-value {
    background-color: rgb(0, 0, 70);
    color: rgb(255, 255, 255);
}

/*
Option control color
*/
option:checked {
    background-color: rgb(0, 0, 70);
    color: rgb(255, 255, 255);
}

    option:checked:hover, select:focus option:checked:hover {
        background-color: rgb(33, 33, 94);
        color: rgb(255, 255, 255);
    }
```

With that, we now have a completed shell for Clok. Similar to the work we did in Chapters 5 through 8, most of the functionality in this application, aside from such things as the SettingsFlyout control we'll add later in this chapter, will be loaded into this shell using page controls, which makes the Navigation App template pretty convenient, in my opinion.

Debugging with the Simulator

Based on the differences between Figure 9-3 and Figure 9-4, you can see why it's a good practice to regularly test your application with different types and sizes of devices. There is no substitute for testing your application on as many real devices—desktops, laptops, and tablets—as possible. Sometimes, though, you don't have easy access to these devices, or perhaps you are actively developing features and not ready to deploy to multiple machines for more rigorous testing. If you don't have access to a variety of hardware to test, Microsoft Windows Simulator can help. The Simulator is software you run on your development machine to allow you to simulate running your application on different devices.

Best of all, you already have the Simulator, because it was installed with Visual Studio. You may have noticed a small menu indicator next to the Debug button in Visual Studio (see Figure 9-6). This menu allows you to set your debug target. By default, Local Machine is selected, but there are two additional options: Remote Machine and Simulator. Select the Simulator and then run your application. The Simulator will open, and your application will be launched (see Figure 9-7).

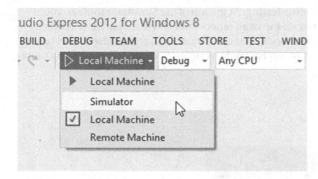

Figure 9-6. *Debugging with the Simulator*

Figure 9-7. *A completed version of Clok in the Simulator*

■ **Note** The Simulator is not a virtual machine, and it is not isolated from your development machine. The Simulator is simply running the same installation of Windows that is installed on your development machine, and it is running with the same credentials you used to launch Visual Studio. Because of this, I've found that I have some programs that run in the background of my development machine that occasionally behave oddly when I launch the Simulator, usually because two instances of that program—one on my development machine and one in the Simulator—are trying to access the same locked resource.

The Simulator provides a number of features to facilitate basic testing. At the top of the Simulator toolbar, you'll find a pushpin icon, which you can toggle to keep the Simulator on top of all other windows (see Figure 9-8). Directly beneath that are four icons that allow you to select an interaction mode. You can choose between mouse mode, basic touch mode, pinch/zoom touch mode, and rotate touch mode. In mouse mode, your application will behave the same in the Simulator as it does on your development machine.

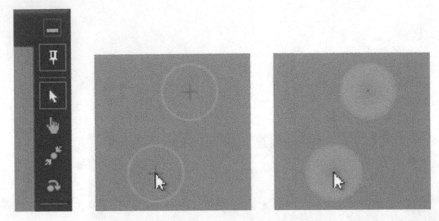

Figure 9-8. Choosing an interaction mode (left); the mouse cursor in touch mode (center) and when pressed (right)

In basic touch mode, your mouse cursor is replaced with a single-target icon, and in pinch/zoom or rotate touch mode it is a double-target icon. These targets indicate where your virtual fingers will touch the screen when you click the mouse. When you click your mouse while in one of the touch modes, your cursor changes again, to indicate that a touch interaction is in progress. In basic touch mode, your mouse behaves as you would probably expect: click your mouse to tap and click and hold to drag or open a context menu.

The pinch/zoom and rotate touch modes are a little trickier to work with at first but will only take a few tries to get used to. You scroll your mouse wheel to move the targets. In pinch/zoom touch mode, this will move the targets closer together or farther apart, and in rotate touch mode, one target will rotate around the other. Once your targets are set how you want, click and hold your mouse button while scrolling with your mouse wheel to actually perform the gesture. My primary development machine is a laptop that does not have a touch-enabled display. For more precise gestures, I've found it easier to use two hands. I use the touch pad button built into my laptop to click while I use the scroll wheel on my mouse to pinch, zoom, or rotate. Your fingers may be more coordinated than mine, though.

The next set of icons, seen in Figure 9-9, allows you to test changes to your simulated device. The first two allow you to rotate the device clockwise or counterclockwise by 90 degrees, cycling between landscape, portrait, landscape-flipped, and portrait-flipped orientations. The third icon in Figure 9-9 provides a way to change the screen resolution of the Simulator. I used this feature when creating the images seen in Figure 9-3 and Figure 9-4. The last icon in this set of buttons provides a way to change the location of the Simulator, which is useful when testing features that use geolocation to determine where the user of your application is located.

Figure 9-9. *Changing device settings*

The remaining toolbar icons are shown in Figure 9-10. The camera icon will take a screenshot of the Simulator, and the gear icon allows you to specify where that screenshot will be stored on the drive of your development machine. Finally, the familiar question mark icon will offer you more help about the various functionality provided by the Simulator.

Figure 9-10. *Changing device settings*

I encourage you to take a few moments to play around in the Simulator. Open other applications you have installed and observe how those applications behave when the screen is rotated or resized. Familiarize yourself with the different interaction modes. While we won't have much need to use the pinch/zoom and rotate interaction modes as we develop Clok, they will surely come in handy as you build more complex applications. As helpful as the Simulator is, it is recommended that you test your application on as many real devices as possible before publishing it to the Windows Store.

■ **Note** Remote Machine debugging is very handy if you have a second device for testing on your network, and I regularly use it to test applications on my tablet. Configuring a remote target for debugging is quick and simple. A good walkthrough is available on MSDN: `http://msdn.microsoft.com/en-us/library/windows/apps/hh441469.aspx`.

Adding Settings Flyouts

As we build Clok through the course of the next several chapters, we'll be adding a number of application-level settings our users can avail themselves of to customize the behavior of the application. In this section, we'll add a SettingsFlyout that we will continue to add settings to throughout the rest of the book. We'll also add some information about Clok to another SettingsFlyout, to give potential users an overview of the application and a way to find more information.

We've already seen how to add an empty `SettingsFlyout` to our application in Chapter 6, and we'll follow the same basic steps in this chapter. However, we'll organize our files in Visual Studio a little differently, to minimize clutter. Let's start by adding a `settings` folder to the root of our project in Visual Studio (see Figure 9-11).

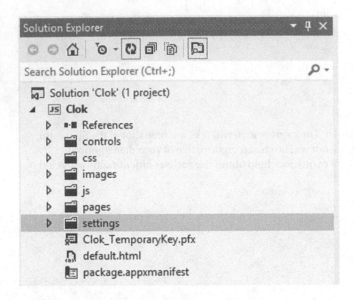

Figure 9-11. *Adding a settings folder in Solution Explorer*

■ **Note** The files that we are using to build our application are just plain old regular HTML, CSS, and JavaScript files. We can organize our project however we see fit, as long as all of the pieces are linked with the correct paths. For example, we could choose to put the CSS files for each `PageControl` into the project's `css` folder. Or, if we were planning to add a large number of pages, we might organize them into subfolders.

The Clok Options SettingsFlyout

Add an HTML file named `options.html` to the `settings` folder. Replace the default contents of that file with the code from Listing 9-8. This will be the `SettingsFlyout` our users will open when they want to change default settings for Clok. We'll add more to it throughout the book.

Listing 9-8. *The HTML Code for options.html*

```
<!DOCTYPE html>
<html>
<head>
    <title>Options</title>
</head>
<body>
    <div id="settingsDiv" data-win-control="WinJS.UI.SettingsFlyout"
        aria-label="Options"
        data-win-options="{settingsCommandId:'options',width:'narrow'}">
```

```
    <div class="win-ui-dark win-header" style="background-color: #000046;">
        <button type="button" class="win-backbutton"
            onclick="WinJS.UI.SettingsFlyout.show()"></button>
        <div class="win-label clok-logo">Options</div>
    </div>
    <div class="win-content">
        <div class="win-settings-section">
            <h3>Settings Section Header</h3>
            <p>Put your settings here.</p>
        </div>
        <div class="win-settings-section">
            <h3>Settings Section Header</h3>
            <p>Put your settings here.</p>
        </div>
    </div>
</div>
</body>
</html>
```

As you review this code, you will see that it is very similar to Listing 6-18. Aside from specifying a narrow width and a different color for the header, the most significant differences are that we've added some placeholder content in a div element with the CSS class win-settings-section. This class is provided by WinJS and is an easy way to apply a style to our SettingsFlyout that is consistent with other Windows Store applications. You can see this CSS rule, and any other CSS rule provided by WinJS, in a file named ui-dark.css. To find this file in Solution Explorer, expand the References folder, then the Windows Library for JavaScript 1.0 folder, and, finally, the css folder (see Figure 9-12). You cannot edit these files, but you can change the styles by adding incremental styles similar to how we used the Theme Roller earlier.

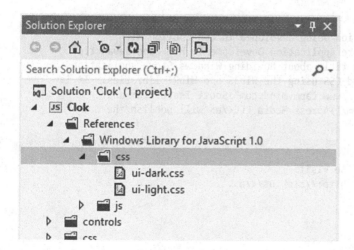

Figure 9-12. *The CSS files provided by WinJS*

The About Clok SettingsFlyout

Most applications you use today have a screen that contains information about the application. Most often, a pop-up window opens with a description of the application and links to find out more about the application or the company that built it. This concept carries over to Windows Store applications, with the pop-up window replaced by a SettingsFlyout. To add this feature to Clok, add an HTML file named about.html to the settings folder. Replace the default contents of that file with the code from Listing 9-9.

Listing 9-9. The HTML Code for about.html

```
<!DOCTYPE html>
<html>
<head>
    <title>About Clok</title>
</head>
<body>
    <div id="settingsDiv" data-win-control="WinJS.UI.SettingsFlyout"
        aria-label="About Clok"
        data-win-options="{settingsCommandId:'about',width:'narrow'}">

        <div class="win-ui-dark win-header" style="background-color: #000046;">
            <button type="button" class="win-backbutton"
                onclick="WinJS.UI.SettingsFlyout.show()">
            </button>
            <div class="win-label clok-logo">About Clok</div>
        </div>
        <div class="win-content">
            <div class="win-settings-section">
                <h3>About Clok</h3>
                <p>
                    Clok is a sample application being developed in conjunction with
                    <em>Beginning Windows Store Application Development: HTML and JavaScript
                    Edition</em>, an upcoming title about building Windows Store applications
                    with HTML,  JavaScript and CSS using the WinJS and WinRT libraries.  It is
                    written by <a href="http://www.tapmymind.com">Scott Isaacs</a> and
                    <a href="http://apress.com/">Apress Media LLC</a> will publish the
                    title in Summer 2013.
                </p>
                <p>
                    For more information, please visit:
                    <a href="http://clok.us/">http://clok.us/</a>.
                </p>
            </div>
        </div>
    </div>
</body>
</html>
```

As you can see, using a SettingsFlyout is an appropriate technique in this case, even though it is not actually used to modify any application settings, as the name might suggest.

Adding the SettingsFlyouts to the Settings Pane

The last step is to register our two SettingsFlyout controls so that Windows displays them on the Settings pane. Open default.js and add the highlighted code from Listing 9-10.

Listing 9-10. Registering Our SettingsFlyouts

```
// SNIPPED

if (app.sessionState.history) {
    nav.history = app.sessionState.history;
}

// add our SettingsFlyout to the list when the Settings charm is shown
WinJS.Application.onsettings = function (e) {
    e.detail.applicationcommands = {
        "options": {
            title: "Clok Options",
            href: "/settings/options.html"
        },
        "about": {
            title: "About Clok",
            href: "/settings/about.html"
        }
    };
    WinJS.UI.SettingsFlyout.populateSettings(e);
};

args.setPromise(WinJS.UI.processAll().then(function () {
    currentTime.winControl.showClockSeconds = false;

    if (nav.location) {
        nav.history.current.initialPlaceholder = true;
        return nav.navigate(nav.location, nav.state);
    } else {
        return nav.navigate(Application.navigator.home);
    }
}));

// SNIPPED
```

Run the application and open the Settings pane. You can open the Settings pane using one of the following methods:

- Moving the mouse to the upper-right corner of the screen to show the Windows charms, then clicking the Settings button

- Swiping in from the right of a touch screen to show the Windows charms, then tapping the Settings button

- Pressing Windows Logo Key+I on a keyboard

Once you've done that, you'll see our two SettingsFlyout controls listed as in Figure 9-13.

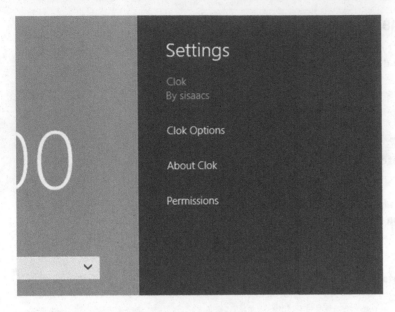

Figure 9-13. *Our SettingsFlyout controls listed in the Settings pane*

Building the Dashboard

So far in this chapter, we've focused on implementing the common design elements of the application—the pieces that will be visible on each screen of Clok. In this section, we're going to start building the user interface for the dashboard, as seen in Figure 9-14.

Figure 9-14. *UI elements on the dashboard*

You can, of course, use any layout techniques you wish in your application, because we're just using HTML and CSS for laying out the elements of our interface. I'm going to take this opportunity to discuss two different layout options available in CSS3, using the Clok dashboard as an example. I'll cover the flexbox layout and the grid layout, both of which are World Wide Web Consortium (W3C) Working Drafts. In other words, it is likely that these CSS3 layouts will become standards that will work across different browsers.

■ **Note** Windows Store applications built with HTML and JavaScript use the same rendering engine as Internet Explorer (IE) 10. As a result, CSS and JavaScript that are supported in IE 10 are also supported in your application.

The Flexbox Layout

The flexbox, or flexible box, layout is a new CSS layout option, enabled by setting the display property of an element to -ms-flexbox. It provides an easy way to indicate that the children of that element are flexible in size, by specifying how they either grow or shrink to fill the available space. The flexbox layout has a lot of options, and dozens of pages could be written about it. Instead of a deep dive into this layout option, I'll just cover, as examples, two use cases. First we'll create the overall page layout for the dashboard by defining flexible regions. Then we will use the flexbox layout again to position the four menu options to match Figure 9-14.

Defining Page Layout with Flexbox

Our dashboard in Figure 9-14 has two areas of content. On the left side, we have four menu options, and to the right of that is a time-entry form. Open home.html and replace the contents of the main section element with the highlighted code from Listing 9-11.

Listing 9-11. The Two Content Areas on the Dashboard

```
<section aria-label="Main content" role="main">
    <div id="mainMenu"></div>
    <div id="timeEntry"></div>
</section>
```

Later in this section, we'll add the menu options to the mainMenu element and the large timer display and form fields to the timeEntry element. Before we add all of those controls, let's work on the layout of these two areas. Add the highlighted code from Listing 9-12 to home.css to add CSS rules to three elements: the main section and each of the two new content areas.

Listing 9-12. Setting Up the Flexbox in CSS

```
.homepage section[role=main] {
    margin-left: 120px;
    width: calc(100% - 120px);
    display: -ms-flexbox;
    -ms-flex-direction: row;
    -ms-flex-align: start;
    -ms-flex-pack: start;
    -ms-flex-wrap: nowrap;
}
```

```
.homepage #mainMenu {
    width: 424px;
    -ms-flex: 0 auto;

    border: 2px solid yellow;   /* temporary */
    height: 500px;              /* temporary */
}

.homepage #timeEntry {
    margin-left: 20px;
    margin-right: 20px;
    -ms-flex: 1 auto;

    border: 2px solid yellow;   /* temporary */
    height: 500px;              /* temporary */
}

@media screen and (-ms-view-state: snapped) {
    .homepage section[role=main] {
        margin-left: 20px;
    }
}

@media screen and (-ms-view-state: portrait) {
    .homepage section[role=main] {
        margin-left: 100px;
    }
}
```

Setting the display property to -ms-flexbox indicates that the main section should be treated as a flexbox container. Setting the -ms-flex-direction property to row results in a horizontal layout of the children of this flexbox. Other choices for this property include column, to orient things vertically, as well as row-reverse and column-reverse, which display the children in the reverse order from how they were defined.

The -ms-flex-align property is used to specify how the children are aligned perpendicular to the -ms-flex-direction. That is, when using row to specify a horizontal layout, the -ms-flex-align property specifies how the children are displayed vertically, and when using column, it specifies how they are displayed horizontally. Because our example has a horizontal layout, setting -ms-flex-align to start will align our two content areas at the top of the container. Other options for this property include end, center, stretch, and baseline.

While the -ms-flex-align property controls the display perpendicular to the layout direction, the -ms-flex-pack property controls the layout parallel to the direction of the layout. Because we have set this property to start, the children of this flexbox will be aligned to the left. Other options for this property include end, center, and justify.

Now that our flexbox container has been defined, let's look at the rules we added for our two content areas. Adding a width setting will keep the Clok menu options on the left, and adding margins to the timeEntry element will prevent the timer and form from butting up against the menu options. The -ms-flex property is the final piece of the magic of the flexbox. Specifying 0 for the mainMenu element will prevent it from growing or shrinking to fit available space, but specifying 1 for the timeEntry element will cause that element to grow to fill the remaining space. If we had two elements with non-zero values, the remaining space would be split proportionally to this value, meaning that if one was set to 1 and another to 2, the second element would flex twice as much as the first.

■ **Note**   A more in-depth discussion of the flexbox layout, including all of the properties used in this chapter, can be found on MSDN: `http://msdn.microsoft.com/en-us/library/ie/hh673531.aspx`.

For both the `mainMenu` and `timeEntry` elements, I have temporarily added a `height` and a `border`, so that we can easily see how the flexbox actually lays out its children. You can see the result in Figure 9-15.

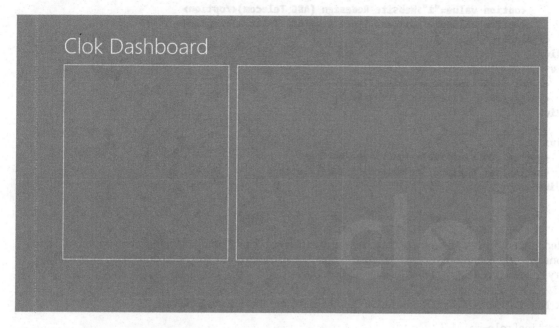

Figure 9-15. *Our initial flexbox layout*

Positioning Menu Options with Flexbox

So far, we've seen an example of using the flexbox layout to create regions within our page. It can also be used to lay out contents within one of these regions. We're also going to use the flexbox to lay out the menu options on the left side of Figure 9-14. First, let's add the HTML. Open `home.html` and replace the contents of the main section element with the highlighted code from Listing 9-13.

Listing 9-13. The Contents of the Clok Dashboard

```
<section aria-label="Main content" role="main">
    <div id="mainMenu">
        <div id="toggleTimerMenuItem" class="mainMenuItem primaryMenuItem"></div>
        <div id="cameraMenuItem" class="mainMenuItem secondaryMenuItem"></div>
        <div id="projectsMenuItem" class="mainMenuItem secondaryMenuItem"></div>
        <div id="timesheetMenuItem" class="mainMenuItem secondaryMenuItem"></div>
    </div>
    <div id="timeEntry">
        <div id="elapsedTime">
            <h2 id="elapsedTimeClock"
```

155

```
                    data-win-control="Clok.UI.Clock"
                    data-win-options="{ mode: Clok.UI.ClockModes.CountUp }"></h2>
        </div>

        <div>
            <label for="project">Project</label>
            <select id="project">
                <option value="">Choose a project</option>
                <option value="1">Website Redesign (ABC Telecom)</option>
                <option value="2">Windows Store App (ABC Telecom)</option>
            </select>
        </div>
        <div>
            <label for="timeNotes">Notes</label>
            <textarea id="timeNotes"></textarea>
        </div>

        <div>
            <button id="saveTimeButton">Save</button>
            <button id="discardTimeButton">Discard</button>
        </div>
    </div>
</div>
</section>
```

I've added four empty div elements to the mainMenu area to serve as placeholders for the menu options. I'll add the actual contents—the icons and text—in the next section. I've also added our timer and time-entry form fields to the timeEntry area. Listing 9-14 contains the code for home.css.

Listing 9-14. New CSS Rules to Lay Out the Menu Options and Time-Entry Form Fields

```
.homepage section[role=main] {
    margin-left: 120px;
    width: calc(100% - 120px);
    display: -ms-flexbox;
    -ms-flex-direction: row;
    -ms-flex-align: start;
    -ms-flex-pack: start;
    -ms-flex-wrap: nowrap;
}

    .homepage #mainMenu {
        width: 424px;
        -ms-flex: 0 auto;

        display: -ms-flexbox;
        -ms-flex-direction: row;
        -ms-flex-align: start;
        -ms-flex-wrap: wrap;
    }
```

```css
        /* all menu buttons */
        .homepage .mainMenuItem {
            border: 2px solid transparent;
            margin: 4px;
            background: rgba(0,0,50,0.65);
        }

        /* just the big menu button */
        .homepage .primaryMenuItem {
            height: 408px;
            width: 408px;
        }

        /* the smaller menu buttons */
        .homepage .secondaryMenuItem {
            height: 128px;
            width: 128px;
        }

    .homepage #timeEntry {
        margin-left: 20px;
        margin-right: 20px;
        -ms-flex: 1 auto;
    }

        .homepage #timeEntry label {
            display: block;
            font-size: 2em;
        }

        .homepage #elapsedTime {
            padding-bottom: 30px;
        }

            .homepage #elapsedTimeClock {
                font-size: 8em;
            }

        .homepage #project {
            width: 400px;
        }

        .homepage #timeNotes {
            width: 400px;
            height: 75px;
        }

@media screen and (-ms-view-state: snapped) {
    .homepage section[role=main] {
        margin-left: 20px;
    }
}
```

```
@media screen and (-ms-view-state: portrait) {
    .homepage section[role=main] {
        margin-left: 100px;
    }
}
```

I've taken out the rules that add the yellow border and height to our two main content areas, but I've also added a number of other rules. The changes we made to the timeEntry div and the controls it contains are pretty straightforward, so I won't cover them here. You'll notice, though, that we've declared that the mainMenu div is another flexbox container by setting the display property to -ms-flexbox. Like the main section, this container is also arranged in a horizontal layout by setting the -ms-flex-direction property to row, and its contents are aligned at the top by setting -ms-flex-align to start. This time, however, we have indicated that items that do not fit on the first row should wrap onto the next row by setting the -ms-flex-wrap property to wrap. Run the application to see our progress so far (Figure 9-16).

Figure 9-16. *Placeholders for our menu options, along with our time-entry form*

We're getting pretty close to our goal pictured in Figure 9-1. We've nested one flexbox container inside of another. This is a powerful way to build complex layouts, and as you'll see in the next section, it is possible to further nest a grid layout within this flexbox container.

The Grid Layout

Similar to the flexbox, the grid layout is another new CSS layout option, enabled by setting the display property of an element to -ms-grid. As the name implies, this layout allows you to indicate that the children of that element are arranged in a grid.

If you were a web developer a decade or more ago, you might be familiar with using HTML table elements to lay out web pages. Before using CSS for web page layout became prominent, this was a common practice. While it allowed simple control of layouts, it fell out of favor for several reasons, notably because it heavily mixed presentation logic with the content of the page. About the same time this shift from using HTML `table` elements for layout to using CSS for layout began, I started spending more of my time working on the back end of web applications and less on the layout. As a result, I still have a lingering fondness for `table`-based layouts, even though I know there are better alternatives.

Fortunately, the grid layout is available now. I, and others like me, can now use familiar table-based concepts to achieve our desired layout but still maintain a separation between our content and our presentation logic, because the grid is specified in CSS now instead of with `table` elements. We'll use the grid layout to add icons and text to each of our menu options. Add the highlighted code from Listing 9-15 to `home.html`. Also, be sure to add the image files referenced here; they are included in the source code that accompanies this book.

Listing 9-15. The Menu Options for the Clok Dashboard

```
<div id="mainMenu">
    <div id="toggleTimerMenuItem" class="mainMenuItem primaryMenuItem">
        <img class="mainMenuItem-image" id="timerImage" src="/images/Clock-Stopped.png" />
        <div class="mainMenuItem-overlay">
            <h4 class="mainMenuItem-title" id="timerTitle">Start Clok</h4>
        </div>
    </div>
    <div id="cameraMenuItem" class="mainMenuItem secondaryMenuItem">
        <img class="mainMenuItem-image" src="/images/Camera.png" />
        <div class="mainMenuItem-overlay">
            <h4 class="mainMenuItem-title">Camera</h4>
        </div>
    </div>
    <div id="projectsMenuItem" class="mainMenuItem secondaryMenuItem">
        <img class="mainMenuItem-image" src="/images/Projects.png" />
        <div class="mainMenuItem-overlay">
            <h4 class="mainMenuItem-title">Projects</h4>
        </div>
    </div>
    <div id="timesheetMenuItem" class="mainMenuItem secondaryMenuItem">
        <img class="mainMenuItem-image" src="/images/Timesheet.png" />
        <div class="mainMenuItem-overlay">
            <h4 class="mainMenuItem-title">Time Sheets</h4>
        </div>
    </div>
</div>
```

For each of the menu options we had previously created as empty `div` elements, we have now added an icon and a label. The code pattern used for each of the four menu options is identical, with the exception that the first has a CSS class of `primaryMenuItem` assigned to it, while the other three use the `secondaryMenuItem` CSS class. All four, regardless of size, have the `mainMenuItem` CSS class assigned. The ability to assign multiple classes to an element allows us to specify CSS rules that apply to all elements, as well as individual rules that apply only to some of the elements. The necessary CSS changes for `home.css` are highlighted in Listing 9-16.

Listing 9-16. CSS to Implement the Grid Layout for Our Menu Options

```css
/* SNIPPED */

.homepage #mainMenu {
    -ms-flex: 0 auto;
    width: 424px;
    display: -ms-flexbox;
    -ms-flex-align: center;
    -ms-flex-direction: row;
    -ms-flex-wrap: wrap;
}

    /* all menu buttons */
    .homepage .mainMenuItem {
        border: 2px solid transparent;
        margin: 4px;
        background: rgba(0,0,50,0.65);
        display: -ms-grid;
        -ms-grid-columns: 1fr;
    }

        .homepage .mainMenuItem:hover {
            cursor: pointer;
            border: 2px solid #ffffff;
        }

        .homepage .mainMenuItem .mainMenuItem-image {
            -ms-grid-row-span: 2;
        }

        .homepage .mainMenuItem .mainMenuItem-overlay {
            -ms-grid-row: 2;
            padding: 6px 15px;
            background: rgba(0,0,35,0.65);
        }

    /* just the big menu button */
    .homepage .primaryMenuItem {
        height: 408px;
        width: 408px;
        -ms-grid-rows: 1fr 70px;
    }

        .homepage .primaryMenuItem .mainMenuItem-image {
            height: 382px;
            width: 382px;
            margin: 10px;
        }
```

```
        .homepage .primaryMenuItem .mainMenuItem-overlay .mainMenuItem-title {
            font-size: 2.5em;
        }

    /* the smaller menu buttons */
    .homepage .secondaryMenuItem {
        height: 128px;
        width: 128px;
        -ms-grid-rows: 1fr 32px;
    }

        .homepage .secondaryMenuItem .mainMenuItem-image {
            height: 128px;
            width: 128px;
            padding: 0;
        }

        .homepage .secondaryMenuItem .mainMenuItem-overlay .mainMenuItem-title {
            font-size: 1em;
        }

.homepage #timeEntry {
    margin-left: 20px;
    margin-right: 20px;
    -ms-flex: 1 auto;
}

/* SNIPPED */
```

Starting at the top of Listing 9-16, the first change we made is to indicate that any of our `mainMenuItem` elements will be grid layout containers, by setting the `display` property to `-ms-grid`. We defined a single column in the `-ms-grid-columns` property. Both the `-ms-grid-columns` property and the `-ms-grid-rows` property (which we will cover in just a moment) can take a variety of different values, including the following:

- One or more specified sizes with units, such as `3px` or `1.5em`

- One or more percentage values

- One or more fractions of the remaining space, such as `1fr`, or `1fr 2fr`

- Any combination of these values, such as `150px 1fr 2fr 150px`. This example would define four columns (`-ms-grid-columns`) or rows (`-ms-grid-rows`) where the first and fourth were each 150 pixels, and one-third of the remaining space would be allocated to the second column or row, and two-thirds would be allocated to the third.

There are a few other options for the `-ms-grid-columns` property and the `-ms-grid-rows` property that I won't cover here, but you can read more about these CSS properties at http://msdn.microsoft.com/en-us/library/windows/apps/hh466340.aspx and http://msdn.microsoft.com/en-us/library/windows/apps/hh466350.aspx.

Next, we've added CSS rules to change the mouse cursor to a pointer and display a white border when the user's mouse hovers over one of these elements. Because we specify with the `-ms-grid-row-span` property that the image will span two rows, and use the `-ms-grid-row` property to place the overlay in the second row, the overlay will be placed on top of the bottom portion of the image. While we set the background color to a semitransparent dark blue here, the exact size and placement of the overlay will be determined when the various `primaryMenuItem` and `secondaryMenuItem` CSS rules are defined in a moment.

■ **Note**   Be careful to note the difference between -ms-grid-rows and -ms-grid-row in this example. The former is applied to the grid container to define how many rows the grid will have. The latter is applied to an item in the grid to indicate the row where that item will be placed. The same advice applies to the -ms-grid-columns and -ms-grid-column CSS properties.

I previously mentioned that while all of our menu items have the mainMenuItem CSS class applied, they also have either the primaryMenuItem class or the secondaryMenuItem class. All of the CSS rules I've covered so far in this section will apply to all of our menu options, regardless of whether they are large or small. You'll notice that we have not specified any sizes for any of the menu options yet. To fix that, we've added a similar set of CSS rules for both the primaryMenuItem class and the secondaryMenuItem class. Listing 9-17 contains a snippet of CSS, taken from Listing 9-16, which defines the various dimensions for the large menu option.

Listing 9-17. CSS Overrides for the Large Menu Option

```
/* just the big menu button */
.homepage .primaryMenuItem {
    height: 408px;
    width: 408px;
    -ms-grid-rows: 1fr 70px;
}

    .homepage .primaryMenuItem .mainMenuItem-image {
        height: 382px;
        width: 382px;
        margin: 10px;
    }

    .homepage .primaryMenuItem .mainMenuItem-overlay .mainMenuItem-title {
        font-size: 2.5em;
    }
```

You can see that this is where we specify the size of the grid rows, indicating that the second row is 70px in height and the first row fills the remaining space. The size of the image and the title text are also set to values appropriate for the large menu option. Referring back to Listing 9-16, you'll see very similar CSS rules for the smaller menu options. I won't cover them in detail here, as they are nearly identical to Listing 9-17, aside from defining smaller dimensions.

If you run Clok again, you'll see all of our menu options in place now (see Figure 9-17). Of course, none of the menu options works yet, but we'll see how to start adding some of that functionality in Chapter 10.

Figure 9-17. Our menu options, each defined with a CSS grid layout

---

■ **Note**   You may be thinking that adding documents and photos to a project doesn't exactly qualify as a time-tracking function. You're correct, but it's a useful feature for a number of reasons, such as keeping track of receipts for expense reporting. More important, it gives us a reason to work with files in our application. We'll look into this further in Chapter 16 and Chapter 22.

Conclusion

We covered a lot of ground in this chapter. We created a few high-level requirements for Clok, the sample application we'll be building throughout the remainder of this book. We created the overall look and feel of our application, which will be automatically applied every time we add a new `PageControl` to Clok. We added two `SettingsFlyout` controls, which will be updated throughout the book as we add features with options that the user can modify. Finally, we added all of the user-interface elements of our application's home page—the Clok dashboard—using the new CSS flexbox and grid layouts. Clok doesn't do anything yet, but it's starting to look like a real application. We'll start adding some basic functionality in Chapter 10, including some useful animations to provide visual feedback to our users when they perform certain tasks.

CHAPTER 10

■ ■ ■

Transitions and Animations

Subtle animations exist throughout Windows 8. When switching to the Start screen, the tiles zoom in to populate the familiar grid, and they react to being clicked or touched. An activated Search or Settings pane slides out from the side of the screen like a drawer. Likewise, `AppBar` controls slide in from the top or bottom of the screen. I used the word *subtle* to describe these animations. What I meant is that, in day-to-day use, you are more likely to notice if the animations have been removed than that they existed in the first place.

We could certainly build an application with no animations, but many good applications make use of animations to provide the user intuitive feedback about a change that is occurring or about an action he or she just initiated. Good animations are short and happen quickly. Additionally, they often simulate some real-world movement, as in the way a button appears to move away when it is pressed. The thing to keep in mind when adding animation to your application is that the animation should not distract the user from the primary purpose of your application.

Transitions and Animations: What's the Difference

Until this point, I've used the word *animation* in a general sense to mean "something on the screen that is moving," but that terminology is not technically correct. In reality, Windows Store applications can define two different types of motion: CSS Transitions and CSS Animations, or, simply, transitions and animations. The two are similar in many ways. Both transitions and animations can create motion on the screen over some period of time, as they modify CSS properties of an HTML element in your application, such as size, color, rotation, position, perspective, and transparency.

Transitions and animations differ in a few ways, though. The most notable difference is that animations can define keyframes, which allow you more control over how the CSS properties for the animated element change over time. For example, by defining keyframes, a single animation can change the color of an element from white to yellow and then to red, before resetting back to white. You'll see a similar example later in this chapter.

Animations allow you to specify values for various CSS properties at different points of the animation. Transitions, on the other hand, do not define values for the CSS properties but do define how those CSS properties will transition between the original value and a changed value. For example, we can use a transition to indicate that any time we change the position of an element, it should ease in and out (start off moving slowly then speed up before slowing to a stop) or move at a constant speed from the starting position to the new position.

In practice, animations are often used to provide some feedback, resetting CSS properties to their original state when complete. Transitions, on the other hand, do not automatically reset CSS properties to their original state. So, if we had used a transition to change the color of an element from white to yellow to red, that element would remain red until we changed it back to white.

165

Methods of Animation (and Transition)

So, how do we animate elements of our application? As is common in software development, there are many ways to accomplish this. I'll cover four different techniques in this chapter, as follows:

- Purely in CSS

- Using animations built into the WinJS Animations Library in our JavaScript code

- Using JavaScript to manipulate our CSS programmatically

- Defining our own transitions and animations in JavaScript and executing them in our JavaScript code

Pure CSS Animation

Ultimately, all animations and transitions that I will cover in this chapter are CSS Animations and CSS Transitions. The motion or change on the screen is a result of changing CSS properties and allowing the client to render the change from one value to another in a smooth manner. While I'll cover a few techniques for initiating these animations and transitions from our JavaScript code, some simple, but useful, animations can be defined directly in our CSS.

We're going to add an animation to the timer we created in Clok in Chapter 9 by defining keyframes in home.css. Keyframes allow us to define CSS rules at each of a number of intermediate steps in our animation in a special @keyframes CSS rule, which contains a rule for each step, or frame, we are defining. Add the code from Listing 10-1 to the end of home.css.

Listing 10-1. Defining Keyframes in CSS

```
@keyframes animateTimeIn {
    from, to {
        color: rgba(255, 255, 255, 1);
    }

    50% {
        color: rgba(255, 255, 0, 0.5);
    }
}
```

The first thing to notice is that we have named our @keyframes rule animateTimeIn, so that we can refer to it later. Our initial state is defined in the from rule, and our final state is defined in the to rule. Because both of these are the same, we can declare the rule once, separating the rule names with a comma. That's exactly what we have done in Listing 10-1, setting the foreground color to white in those cases. We have created another rule, which will change the color to a semitransparent yellow halfway through the animation.

▪ **Note** Similar to how we have defined the midpoint of our animation at 50%, you can also use 0% to define the initial state and 100% to define the final state. Those values are equivalent to from and to, respectively.

So far, we have defined what values will change when the animation occurs, but nowhere in our CSS have we mentioned our timer yet. To attach the animation to our timer, we have to add the highlighted code from Listing 10-2 to home.css.

Listing 10-2. Applying Our Keyframe Animation to the Timer

```
.homepage section[role=main] #timeEntry #elapsedTime #elapsedTimeClock {
    font-size: 8em;
    animation: animateTimeIn 750ms ease-in-out 1s 2 normal;
}
```

Adding the `animation` CSS property to this rule allows us to identify which animation we want to apply to the elapsedTimeClock element, by specifying the name we defined in Listing 10-1. Our animation will ease in and out over a period of 750 milliseconds. It will start after a 1 second delay and will repeat twice. This shortcut syntax allows us to define the animation property all in a single line. We could also set each of these properties individually (see Listing 10-3).

Listing 10-3. Long Form Equivalent to Listing 10-2

```
.homepage section[role=main] #timeEntry #elapsedTime #elapsedTimeClock {
    font-size: 8em;
    animation-name: animateTimeIn;
    animation-duration: 750ms;
    animation-timing-function: ease-in-out;
    animation-delay: 1s;
    animation-iteration-count: 2;
    animation-direction: normal;
}
```

■ **Note** A more complete description of these and other CSS animation properties can be found in MSDN at http://msdn.microsoft.com/en-us/library/hh673530.aspx.

When you launch the application now, the timer control will alternate twice between white and yellow (see Figure 10-1). Currently, this isn't very useful, because we are showing the animation every time the application launches. However, imagine a scenario where we start Clok, and the timer is already running, or perhaps the timer isn't running but has a value that hasn't been saved yet. Using this animation, or a similar animation, in those unique situations could be a subtle way to alert the user that the application is currently in an "in progress" state.

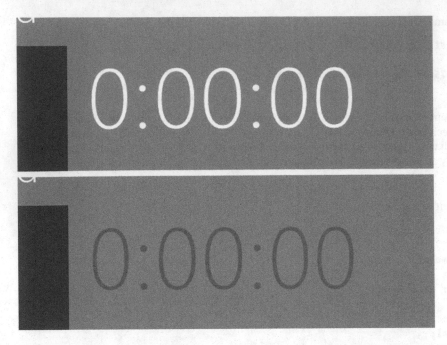

Figure 10-1. *Our timer in its initial state (top) and with a modified color (bottom). The color in the bottom image is different from how it will appear in our application. It has been darkened for additional contrast in the print book*

Pure CSS Transition

In addition to defining animations in CSS, you can also define transitions. It is important to note that a CSS transition itself does not create motion on the screen. You cannot, for example, specify a new color using the transition property. What transitions actually do is define how the target element changes from its current style to its new style. What this means is that you must have two sets of CSS rules defined for the target element: for the beginning and for the end of the transition.

Because we have three menu options that haven't been implemented yet, we'll add a transition that changes them when users hover their mouse over them. The first thing we have to do is add another CSS class to the menu options we haven't implemented yet. Modify home.html by adding notImplemented to the class attribute for the three smaller menu options (see highlighted code in Listing 10-4).

Listing 10-4. Marking Menu Options As Not Implemented

```
<div id="cameraMenuItem" class="mainMenuItem secondaryMenuItem notImplemented">
    <img class="mainMenuItem-image" src="/images/Camera.png" />
    <div class="mainMenuItem-overlay">
        <h4 class="mainMenuItem-title">Camera</h4>
    </div>
</div>
<div id="projectsMenuItem" class="mainMenuItem secondaryMenuItem notImplemented">
    <img class="mainMenuItem-image" src="/images/Projects.png" />
    <div class="mainMenuItem-overlay">
        <h4 class="mainMenuItem-title">Projects</h4>
    </div>
</div>
```

```
<div id="timesheetMenuItem" class="mainMenuItem secondaryMenuItem notImplemented">
    <img class="mainMenuItem-image" src="/images/Timesheet.png" />
    <div class="mainMenuItem-overlay">
        <h4 class="mainMenuItem-title">Time Sheets</h4>
    </div>
</div>
```

Now that we've indicated which menu options should have the transition applied, we have to define the CSS rules that will be in effect when the transition has been completed. Add the CSS code from Listing 10-5 to home.css.

Listing 10-5. *Adding CSS for the Menu Options That Aren't Implemented*

```css
/* buttons that haven't been implemented yet */
.homepage .mainMenuItem.notImplemented:hover {
    cursor: default;
    border: 2px solid transparent;
    background: rgba(50,50,50,0.65);
    background-image: url('/images/Thumb-Down.png');
}

    .homepage .mainMenuItem.notImplemented:hover .mainMenuItem-image {
        visibility: hidden;
    }

    .homepage .mainMenuItem.notImplemented:hover .mainMenuItem-overlay {
        background: rgba(35,35,35,0.65);
    }

    .homepage .mainMenuItem.notImplemented:hover .mainMenuItem-overlay .mainMenuItem-title {
        display: none;
    }

    .homepage .mainMenuItem.notImplemented:hover .mainMenuItem-overlay::after {
        content: 'Coming Soon';
    }
```

If you run Clok now, any time you hover your mouse over one of the three smaller menu options, the background color will change to gray, and the icon will change to a "thumbs down" icon. Additionally, the descriptive text will change to read "Coming Soon." Once you move your mouse away, the menu option returns to its normal state. Figure 10-2 shows both states of the Time Sheets button.

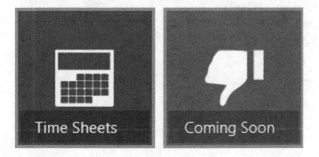

Figure 10-2. *Normal state of a menu option that is not implemented (left) and the hover state of the same menu option (right)*

When you ran the application and moved your mouse over the Time Sheets option, you probably noticed that, although the styles changed, it was an abrupt change. That's because, so far, we have only defined the final state of the CSS, but we haven't indicated how the CSS should transition from the initial state to the final state. Let's add one more line of code to home.css. The highlighted line of code in Listing 10-6 will cause the background color to gently transition from the default blue color to a gray color.

Listing 10-6. Setting Up a Short Transition Between the Initial CSS Rules and the Rules for the Hover State

```
.homepage .mainMenuItem.notImplemented:hover {
    cursor: default;
    border: 2px solid transparent;
    background: rgba(50,50,50,0.65);
    background-image: url('/images/Thumb-Down.png');
    transition: background 500ms ease-in-out 0s;
}
```

I encourage you to play around with the CSS a bit before continuing. For example, you may also want to add a transition to the background color of the overlay, because currently, it still changes immediately from the dark blue to dark gray. Documentation for the CSS transition property, and other related properties, can be found at http://msdn.microsoft.com/en-us/library/hh673535.aspx.

WinJS Animations Library

As you use Windows 8, you'll find that there are a number of common animations. WinJS makes many of these available through an Animations Library, and we can use them in our applications to provide visual feedback that is consistent with other Windows Store applications, as well as with Windows itself. There are, for example, predefined animations for adding an item to a ListView control, for fading something into or out of view, and for having an element react to being clicked or touched. We'll use this library to animate our menu options when the user presses one. Replace the page definition in home.js with the code from Listing 10-7.

Listing 10-7. Adding Pointer Animations

```
WinJS.UI.Pages.define("/pages/home/home.html", {
    ready: function (element, options) {
        this.initializeMenuPointerAnimations();
    },

    initializeMenuPointerAnimations: function () {
        var buttons = WinJS.Utilities.query(".mainMenuItem");
        buttons.listen("MSPointerDown", this.pointer_down, false);
        buttons.listen("MSPointerUp", this.pointer_up, false);
        buttons.listen("MSPointerOut", this.pointer_up, false);
    },

    pointer_down: function (e) {
        WinJS.UI.Animation.pointerDown(this);
        e.preventDefault();
    },
```

```
      pointer_up: function (e) {
         WinJS.UI.Animation.pointerUp(this);
         e.preventDefault();
      },
});
```

In the new initializeMenuPointerAnimations method, we find all of our menu option buttons—those HTML elements with the mainMenuItem CSS class. For each of the items we find, we listen for the MSPointerDown and MSPointerUp events, which represent mouse or touch interactions. We have created two functions, named pointer_down and pointer_up, to handle these events by animating the clicked or touched item with a call to the appropriate method in the WinJS Animations Library: either WinJS.UI.Animation.pointerDown or WinJS.UI.Animation.pointerUp. If you look closely at Figure 10-3, you can see how the button slightly shrinks in size when pressed, to give the appearance of being pushed away. The effect is much more obvious when interacting with the application.

Figure 10-3. Pushing our button away

Additionally, we are handling the MSPointerOut event as if it were an MSPointerUp event. If we ignore that event, it would be easy to get a menu option stuck in the pressed state by, for example, clicking it and sliding the mouse off of it before releasing the mouse button.

We've only covered two of the animations in the Animations Library here. There are several others available, and you can read more about them on MSDN at http://msdn.microsoft.com/en-us/library/windows/apps/br229780.aspx.

Using JavaScript to Manipulate CSS

As we saw in previous sections, configuring animations and transitions directly within CSS is simple, and using the WinJS Animations Library is about as trivial. Sometimes, though, you need a little more control. For example, you might want to let users specify the color to use in the animation above. Instead of yellow, they may choose orange. Or they may choose #E3A238. Or you may want to run some code after the animation or transition has completed, which is what we're going to do in this section.

We're going to add a CSS transition to Clok that gets triggered when users save their time entry. An animation might not be necessary in this situation, but it's helpful to provide feedback to users, especially those interacting with Clok via touch. If we simply save the data and reset the form, users might not be confident that their data was saved, because that would visually appear the same as when they discarded their time entry. To provide clear feedback, we'll use CSS Transitions to shrink the form and animate it toward the Time Sheets menu option, to indicate that their entry has been saved to their time sheet. Figure 10-4 shows the time-entry form after a user has entered some notes and is pressing the Save button. Let's see what we have to add to make something interesting happen after he or she presses the Save button.

Figure 10-4. *A Clok user saving her time entry*

First Things First: Making the Timer Tick

Before we can add the code to add this transition, we have some setup work to do. Update the page definition in home.js with the highlighted code from Listing 10-8. This code isn't specific to the transition we are going to add, so I won't cover it in detail, but it is required to configure basic form behavior. As you scroll through this code, you'll see the familiar concepts of handling events and changing the value and state of controls that I covered in Chapter 8 when we created our custom clock control. You'll see code that starts the timer when the Clok user presses the Start Clok menu option, then stops the timer when he presses the Stop Clok menu option. There is some logic to prevent the user from saving an entry without a project selected, as well as preventing him from either saving or discarding a timer with no elapsed time. Currently, both the Save button and Discard button simply reset the form. While this is the correct action for the Discard button, we've left ourselves a comment to record the time entry when the user presses the Save button. I'll cover that in Chapter 12.

Listing 10-8. Preparing Our JavaScript to Handle Time-Entry Form Events

```
WinJS.UI.Pages.define("/pages/home/home.html", {
    ready: function (element, options) {
        this.initializeMenuPointerAnimations();

        toggleTimerMenuItem.onclick = this.toggleTimerMenuItem_click.bind(this);
```

```
        project.onchange = this.project_change.bind(this);
        saveTimeButton.onclick = this.saveTimeButton_click.bind(this);
        discardTimeButton.onclick = this.discardTimeButton_click.bind(this);

        this.setupTimerRelatedControls();
    },

initializeMenuPointerAnimations: function () {
    var buttons = WinJS.Utilities.query(".mainMenuItem");
    buttons.listen("MSPointerDown", this.pointer_down, false);
    buttons.listen("MSPointerUp", this.pointer_up, false);
    buttons.listen("MSPointerOut", this.pointer_up, false);
},

pointer_down: function (e) {
    WinJS.UI.Animation.pointerDown(e.srcElement);
    e.preventDefault();
},

pointer_up: function (e) {
    WinJS.UI.Animation.pointerUp(e.srcElement);
    e.preventDefault();
},

timerIsRunning: false,

toggleTimerMenuItem_click: function (e) {
    this.toggleTimer();
},

project_change: function (e) {
    this.enableOrDisableButtons();
},

discardTimeButton_click: function (e) {
    this.discard();
},

saveTimeButton_click: function (e) {
    this.save();
},

save: function () {
    // TODO: save the time entry
    this.resetTimer()
},

discard: function () {
    this.resetTimer()
},

toggleTimer: function () {
```

```
            this.timerIsRunning = !this.timerIsRunning;
            this.setupTimerRelatedControls();
    },

    resetTimer: function () {
        this.timerIsRunning = false;
        elapsedTimeClock.winControl.reset();
        project.selectedIndex = 0;
        timeNotes.value = "";

        this.setupTimerRelatedControls();
    },

    setupTimerRelatedControls: function () {
        if (this.timerIsRunning) {
            elapsedTimeClock.winControl.start();
            timerImage.src = "/images/Clock-Running.png";
            timerTitle.innerText = "Stop Clok";
        } else {
            elapsedTimeClock.winControl.stop();
            timerImage.src = "/images/Clock-Stopped.png";
            timerTitle.innerText = "Start Clok";
        }

        this.enableOrDisableButtons();
    },

    enableOrDisableButtons: function () {
        if ((project.value !== "")
                && (!this.timerIsRunning)
                && (elapsedTimeClock.winControl.counterValue > 0)) {
            saveTimeButton.disabled = false;
        } else {
            saveTimeButton.disabled = true;
        }

        discardTimeButton.disabled = (this.timerIsRunning)
                || (elapsedTimeClock.winControl.counterValue <= 0);
    },
});
```

Adding CSS Transition with JavaScript

If you were to run Clok now, the app would probably behave as you expect. You could start and stop the timer and save a valid time entry. Now let's look at Listing 10-9 to find the code we need to add to our save method to trigger the transition.

Listing 10-9. Our Updated Save Method

```
save: function () {
    // TODO: save the time entry

    timeEntry.style.transition = 'color 5ms ease 0s, '
        + 'transform 500ms ease 0s, opacity 500ms ease 0s';

    timeEntry.style.transform = 'scale3d(0,0,0)';
    timeEntry.style.opacity = '0';
    timeEntry.style.color = '#00ff00';
    timeEntry.style.transformOrigin = "-130px 480px";

    var self = this;
    var transitionend = function (e1) {
        if (e1.propertyName === "transform") {
            timeEntry.removeEventListener('transitionend', transitionend);
            self.resetTimer();
        }
    };
    timeEntry.addEventListener('transitionend', transitionend, false);
},
```

The first line of code we've added here is to define our transition. This line will animate any change to the color, transform, or opacity CSS properties, gradually changing them over the specified time for each property, 5ms for color and 500ms for transform and opacity. Next, we specify new values for each of these properties, indicating that our time-entry form should shrink and fade while changing the text color to green, to indicate success. The transformOrigin property allows us to indicate the point around which the transition will occur. In this case, we have indicated that the center of our transition is 130 pixels to the left and 480 pixels below the top left corner of the time-entry form. These numbers were selected based on the size we previously defined for the menu options and will set the origin of our transition on top of the Time Sheets button.

Next, we create an inline function named transitionend to handle an event of the same name. As you might guess, this event is raised when the transition completes. We have three transitions happening at once, and the color, transform, and opacity transitions each raise this event when they complete, each at different times. Our handler function ignores the color and opacity completion events, but when the transform transition completes, our handler resets the form and stops listening for subsequent transition completion events. Because the opacity transition has the same duration as the transform transition, listening for that one to complete would be equivalent.

■ **Note** If this transition were the only one we were going to add to Clok, we wouldn't need to worry about removing the event listener like this. However, without doing that, any subsequent transition would also trigger the transitionend event handler, which could lead to unexpected results.

Now when we run Clok and saved our time entry, we can clearly see that our time entry was saved to our time sheet (see Figure 10-5).

Figure 10-5. *A successfully completed time-entry form saving to our time sheet*

The transition is pretty slick, and Clok is starting to come together as a useful little application. We have one small problem now, though. Once the entry is saved, the form is gone. We could make the user close Clok and relaunch it if he wanted to record time for another project, but that would be a pretty poor experience. Fortunately, just as easily as we animated our time-entry form away, we can reset the form to its original state. Listing 10-10 does just that. I've added a new resetTimerStyles method to reset all of the styles back to their original values and clear the transition. Then I call this method from the existing resetTimer method.

Listing 10-10. Putting Things Back Where They Belong

```
resetTimer: function () {
    this.timerIsRunning = false;
    elapsedTimeClock.winControl.reset();
    project.selectedIndex = 0;
    timeNotes.value = "";

    this.resetTimerStyles();
    this.setupTimerRelatedControls();
},

resetTimerStyles: function () {
    timeEntry.style.transition = 'none';
    timeEntry.style.transformOrigin = "50% 50%";
    timeEntry.style.transform = 'scale3d(1,1,1)';
    timeEntry.style.opacity = '1';
    timeEntry.style.color = '#ffffff';
},
```

The executeTransition and executeAnimation Methods

In the previous section, we saw how we could create a transition by modifying the various CSS style properties of the element we want to animate. This is pretty convenient and straightforward. However, there is something else to keep in mind. In the Ease of Access control panel, Windows 8 allows users to disable unnecessary animations (see Figure 10-6). Some users may turn animations off, because the computer they use becomes slow when animations are enabled. Others may do so simply because they don't want to be distracted by animations. Whatever the reason, if an animation (or transition) is not critical to the functionality of your application, you should respect the user's choice and not initiate the animation.

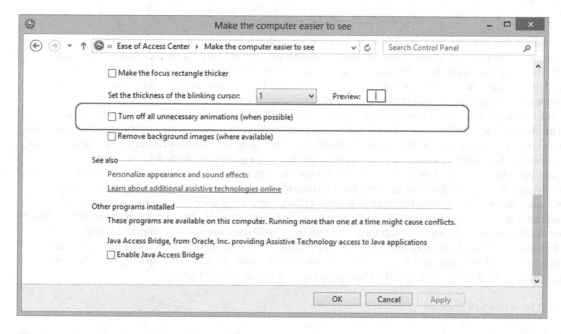

Figure 10-6. Disable unnecessary animations

So how do we check this value? The Windows Runtime (WinRT) defines a class that we can use. The `Windows.UI.ViewManagement.UISettings` class provides an easy way to access a number of common user-interface settings (see Listing 10-11). Once we have an instance of this class, we can check a property named `animationsEnabled`, which directly corresponds to the setting in Figure 10-6.

Listing 10-11. Example of Checking the User's Preference

```
var uiSettings = new Windows.UI.ViewManagement.UISettings();
if (uiSettings.animationsEnabled) {
    // perform animation or transition
    myElement.style.transition = "opacity 500ms ease 0s";
    timeEntry.style.opacity = "0.5";
}
```

Additionally, WinJS provides a function, `WinJS.UI.isAnimationEnabled`, that examines that setting and, in combination with some other criteria, determines if an animation should occur. A description of the criteria that determine the value of `isAnimationEnabled` can be found on MSDN: http://msdn.microsoft.com/en-us/library/windows/apps/hh779793.aspx. The `isAnimationEnabled` function is used internally by the Animations Library and the ListView control, and it gives you the information you need to maintain consistency in your animations. While not possible with animations declared purely in CSS, Listing 10-12 gives a hypothetical example of how we might modify the code in Listing 10-9 to check this function before initiating our transition.

Listing 10-12. Hypothetical Changes to Our Save Method

```
save: function () {
    if (WinJS.UI.isAnimationEnabled()) {
        // SNIPPED
    }
},
```

The downside to this practice is that you have to check this function any time you use JavaScript to define a custom CSS Transition or CSS Animation. I mentioned that the Animations Library checks this method internally, so the pointerDown and pointerUp animations we created earlier automatically take the control panel setting into account when creating the animations. It would be convenient to be able to declare custom animations and transitions that automatically check the isAnimationEnabled function for us.

Fortunately, this is possible. The Animations Library uses two WinJS methods internally to perform transitions and animations. The check of the isAnimationEnabled function happens within these two methods, and they are exposed for us to use in our own applications as well. We can use WinJS.UI.executeTransition and WinJS.UI.executeAnimation to set up one or more transitions and animations, respectively, to perform on a particular element in our page.

Let's look at an example. In the last section, we added a transition to provide feedback to the user when she saves her time entry. In this section, we'll add a transition for the Discard button as well. Saving an entry animated the form into the Time Sheets menu option. When I think of discarding something, such as an empty water bottle, I picture myself tossing it into a recycle bin. We don't have the concept of a recycle bin in Clok; however, we can create an analogy for tossing something away. As with the save animation, we'll have our discard animation shrink the form, but instead of animating toward a menu option, we'll just have it spin as it shrinks into the background, and instead of turning green to indicate success, we'll have the text change to red to indicate that we are getting rid of this entry. Update the discard method in home.js with the highlighted code from Listing 10-13.

Listing 10-13. A New Discard Method

```
discard: function () {
    var self = this;

    var slideTransition = WinJS.UI.executeTransition(
        timeEntry,
        [
            {
                property: "transform",
                delay: 0,
                duration: 500,
                timing: "ease",
                from: "rotate(0deg) scale3d(1,1,1)",
                to: "rotate(720deg) scale3d(0,0,0)"
            },
            {
                property: "opacity",
                delay: 0,
                duration: 500,
                timing: "ease",
```

```
                from: 1,
                to: 0
            },
            {
                property: "color",
                 delay: 0,
                duration: 5,
                timing: "ease",
                from: '#ffffff',
                to: '#ff0000'
            }
        ]).done(function () { self.resetTimer(); });
},
```

Here we're using the executeTransition method to perform three different transitions on our timeEntry element.

- We're spinning the form twice by transforming the angle of rotation from 0 degrees to 720 degrees.

- We're fading the form by changing its opacity.

- We're changing the text color from white to red.

Then, once the transition is done, the timer and form are reset. The result is that Clok now gives the user feedback confirming that we have intentionally cleared the form when she presses the Discard button (see Figure 10-7).

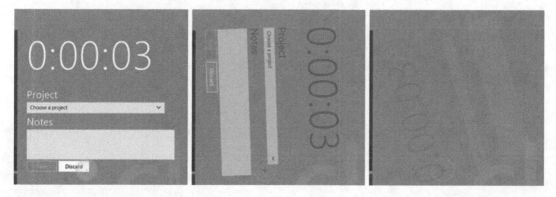

Figure 10-7. *The discard animation*

Conclusion

You've seen in this chapter that there are a number of ways to provide visual, animated feedback to our users. While excessive animations are a distraction, subtle animations representing the action that the user has performed can provide confidence to our users that our application has behaved as intended.

Our choices of animation techniques include simple animations defined purely in CSS, using one of the several predefined animations in the WinJS Animations Library, using JavaScript to programmatically modify the CSS styles associated with an element, or by using the low-level executeTransition or executeAnimation methods from WinJS. While there may be a place for each of these in our applications, we should be aware that the user may prefer not to see unnecessary animations for one reason or another, and we should let this fact influence our decision concerning which method of animation we should use.

CHAPTER 11

■ ■ ■

Data-Binding Concepts

It goes without saying that data is an integral part of nearly every useful application. Clok, our sample application, is no different. This chapter will cover various techniques for displaying data in your application—a process called *data binding*. Chapters 14, 15 and 16 will cover working with data from a variety of different sources, as well as different ways to save your data. To keep things simple in this chapter, however, we're going to work with data that is stored in memory. This has the side effect of preventing our changes from persisting after we close the application, but I'll address that in Chapter 14.

We are going to build our data model as a handful of classes in JavaScript. These classes will define the structure of our data, as well as how to work with it. Let's get started building the data model that we will continue to expand upon throughout the book.

Our Data Model

In this chapter, we'll build a class to model the project and client data, as well as a separate storage class for working with our in-memory database. This storage class will allow us to create, read, update, and delete data—concepts collectively referred to as CRUD operations. Although we are creating these classes to manage our in-memory data, we will continue to use them as we upgrade Clok to take advantage of other data sources.

As we continue to build Clok, we will be adding a number of files to our Visual Studio project. So, as a means of keeping more organized, let's create a new folder for our data model code. If it's not already open, open your Clok project in Visual Studio. Then add a folder named data to the Solution Explorer (see Figure 11-1). We'll be using this folder for the classes we create in this chapter, as well as any other files we add to perform different data-access functions throughout the book.

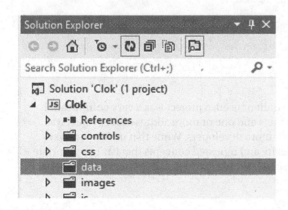

Figure 11-1. *Adding a data folder to our project*

■ **Note**   There's nothing special about a folder named `data`, and there's no reason you couldn't put the files we'll be working with somewhere else, as long as you reference them correctly when we get to that topic later in this chapter. So, if you, or the team you work on, have other conventions, you'll be able to follow those while building Windows Store applications. The files could be placed anywhere within the Visual Studio project, but for the rest of this book, we'll place them in this new `data` folder.

Project Class

Our time-keeping application will have two primary types of objects: projects and time entries. I won't be covering time entries in this chapter, but we will be defining a class to represent projects. We'll keep it pretty simple to start. Add a new JavaScript File to the `data` folder and name it `project.js` (see Figure 11-2).

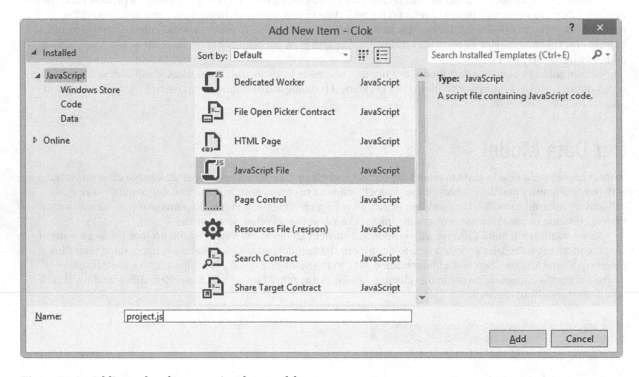

Figure 11-2. *Adding a class for our project data model*

In other project-management and time-recording systems I've built or used, a project was a very complicated concept. A project belonged to a client, which had one or more contacts and one or more addresses. A project was made up of multiple tasks, each of which could be assigned to one or more developers. While that makes for a very robust project-management application, it creates a level of complexity and repeated concepts that isn't appropriate for this book. So, we'll consolidate all of that functionality into our single, simple `Project` class, which we define in `project.js` by adding the code from Listing 11-1.

Listing 11-1. Defining Our Project Class

```
(function () {
    "use strict";

    var projectClass = WinJS.Class.define(
        function constructor() {

            // define and initialize properties
            this.id = (new Date()).getTime();
            this.name = "";
            this.projectNumber = "";
            this.status = "active";
            this.description = "";
            this.startDate = new Date();
            this.dueDate = new Date();
            this.clientName = "";
            this.contactName = "";
            this.address1 = "";
            this.address2 = "";
            this.city = "";
            this.region = "";
            this.postalCode = "";
            this.email = "";
            this.phone = "";
        },
        {
            // instance members
        },
        {
            // static members
        }
    );

    WinJS.Namespace.define("Clok.Data", {
        Project: projectClass,
    });

})();
```

As in previous chapters, we define a class using the WinJS.Class.define method within a self-executing function, and then we expose it for use in our application as Clok.Data.Project, using the WinJS.Namespace.define method. The class itself is pretty simple, defining a number of properties and their initial values, mostly empty strings. I would like to explain one thing in particular about this code.

Traditional relational database engines, such as Microsoft SQL Server or Oracle, allow developers to create an identity field as a unique identifier for an object. These are commonly represented as an integer that automatically increments for each new record in the database or a globally unique identifier (GUID), such as C9EFEADF-A6BB-455A-8A9A-CD0BC5A588CB. IndexedDB, which I will introduce in Chapter 14, also supports an automatcially incrementing identity field. However, because Clok data may eventually need to be synchronized between multiple computers, a GUID is preferred to prevent identity conflicts. While JavaScript can create a random string of characters that looks like a GUID, it's not really globally unique, and duplicate values could occur. In the absence of real identity functionality in our in-memory example, I have used the getTime method that is part of JavaScript's Date class. This method returns the number of milliseconds that have passed since January 1, 1970. While it's not a perfect replacement for an identity field, it will work well enough, as long as we don't create more than one project in the same millisecond. I'll revisit this in Chapter 18, where you'll see how to use an external library to generate a GUID for us.

Storage Class

You might have noticed that our Project class doesn't contain any methods for CRUD operations. It's just a simple class defining some properties. Because we will need some way to store and retrieve this data, we'll create a Storage class to handle those operations for us. Add the code in Listing 11-2 to a new JavaScript file named storage.js in the data folder you created earlier in this chapter.

Listing 11-2. Defining Our Storage Class

```
(function () {
    "use strict";

    var storage = WinJS.Class.define(
        function constructor() {
        },
        {
            // instance members
        },
        {
            // static members
            projects: new WinJS.Binding.List([]),
        }
    );

    WinJS.Namespace.define("Clok.Data", {
        Storage: storage,
    });

})();
```

At this point, our new Clok.Data.Storage class is pretty light. Aside from the boilerplate code to create a class with WinJS, we've defined only a single static property, named projects, as an empty WinJS.Binding.List that will store all of the Project objects our users will create. You've seen this List class in Chapter 7, when you first looked at the ListView control. While we could use regular JavaScript arrays to store this data, the List provides a number of additional benefits. Some of these benefits that I will cover in this chapter include support for grouping (which I also covered in Chapter 7) and the ability to create live filtered and sorted views of the data in the List. It also implements the necessary functionality to support binding in Windows Store applications. As we build Clok, both in this chapter and in subsequent chapters, we'll keep coming back to this class to add more functionality.

Referencing Our Data Classes

So, we have a Project class and a Storage class. Now we have to make those classes available to the rest of Clok. Because every screen we create will have to access these classes, the quickest and easiest way to accomplish that is to add script references to default.html. Remember that default.html is the first page that loads when our application launches, and all other pages we create are loaded within that page. If you're familiar with the concept of master pages from ASP.NET development, you can think of default.html as the master page for our application. The important thing to take away is that, because we are using the Navigation App template for Clok, default.html is always loaded, so the code in any scripts we reference in it will always be available to use. Add the highlighted code in Listing 11-3 to the head section of default.html.

Listing 11-3. Referencing Our New Classes in default.html

```
<head>
    <meta charset="utf-8" />
    <title>Clok</title>

    <!-- WinJS references -->
    <link href="//Microsoft.WinJS.1.0/css/ui-dark.css" rel="stylesheet" />
    <script src="//Microsoft.WinJS.1.0/js/base.js"></script>
    <script src="//Microsoft.WinJS.1.0/js/ui.js"></script>
    <script src="/js/extensions.js"></script>
    <script src="/js/debug.js"></script>

    <!-- Clok references -->
    <link href="/css/default.css" rel="stylesheet" />
    <link href="/css/themeroller.css" rel="stylesheet" />
    <script src="/js/default.js"></script>
    <script src="/js/navigator.js"></script>
    <script src="/controls/js/clockControl.js"></script>

    <script src="/data/project.js"></script>
    <script src="/data/storage.js"></script>
</head>
```

■ **Note**   If you have decided to use a folder other than `data` to store your data model scripts, be sure to modify
Listing 11-3 accordingly.

Temporary Data

To keep things a bit simpler in this chapter about binding data to your UI, we won't actually be reading and writing data to any kind of persistent storage. I'll get to that in Chapter 14 and Chapter 15. We do need some data, however, to build our understanding of how data binding works. To accomplish that, we're going to hard-code a handful of projects by adding the code from Listing 11-4 at the very end of `storage.js`.

Listing 11-4. Temporarily Adding Hard-Coded Data

```
// add temp data
(function () {
    var createProject = function (name, projectNumber, clientName, id, status) {
        var newProject = new Clok.Data.Project();
        newProject.id = id;
        newProject.name = name;
        newProject.projectNumber = projectNumber;
        newProject.clientName = clientName;
        newProject.status = status || newProject.status;

        return newProject;
    }
```

```
    var projects = Clok.Data.Storage.projects;

    var name1 = "Windows Store App";
    var name2 = "Mobile Website";
    var name3 = "Website Redesign";
    var name4 = "Employee Portal";

    var client1 = "Northwind Traders";
    var client2 = "Contoso Ltd.";
    var client3 = "AdventureWorks Cycles";
    var client4 = "TailSpin Toys";
    var client5 = "A. Datum Corporation";
    var client6 = "Woodgrove Bank";
    var client7 = "Fabrikam, Inc.";

    projects.push(createProject(name1, "2012-0003", client1, 1368296808745, "inactive"));
    projects.push(createProject(name2, "2012-0008", client2, 1368296808746, "inactive"));
    projects.push(createProject(name3, "2012-0011", client1, 1368296808747, "inactive"));
    projects.push(createProject(name1, "2012-0017", client3, 1368296808748));
    projects.push(createProject(name3, "2012-0018", client4, 1368296808749, "deleted"));
    projects.push(createProject(name1, "2012-0023", client5, 1368296808750, "deleted"));
    projects.push(createProject(name3, "2012-0027", client6, 1368296808751, "inactive"));
    projects.push(createProject(name3, "2012-0030", client7, 1368296808752, "inactive"));
    projects.push(createProject(name3, "2012-0033", client3, 1368296808753));
    projects.push(createProject(name2, "2012-0039", client1, 1368296808754, "inactive"));
    projects.push(createProject(name4, "2012-0042", client3, 1368296808755, "inactive"));
    projects.push(createProject(name3, "2012-0050", client5, 1368296808756, "inactive"));
    projects.push(createProject(name1, "2012-0053", client4, 1368296808757, "inactive"));
    projects.push(createProject(name2, "2013-0012", client5, 1368296808758));
    projects.push(createProject(name2, "2013-0013", client7, 1368296808759));
    projects.push(createProject(name4, "2013-0016", client1, 1368296808760, "deleted"));
    projects.push(createProject(name4, "2013-0017", client6, 1368296808761));
    projects.push(createProject(name3, "2013-0018", client2, 1368296808762));
})();
```

In summary, the createProject method is a means to make it easier to create our temporary projects with a single line of code. All of the name and client variables are only to ensure consistency and make each line shorter and easier to read. The push method adds a new Project to the end of the List we created in our Storage class.

Manual Binding a Drop-Down List

Now that we have our data classes, and some actual data, defined, let's get some of it to show on the screen. We'll start by doing some manual data binding. By that I mean that we will explicitly set the value of a control instead of using binding functionality included in WinJS to set the values of our controls for us. While using WinJS binding functionality is often easier than setting the value of your control explicitly, especially if you have several controls, sometimes there is a legitimate need for doing it manually. One case in particular is binding the items in a drop-down list to your data.

While many controls you will use to build Windows Store applications with HTML and JavaScript support the WinJS binding functionality, one in particular that doesn't is the list of items in a drop-down list. In order to bind the choices in a drop-down list to our data, we'll do it in a more manual manner. First, let's see what we're working with. In Chapter 9 (Listing 9-13), we hard-coded the project drop-down list on the Clok dashboard in home.html with option elements to include the two projects shown in Figure 11-3.

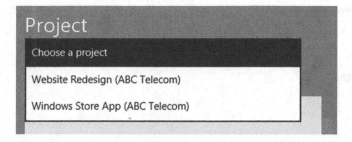

Figure 11-3. *Projects hard-coded in home.html*

For some drop-down lists, it is appropriate to have the data hard-coded. For example, if your drop-down list was a list of months, or states in the United States, or chapters in a specific book, or anything else that rarely changes, it would be perfectly valid to hard-code the drop-down list options, as we have done so far. Clearly, however, for a list of projects that your user is currently working on, hard-coding them is not a good choice.

Before we get to the task of binding data to the project drop-down list, I'd like to describe a technique that I've glossed over a few times, to help reduce some unnecessary code duplication. In general, I prefer descriptive namespace and class names, because they make the purpose of the code more clear, both to other developers and to me, in the future. That's why I used the names Clok.Data.Storage and Clok.Data.Project in earlier examples. However, I don't want to have to type the full name each time, so I've borrowed the practice of aliasing these namespaces or classes from the project templates included with Visual Studio. If you open default.js, you will see the code in Listing 11-5 near the top of the file.

Listing 11-5. Some Common Aliases in Our Project Template

```
var app = WinJS.Application;
var activation = Windows.ApplicationModel.Activation;
var nav = WinJS.Navigation;
```

While this step isn't necessary, it does make the rest of our code easier to read and write. Instead of typing WinJS.Navigation.navigate, we can now type nav.navigate when we are working in default.js. We can bring this concept into our home.js file as well, by adding the highlighted code in Listing 11-6 near the top of the file.

Listing 11-6. Adding Aliases in home.js

```
(function () {
    "use strict";

    var nav = WinJS.Navigation;
    var storage = Clok.Data.Storage;

    WinJS.UI.Pages.define("/pages/home/home.html", {

// SNIPPED
```

Now, let's take advantage of the new storage alias when we add some functionality, to show only projects that have their status set to active in this drop-down list. Add the bindListOfProjects function defined in Listing 11-7 to home.js.

Listing 11-7. New Function to Populate the Project Drop-Down List

```
bindListOfProjects: function () {
    project.options.length = 1;

    var activeProjects = storage.projects.filter(
        function (p) { return p.status === "active"; }
    );

    activeProjects.forEach(function (item) {
        var option = document.createElement("option");
        option.text = item.name + " (" + item.projectNumber + ")";
        option.title = item.clientName;
        option.value = item.id;
        project.appendChild(option);
    });
},
```

The first line removes all of the choices from `projects`, leaving only the "Choose a project" option. We use the `filter` method of the `WinJS.Binding.List` to get an array of projects that have an active status. For each active project, we create a new `option` and add it to the `project` drop-down list. Now, we just have to call this method. To do that, add the highlighted code from Listing 11-8 to the ready function in `home.js`.

Listing 11-8. Calling the New Function

```
ready: function (element, options) {
    this.initializeMenuPointerAnimations();

    toggleTimerMenuItem.onclick = this.toggleTimerMenuItem_click.bind(this);

    this.bindListOfProjects();
    project.onchange = this.project_change.bind(this);
    saveTimeButton.onclick = this.saveTimeButton_click.bind(this);
    discardTimeButton.onclick = this.discardTimeButton_click.bind(this);

    this.setupTimerRelatedControls();
},
```

Now, when you run Clok, you should see some of the projects we added in Listing 11-4 in the drop-down list (see Figure 11-4). Although we hard-coded our data into `storage.js` earlier in this chapter, this drop-down list is loaded dynamically. When we later change Clok to use persistent storage and remove the hard-coded projects, this functionality will still continue to work.

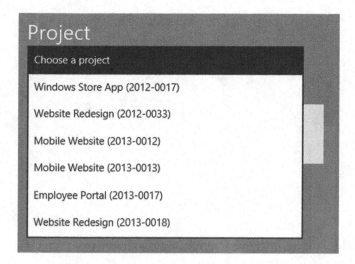

Figure 11-4. *Projects added from our data source*

Binding Grouped Data to a ListView

To make Clok a useful application, the user will require a way to view a list of all of his or her projects. This is the perfect opportunity to use data-binding functionality from WinJS. In fact, because we designed our `Project` class and `Storage` class to use `WinJS.Binding.List` to store our projects, adding a `ListView` to display them will be very similar to the `ListView` example in Chapter 7.

Creating and Connecting the Page Control

Start by adding a new folder named `projects` to the pages folder, then add a new page control named `list.html` to the `projects` folder. When you're done, your Solution Explorer should look similar to Figure 11-5.

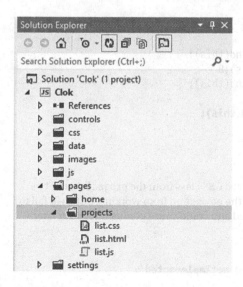

Figure 11-5. *Adding a page control for a list of projects*

Now, we have to modify the Clok dashboard, so that the Projects menu option (Figure 11-6) will navigate to our new page control.

Figure 11-6. *Projects menu option*

Open home.js and add the projectsMenuItem_click function in Listing 11-9 after the definition of the enableOrDisableButtons function.

Listing 11-9. Defining an Event Handler

```
projectsMenuItem_click: function (e) {
    nav.navigate("/pages/projects/list.html");
},
```

Next, modify the ready function, by adding the highlighted line of code from Listing 11-10.

Listing 11-10. Wiring the Event Handler to the Menu Projects Option

```
ready: function (element, options) {
    this.initializeMenuPointerAnimations();

    toggleTimerMenuItem.onclick = this.toggleTimerMenuItem_click.bind(this);

    this.bindListOfProjects();
    project.onchange = this.project_change.bind(this);
    editProjectButton.onclick = this.editProjectButton_click.bind(this);
    saveTimeButton.onclick = this.saveTimeButton_click.bind(this);B
    discardTimeButton.onclick = this.discardTimeButton_click.bind(this);

    projectsMenuItem.onclick = this.projectsMenuItem_click.bind(this);

    this.setupTimerRelatedControls();
},
```

The last thing to remember is that we should remove the notImplemented CSS class from the projectsMenuItem div in home.html (highlighted in Listing 11-11). Leaving this won't prevent the navigation from working, but if we fail to remove it, the mouseover animation we added in Chapter 10 will be retained and could cause confusion for our users.

Listing 11-11. The CSS Class That Should Be Removed

```
<div id="projectsMenuItem" class="mainMenuItem secondaryMenuItem notImplemented">
```

Adding the ListView and Binding the Data

At this point, we can navigate to the Projects page, but there isn't much to see. To make this page useful, we'll add a ListView, to display an item for each Clok.Data.Project object in our data. At the same time, we'll also group the projects by the first letter of their clientName property and add a SemanticZoom control, which will come in handy when the user has many projects. We have to revisit storage.js, to add support for grouping our project data. Open that file and add the highlighted code from Listing 11-12.

Listing 11-12. Adding Support for Grouping Projects

```
// SNIPPED

{
    // static members
    projects: new WinJS.Binding.List([]),

    compareProjectGroups: function (left, right) {
        return left.toUpperCase().charCodeAt(0) - right.toUpperCase().charCodeAt(0);
    },
    getProjectGroupKey: function (dataItem) {
        return dataItem.clientName.toUpperCase().charAt(0);
    },
    getProjectGroupData: function (dataItem) {
        return {
            name: dataItem.clientName.toUpperCase().charAt(0)
        }
    },
    groupedProjects: {
        get: function () {
            var grouped = storage.projects.createGrouped(
                    storage.getProjectGroupKey,
                    storage.getProjectGroupData,
                    storage.compareProjectGroups);

            return grouped;
        }
    },
}

// SNIPPED
```

This code should seem familiar, because we used very similar code in Chapter 7 to add grouping support to our animal data in that chapter. In fact, any time you want to be able to group data in a WinJS.Binding.List in a ListView, you will have to call the createGrouped method of the List. This function returns a live view of the data in your List, which means that, by adding or modifying the underlying data, the grouped view is also changed. More information about the createGrouped function is available on MSDN: http://msdn.microsoft.com/en-us/library/windows/apps/hh700742.aspx.

Also familiar is the HTML code needed to display the ListView with SemanticZoom. Replace the body element in list.html with the code from Listing 11-13.

Listing 11-13. Adding a ListView to Display Projects

```
<body>
    <div class="list fragment">
        <header aria-label="Header content" role="banner">
            <button class="win-backbutton" aria-label="Back" disabled type="button"></button>
            <h1 class="titlearea win-type-ellipsis">
                <span class="pagetitle">Projects</span>
            </h1>
        </header>
        <section aria-label="Main content" role="main">
            <div id="listViewHeaderTemplate"
                    data-win-control="WinJS.Binding.Template"
                    style="display: none">
                <div class="listViewHeader">
                    <h1 data-win-bind="innerText: name"></h1>
                </div>
            </div>

            <div id="listViewTemplate"
                    data-win-control="WinJS.Binding.Template"
                    style="display: none">
                <div class="listViewItem">
                    <h4 data-win-bind="innerText: name"></h4>
                    <h6>
                        <span data-win-bind="innerText: projectNumber"></span>
                        (<span data-win-bind="innerText: status"></span>)
                    </h6>
                    <h6 data-win-bind="innerText: clientName"></h6>
                </div>
            </div>

            <div id="semanticZoomTemplate"
                    data-win-control="WinJS.Binding.Template"
                    style="display: none">
                <div class="semanticZoomItem">
                    <h2 class="semanticZoomItemText" data-win-bind="innerText: name"></h2>
                </div>
            </div>

            <div id="semanticZoom" data-win-control="WinJS.UI.SemanticZoom">

                <!-- zoomed in -->
                <div id="listView"
                    class="win-selectionstylefilled"
                    data-win-control="WinJS.UI.ListView"
                    data-win-options="{
                        itemTemplate: select('#listViewTemplate'),
                        groupHeaderTemplate: select('#listViewHeaderTemplate'),
                        selectionMode: 'none',
                        tapBehavior: 'invoke',
                        swipeBehavior: 'none',
```

```
                        itemDataSource: Clok.Data.Storage.groupedProjects.dataSource,
                        groupDataSource: Clok.Data.Storage.groupedProjects.groups.dataSource
                    }">
                </div>

                <!-- zoomed out -->
                <div id="zoomedOutListView"
                    data-win-control="WinJS.UI.ListView"
                    data-win-options="{
                        itemTemplate: select('#semanticZoomTemplate'),
                        selectionMode: 'none',
                        tapBehavior: 'invoke',
                        swipeBehavior: 'none',
                        itemDataSource: Clok.Data.Storage.groupedProjects.groups.dataSource
                    }">
                </div>
            </div>
        </section>
    </div>
</body>
```

Finally, we have to style the ListView, by adding the code in Listing 11-14 to list.css.

Listing 11-14. CSS to Style the ListView

```css
.listViewHeader {
    width: 50px;
    height: 50px;
    padding: 8px;
}

.listViewItem {
    width: 250px;
    height: 75px;
    padding: 5px;
    overflow: hidden;
}

#listView {
    height: 400px;
    width: 100%;
}

#zoomedOutListView {
    height: 400px;
    width: 100%;
}

#semanticZoom {
    height: calc(100% - 30px);
    width: calc(100% - 120px);
}
```

```
.semanticZoomItem {
    color: #ffffff;
    background-color: #000046;
    width: 50px;
    height: 40px;
    padding: 5px 15px;
}
```

If you view this page in Clok now, you'll see a ListView similar to that in Figure 11-7. It's pretty good but not great. The biggest issue with it is that it will show projects that have been deleted, but we can fix that.

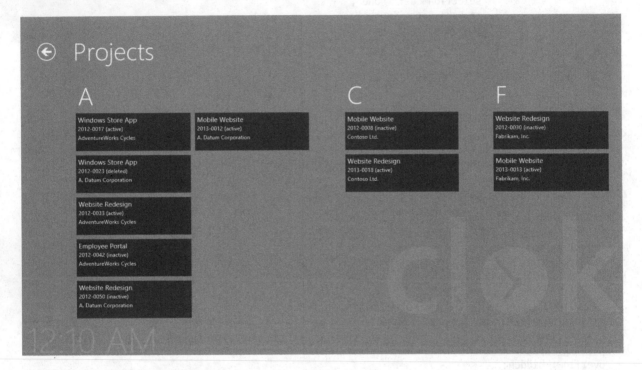

Figure 11-7. *ListView with all projects*

Binding Filtered Data to a ListView

In Clok, we can't actually delete projects, because, once we build the functionality, we could possibly have time entries associated with the project. Instead, we have given the project a deleted status and kept it from being displayed via logic in our code. Additionally, projects can be active or inactive, and once our user has several projects, a helpful feature would be to allow him or her to filter projects by status.

Displaying Filtered Data

The WinJS.Binding.List class has a createFiltered method, which returns a subset of the data in your List, which satisfies a filter condition you can define in JavaScript. Like the createGrouped method, createFiltered returns a live view of your List, which means that adding or modifying the underlying data, the filtered view is also changed.

More information about the createFiltered function is available on MSDN: http://msdn.microsoft.com/en-us/library/windows/apps/hh700741.aspx. Modify storage.js by adding the highlighted code from Listing 11-15, taking note to put it outside the class definition.

Listing 11-15. Adding a Group and Filter Method

```
var storage = WinJS.Class.define(
    // SNIPPED
);

storage.projects.getGroupedProjectsByStatus = function (statuses) {
    var filtered = this
        .createFiltered(function (p) {
            return statuses.indexOf(p.status) >= 0;
        });

    var grouped = filtered
        .createGrouped(
            storage.getProjectGroupKey,
            storage.getProjectGroupData,
            storage.compareProjectGroups);

    return grouped;
};

WinJS.Namespace.define("Clok.Data", {
    Storage: storage,
});
```

Thanks to the dynamic nature of JavaScript, we are able to define a new function named getGroupedProjectsByStatus and add it to our existing projects variable. This function accepts an array of project statuses that the user wants to see. Because getGroupedProjectsByStatus is added to projects, the this JavaScript keyword refers to the current List of projects. We use the createFiltered method to return a subset of the current projects matching our filtering function—those that have a status specified in the statuses parameter. Once we have a filtered list, we group them, using the same createGrouped method we used in the last section.

In order to bind our ListView to the results of this function, we have to change our existing code, so that the data sources are set in our JavaScript code. Modify the ready function in list.js with the code from Listing 11-16 to accomplish that.

Listing 11-16. Setting ListView Data Sources in JavaScript

```
ready: function (element, options) {
    this.filteredProjects =
        storage.projects.getGroupedProjectsByStatus(["active", "inactive"]);

    listView.winControl.itemDataSource = this.filteredProjects.dataSource;
    listView.winControl.groupDataSource = this.filteredProjects.groups.dataSource;
    zoomedOutListView.winControl.itemDataSource = this.filteredProjects.groups.dataSource;
},
```

> ■ **Note** Remember to define the storage alias in list.js like you did in home.js in Listing 11-6.

Because we're setting the ListView data sources in our code, we can remove them from our HTML markup. Remove the highlighted code in Listing 11-17 from list.html.

Listing 11-17. Remove the Data Sources from list.html

```
<!-- zoomed in -->
<div id="listView"
    class="win-selectionstylefilled"
    data-win-control="WinJS.UI.ListView"
    data-win-options="{
        itemTemplate: select('#listViewTemplate'),
        groupHeaderTemplate: select('#listViewHeaderTemplate'),
        selectionMode: 'none',
        tapBehavior: 'invoke',
        swipeBehavior: 'none',
        itemDataSource: Clok.Data.Storage.groupedProjects.dataSource,
        groupDataSource: Clok.Data.Storage.groupedProjects.groups.dataSource
}">
</div>

<!-- zoomed out -->
<div id="zoomedOutListView"
    data-win-control="WinJS.UI.ListView"
    data-win-options="{
        itemTemplate: select('#semanticZoomTemplate'),
        selectionMode: 'none',
        tapBehavior: 'invoke',
        swipeBehavior: 'none',
        itemDataSource: Clok.Data.Storage.groupedProjects.groups.dataSource
    }">
</div>
```

> ■ **Note** Don't forget also to remove the trailing comma from the last item in the data-win-options attribute—in this example, the comma after the swipeBehavior option.

Binding Other Control Properties

At this point, your Projects page should only show active and inactive projects, and you shouldn't see any deleted projects, but we can improve the user experience by styling each of these differently. WinJS data binding is pretty powerful and can help us accomplish this pretty easily. In addition to binding data that is displayed on the screen, you can also bind other properties of your controls to your data source. For example, we can bind the className property of our ListView template to the status property of our Project class. Assuming you had created CSS rules for .active and .inactive to change the background color of the item, you could modify list.html by adding the highlighted code in Listing 11-18.

Listing 11-18. Binding the CSS Class via the className Property

```
<div class="listViewItem" data-win-bind="className: status">
```

However, when we run Clok now, we don't quite see what we expected. As you can see in Figure 11-8, we lost the styling we had previously defined in Listing 11-14, which set CSS properties such as width and height. That's because by binding the className property, we have replaced the listViewItem class with either the active or inactive class.

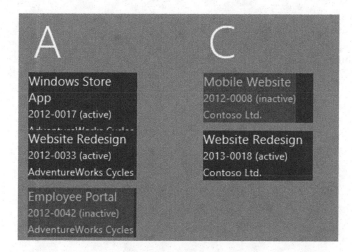

Figure 11-8. *This isn't what we had in mind*

At this point, we have a couple of options. The most straightforward option would be to add the additional CSS definitions to both our active and inactive CSS classes. That wouldn't be so bad in this case, because that's only two classes, but my preference would be not to have to duplicate those settings. Besides, if we did that, then I wouldnt be able to illustrate this next option.

In order to achieve the formatting we intended, we have to make sure that the original CSS settings in the listViewItem class are not overwritten when we bind a value to the className property. The method I'm going to illustrate here takes advantage of data- attributes supported in HTML5. We've been using these attributes since Chapter 5, when we started adding data-win-control to HTML elements to have WinJS treat them as controls rather than as div elements. Additionally, we've also used data-win-options to initialize our controls with default settings and data-win-bind to configure binding. What you may or may not know is that you can create your own data- attributes in HTML5, and we're going to take advantage of that to fix our ListView styling issue. Modify list.html once again with the highlighted code in Listing 11-19.

Listing 11-19. Binding the CSS Class via the className Property

```
<div data-class="listViewItem" data-win-bind="className: status">
```

The only difference from Listing 11-18 is changing the class attribute to our custom data-class attribute. Now, we only have to modify our CSS accordingly, which is a two-part process. First, remove the code in Listing 11-20 from list.css.

Listing 11-20. Remove This from list.css.

```
.listViewItem {
    width: 250px;
    height: 75px;
    padding: 5px;
    overflow: hidden;
}
```

In place of the removed code, add the code from Listing 11-21 to list.css.

Listing 11-21. New CSS Rules for Our data-class Attribute

```
[data-class=listViewItem] {
    width: 250px;
    height: 75px;
    padding: 5px;
    overflow: hidden;
}

    [data-class=listViewItem].active {
        background-color: #000046;
    }

    [data-class=listViewItem].inactive {
        background-color: #464646;
        color: #cccccc;
    }
```

■ **Note**   You can use the [attributeName=attributeValue] CSS selector syntax to style elements based on attributes.

You'll see that the new rule for [data-class=listViewItem] is identical to the .listViewItem rule we removed. Setting this custom attribute and targeting it instead from our CSS means that the className property no longer has a value defined. In this case, this gives us the benefit of not having to worry about removing CSS rules that we wish to retain. Then our new rules add appropriate styling, based on whether the className property is set to active or inactive in the data-binding process. See the results in Figure 11-9.

Figure 11-9. Projects filtered and styled, based on status

Using WinJS.Binding.as

Our Projects page now correctly hides deleted projects and displays only active and inactive projects. It also styles them differently, based on their status. As the user's list of projects grows, however, this page could become unnecessarily long. To remedy this, let's add some functionality that will allow the user to specify if he or she wants to see only active projects, only inactive projects, or both active and inactive projects. First, we need some buttons that users can click to indicate how they want to filter their projects. Add the highlighted code from Listing 11-22 to list.html.

Listing 11-22. Adding Buttons to Filter the List of Projects

```
<div id="semanticZoomTemplate" data-win-control="WinJS.Binding.Template" style="display: none">
    <div class="semanticZoomItem">
        <h2 class="semanticZoomItemText" data-win-bind="innerText: name"></h2>
    </div>
</div>

<div id="filters">
    <button id="allProjectsButton" class="selected">All projects</button>
    <button id="activeProjectsButton">Only active projects</button>
    <button id="inactiveProjectsButton">Only inactive projects</button>
</div>

<div id="semanticZoom" data-win-control="WinJS.UI.SemanticZoom">
<!-- SNIPPED -->
</div>
```

We could leave these filter buttons with their default style, but a better user experience (in my opinion, at least) would be to remove the border from the button and boldface the text of the currently selected filter button. So, add the code from Listing 11-23 to list.css.

Listing 11-23. CSS to Style the Filter Buttons

```
#filters {
    height: 30px;
}


    #filters button {
        border: 0px;
        font-weight: normal;
    }


        #filters button.selected {
            font-weight: bold;
        }
```

Now that we have the UI in place, we have some work, and rework, to do in our JavaScript, to wire all the pieces together. Replace the entire page definition in list.js with the code from Listing 11-24.

Listing 11-24. Our New Page Definition

```
WinJS.UI.Pages.define("/pages/projects/list.html", {
    ready: function (element, options) {
        allProjectsButton.onclick = this.allStatusFilter_click.bind(this);
        activeProjectsButton.onclick = this.activeStatusFilter_click.bind(this);
        inactiveProjectsButton.onclick = this.inactiveStatusFilter_click.bind(this);

        this.filter = WinJS.Binding.as({ value: ["active", "inactive"] });
        this.filter.bind("value", this.filter_value_changed.bind(this));
    },

    allStatusFilter_click: function (e) {
        this.filter.value = ["active", "inactive"];
        this.setSelectedButton(allProjectsButton);
    },

    activeStatusFilter_click: function (e) {
        this.filter.value = ["active"];
        this.setSelectedButton(activeProjectsButton);
    },

    inactiveStatusFilter_click: function (e) {
        this.filter.value = ["inactive"];
        this.setSelectedButton(inactiveProjectsButton);
    },

    setSelectedButton: function (btnToSelect) {
        WinJS.Utilities.query("#filters button").removeClass("selected");
        WinJS.Utilities.addClass(btnToSelect, "selected");
    },
```

```
filter_value_changed: function (e) {
    this.filteredProjects = storage.projects.getGroupedProjectsByStatus(this.filter.value);

    listView.winControl.itemDataSource = this.filteredProjects.dataSource;
    listView.winControl.groupDataSource = this.filteredProjects.groups.dataSource;
    zoomedOutListView.winControl.itemDataSource = this.filteredProjects.groups.dataSource;
},

});
```

The first thing to notice is that we've added functions to handle the click event from each of our new filter buttons. They're pretty self-explanatory: they set the value of some variable named filter, which I'll discuss in a moment, and then they set the clicked button as the currently selected one, using a few methods in the WinJS. Utilities namespace. You'll also see a new function, named filter_value_changed, which looks pretty similar to the code we added in Listing 11-16, aside from the fact that it also refers to the filter variable. The interesting part here is the definition of filter. I've copied this interesting part in Listing 11-25.

Listing 11-25. The Most Interesting Part of Listing 11-24

```
this.filter = WinJS.Binding.as({ value: ["active", "inactive"] });
this.filter.bind("value", this.filter_value_changed.bind(this));
```

We've defined filter as a new variable with which to take an object with a value property containing a status array and wrap it with a call to WinJS.Binding.as. The as method takes whatever parameter it receives and returns an observable version of that parameter. What does that mean? In short, when something is observable, then anything that is observing it, such as controls that are bound to it, is notified when the observable object changes. In our example, we bind the value property of our filter to filter_value_changed, and whenever value changes, the filter_value_changed function is called.

So, when our button-click handlers change the filter.value, filter_value_changed is called and rebinds the ListView data sources to a filtered list of projects. More information about the as method is available on MSDN: http://msdn.microsoft.com/en-us/library/windows/apps/br229801.aspx.

■ **Note** The second line of Listing 11-25 contains calls to two different bind methods. The first, this.filter.bind, configures an observer for the value property as the address of the filter_value_changed function. The second, this.filter_value_changed.bind, identifies what the this JavaScript keyword will refer to within that method, in this case, the page definition itself, which is the value of this in the ready function.

Now, when you run Clok and navigate to the Projects page, you will initially see a screen like Figure 11-10, showing all active and inactive projects. This is the same as that we saw in Figure 11-9, with the addition of our new filter buttons.

Figure 11-10. Projects page, with new filter buttons

Now, click on the second filter button to see only the active projects. The page will update to match Figure 11-11, with the second button selected and the inactive projects removed from the ListView.

Figure 11-11. Only the active projects are displayed

Setting a Data Context

Now that we have a nicely working project list, the next logical step would be to add a page for project details. This page will allow the user to view and edit an existing project, as well as create a new project. An HTML form, however, doesn't have a property for data source. So, we'll take a look at how we can effectively set the data source for a form, or any arbitrary HTML element for that matter, by setting a data context. First, however, we have some quick setup work to complete.

Adding a Project Detail Page

Add a new page-control item named `detail.html` to the same `projects` folder that we created earlier in this chapter. When you're done, your Solution Explorer should look similar to Figure 11-12.

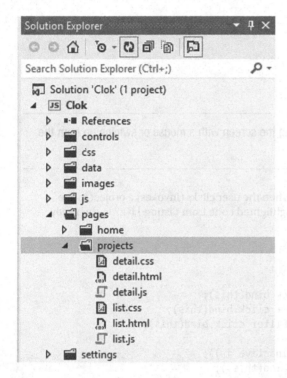

Figure 11-12. Two page controls in the projects folder

There will be two ways for a user to reach the project detail page: by editing an existing project and by adding a new project. We have to add the navigation for both of these options to the project list page. To keep in line with Windows Store application guidelines, we'll add an `AppBar` with an `AppBarCommand` button to add a new project to the project list page. Add the highlighted code in Listing 11-26 immediately after the body element in `list.html`.

Listing 11-26. Adding an AppBar to the Project List Page

```
<body>
    <div id="projectListAppBar"
         class="win-ui-dark"
         data-win-control="WinJS.UI.AppBar">

        <button
            data-win-control="WinJS.UI.AppBarCommand"
            data-win-options="{
                id:'addProjectCommand',
                label:'Add',
                icon:'add',
                section:'global',
                tooltip:'Add'}">
        </button>
    </div>

<!-- SNIPPED -->
</body>
```

■ **Note**   Remember that the app bar can be opened by right-clicking the screen with a mouse or swiping up from the bottom edge of a touch screen.

Adding a click-event handler for this button, and another for when the user clicks (invokes) a project in the ListView, should be getting pretty familiar at this point. Add the highlighted code from Listing 11-27 to the ready function in list.js.

Listing 11-27. Wiring Up Event Handlers

```
ready: function (element, options) {
    allProjectsButton.onclick = this.allStatusFilter_click.bind(this);
    activeProjectsButton.onclick = this.activeStatusFilter_click.bind(this);
    inactiveProjectsButton.onclick = this.inactiveStatusFilter_click.bind(this);

    this.filter = WinJS.Binding.as({ value: ["active", "inactive"] });
    this.filter.bind("value", this.filter_value_changed.bind(this));

    addProjectCommand.onclick = this.addProjectCommand_click.bind(this);
    listView.winControl.oniteminvoked = this.listView_itemInvoked.bind(this);
},
```

■ **Note**   The ListView raises the itemInvoked event when the user clicks an item in the ListView. This event is very similar to a click event but also includes information about which item was clicked.

Defining those event handlers is also pretty straightforward. Add the code from Listing 11-28 after the ready function in list.js.

Listing 11-28. Defining the Event Handlers That Navigate to the Project Detail Page

```
addProjectCommand_click: function (e) {
    WinJS.Navigation.navigate("/pages/projects/detail.html");
},

listView_itemInvoked: function (e) {
    var item = this.filteredProjects.getAt(e.detail.itemIndex);
    WinJS.Navigation.navigate("/pages/projects/detail.html", { id: item.id });
},
```

When `addProjectCommand` is clicked, Clok performs a simple navigation to the project detail page. When an item in the `ListView` is invoked, we use the `itemIndex` property to determine which project was selected and then navigate to the project detail page with an initial state that includes the `id` of the selected `Project` object.

Adding a Form to the Project Detail Page

Now that we can navigate to the project detail page, it's time to add a form to that page. We'll use this form to view, edit, and add projects to Clok. Replace the body element in `detail.html` with the code from Listing 11-29.

Listing 11-29. Project Detail Form

```
<body>
    <div id="projectDetailAppBar"
            class="win-ui-dark"
            data-win-control="WinJS.UI.AppBar"
            data-win-options="{ sticky: true }">

        <button
            data-win-control="WinJS.UI.AppBarCommand"
            data-win-options="{
                id:'saveProjectCommand',
                label:'Save',
                icon:'save',
                section:'selection',
                tooltip:'Save'}">
        </button>
        <hr
            data-win-control="WinJS.UI.AppBarCommand"
            data-win-options="{type:'separator',section:'selection'}" />
        <button
            data-win-control="WinJS.UI.AppBarCommand"
            data-win-options="{
                id:'deleteProjectCommand',
                label:'Delete',
                icon:'delete',
                section:'selection',
                tooltip:'Delete',
                disabled: true}">
        </button>
    </div>
```

```
<div class="detail fragment">
    <header aria-label="Header content" role="banner">
        <button class="win-backbutton" aria-label="Back" disabled type="button"></button>
        <h1 class="titlearea win-type-ellipsis">
            <span class="pagetitle">Project Detail</span>
        </h1>
    </header>
    <section aria-label="Main content" role="main">
        <form id="projectDetailForm" onsubmit="return false;">
            <div class="formField" style="-ms-grid-row: 1; -ms-grid-column: 1;">
                <label for="projectName">Project Name</label><br />
                <input type="text" id="projectName"
                    maxlength="75"
                    required
                    autofocus
                    data-win-bind="value: name">
            </div>
            <div class="formField" style="-ms-grid-row: 1; -ms-grid-column: 3;">
                <label for="projectNumber">Project Number</label><br />
                <input type="text" id="projectNumber"
                    maxlength="25"
                    required
                    data-win-bind="value: projectNumber">
            </div>
            <div class="formField" style="-ms-grid-row: 1; -ms-grid-column: 5;">
                <label for="projectStatus">Status</label><br />
                <div id="projectStatus"
                    data-win-control="WinJS.UI.ToggleSwitch"
                    data-win-options="{
                        labelOn: 'Active',
                        labelOff: 'Inactive'
                    }"></div>
            </div>

            <div class="formField"
                    style="-ms-grid-row: 2; -ms-grid-column: 1; -ms-grid-column-span: 3;">
                <label for="projectDescription">Description</label><br />
                <textarea id="projectDescription"
                    data-win-bind="value: description"></textarea>
            </div>

            <div class="formField" style="-ms-grid-row: 3; -ms-grid-column: 1;">
                <label for="startDate">Start Date</label><br />
                <div id="startDate"
                    data-win-control="WinJS.UI.DatePicker"
                    data-win-bind="winControl.current: startDate"></div>
            </div>
```

```
<div class="formField" style="-ms-grid-row: 3; -ms-grid-column: 3;">
    <label for="dueDate">Due Date</label><br />
    <div id="dueDate"
        data-win-control="WinJS.UI.DatePicker"
        data-win-bind="winControl.current: dueDate"></div>
</div>
<div class="formField" style="-ms-grid-row: 4; -ms-grid-column: 1;">
    <label for="clientName">Client Name</label><br />
    <input type="text" id="clientName"
        maxlength="50"
        required
        data-win-bind="value: clientName">
</div>
<div class="formField" style="-ms-grid-row: 4; -ms-grid-column: 3;">
    <label for="contactName">Contact Name</label><br />
    <input type="text" id="contactName"
        maxlength="50"
        data-win-bind="value: contactName">
</div>
<div class="formField"
        style="-ms-grid-row: 5; -ms-grid-column: 1; -ms-grid-column-span: 3;">
    <label for="address1">Address</label><br />
    <input type="text" id="address1"
        maxlength="60"
        placeholder="Line 1 (e.g., 1234 Maple St.)"
        data-win-bind="value: address1"><br />
    <input type="text" id="address2"
        maxlength="60"
        placeholder="Line 2 (e.g., Suite A)"
        data-win-bind="value: address2"><br />
    <input type="text" id="city"
        maxlength="35"
        placeholder="City"
        data-win-bind="value: city">
    <input type="text" id="region"
        maxlength="25"
        placeholder="State/Region"
        data-win-bind="value: region">
    <input type="text" id="postalCode"
        maxlength="12"
        placeholder="Postal Code"
        data-win-bind="value: postalCode">
</div>
<div class="formField" style="-ms-grid-row: 6; -ms-grid-column: 1;">
    <label for="contactEmail">Email</label><br />
    <input type="email" id="contactEmail"
        maxlength="75"
        data-win-bind="value: email">
</div>
<div class="formField" style="-ms-grid-row: 6; -ms-grid-column: 3;">
    <label for="phone">Phone</label><br />
```

```
                        <input type="tel" id="phone"
                            maxlength="25"
                            data-win-bind="value: phone">
                </div>
            </form>
        </section>
    </div>
</body>
```

■ **Note** The use of the `placeholder` attribute in the various address fields provides a nice watermark effect to those fields. The placeholder text is shown in empty fields and disappears when the user clicks the field. This is an easy, compact way to provide simple instructions, or example input, to your user.

That was a lot of code, but as you look at it, a lot of it is self-explanatory. We create an AppBar with two AppBarCommand controls, and then we create a form with a number of fields. We've added some CSS classes, so that we can style the form fields in CSS, which we will do shortly. That's all fine, but it's not really anything new. There are two topics that I want to specifically address in this section, both illustrated in Listing 11-30.

Listing 11-30. The Project Name Field Is Required

```
<input type="text" id="projectName"
    maxlength="75"
    required
    autofocus
    data-win-bind="value: name">
```

With the exception of the Status field, which I'll address in an upcoming section, each of the fields on the page has a binding defined in its `data-win-bind` attribute. The syntax is exactly the same as that we saw in Listing 11-13. Additionally, we've marked three of the fields with the `required` attribute—Project Name, Project Number and Client Name—and we'll take advantage of this attribute when validating the data that the user enters.

I'll come back to both of these attributes in a moment. Before I get to that, however, let's make this form look nice with some CSS. Add the code from Listing 11-31 to `detail.css`.

Listing 11-31. Styling the Project Detail Form

```
#projectDetailForm {
    display: -ms-grid;
    -ms-grid-columns: 2fr 20px 1fr 20px 1fr;
    max-width: 900px;
}

    #projectDetailForm .formField {
        padding-bottom: 10px;
    }

        #projectDetailForm .formField input:invalid,
        #projectDetailForm .formField textarea:invalid,
```

```
        #projectDetailForm .formField select:invalid {
            border: 5px solid red;
            background-color: #EE9090;
        }

#projectName, #clientName, #contactName, #contactEmail {
    width: 430px;
}

#projectDescription {
    height: 60px;
    width: calc(90vw - 120px);
}

#projectNumber, #phone {
    width: 200px;
}

#address1, #address2 {
    width: 600px;
}

#city {
    width: 265px;
}

#region {
    width: 175px;
}

#postalCode {
    width: 140px;
}
```

Again, that's several lines of code, but it's pretty simple. We use Grid Layout to create five columns in our form, and we're using three of them for the form contents and the other two to add spacing between the columns. The bulk of the remaining CSS is used to set dimensions on the different fields, identifying each field by its id attribute.

Using CSS to Style Required and Invalid Fields

One thing that you might not be familiar with in Listing 11-31 is the use of the :invalid CSS pseudo-class. The CSS rule we created using :invalid will highlight any invalid fields with a thick red border. Because we marked three fields, as required, HTML5 automatically validates those fields for us and adds the :invalid pseudo-class when those fields are empty. Additionally, because we set its type attribute to email, HTML5 automatically validates that our Email field contains any text that it is a valid e-mail address. See Figure 11-13 for an example of this.

Figure 11-13. *Because Project Name and Project Number are required, they are invalid*

This works great as an indicator to our users that something they entered, or didn't enter, is not allowed. Unfortunately for the user experience, when adding a new project, as soon as the project detail page loads, the fields already appear to be in error. While it is technically true that a project must have a name, it's an abrupt experience to the user. So, we'll make a small modification that will serve two purposes: indicating which fields are required, and not indicating that they are invalid until the user interacts with the form. Take a look at a snippet from a modified detail.html file in Listing 11-32.

Listing 11-32. Modified Project Name Field

```
<div class="formField required" style="-ms-grid-row: 1; -ms-grid-column: 1; ">
    <label for="projectName">Project Name</label><br />
    <input type="text" id="projectName"
        maxlength="75"
        autofocus
        data-win-bind="value: name">
</div>
```

See the difference? We removed the required attribute from the input control, and we added an additional CSS class named required to the div element that contains the control. Make the same change to the Project Number and Client Name fields as well. Then modify detail.css by adding the highlighted code from Listing 11-33.

Listing 11-33. A New CSS Rule for Required Fields

```
#projectDetailForm .formField {
    padding-bottom: 10px;
}

#projectDetailForm .formField.required input,
#projectDetailForm .formField.required textarea,
#projectDetailForm .formField.required select {
    border: solid green;
    background-color: lightgreen;
}

#projectDetailForm .formField input:invalid,
#projectDetailForm .formField textarea:invalid,
#projectDetailForm .formField select:invalid {
    border: 5px solid red;
    background-color: #EE9090;
}
```

Now, when we run Clok and add a new project, the required fields are highlighted with a thinner green border and a green background (see Figure 11-14).

Figure 11-14. *These fields are required but not yet considered invalid*

The required CSS class is not special, however. You might notice as you use this form that, no matter what you do at this point, the fields never appear invalid, as they did in Figure 11-13. That's because applying a CSS class named required doesn't actually make fields required. What should happen is that the required fields are green when they are valid and red when invalid. Replace the page definition in detail.js with the code in Listing 11-34.

Listing 11-34. Configuring the AppBarCommand Controls

```
ready: function (element, options) {
    this.configureAppBar(options && options.id);
    saveProjectCommand.onclick = this.saveProjectCommand_click.bind(this);
},

saveProjectCommand_click: function (e) {
    WinJS.Utilities
        .query(".required input, .required textarea, .required select")
        .setAttribute("required", "required");
},

configureAppBar: function (existingId) {
    var fields = WinJS.Utilities.query("#projectDetailForm input, "
        + "#projectDetailForm textarea, "
        + "#projectDetailForm select");

    fields.listen("focus", function (e) {
        projectDetailAppBar.winControl.show();
    }, false);

    if (existingId) {
        deleteProjectCommand.winControl.disabled = false;
    }
},
```

The approach taken here is to add the required attribute to our required fields only after the user first attempts to save the form. Until then, we won't bother them by emphasizing that any empty required fields are invalid. We do this by querying for fields that have the required CSS class and adding the required attribute to them when the user clicks the Save button. Additionally, for good measure, we've added some code to show the AppBar when the user has given focus to a field, and we enable the Delete button only if we are editing an existing project.

Now, when we run Clok and add a new project, the style of the required fields is as expected. When the fields are valid, or before the user attempts to save the form for the first time, the fields are green. After the first attempt to save the form, any invalid fields are highlighted in red and given a thicker border (see Figure 11-15).

Figure 11-15. One valid field and one invalid field

Setting the Data Context for the Form

Back in Listing 11-28, we indicated that if we wanted to add a new project, we would simply navigate to detail.html. However, if we wanted to edit an existing project, we would initialize the page with an object containing the id of the Project object we wanted to edit. At the moment, we don't have an easy way to retrieve a Project object for a specific id, so let's fix that. Add the highlighted code in Listing 11-35 to storage.js.

Listing 11-35. New Method to Get a Project by id

```
storage.projects.getGroupedProjectsByStatus = function (statuses) {
    // SNIPPED
};


storage.projects.getById = function (id) {
    if (id) {
        var matches = this.filter(function (p) { return p.id === id; });
        if (matches && matches.length === 1) {
            return matches[0];
        }
    }
    return undefined;
};

WinJS.Namespace.define("Clok.Data", {
    Storage: storage,
});
```

Back in Listing 11-29, when we defined our form in detail.html, we specified a data-win-bind attribute for all of our fields. With our new getById function defined, we can now make a few small changes to detail.js, to complete the data binding for existing projects. First, as we did in Listing 11-6, let's add an alias for Clok.Data.Storage to detail.js (see Listing 11-36).

Listing 11-36. Adding Aliases to Simplify Our Code

```
var storage = Clok.Data.Storage;

WinJS.UI.Pages.define("/pages/projects/detail.html", {
    // SNIPPED
});
```

Next, add the highlighted code from Listing 11-37 to the ready function in detail.js.

Listing 11-37. Setting the Data-Binding Context with processAll

```
ready: function (element, options) {
    this.currProject = storage.projects.getById(options && options.id)
        || new Clok.Data.Project();

    this.configureAppBar(options && options.id);

    saveProjectCommand.onclick = this.saveProjectCommand_click.bind(this);
```

```
    var form = document.getElementById("projectDetailForm");
    WinJS.Binding.processAll(form, this.currProject);
},
```

While the templates used with a ListView inherit a data context, as a result of being contained within the data-bound ListView, our form is not bound to any data. The code we added creates a property named currProject. If the requested Project exists, currProject is set to that object. Otherwise, it is set to a new, empty Project object. The magic, however, occurs in the call to WinJS.Binding.processAll. This method configures our currProject property as the data context for our form. So, any controls within projectDetailForm that have data-win-bind attribute set are bound to currProject.

As a result, for example, because the data-win-bind attribute of the Project Name field is set to "value: name", the value property on that input field will be mapped to the name property of currProject. Now, when we run Clok and click an existing project, the form is populated (see Figure 11-16). Any properties of the project that we set in our temporary data earlier in this chapter are populated on the form.

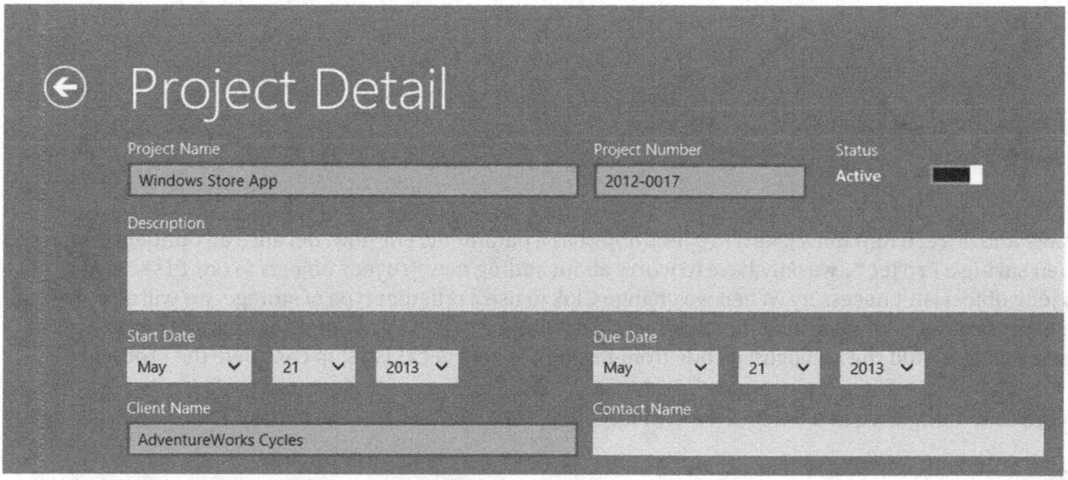

Figure 11-16. Editing an existing project

Saving and Deleting Projects

Before we address the fact that the Status field is not bound to anything, let's wrap up this section by allowing the user to save and delete projects. The first step is to define two new functions in storage.js, by adding the highlighted code from Listing 11-38.

Listing 11-38. Functions to Save and Delete a Project

```
storage.projects.getById = function (id) {
    if (id) {
        var matches = this.filter(function (p) { return p.id === id; });
        if (matches && matches.length === 1) {
            return matches[0];
        }
    }
    return undefined;
};
```

```javascript
storage.projects.save = function (p) {
    if (p && p.id) {
        var existing = storage.projects.getById(p.id);
        if (!existing) {
            storage.projects.push(p);
        }
    }
};

storage.projects.delete = function (p) {
    if (p && p.id) {
        var existing = storage.projects.getById(p.id);
        if (existing) {
            existing.status = "deleted";
            storage.projects.save(existing);
        }
    }
};

WinJS.Namespace.define("Clok.Data", {
    Storage: storage,
});
```

Both the save and delete functions take a Project object as a parameter. For now, because all our data is stored in memory, when saving a Project, we only have to worry about adding new Project objects to our List. Saving an existing Project object isn't necessary. When we change Clok to use a different type of storage, we will also implement the necessary code for persisting those changes. Deleting a Project is as simple as changing its status to deleted and then saving it. Add the highlighted code from Listing 11-39 to detail.js, to complete the process.

Listing 11-39. Implementing Save and Delete Functionality

```javascript
ready: function (element, options) {
    this.currProject = storage.projects.getById(options && options.id)
        || new Clok.Data.Project();

    this.configureAppBar(options && options.id);

    saveProjectCommand.onclick = this.saveProjectCommand_click.bind(this);
    deleteProjectCommand.onclick = this.deleteProjectCommand_click.bind(this);

    var form = document.getElementById("projectDetailForm");
    WinJS.Binding.processAll(form, this.currProject);
},

saveProjectCommand_click: function (e) {
    WinJS.Utilities
        .query(".required input, .required textarea, .required select")
        .setAttribute("required", "required");
```

```
    if (projectDetailForm.checkValidity()) {
        this.populateProjectFromForm();
        storage.projects.save(this.currProject);
        WinJS.Navigation.back();
    }
},

deleteProjectCommand_click: function (e) {
    storage.projects.delete(this.currProject);
    WinJS.Navigation.back();
},

populateProjectFromForm: function () {
    this.currProject.name = document.getElementById("projectName").value;
    this.currProject.projectNumber = document.getElementById("projectNumber").value;
    this.currProject.status = (projectStatus.winControl.checked) ? "active" : "inactive";
    this.currProject.description = document.getElementById("projectDescription").value;
    this.currProject.startDate = startDate.winControl.current;
    this.currProject.dueDate = dueDate.winControl.current;
    this.currProject.clientName = document.getElementById("clientName").value;
    this.currProject.contactName = document.getElementById("contactName").value;
    this.currProject.address1 = document.getElementById("address1").value;
    this.currProject.address2 = document.getElementById("address2").value;
    this.currProject.city = document.getElementById("city").value;
    this.currProject.region = document.getElementById("region").value;
    this.currProject.postalCode = document.getElementById("postalCode").value;
    this.currProject.email = document.getElementById("contactEmail").value;
    this.currProject.phone = document.getElementById("phone").value;
},
```

Because WinJS binding is not two-way—that is, changes to our data-bound form fields are not automatically reflected in the underlying data context—we use the populateProjectFromForm function to set the values our currProject based on what the user has provided in each of the form fields. The click-event handlers for both saving and deleting a Project object call the appropriate method that we just defined in Listing 11-38 and then return the user to the page that he or she was previously viewing. The most notable item here is the call to projectDetailForm. checkValidity. This method checks the status of each field in projectDetailForm, to make sure that they are all valid. In this case, it checks to make sure that required fields have a value and e-mail addresses are in the correct format. Then, it only saves the Project object if every field is valid.

Run Clok and make changes to some projects and delete some other projects. Aside from the Status field, which we'll address next, everything should be working as expected. Compare Figure 11-17 to Figure 11-10, and you'll see that I have changed the name of one project and deleted another.

Figure 11-17. *A project has been edited, and another has been deleted*

Because we have encapsulated all data access into `Clok.Data.Storage`, when we start persisting our data, instead of keeping it in memory, we should only have to make changes to `storage.js`, and the rest of our application should more or less stay the same.

Binding Converters

You've surely noticed that the Status field isn't bound to anything yet. We are already saving any value that users select for this field when they click the Save button, but we aren't showing the correct value when they choose to edit an existing project. The reason we left this to the end is to illustrate binding converters. There are three possible values for status (`active`, `inactive`, and `deleted`), but the `ToggleSwitch` control we are using to display this field only has two possible states. Binding converters allow us to bind to some data but apply some logic to it before the binding occurs. In a nutshell, they *convert* the value we are binding to a format that the bound control requires. In this case, we will convert a `status` to a Boolean, where an active status is `true` and anything else is `false`.

Defining a binding converter is not much different than defining a function. In fact, it can be done by simply wrapping a function definition in a call to `WinJS.Binding.converter` in `project.js` (see Listing 11-40).

Listing 11-40. Our Binding Converter and a New Enumeration

```
var statuses = Object.freeze({
    Active: "active",
    Inactive: "inactive",
    Deleted: "deleted",
});

var projectStatusToBoolConverter = WinJS.Binding.converter(function (status) {
    return (status === Clok.Data.ProjectStatuses.Active);
});
```

```
WinJS.Namespace.define("Clok.Data", {
    Project: projectClass,
    ProjectStatuses: statuses,
    ProjectStatusToBoolConverter: projectStatusToBoolConverter,
});
```

In this code, we've also created a `ProjectStatuses` enumeration, to define the possible statuses a `Project` object can have. Then, we add both this new enumeration and the converter to the `Clok.Data` namespace.

■ **Note** In the sample project that accompanies this book, I have changed all of the hard-coded status strings throughout the project to use the `ProjectStatuses` enumeration instead. Because the enumeration values are the same as the hard-coded strings, this change is not required. However, I prefer it for consistency, as well as for safeguarding against odd behavior caused by typos.

Now, we can bind the `projectStatus` `ToggleSwitch` to the `status` property of the current data context. Add the highlighted code from Listing 11-41 to `detail.html`.

Listing 11-41. Binding with a Converter

```
<div id="projectStatus"
    data-win-control="WinJS.UI.ToggleSwitch"
    data-win-options="{ labelOn: 'Active', labelOff: 'Inactive' }"
    data-win-bind="winControl.checked: status Clok.Data.ProjectStatusToBoolConverter"></div>
```

By specifying a binding converter after the data-binding property, WinJS will call `Clok.Data.ProjectStatusToBoolConverter` with `status` as a parameter and will bind the result of that to the `checked` property of the `ToggleSwitch` control.

Now, when you run Clok and select different projects from the list of projects, the Status `ToggleSwitch` will be correctly populated. Because we already implemented functionality to save changes to projects, you can switch a project from active to inactive, or vice versa, and see the change reflected in the list of projects.

A Simple MapReduce Example

I've covered a lot in this chapter, but there is one more feature I'd like to add to the Project Detail screen before wrapping up. Because we have a simplified concept of a project, compared to other project-management systems, we can enter any value we wish in the Client Name field when adding or editing a project. While this is important to allow us to define new clients, it would be nice to provide hints to the user when typing in the Client Name field. We want to make it as easy as possible to prevent misspelled, or differently spelled, client names.

HTML5 has a `datalist` control. It is similar to a drop-down list created with a `select` element, in that you add `option` elements to it, except that it doesn't display anything on its own. It is used to define a list of values and to then attach that list to another element. Add the highlighted code from Listing 11-42 to `detail.html`.

Listing 11-42. Adding a Datalist to Provide Hints in the Client Name Field

```
<input type="text" id="clientName"
    maxlength="50"
    list="clientList"
    data-win-bind="value: clientName">
<datalist id="clientList"></datalist>
```

This code will take any items we add to clientList and offer them to users as hints when they are entering a value for Client Name. At the moment, there are no items in the datalist, so no hints will display. The ideal situation would be to populate clientList with all of the clients that we have already defined in Clok. We can use the map method of the WinJS.Binding.List class to create an array that contains our users' clients. Add the highlighted code from Listing 11-43 to storage.js.

Listing 11-43. Using the Map Method

```
projects: new WinJS.Binding.List([]),
clients: {
    get: function () {
        return new WinJS.Binding.List(storage.projects
            .map(function (p) { return p.clientName; })
        );
    }
},
compareProjectGroups: function (left, right) {
    return left.toUpperCase().charCodeAt(0) - right.toUpperCase().charCodeAt(0);
},
```

Now that we have a clients property, we only have to use this to populate the datalist control we created in Listing 11-42. Add the highlighted code from Listing 11-44 to detail.js.

Listing 11-44. Binding Clients to the Datalist

```
ready: function (element, options) {
    this.currProject = storage.projects.getById(options && options.id)
        || new Clok.Data.Project();

    this.configureAppBar(options && options.id);

    var form = document.getElementById("projectDetailForm");
    WinJS.Binding.processAll(form, this.currProject);

    this.bindClients();

    saveProjectCommand.onclick = this.saveProjectCommand_click.bind(this);
    deleteProjectCommand.onclick = this.deleteProjectCommand_click.bind(this);
},

bindClients: function () {
    storage.clients.forEach(function (item) {
        var option = document.createElement("option");
        option.textContent = item;
        option.value.textContent = item;
        clientList.appendChild(option);
    });
},

saveProjectCommand_click: function (e) {
    // SNIPPED
},
```

As I mentioned, the datalist control is very similar to the drop-down list control created from the select element. Neither the datalist nor select supports WinJS data binding, which is unfortunate, in my opinion, so in both cases, we bind data by manually creating an option element for each item in our data source. Note the similarities between Listing 11-44 and Listing 11-7.

With that, run Clok and add a new project. Does it work like you expected? It's not what I had in mind. Our datalist has a client for each of the user's projects, but if a client has more than one project, that client is in the list more than once. For example, Northwind Traders has four projects, so typing the letter N into the Client Name field results in a datalist like that shown in Figure 11-18.

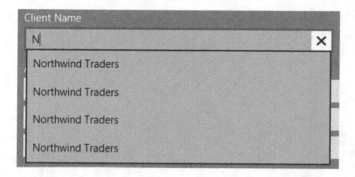

Figure 11-18. *Client Name, with an overly populated datalist*

While this alone could be helpful, the datalist will become unhelpful as more and more projects are added. A better choice would be to show only each client once in the datalist, regardless of how many projects the user has for that client.

If you're familiar with MapReduce, you surely know what's coming next. If not, a short, nontechnical description is that it transforms one set of data, potentially very large, into a meaningful summary of that data. For example, given several exam scores for all students at a university, MapReduce might be used to get a subset of all students that includes their GPAs for the semester. While the concepts are consistent, MapReduce implementations vary between languages and platforms. Much more detailed information about MapReduce concepts can be found online. In particular, the map and reduce functions of the WinJS.Binding.List class are documented on MSDN at http://msdn.microsoft.com/en-us/library/windows/apps/hh700766.aspx and http://msdn.microsoft.com/en-us/library/windows/apps/hh700784.aspx. In any case, we've only done the mapping part so far. We want to reduce our list of clients to include only one item per client. Add the highlighted code from Listing 11-45 to storage.js.

Listing 11-45. Sorting Then Reducing Our Mapped Clients

```
clients: {
    get: function () {
        return new WinJS.Binding.List(storage.projects
            .map(function (p) { return p.clientName; })
            .sort()
            .reduce(function (accumulated, current) {
                if (current !== accumulated[accumulated.length - 1]) {
                    accumulated[accumulated.length] = current;
                }
                return accumulated;
            }, [])
        );
    }
},
```

After mapping our projects to a list of clients, we first sort the result, then call the reduce method. The reduce method calls the specified callback function for each item in the mapped results. In this example, it adds the client currently being evaluated, the current variable, to a growing array of clients, the accumulated variable, but only if that client is not already in accumulated. The reduce method also takes an initial value for the accumulated result, which, in our example, is an empty array, [].

Run Clok and add a new project. When you first click the Client Name field, a list of all clients the user has defined is displayed, in case your new project is for one of those clients (see Figure 11-19).

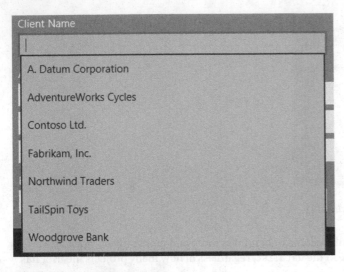

Figure 11-19. *Existing clients*

As you start typing in the Client Name field, the datalist is automatically filtered to show only hints that match the text you've entered so far (see Figure 11-20).

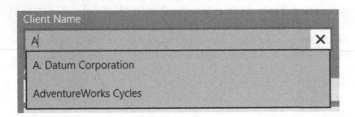

Figure 11-20. *Filtered and unique hints*

■ **Note** The code in this section has intentionally included clients for all projects in Clok, including deleted projects. If you'd prefer only to include clients with active or inactive projects, then you will have to change your mapping method to return only p.clientName, if p.status has an appropriate value.

Conclusion

I have covered a lot in this chapter. There are many techniques for binding data to your user interface, and I've covered several here. Although we are currently using in-memory data for Clok, all of the data-binding code that we've created in this chapter will continue to work as we upgrade our `Clok.Data.Storage` class to persist data in a more meaningful manner. Data binding can be simple, but it is an enormous topic, and there is a lot of information that is not appropriate to cover in this book. If you are interested in additional information, more is available on MSDN at `http://msdn.microsoft.com/en-us/library/windows/apps/br229775.aspx`.

CHAPTER 12

■ ■ ■

Promises

Have you ever been frustrated when an application you were using temporarily froze while it was performing some task? Maybe it froze while you were searching its data or perhaps performing a long calculation. There are many factors that could cause an application to become unresponsive, but it is usually the result of doing something intensive on the same thread that is responsible for updating the user interface (UI). That means that when this long-running code is executing, the UI is unable to update, causing a perceived application freeze.

Clearly, this isn't something we want in our applications. Fortunately, there are a few techniques that allow you to minimize this occurrence in your code. In this chapter, I will cover promises, and in Chapter 13, I will cover web workers. Promises allow you to write code to do something with a value you don't yet have. Web workers allow you to create new threads to perform long-running operations.

To keep applications responsive, the WinJS library makes heavy use of promises. In fact, simply by creating a new project in Visual Studio using one of the project templates covered in Chapter 4, your project will contain code dealing with promises. In the context of Clok, the sample time-tracking application we started building in Chapter 9, we will explore promises, as we add functionality to allow use to save and view time entries. I'll give an overview of promises, including how to work with promises returned from functions you might call, as well as how to create them in your own code. First, though, a little background.

What Are Promises

In short, a promise represents a value that might not exist yet. What does that mean? If you have an operation that runs asynchronously, such as requesting remote data over HTTP, instead of blocking and waiting for that operation to complete, you can use a promise to represent the data that you will ultimately receive from that HTTP request. If you do this, then the rest of your code can continue to execute, and when the promise has been fulfilled, a specified function executes to process the result of the asynchronous (async) operation. Listing 12-1 demonstrates a potential implementation for getting remote data over HTTP with promises.

Listing 12-1. A Pseudo–Code Promise Example

```
var myPromise = getJsonDataAsync();
myPromise.then(
    function doSomethingWithTheData(data) { /*  */ },
    function logError(e) { /*  */ }
);
```

Clearly, this code is missing some context, but it does illustrate how to work with promises. Assume the function getJsonDataAsync has been defined and returns a promise object. Once the data has been received, the promise executes its then function, passing along the data as a parameter, so that it can be processed in doSomethingWithTheData. Alternatively, if there were an error in the promise, the logError function is executed instead.

223

It is important to point out that, in Listing 12-1, the function getJsonDataAsync does not return the data we requested. It returns a promise. A promise is not the actual result of your async operation. It is a separate object that can exist in one of three states: unfulfilled, fulfilled, or rejected. An unfulfilled promise implies that the async work has not yet been completed. A fulfilled promise means the work completed without error. A rejected promise is one that completed, but has errors.

Promises can be a tricky thing to wrap your head around. It doesn't help that there are numerous different JavaScript implementations of promises available in different libraries, such as jQuery or Dojo, each potentially with slightly different implementations. Fortunately, while not a standard, the CommonJS Promises/A specification (http://wiki.commonjs.org/wiki/Promises/A) is popular and has been implemented by a number of different promises libraries. In fact, the WinJS implementation of promises follows this specification.

As I mentioned, the code in Listing 12-1 is missing some context, so let's add a little by defining the getJsonDataAsync function, as seen in Listing 12-2. This is a common pattern for creating functions that return Promise objects.

Listing 12-2. Extending the Promise Previous Example

```
function getJsonDataAsync() {
    return new WinJS.Promise(function init(oncomplete, onerror) {
        setTimeout(function () {
            try {
                var data = getTheData();
                oncomplete(data);
            }
            catch (e) {
                onerror(e);
            }
        }, 1000);
    });
}
```

So what's going on here? Well, I've combined a number of statements into a single return statement in Listing 12-2. While this is a common technique when defining a Promise, it can be a little complicated when being introduced to the topic. In this example, the task of actually getting the data I need happens in the call to getTheData, but I need the getJsonDataAsync to return a Promise object. The Promise constructor takes an initializer function, init in this example, as its first parameter. This init function accepts two functions as parameters. The first, oncomplete, is the function to call when the Promise has successfully completed, passing along the data I need. The second init parameter, onerror, is the function to call when there is an error. I've wrapped the contents of the init function in a call to setTimeout, so that it executes asynchronously after one second.

■ **Note** The Promise constructor can optionally take another function as a second paramater, which will be executed if the promise should be canceled. Additionally, the init function can optionally take a third parameter, which can be used to report the progress of the Promise to the calling code. See MSDN for more details about these optional parameters: http://msdn.microsoft.com/en-us/library/windows/apps/br211866.aspx.

The Promise class defines two functions for working with the results of your async method: then and done. These two functions are very similar. They both can accept up to three functions as parameters: a function to call on successful completion of the promise, one to call when there is an error, and one to report the progress of the async code. In fact, in some cases, you could use then in place of done. There are two main differences between them.

The first is that the then function returns another Promise, allowing you to chain multiple then statements to one another. The done function, on the other hand, doesn't return anything. Listing 12-3 illustrates an example where the results of our Promise are passed to the first then function, and the results of that are passed to a second then function and, ultimately, to the done function. In this example, only the functions that handle promise completion are supplied to then and done.

Listing 12-3. Example of Promise Chaining

```
getRemoteData()
    .then(function processTheData(data) {
        // ...
    })
    .then(function postProcessedDataToServer(data) {
        // ...
    })
    .done(function updateUserInterfaceWithPostStatus(data) {
        // ...
    });
```

The second significant difference between then and done is related to error handling. If an error handling function is not supplied to then, any errors will be passed along to the next statement in the chain. If an error handling function is not supplied to done, any errors will cause an exception to be raised in your application.

Back to our example in Listing 12-1 and Listing 12-2, the data that is returned from getTheData in Listing 12-2 is passed to the oncomplete function, which maps to the first parameter of the then function, doSomethingWithTheData, in Listing 12-1. Any errors are passed to the onerror function, which maps to the second parameter of the then function, logError, in Listing 12-1. The result is that I can request the data I need and specify what I want to do with it before I actually have it. You'll see some fully-implemented examples of working with promises later in this chapter.

One thing to remember as you work with promises is that JavaScript is not a multi-threaded language by default. While the purpose of promises is to handle the results of async functions, I want to be clear that simply having a promise object does not mean that your code is executing on a different thread. Restated a different way, async code does not necessarily run on a different thread. It just runs at a different time. It is very common for async code to execute on a different thread, but as you will see later in this chapter, it is possible that your UI can still become unresponsive, even when using promises, because the async code is executing on the UI thread.

In the rest of this chapter, I'll introduce you to promises within the context of Clok, the sample application we've been assembling over the last few chapters. While the purpose of this chapter is to cover the WinJS.Promise class, there will be a significant amount of code throughout the chapter that is not inherently related to promises on its own. This code is required, however, to build a meaningful sample. By the end of this chapter, you'll see a few different techniques for working with promises, and Clok will be much farther along the path to becoming a useful Windows Store application.

Recording Time Entries

Our sample application, Clok, needs the ability to save time entries. You might remember that the time-entry form we created on the Clok dashboard screen doesn't actually do anything yet. It only animates away and resets. We have to add functionality to save those time entries, and, fortunately for Chapter 12 (this chapter), that's a great opportunity to take advantage of promises. There are three steps we have to take in order to allow users to record time entries.

1. We have to replace the current clock on the Clok dashboard screen with a new timer control.

2. We have to update our data model to support time entries in addition to projects.

3. We have to add code to actually save a new time entry when the user clicks the Save button.

New Timer Control

Before we can save a time entry, we have to make some changes to the timer we have on the Clok dashboard screen. While the current Clok.UI.Clock control helped illustrate how to create custom controls, it isn't really very practical to have a single control with multiple resposibilities: displaying the current time and displaying elapsed time. We're going to split that control into two different controls, each specialized for its given purpose. The current control will still exist but will have timer-related functionality removed, and a new Clok.UI.Timer control will be created to calculate and display elpased time.

Instead of storing a single value for elapsed time, this new Timer control will keep track of when it is started and stopped and calculate the elapsed time from these values. Later, this will allow our users to start the timer, then close Clok. When they return later, the timer will still appear to be running, displaying the total time elapsed since the user started the timer, even though the application was not running during this time. I'll cover this in Chapter 17. In the meantime, let's create our new Timer control. Add a new JavaScript file named timerControl.js to the controls/js folder in your Visual Studio project. Add the code from Listing 12-4 to this new file.

Listing 12-4. Our New Timer Control

```
(function () {
    "use strict";

    var controlDefinition = WinJS.Class.define(
        function Control_ctor(element, options) {
            this.element = element || document.createElement("div");
            this.element.winControl = this;

            // Set option defaults
            this._startStops = [];

            // Set user-defined options
            WinJS.UI.setOptions(this, options);

            this._init();
        },
        {
            _intervalId: 0,

            isRunning: {
                get: function () {
                    return (this.startStops.length > 0
                        && this.startStops[this.startStops.length - 1]
                        && this.startStops[this.startStops.length - 1].startTime
                        && !this.startStops[this.startStops.length - 1].stopTime);
                }
            },

            startStops: {
                get: function () {
                    return this._startStops;
                },
                set: function (value) {
                    this._startStops = value;
                }
            },
```

```
        timerValue: {
            get: function () {
                if (this.startStops.length <= 0) {
                    return 0;
                } else {
                    var val = 0;

                    for (var i = 0; i < this.startStops.length; i++) {
                        var startStop = this.startStops[i];
                        if (startStop.stopTime) {
                            val += (startStop.stopTime - startStop.startTime);
                        } else {
                            val += ((new Date()).getTime() - startStop.startTime);
                        }
                    }

                    return Math.round(val / 1000);
                }
            }
        },

        timerValueAsTimeSpan: {
            get: function () {
                return Clok.Utilities.SecondsToTimeSpan(this.timerValue);
            }
        },

        _init: function () {
            this._updateTimer();
        },

        start: function () {
            if (!this.isRunning) {
                this._intervalId = setInterval(this._updateTimer.bind(this), 250);
                this.startStops[this.startStops.length] = {
                    startTime: (new Date()).getTime()
                };
                this.dispatchEvent("start", {});
            }
        },

        stop: function () {
            if (this.isRunning) {
                clearInterval(this._intervalId);
                this._intervalId = 0;
                this.startStops[this.startStops.length - 1]
                    .stopTime = (new Date()).getTime();
                this._updateTimer();
                this.dispatchEvent("stop", {});
            }
        },
```

```
                    reset: function () {
                        this._startStops = [];
                        this._updateTimer();
                        this.dispatchEvent("reset", {});
                    },

                    _updateTimer: function () {
                        var ts = this.timerValueAsTimeSpan;

                        var sec = ts[2];
                        var min = ts[1];
                        var hr = ts[0];

                        min = ((min < 10) ? "0" : "") + min;
                        sec = ((sec < 10) ? "0" : "") + sec;

                        var formattedTime = new String();
                        formattedTime = hr + ":" + min + ":" + sec;

                        this.element.textContent = formattedTime;
                    },

                }
            );

        WinJS.Namespace.define("Clok.UI", {
            Timer: controlDefinition,
        });

        WinJS.Class.mix(Clok.UI.Timer,
            WinJS.Utilities.createEventProperties("start"),
            WinJS.Utilities.createEventProperties("stop"),
            WinJS.Utilities.createEventProperties("reset"),
            WinJS.UI.DOMEventMixin);

})();
```

That's a fair amount of code, but you've already seen most of it, so I won't discuss it in great detail. I'll only point out that there is a new property named startStops that contains an array of times at which the timer is started and stopped. Each time the timer is started, a new item is added to startStops, with only a startTime defined. When the timer is stopped, the stopTime is defined for the most recent item in the array. The startStops property is then used to determine the value of the isRunning and timerValue properties. Note that because the getTime method of the Date object returns a number of milliseconds, I've divided the difference by 1000 in timerValue before returning.

You'll also see a call to a new function, Clok.Utilities.SecondsToTimeSpan. Add a file named utilities.js to the js folder and add the code from Listing 12-5.

Listing 12-5. Our Utilities Class

```
(function () {
    "use strict";

    var utilClass = WinJS.Class.define(
        function constructor() { },
        { /* no instance members */ },
        {
            // static members
            SecondsToTimeSpan: function (totalSec) {
                if (!isNaN(totalSec)) {
                    var sec = totalSec % 60;
                    var min = ((totalSec - sec) / 60) % 60;
                    var hr = ((totalSec - sec - (60 * min)) / 3600);

                    return [hr, min, sec];
                }
                return [0, 0, 0];
            },

            TimeSpanToSeconds: function (timespan) {
                if (isNaN(timespan)) {
                    return (timespan[0] * 3600) + (timespan[1] * 60) + (timespan[2]);
                }
                return 0;
            },

        }
    );

    WinJS.Namespace.define("Clok", {
        Utilities: utilClass,
    });

})();
```

Only a few small changes remain to swap out our old Clock control for our new Timer control. Add the highlighted code from Listing 12-6 to default.html, so that our new classes are available throughout the application.

Listing 12-6. Adding Script References in default.html

```
<link href="/css/default.css" rel="stylesheet" />

<script src="/js/default.js"></script>
<script src="/js/navigator.js"></script>
<script src="/js/utilities.js"></script>

<script src="/controls/js/timerControl.js"></script>
<script src="/controls/js/clockControl.js"></script>
```

```
<script src="/data/project.js"></script>
<script src="/data/storage.js"></script>
```

Next, open home.html and replace the Clock control with our new Timer control. This change is highlighted in Listing 12-7.

Listing 12-7. Switching to Our New Control

```
<div id="elapsedTime">
    <h2 id="elapsedTimeClock"
        data-win-control="Clok.UI.Timer"></h2>
</div>
```

Finally, we have to make two small changes to home.js. When splitting the timer functionality out into its own class, I changed the name of the counterValue property to timerValue. So, Listing 12-8 highlights the two places we have to change that in the enableOrDisableButtons function in home.js.

Listing 12-8. Updating home.js with a New Property Name

```
enableOrDisableButtons: function () {
    if ((project.value !== "")
            && (!this.timerIsRunning)
            && (elapsedTimeClock.winControl.timerValue > 0)) {
        saveTimeButton.disabled = false;
    } else {
        saveTimeButton.disabled = true;
    }

    discardTimeButton.disabled = (this.timerIsRunning)
            || (elapsedTimeClock.winControl.timerValue <= 0);

    editProjectButton.disabled =
        (project.options[project.selectedIndex].value === "");
},
```

Now, if you run Clok, it should look and behave exactly as it did before. While this change doesn't seem to make any difference at this point, the Timer control functionality now mirrors the user's behavior. The user can start and stop the timer, and the Timer control now keeps track of each time that happens. Additionally, this change is critical for functionality you will build in Chapter 15 to allow the user to close Clok and return later with the timer still intact.

■ **Note**   In this chapter, I've illustrated the code for the new Clok.UI.Timer control but have not shown the modified Clok.UI.Clock control. Leaving the unnecessary timer-related functionality in this control will not prevent Clok from functioning as expected, but keeping your code base clean is a good practice that will improve maintainability in the future. So, if you're interested in seeing the modified code, the source code available with this book contains a version with the timer-related functionality removed. You can find the code samples for this chapter on the Source Code/Downloads tab of the book's Apress product page (www.apress.com/9781430257790).

Updating Our Data Model

In order to save time entries, updates are needed in the Clok data model. A new timeEntry class is needed, as well as changes to the storage class, to work with timeEntry objects. Create a new file named timeEntry.js in the data folder of your Visual Studio project. Add the code in Listing 12-9 to timeEntry.js.

Listing 12-9. A Class for Time Entries

```
(function () {
    "use strict";

    var timeEntryClass = WinJS.Class.define(
        function constructor() {

            // define and initialize properties
            this.id = (new Date()).getTime();
            this._projectId = -1;
            this._dateWorked = (new Date()).removeTimePart();
            this.elapsedSeconds = 0;
            this.notes = "";
        },
        {
            // instance members
            projectId: {
                get: function () {
                    return this._projectId;
                },
                set: function (value) {
                    this._projectId =
                        (value && !isNaN(value) && Number(value))
                            || this._projectId;
                }
            },

            dateWorked: {
                get: function () {
                    return this._dateWorked;
                },
                set: function (value) {
                    this._dateWorked = value.removeTimePart();
                }
            },

            project: {
                get: function () {
                    var p = Clok.Data.Storage.projects.getById(this.projectId);
                    return p;
                }
            },
        },
```

```
        {
            // static members
        }
    );

    WinJS.Namespace.define("Clok.Data", {
        TimeEntry: timeEntryClass,
    });
})();
```

■ **Note**   Be sure to add a script reference to /data/timeEntry.js in default.html.

You probably noticed that I've structured the timeEntry a little differently from the project class in Chapter 11. I've explicitly defined get and set functions for some of the timeEntry properties. This allows validation of the values being assigned to these properties. Specifically, I verify that the value supplied for projectId is a number, before setting the projectId property's value. Additionally, I use a method on the Date class named removeTimePart, so that dates are saved without times. Saving "12/1/2013" instead of "12/1/2013 4:05 PM," for example, simplifies filtering time entries, which I will cover later in this chapter.

Unfortunately, the Date class does not actually have a method named removeTimePart. In order to get this to work, I added some functions to Date.prototype. If you're familiar with JavaScript, you probably already know how to use prototype. In case you're coming form a different background, I'll summarize. Because JavaScript is a dynamic language, we can add members (properties and methods) to an individual object after it has been created. I never called it out, but that is exactly what I've done when defining properties on our data-model classes, such as when I initialize the notes property of the this object in Listing 12-9, even though it doesn't have an explicit definition.

In addition to adding members to instances of objects, we can also add members to the class definition itself, after it has been created. When this is done, any instances of that class also contain that new member. Create a file named extensions.js in the js folder of your Visual Studio project. Add the code in Listing 12-10 to extensions.js.

Listing 12-10. Extending the Date Class

```
Date.prototype.removeTimePart = function () {
    var year = this.getFullYear();
    var month = this.getMonth();
    var date = this.getDate();

    return new Date(year, month, date);
}
```

■ **Note**   If you are familiar with C#, this has a similar feel to extension methods. It's not really the same thing, because in JavaScript we are changing the class definition. With C# extension methods, however, the compiler does some magic to make our extension methods appear to be members of the class, without actually changing the class defintion.

Our Clok.Data.Storage class also requires a few updates, to allow us to save timeEntry objects. Open storage.js and add the highlighted code in Listing 12-11 after the groupedProjects function definition.

Listing 12-11. Adding an Empty List to Store Time Entries

```
groupedProjects: {
    // SNIPPED
},

timeEntries: new WinJS.Binding.List([]),
```

We also need a save method, such as we added for projects in Chapter 11. Add the highlighted code in Listing 12-12 to storage.js, after the storage.projects.delete function definition.

Listing 12-12. Adding Methods to Get and Save Time Entries to Our Storage Class

```
storage.projects.delete = function (p) {
    // SNIPPED
};

storage.timeEntries.getById = function (id) {
    if (id) {
        var matches = this.filter(function (te) { return te.id === id; });
        if (matches && matches.length === 1) {
            return matches[0];
        }
    }
    return undefined;
};

storage.timeEntries.save = function (te) {
    if (te && te.id) {
        var existing = storage.timeEntries.getById(te.id);
        if (!existing) {
            storage.timeEntries.push(te);
        }
    }
};
```

Saving Time Entry from Clok Dashboard

While we still aren't persisting our data anywhere, we now have the code in place to save timeEntry objects in-memory in the same manner we have been saving project objects. I'll cover more persistent storage options in Chapter 14. We are finally ready, however, to actually introduce promises to Clok.

Actually, we already have. Take a look at the discard function in home.js. The call to WinJS.UI.executeTransition actually returns a Promise object (see Listing 12-13).

Listing 12-13. We've Already Seen Promises

```
var slideTransition = WinJS.UI.executeTransition(
    // SNIPPED
]).done(function () { self.resetTimer(); });
```

When the Promise returned by WinJS.UI.executeTransition has successfully completed, the anonymous function we pass to the done function resets the timer. That was a pretty basic-use case for promises. When we implement the ability to save a time entry, we can take advantage of promises in a different way, as we make some changes to the save function in home.js. Replace the save function with the code from Listing 12-14.

Listing 12-14. Modified Save Function

```
save: function () {
    var self = this;

    var transitionPromise = new WinJS.Promise(function (comp, err, prog) {
        timeEntry.style.transition = 'color 5ms ease 0s, '
            + 'transform 500ms ease 0s, opacity 500ms ease 0s';

        timeEntry.style.transformOrigin = "-130px 480px";
        timeEntry.style.transform = 'scale3d(0,0,0)';
        timeEntry.style.opacity = '0';
        timeEntry.style.color = '#00ff00';

        var self = this;
        var transitionend = function (e1) {
            if (e1.propertyName === "transform") {
                timeEntry.removeEventListener('transitionend', transitionend);
                comp();
            }
        };

        timeEntry.addEventListener('transitionend', transitionend, false);
    });

    var savePromise = new WinJS.Promise(function (comp, err, prog) {
        var timeEntry = new Clok.Data.TimeEntry();
        timeEntry.projectId = Number(project.options[project.selectedIndex].value);
        timeEntry.dateWorked = new Date(elapsedTimeClock.winControl.startStops[0].startTime);
        timeEntry.elapsedSeconds = elapsedTimeClock.winControl.timerValue;
        timeEntry.notes = timeNotes.value;

        storage.timeEntries.save(timeEntry);

        comp();
    });

    WinJS.Promise.join([transitionPromise, savePromise]).done(function () {
        self.resetTimer();
    });
},
```

The first thing you'll notice is that we wrapped the code that performs the CSS transition in a Promise object named transitionPromise. Instead of calling self.resetTimer in the transitionend event handler, we call the comp handler of the promise's initializer. Next, we have some code to actually save the time entry. Creating and saving a new timeEntry object is pretty straightforward on its own. In Listing 12-14, we've also wrapped this functionality in a Promise object named savePromise.

Now we have two Promise objects. When both have completed—the animation is over and the time entry has been saved—then the timer should be reset. The Promise class has a join method that offers precisely this functionality. You can pass an array of Promise objects to the join method, and the join method will return a new Promise that is fulfilled when each Promise in that array has completed successfully. So, the call to self.resetTimer doesn't occur until both the animation has completed and the time entry has been saved.

■ **Note** In addition to `WinJS.Promise.join`, to create a new `Promise` that is fulfilled when each of a number of other promises has been fulfilled, you can use the `WinJS.Promise.any` function to create a new `Promise` that is fulfilled when any one of a list of promises has been fulfilled. As with `join`, `any` accepts an array of `Promise` objects as its parameter.

We've done a lot of good work so far in this chapter. We changed our timer control, updated our data model, and added code to save time entries, taking advantage of promises in the process. Yet, when running Clok at this point, everything appears on the surface to be exactly the same as it was at the end of Chapter 11. The timer still starts ticking when the user clicks the Start menu option, and it stops when he or she clicks the Stop menu option. When the user clicks the Save or Discard buttons, the form still animates and then resets. Even though we've added functionality to save that time entry, there's no way to tell from the user's perspective that anything is different. Let's fix that.

Viewing Time Entries

Now that users can save time entries from the Clok dashboard screen, they need a way to view them. In this section, we'll add a page from which to view a list of saved time entries, as well as a few different ways to filter the list.

Temporary Data

While we could use the functionality we just added to load a few `timeEntry` objects, having to do that each time we test the application would get old quickly. So, before we build our new page for viewing time entries, let's hard-code a few `timeEntry` objects by adding the code from Listing 12-15 at the very end of `storage.js`.

Listing 12-15. Temporarily Adding Hard-Coded Data

```
(function () {
    var createTime = function (id, projectId, dateWorked, elapsedSeconds, notes) {
        var newTimeEntry = new Clok.Data.TimeEntry();
        newTimeEntry.id = id;
        newTimeEntry.projectId = projectId;
        newTimeEntry.dateWorked = dateWorked;
        newTimeEntry.elapsedSeconds = elapsedSeconds;
        newTimeEntry.notes = notes;

        return newTimeEntry;
    }

    var time = Clok.Data.Storage.timeEntries;

    var date1 = (new Date()).addMonths(-1).addDays(1);
    var date2 = (new Date()).addMonths(-1).addDays(2);
    var date3 = (new Date()).addMonths(-1).addDays(3);

    var timeId = 1369623987766;
    time.push(createTime(timeId++, 1368296808757, date1, 10800, "Lorem ipsum dolor sit."));
    time.push(createTime(timeId++, 1368296808757, date2, 7200, "Amet, consectetur euismod."));
    time.push(createTime(timeId++, 1368296808757, date3, 7200, "Praesent congue diam."));
    time.push(createTime(timeId++, 1368296808760, date2, 7200, "Curabitur euismod mollis."));
```

```
        time.push(createTime(timeId++, 1368296808759, date1, 7200, "Donec sit amet porttitor."));
        time.push(createTime(timeId++, 1368296808758, date3, 8100, "Praesent congue euismod."));
        time.push(createTime(timeId++, 1368296808758, date2, 14400, "Curabitur euismod mollis."));
        time.push(createTime(timeId++, 1368296808761, date1, 7200, "Donec sit amet porttitor."));
        time.push(createTime(timeId++, 1368296808748, date3, 7200, "Praesent euismod diam."));
        time.push(createTime(timeId++, 1368296808748, date2, 7200, "Curabitur euismod mollis."));
        time.push(createTime(timeId++, 1368296808748, date1, 7200, "Donec sit amet porttitor."));
        time.push(createTime(timeId++, 1368296808746, date2, 8100, "Congue euismod diam."));
        time.push(createTime(timeId++, 1368296808753, date2, 14400, "Curabitur euismod mollis."));
        time.push(createTime(timeId++, 1368296808753, date1, 7200, "Donec sit amet porttitor."));
        time.push(createTime(timeId++, 1368296808761, date2, 10800, "Donec semper risus nec."));
})();
```

We will have to remove this code later, once we start persisting our data, but in the meantime, it's nice to have some test data in the application, as we're developing. This self-executing function is very similar to the code added in Chapter 11 for hard-coding temporary projects to Clok.

One thing you might have noticed, however, is the use of two additional functions I've added to the Date class's prototype: addMonths and addDays. Using these functions when creating temporary data will ensure that we will always have recent test data, regardless of when we test. Let's define these functions, as well as one named addYears for good measure. Add the code from Listing 12-16 to extensions.js.

Listing 12-16. Further Extending the Date Class

```
Date.prototype.addDays = function (n) {
    var year = this.getFullYear();
    var month = this.getMonth();
    var date = this.getDate();

    date += n;

    return new Date(year, month, date);
}

Date.prototype.addMonths = function (n) {
    var year = this.getFullYear();
    var month = this.getMonth();
    var date = this.getDate();

    month += n;

    return new Date(year, month, date);
}

Date.prototype.addYears = function (n) {
    var year = this.getFullYear();
    var month = this.getMonth();
    var date = this.getDate();

    year += n;

    return new Date(year, month, date);
}
```

When I first saw this technique for shifting a date by adding a value to one of the date parts, I became concerned about what might happen if, for example, I added 30 days to May 24th. There's no such date as May 54th. Fortunately, the JavaScript Date constructor is capable of handling this, and would return June 23rd in this instance.

■ **Note** Many programming languages and frameworks provide methods for easily working with dates and times like this. JavaScript doesn't have a convenient way to work with dates by default. These simple methods meet some common needs that we have in Clok. Additionally, WinRT provides some ability to format dates via the `Windows.Globalization.DateTimeFormatting` namespace. If you are looking for additional functionality, many libraries are available. A popular one is the Moment.js library, which can be found online at `www.momentjs.com`.

List Time Entries

Now that we have some temporary data loaded, let's define how the UI should appear when the user is viewing a list of time entries. The Mail application that comes with Windows 8 uses a "split layout," very similar in structure to the project Visual Studio creates when you select the Split App template we covered in Chapter 4. In the Mail application, a list of messages is visible on the left, and the message detail is visible on the right side of the screen (see Figure 12-1).

Figure 12-1. *The Windows Mail application*

I'd like to use a similar layout for viewing time entries in Clok. When I was planning the content for this book, I made mock-ups of how various screens in Clok might appear. Figure 12-2 is an early mock-up of the screen we are about to build. I've since added a few updates to Clok that vary a little from this mock-up, but it's still fairly close.

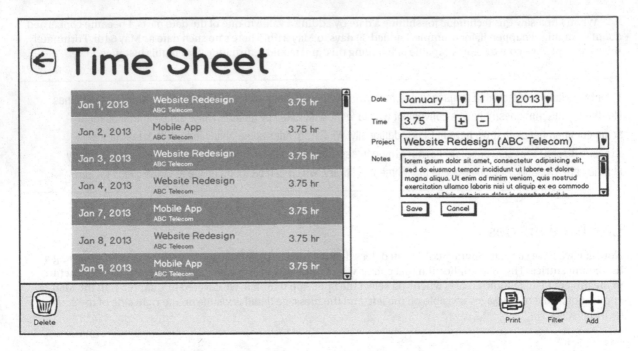

Figure 12-2. *An early mock-up of the Clok time entries screen*

■ **Note** To create my mock-ups for Clok, I used a popular wireframing tool called Balsamiq Mockups. More info about this great tool is available from the Balsamiq web site, at `www.balsamiq.com/products/mockups`. Working with wireframes or mock-ups is a good, quick way to make sure that you know what you are about to build. I highly suggest working from mock-ups, even if they are photos of drawings on a whiteboard, which, coincidentally, is a feature we will be adding to Clok in Chapter 22.

On the left side, users will see a list of previous time entries, which they can filter using the Filter app bar command. On the right, they'll be able to edit an existing one. Deleting time entries is a scenario I'll cover later in this chapter, but I won't actually cover editing existing time entries or adding a time entry from this screen in the text of this book. The code to do that is similar to the code that allows a user to edit or add projects. The source code that accompanies this book does have a completed version of the Time Sheets screen, including the ability to edit time entries or add new ones from this screen. (See the Source Code/Downloads tab of the book's Apress product page [www.apress.com/9781430257790].)

Creating and Connecting the Page Control

The first thing to do is create a folder named `timeEntries` in the pages folder of your Visual Studio project. Within the `timeEntries` folder, add a new page control named `list.html` (see Figure 12-3).

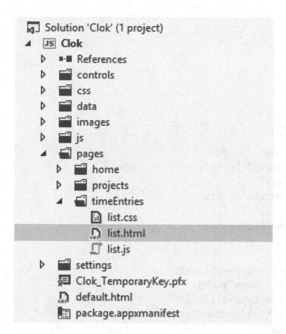

Figure 12-3. Solution Explorer with new page control for time entries

Now we have to modify the Clok dashboard screen so that the Time Sheets menu option (Figure 12-4) will navigate to our new page control. Refer to Chapter 11, specifically to Listing 11-9, Listing 11-10, and Listing 11-11, if you need a quick reminder on how to wire up this navigation.

Figure 12-4. Time Sheets menu option

For this section, we'll start with the only list of time entries on the left side of the screen. Later, we'll add the app bar commands for filtering and deleting time entries. To get started, replace the entire contents of the body element in list.html with the code from Listing 12-17.

Listing 12-17. New Contents for list.html

```
<div class="timeEntryListPage fragment">
    <header aria-label="Header content" role="banner">
        <button class="win-backbutton" aria-label="Back" disabled type="button"></button>
        <h1 class="titlearea win-type-ellipsis">
```

```
                <span class="pagetitle">Time Sheets</span>
        </h1>
    </header>
    <section aria-label="Main content" role="main">
        <div id="timeEntryTemplate"
                data-win-control="WinJS.Binding.Template"
                style="display: none">
            <div class="timeEntryItem">
                <div class="timeEntryItem-dateWorked">
                    <h5 class="timeEntryItem-dateWorked-mon"
                        data-win-bind="textContent: dateWorked "></h5>
                    <h2 class="timeEntryItem-dateWorked-day"
                        data-win-bind="textContent: dateWorked"></h2>
                    <h5 class="timeEntryItem-dateWorked-year"
                        data-win-bind="textContent: dateWorked"></h5>
                </div>
                <div class="timeEntryItem-projectInfo">
                    <h3 class="timeEntryItem-projectName win-type-ellipsis"
                        data-win-bind="textContent: project.name"></h3>
                    <h6 class="timeEntryItem-clientName win-type-ellipsis"
                        data-win-bind="textContent: project.clientName"></h6>
                    <h6 class="timeEntryItem-projectNumber"
                        data-win-bind="textContent: project.projectNumber"></h6>
                </div>
                <div class="timeEntryItem-timeWorked">
                    <h2 class="timeEntryItem-timeWorked-elapsed"
                        data-win-bind="textContent: elapsedSeconds"></h2>
                    <h5>hours</h5>
                </div>
            </div>
        </div>

        <div id="timeEntriesContainer">
            <div id="timeEntriesListViewPane">
                <div
                    id="timeEntriesListView"
                    class="itemlist win-selectionstylefilled"
                    data-win-control="WinJS.UI.ListView"
                    data-win-options="{
                        itemTemplate: select('#timeEntryTemplate'),
                        selectionMode: 'multi',
                        swipeBehavior: 'select',
                        tapBehavior: 'directSelect'
                    }">
                </div>
                <div id="noMatchesFound">No data found.  Try adjusting the filters.</div>
                <div id="searchInProgress">
                    Searching for time entries...<br />
                    <progress />
                </div>
```

```
            <div id="searchError">There was an error searching for time entries.</div>
        </div>
        <div id="timeEntryDetailPane">
            <!-- edit form goes here -->
        </div>
      </div>
    </section>
</div>
```

By this point, you are probably pretty familiar with what this code is doing. I've added a WinJS.Binding.Template named timeEntryTemplate, and I've defined two regions on the page. The second is the timeEntryDetailPane div element, which is currently empty. I'll come back to that later in this chapter. The region we're working with in this section is the timeEntriesListViewPane div element. Within that region, I've added a ListView as well as a few other div elements for displaying different statuses to the user. I have set a few different properties on the ListView this time. The highlighted code shows the settings used to have this ListView behave as expected. In this case, we are allowing the user to select multiple items, by either swiping items on a touch-enabled display or right-clicking with a mouse. Additionally, if the user taps or clicks a single item, that item will be selected, and any others will be deselected. Next, replace the entire contents of list.css with the code from Listing 12-18.

Listing 12-18. New Contents for list.css

```css
.timeEntryListPage section[role=main] {
    margin-left: 120px;
    width: calc(100% - 120px);
}


.hidden {
    display: none;
}


#timeEntriesContainer {
    display: -ms-flexbox;
    -ms-flex-align: start;
    -ms-flex-pack: start;
    -ms-flex-direction: row;
    -ms-flex-wrap: nowrap;
    height: 100%;
}


#timeEntriesListViewPane {
    -ms-flex: 0 auto;
    width: 600px;
    height: 100%;
}


#timeEntriesListView {
    height: 100%;
}

    #timeEntriesListView .win-container {
        background-color: #46468C;
    }
```

```css
#timeEntriesListView .timeEntryItem {
    display: -ms-grid;
    -ms-grid-columns: auto 1fr 150px;
}

#timeEntriesListView .timeEntryItem-dateWorked {
    -ms-grid-column: 1;
    margin: 5px;
    width: 75px;
    height: 75px;
    text-align: center;
    background-color: #8C8CD2;
}

#timeEntriesListView .timeEntryItem-dateWorked-day {
    font-weight: bold;
}

#timeEntriesListView .timeEntryItem-projectInfo {
    -ms-grid-column: 2;
    margin: 5px;
}

#timeEntriesListView .timeEntryItem-projectName {
    font-size: 1.25em;
}

#timeEntriesListView .timeEntryItem-timeWorked {
    -ms-grid-column: 3;
    height: 100%;
    margin-left: 5px;
    margin-right: 10px;
    text-align: right;
    display: -ms-flexbox;
    -ms-flex-pack: center;
    -ms-flex-direction: column;
}

#timeEntriesListView .timeEntryItem-timeWorked-elapsed {
    font-weight: bold;
}

@media screen and (-ms-view-state: snapped) {
    .timeEntryListPage section[role=main] {
        margin-left: 20px;
        margin-right: 20px;
    }
}
```

```
@media screen and (-ms-view-state: fullscreen-portrait) {
    .timeEntryListPage section[role=main] {
        margin-left: 100px;
        margin-right: 100px;
    }
}
```

Again, there's nothing here you haven't seen before. I've merely added CSS, to display the page using the flexbox layout, and some rules, to style the various parts of timeEntryTemplate.

Getting Time-Entry Data

So far, there's still really nothing to see. If you run Clok now, you'll see an empty Time Sheets page, similar to Figure 12-5.

Figure 12-5. *Our work in progress. Nothing to see yet*

■ **Note**   In all of our code and technical discussions, I have used the term *time entry* to refer to this section of the application. However, *Time Sheets* is a more meaningful name to users. Remember: While you should use names and terminology that are meaningful to developers when communicating with developers, you should be sure to use names and terminology that are meaningful to your users in your user interface and any nontechnical documentation. The terms don't have to match, if there's a good reason for them to be different.

In Chapter 11, we added functions to storage.js to allow us to specify a filter for projects. Those functions ultimately returned a filtered and sorted list of projects to which we bound a ListView on the Projects page. Now, we are going to do something similar for time entries. Add the highlighted code in Listing 12-19 to storage.js, after the definition of timeEntries.

Listing 12-19. A Time Entry Comparer for storage.js

```
timeEntries: new WinJS.Binding.List([]),

compareTimeEntries: function (left, right) {
    // first sort by date worked...
    var dateCompare = left.dateWorked.getTime() - right.dateWorked.getTime();
    if (dateCompare !== 0) {
        return dateCompare;
    }

    // then sort by client name...
    if (left.project.clientName !== right.project.clientName) {
        return (left.project.clientName > right.project.clientName) ? 1 : -1;
    }

    // then sort by project name...
    if (left.project.name !== right.project.name) {
        return (left.project.name > right.project.name) ? 1 : -1;
    }

    return 0;
},
```

■ **Note** Comparison functions should return either -1, 0, or 1. If the two values being compared are equal, the function should return 0. If the first value should be greater, or after, the second function, return 1. If the second function is greater than the first, return -1.

In this case, we decided to use a more complex sort definition. Time entries will first be sorted by date, then by the client's name, and finally by the name of the project itself. Next, in storage.js, add the highlighted code from Listing 12-20, before the definition of timeEntries.getById.

Listing 12-20. The Time-Entry Search Function

```
storage.timeEntries.getSortedFilteredTimeEntriesAsync = function (begin, end, projectId) {
    var filtered = this
        .createFiltered(function (te) {
            if (begin) {
                if (te.dateWorked < begin) return false;
            }

            if (end) {
                if (te.dateWorked >= end.addDays(1)) return false;
            }
```

```
        if (projectId && !isNaN(projectId) && Number(projectId) > 0) {
            if (te.projectId !== Number(projectId)) return false;
        }

        if (te.project.status !== Clok.Data.ProjectStatuses.Active) return false;

        return true;
    });

    var sorted = filtered.createSorted(storage.compareTimeEntries);

    return sorted;
};

storage.timeEntries.getById = function (id) {
    if (id) {
        var matches = this.filter(function (te) { return te.id === id; });
        if (matches && matches.length === 1) {
            return matches[0];
        }
    }
    return undefined;
};
```

While we only allow users to filter a list of projects by status, it makes sense to allow them to filter time entries by date and project. So, getSortedFilteredTimeEntriesAsync accepts three parameters: begin and end, to define a date range, and projectId, to limit the list of time entries to those for a single project. For this first iteration, we won't be using those filters, and all time entries will be displayed. We'll add filtering in an upcoming section of this chapter, once we get the unfiltered list to display properly. To that end, add the highlighted code from Listing 12-21 to list.js.

Listing 12-21. Adding Aliases to Make Subsequent Code Easier to Write

```
(function () {
    "use strict";

    var data = Clok.Data;
    var storage = data.Storage;

    WinJS.UI.Pages.define("/pages/timeEntries/list.html", {
        // SNIPPED
    });
})();
```

Replace the default contents of the page definition in list.js with the code from Listing 12-22.

Listing 12-22. The Page Definition for Our First Iteration

```
ready: function (element, options) {

    this.setupListViewBinding(options);

    timeEntriesListView.winControl.layout = new WinJS.UI.ListLayout();

},
```

```
setupListViewBinding: function (options) {
    var results = storage.timeEntries.getSortedFilteredTimeEntriesAsync();

    if (results.length <= 0) {
        this.updateResultsArea(noMatchesFound);
    } else {
        this.updateResultsArea(timeEntriesListView);
    }

    timeEntriesListView.winControl.itemDataSource = results.dataSource;
},

updateResultsArea: function (div) {
    var allDivs = WinJS.Utilities.query("#timeEntriesListView, "
        + "#noMatchesFound, "
        + "#searchError, "
        + "#searchInProgress");

    allDivs.addClass("hidden");
    if (div) {
        WinJS.Utilities.removeClass(div, "hidden");
    }

    timeEntriesListView.winControl.forceLayout();
},
```

Because this is largely similar to what I've already explained in Chapters 7 and 11, I'll just quickly point out a few things. I have set the ListView control to use a ListLayout, instead of the default GridLayout. As the name suggests, the items in our ListView will be displayed in a list from top to bottom, instead of in a grid from left to right, as on the Projects page. I've also added a function named updateResultsArea, which will show or hide the ListView and the various status div elements added in Listing 12-17, by adding or removing a CSS class named hidden, which was defined in Listing 12-18. Finally, within the updateResultsArea function, I call the forceLayout method of the ListView. When a ListView is hidden, WinJS stops tracking layout information, so you should call this method whenever you change the display of a ListView. More information about forceLayout can be found on MSDN at http://msdn.microsoft.com/en-us/library/windows/apps/hh758352.aspx.

Run Clok and navigate to the Time Sheets page. You should see all of the temporary data we added earlier, in a mostly well-formatted list (see Figure 12-6). Mostly. We still have a bit more to add to format dates and times appropriately.

To fix the date and time format issues, we'll make use of binding converters again. Let's define a few converters by adding the highlighted code in Listing 12-23 to timeEntry.js.

Figure 12-6. *Needs a little work, but almost there*

Listing 12-23. Binding Converters for Dates and Times

```
var secondsToHoursConverter = WinJS.Binding.converter(function (s) {
    return (s / 3600).toFixed(2);
});

var dateToDayConverter = WinJS.Binding.converter(function (dt) {
    return formatDate("day", dt);
});

var dateToMonthConverter = WinJS.Binding.converter(function (dt) {
    return formatDate("month.abbreviated", dt);
});

var dateToYearConverter = WinJS.Binding.converter(function (dt) {
    return formatDate("year", dt);
});

var formatDate = function (format, dt) {
    var formatting = Windows.Globalization.DateTimeFormatting;
    var formatter = new formatting.DateTimeFormatter(format)
    return formatter.format(dt);
}

WinJS.Namespace.define("Clok.Data", {
    TimeEntry: timeEntryClass,
    DateToDayConverter: dateToDayConverter,
```

247

```
        DateToMonthConverter: dateToMonthConverter,
        DateToYearConverter: dateToYearConverter,
        SecondsToHoursConverter: secondsToHoursConverter,
});
```

Next, specify which converter to use for each of the data-bound elements in list.html (see highlighted code in Listing 12-24).

Listing 12-24. Using the New Converters

```
<div class="timeEntryItem">
    <div class="timeEntryItem-dateWorked">
        <h5 class="timeEntryItem-dateWorked-mon"
            data-win-bind="textContent: dateWorked Clok.Data.DateToMonthConverter"></h5>
        <h2 class="timeEntryItem-dateWorked-day"
            data-win-bind="textContent: dateWorked Clok.Data.DateToDayConverter"></h2>
        <h5 class="timeEntryItem-dateWorked-year"
            data-win-bind="textContent: dateWorked Clok.Data.DateToYearConverter"></h5>
    </div>
    <div class="timeEntryItem-projectInfo">
        <h3 class="timeEntryItem-projectName win-type-ellipsis"
            data-win-bind="textContent: project.name"></h3>
        <h6 class="timeEntryItem-clientName win-type-ellipsis"
            data-win-bind="textContent: project.clientName"></h6>
        <h6 class="timeEntryItem-projectNumber"
            data-win-bind="textContent: project.projectNumber"></h6>
    </div>
    <div class="timeEntryItem-timeWorked">
        <h2 class="timeEntryItem-timeWorked-elapsed"
            data-win-bind="textContent: elapsedSeconds Clok.Data.SecondsToHoursConverter"></h2>
        <h5>hours</h5>
    </div>
</div>
```

If you run Clok again, the list of time entries should have a slightly different format than the mock-up in Figure 12-2, but the current state in Figure 12-7 looks pretty good.

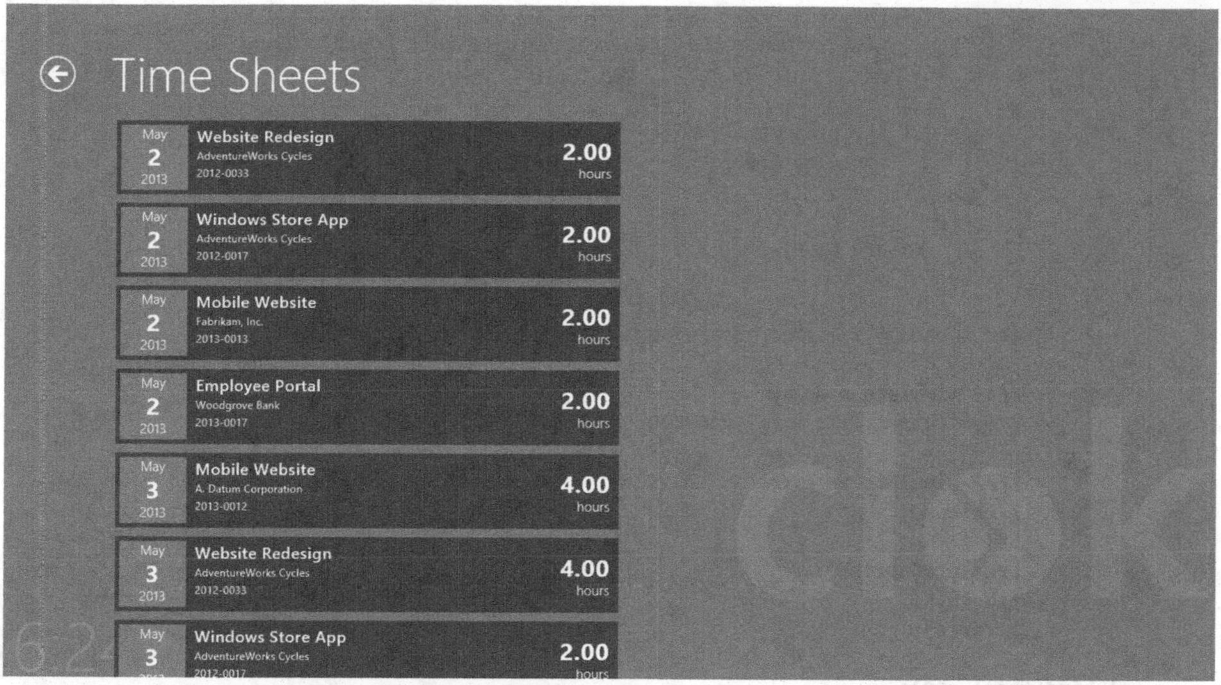

Figure 12-7. A nicely formatted list of time entries

Getting Time-Entry Data, This Time with Promises

The current state of the application works very well, as it does when filtering a few time-entry records that are already in memory. In reality, however, your application may be retrieving its data from a remote source that takes a few seconds or more to respond. We'll handle that by returning a WinJS.Promise object from the getSortedFilteredTimeEntriesAsync function. Change the getSortedFilteredTimeEntriesAsync function in storage.js, so that it matches the code in Listing 12-25, taking note of the highlighted code.

Listing 12-25. Returning a Promise

```
storage.timeEntries.getSortedFilteredTimeEntriesAsync = function (begin, end, projectId) {
    return new WinJS.Promise(function (complete, error) {
        setTimeout(function () {
            try {
                var filtered = this
                    .createFiltered(function (te) {
                        if (begin) {
                            if (te.dateWorked < begin) return false;
                        }

                        if (end) {
                            if (te.dateWorked >= end.addDays(1)) return false;
                        }
```

```
                         if (projectId && !isNaN(projectId) && Number(projectId) > 0) {
                             if (te.projectId !== Number(projectId)) return false;
                         }

                         if (te.project.status !== Clok.Data.ProjectStatuses.Active) {
                             return false;
                         }

                         return true;
                    });

                var sorted = filtered.createSorted(storage.compareTimeEntries);

                //// simulate a delay
                //for (var i = 1; i <= 50000000; i++) { }

                //// simulate an error
                //throw 0;

                complete(sorted);
            } catch (e) {
                error(e);
            }
        }.bind(this), 10);
    }.bind(this));
};

storage.timeEntries.getById = function (id) {
    // SNIPPED
};
```

The body of the method is mostly the same as it was before. I simply wrapped the previous method body in a new Promise. Instead of returning sorted, I pass sorted to the complete method provided in the Promise constructor. The call to setTimeout causes this code to return immediately and then be executed asynchronously.

The Complete Handler

You might have noticed a few commented statements in Listing 12-25. One we will use to simulate a delay obtaining the results, and the other we will use to simulate an error. For now, uncomment the simulated delay (see Listing 12-26). After working through the rest of the code in this section, you'll need to come back to this line of code and re-comment it or delete it.

Listing 12-26. Simulating a Delay

```
//// simulate a delay
for (var i = 1; i <= 50000000; i++) { }
```

■ **Note**   This is an imprecise way to simulate a delay. Depending on your computer, you may have to adjust the upper end of the loop: too small, and you won't see the progress bar; too large, and you'll become frustrated at how long you see the progress bar.

Now that the getSortedFilteredTimeEntriesAsync function returns a Promise, we have to change the way we do data binding in list.js. Update setupListViewBinding with the code from Listing 12-27.

Listing 12-27. Binding When the Promise Is Fulfilled

```
setupListViewBinding: function (options) {
    this.updateResultsArea(searchInProgress);

    storage.timeEntries.getSortedFilteredTimeEntriesAsync()
        .then(
            function complete(results) {
                if (results.length <= 0) {
                    this.updateResultsArea(noMatchesFound);
                } else {
                    this.updateResultsArea(timeEntriesListView);
                }
                timeEntriesListView.winControl.itemDataSource = results.dataSource;
            }.bind(this),
            function error(results) {
                this.updateResultsArea(searchError);
            }.bind(this)
        );
},
```

Let's walk through this version of setupListViewBinding. The first statement will display a message to the user, indicating that a search is in progress. Calling getSortedFilteredTimeEntriesAsync returns a Promise, not data, so I've handled the data binding in one of the parameters of the then method. The first parameter is the function to call when the promise has been fulfilled and results are available. If there are results, I display the ListView, and if not, I display an appropriate message to the user.

■ **Note**   In this example, I've named the two handler functions complete and error. In reality, you can name these anything that makes sense to you. The name is irrelevant. In fact, you can completely omit the name. For example, I could have written function (results) {...} instead of function complete(results) {...}. The name is there, in this case, to make it easier to understand.

Run Clok now. Assuming you have set the simulated delay to an appropriate number in Listing 12-26, you will see an "in progress" message and progress bar (see Figure 12-8) and, ultimately, the same list of time entries you saw earlier in Figure 12-7.

Figure 12-8. *Searching for time entries—a simulated delay*

At this point, we've seen the Time Sheets page in its "in progress" state and its "results found" state. Let's make a quick, temporary change, so that we can make sure the "no results found" state also works as expected. For this test, change the call to getSortedFilteredTimeEntriesAsync in list.js, so that it searches for time entries after some date in the distant future (see highlighted code in Listing 12-28).

Listing 12-28. Specify a Value for the Begin Parameter to Some Date in the Distant Future

```
storage.timeEntries.getSortedFilteredTimeEntriesAsync(new Date("1/1/2500"))
```

The Promise object returned from getSortedFilteredTimeEntriesAsync will still be fulfilled and will complete successfully. However, because we didn't define any entries that far in advance in our temporary data, no results will be found (see Figure 12-9).

Figure 12-9. *No time entries were found after 1/1/2500*

The Error Handler

So far, so good. The only case we haven't yet handled is when the `Promise` object that is returned from `getSortedFilteredTimeEntriesAsync` is in the error state. Because you no longer have to simulate delays when retrieving time-entry data, you can now delete, or re-comment, the code in Listing 12-26. Also, be sure to undo the change made in Listing 12-28, to test returning a promise with no results found. Now, we want to simulate an error, so switch back to `storage.js` and uncomment the code in Listing 12-29.

Listing 12-29. Simulating an Error

```
//// simulate an error
throw 0;
```

Now, when you run Clok, the error handler defined in Listing 12-27 will get called, instead of the `complete` handler. In Clok, we simply display a friendly message to the user (see Figure 12-10). In other applications, we might use this to log the error or report info about the error back to our development team.

Figure 12-10. *There was an error*

At this point you've implemented code that handles all of the possible various states the Time Sheets page might be in: searching, results were found and displayed, no results were found, and error states. Go ahead and delete, or re-comment, the code in Listing 12-29, because there is no longer a need to simulate an error.

Filtering Time Entries

I've already mentioned that `getSortedFilteredTimeEntriesAsync` can filter time entries by date or project. In fact, we used this feature in Listing 12-28 to do some testing. Now it's time to add features to Clok, so that the user can filter time entries in a meaningful manner. In this section, we'll give the user two ways to filter the data. First, we'll add a button to the Project Detail page, to see time entries for the selected project. Then, we'll add some filtering controls to the Time Sheets page, so the user can specify a date range or a project when viewing time entries.

Filtering from Project Detail

You may have wondered why I was passing the page's `options` parameter to the `setupListViewBinding` function in Listing 12-27. When we navigate to the Time Sheets page from the Project Detail page, the currently selected project must be provided, and it will be passed along in this `options` object. Before we modify the Project Detail page, let's make some needed changes to the `list.js` file in the `timeEntries` folder. Make the changes highlighted in Listing 12-30 to `list.js`.

Listing 12-30. Changes to list.js

```
setupListViewBinding: function (options) {
    this.filter = WinJS.Binding.as({
        startDate: (options && options.startDate) || (new Date()).addMonths(-1),
        endDate: (options && options.endDate) || new Date().removeTimePart(),
        projectId: (options&& options.projectId) || -1
    });

    this.filter.bind("startDate", this.filter_changed.bind(this));
    this.filter.bind("endDate", this.filter_changed.bind(this));
    this.filter.bind("projectId", this.filter_changed.bind(this));
},

filter_changed: function (e) {
    this.updateResultsArea(searchInProgress);

    storage.timeEntries.getSortedFilteredTimeEntriesAsync(
            this.filter.startDate,
            this.filter.endDate,
            this.filter.projectId)
        .then(
            function complete(results) {
                if (results.length <= 0) {
                    this.updateResultsArea(noMatchesFound);
                } else {
                    this.updateResultsArea(timeEntriesListView);
                }
                timeEntriesListView.winControl.itemDataSource = results.dataSource;
            }.bind(this),
            function error(results) {
                this.updateResultsArea(searchError);
            }.bind(this)
        );
},
```

This code specifies a new definition for setupListViewBinding, which declares an observable filter property. Also, the previous definition for the setupListViewBinding function has moved to a new handler function named filter_changed. This is very similar to what we did in Chapter 11 for filtering projects. The difference is that on this page, the filter observable object has three properties that could change: startDate, endDate, and projectId. When any one of those properties changes, the new filter_changed function is called, and a new set of time entries is retrieved. The only difference between the new filter_changed function and the previous setupListViewBinding function is that the various filter properties are provided as parameters in the call to getSortedFilteredTimeEntriesAsync.

■ **Note** If I didn't already know the requirements for functionality that we'll be adding in the next section, the code in Listing 12-30 could have been a little simpler. However, because we will take advantage of all of these changes in the next section, I added them now.

So, our Time Sheets page is now configured to support filtering from various locations within Clok. Now we just have to add the functionality to allow the user to request a filtered list of time entries. Open the detail.html file in the projects folder and add the highlighted code from Listing 12-31 inside projectDetailAppBar.

Listing 12-31. *Adding a Time Sheet Button to the App Bar*

```html
<div id="projectDetailAppBar"
     class="win-ui-dark"
     data-win-control="WinJS.UI.AppBar"
     data-win-options="{ sticky: true }">

    <!-- SNIPPED -->
    <hr
        data-win-control="WinJS.UI.AppBarCommand"
        data-win-options="{type:'separator',section:'selection'}" />
    <button
        data-win-control="WinJS.UI.AppBarCommand"
        data-win-options="{
            id:'goToTimeEntriesCommand',
            label:'Time Sheet',
            icon:'url(/images/Timesheet-small-sprites.png)',

            section:'selection',
            tooltip:'Time Entries',
            disabled: true}">
    </button>
</div>
```

Notice that I specified the path to an image for the icon property of this new AppBarCommand. In addition to all of the icons defined in the WinJS.UI.AppBarIcon enumeration, AppBarCommand objects can use custom images. For Clok, I created a specially formatted image named Timesheet-small-sprites.png (see Figure 12-11).

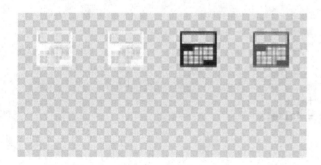

Figure 12-11. *Image used for AppBarCommand icon*

This image has a transparent background and consists of two rows, each with four versions of the icon. The first row is used when the AppBarCommand is in its normal state, and the second row is used when it is in its toggled state. Because this AppBarCommand doesn't require a toggled state, I didn't bother to create the images in the second row. Each icon is 40×40 pixels, making the entire image 160×80. From left to right, the four images on each row are used for the default state of the button, the hover state, the active state (when it is being clicked), and the disabled state.

Because WinJS automatically adds the ring around the image, only the icon itself is required. Documentation for the AppBarCommand.icon property is available on MSDN at http://msdn.microsoft.com/en-us/library/windows/apps/ hh700483.aspx. Additionally, I found this blog article particularly helpful when I was first researching this: http://blogs.msdn.com/b/shawnste/archive/2012/06/16/custom-appbar-sprite-icons-for-your-windows-8- metro-style-html-app.aspx.

The last step is to wire up goToTimeEntriesCommand in detail.js. Update detail.js with the highlighted code from Listing 12-32.

Listing 12-32. Wiring Up the New AppBarCommand

```
ready: function (element, options) {
    // SNIPPED
    saveProjectCommand.onclick = this.saveProjectCommand_click.bind(this);
    deleteProjectCommand.onclick = this.deleteProjectCommand_click.bind(this);
    goToTimeEntriesCommand.onclick = this.goToTimeEntriesCommand_click.bind(this);
},

// SNIPPED

deleteProjectCommand_click: function (e) {
    storage.projects.delete(this.currProject);
    WinJS.Navigation.back();
},

goToTimeEntriesCommand_click: function (e) {
    if (this.currProject && this.currProject.id) {
        WinJS.Navigation.navigate("/pages/timeEntries/list.html",
            { projectId: this.currProject.id });
    }
},

// SNIPPED

configureAppBar: function (existingId) {

    // SNIPPED

    if (existingId) {
        deleteProjectCommand.winControl.disabled = false;
        goToTimeEntriesCommand.winControl.disabled = false;
    }
},

// SNIPPED
```

We're finally ready to test these changes. Run Clok now and go to the Project Detail page for an existing project. If you look at the app bar, you should see that the Time Sheet command is enabled (see Figure 12-12).

Figure 12-12. *New AppBarCommand on the Project Detail page*

The code we added in Listing 12-31 and Listing 12-32 will cause this button to be disabled when adding a new project, and it will be enabled when viewing details of an existing project. As you probably expect, clicking the new button will navigate to the Time Sheets page, supplying the `projectId` for the currently selected project as the navigation option (see Figure 12-13).

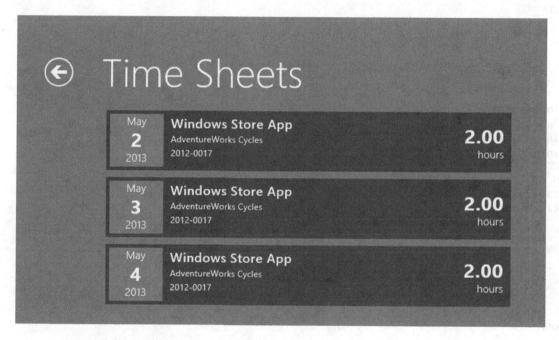

Figure 12-13. *Time entries for the selected project*

Filtering with the App Bar

It's pretty handy to be able to see a list of time entries for a single project. As a Clok user, I can see myself using that functionality fairly often. However, there's currently no way to filter the list of time entries by date, and in order to see entries for a different project, you have to navigate back to the Projects page, select a different project from the list, and then click the Time Sheet button. It's good functionality, but it's not enough. We must add a way to filter the time entries on the Time Sheets page itself. Add the code in Listing 12-33 after the opening body element in `list.html`.

Listing 12-33. Adding an App Bar and a Flyout

```html
<div id="filterFlyout"
    data-win-control="WinJS.UI.Flyout">

    <label for="filterStartDate">From</label><br />
    <div id="filterStartDate" data-win-control="WinJS.UI.DatePicker"></div>

    <br />

    <label for="filterEndDate">To</label><br />
    <div id="filterEndDate" data-win-control="WinJS.UI.DatePicker"></div>

    <hr />

    <label for="filterProjectId">Project</label><br />
    <select id="filterProjectId">
        <option value="-1">All projects</option>
    </select>

    <br />

    <button id="clearFilterButton">&#xe106; Clear Filter</button>
</div>

<div id="timeEntryAppBar"
    class="win-ui-dark"
    data-win-control="WinJS.UI.AppBar"
    data-win-options="{ sticky: true }">

    <button
        data-win-control="WinJS.UI.AppBarCommand"
        data-win-options="{
            id:'filterTimeEntriesCommand',
            label:'Filter',
            icon:'filter',
            type: 'flyout',
            flyout: 'filterFlyout',
            section:'global',
            tooltip:'Filter'}">
    </button>
</div>
```

I've added an AppBar to the Time Sheets page, and it contains a Filter button. Clicking the Filter button will open a flyout with a few options for filtering the time entries shown in the ListView. Now, add the simple CSS in Listing 12-34 to list.css.

Listing 12-34. Styling the Clear Filter Button

```css
#clearFilterButton {
    border: 0px;
    background-color: transparent;
    float: right;
}

    #clearFilterButton:active {
        color: #666666;
    }
```

With these controls in place, their initial values have to be set to match the current value of filter. Additionally, we have to update filter when the value of any of these controls is changed. Both of those tasks will be accomplished by adding the highlighted code in Listing 12-35 to the setupListViewBinding function in list.js.

Listing 12-35. Wiring Up the Controls Used for Filtering

```javascript
setupListViewBinding: function (options) {
    this.filter = WinJS.Binding.as({
        startDate: (options && options.startDate) || (new Date()).addMonths(-1),
        endDate: (options && options.endDate) || new Date().removeTimePart(),
        projectId: (options && options.projectId) || -1
    });

    this.filter.bind("startDate", this.filter_changed.bind(this));
    this.filter.bind("endDate", this.filter_changed.bind(this));
    this.filter.bind("projectId", this.filter_changed.bind(this));

    filterStartDate.winControl.current = this.filter.startDate;
    filterEndDate.winControl.current = this.filter.endDate;
    filterProjectId.value = this.filter.projectId;

    filterStartDate.winControl.onchange = this.filterStartDate_change.bind(this);
    filterEndDate.winControl.onchange = this.filterEndDate_change.bind(this);
    filterProjectId.onchange = this.filterProjectId_change.bind(this);
    clearFilterButton.onclick = this.clearFilterButton_click.bind(this);
},
```

Next, we must define the event handlers referenced in Listing 12-35. Additionally, we have to populate the Project filter drop-down list with the currently active projects, much like the drop-down list on the Clok dashboard screen. After the definition of filter_changed, add the new event handlers and the new bindListOfProjects function, as shown in Listing 12-36.

Listing 12-36. New Functions in list.js

```javascript
filter_changed: function (e) {
    // SNIPPED
},

filterStartDate_change: function (e) {
    this.filter.startDate = filterStartDate.winControl.current;
},
```

```
filterEndDate_change: function (e) {
    this.filter.endDate = filterEndDate.winControl.current;
},

filterProjectId_change: function (e) {
    this.filter.projectId = filterProjectId.value;
},

clearFilterButton_click: function (e) {
    filterStartDate.winControl.current = new Date().addMonths(-1);
    filterEndDate.winControl.current = new Date().removeTimePart();
    filterProjectId.value = -1;

    this.filterStartDate_change();
    this.filterEndDate_change();
    this.filterProjectId_change();
},

bindListOfProjects: function (selectControl) {
    selectControl.options.length = 1;

    var activeProjects = storage.projects.filter(function (p) {
        return p.status === Clok.Data.ProjectStatuses.Active;
    });

    activeProjects.forEach(function (item) {
        var option = document.createElement("option");
        option.text = item.name + " (" + item.projectNumber + ")";
        option.title = item.clientName;
        option.value = item.id;
        selectControl.appendChild(option);
    });
},
```

When any one of the filter controls is changed, the corresponding property on the current filter object is set, which will trigger the filter_change method. Clicking the Clear Filter button simply resets the filter controls to default values and updates the current filter object. The bindListOfProjects function is almost identical to the function of the same name in home.js. The only difference is that a drop-down list control is provided as a parameter to the function, which allows bindListOfProjects to be reused when implementing the functionality to edit existing time entries, which can be seen in the source code that accompanies this book. The final change needed is to call the bindListOfProjects function in the ready function. Add the highlighted code in Listing 12-37 to the ready function in list.js.

Listing 12-37. Adding Projects to filterProjectId

```
ready: function (element, options) {

    this.bindListOfProjects(filterProjectId);

    this.setupListViewBinding(options);

    timeEntriesListView.winControl.layout = new WinJS.UI.ListLayout();

},
```

With that, you now have a fully functional filter on the Time Sheets page. Run Clok and try it out. Select different dates, select a project, and click the Clear Filter button. As soon as you make a change to one of the filter controls, the ListView is immediately updated with matching results (see Figure 12-14).

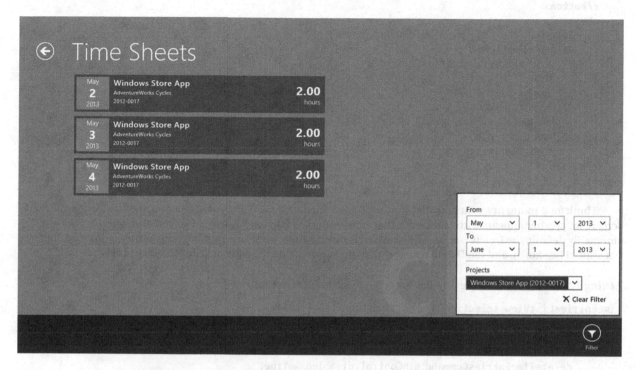

Figure 12-14. *The filter flyout in use on the Time Sheets page*

Deleting Time Entries

We can create, and we can read, time entries; we've implemented half of the CRUD operations. Let's give the user the ability to delete now. Back in Listing 12-17, we configured the ListView to support multiple selections. We're going to take advantage of that in this section by allowing the user to select one or more time entries to delete. Let's start by adding a Delete button to the app bar. Add the highlighted code from Listing 12-38 within the timeEntryAppBar control in list.html.

Listing 12-38. Adding a Delete Button to the App Bar

```
<div id="timeEntryAppBar"
    class="win-ui-dark"
    data-win-control="WinJS.UI.AppBar"
    data-win-options="{ sticky: true }">

    <button
        data-win-control="WinJS.UI.AppBarCommand"
        data-win-options="{
            id:'deleteTimeEntriesCommand',
            label:'Delete',
            icon:'delete',
```

```
            section:'selection',
            tooltip:'Delete',
            disabled: true}">
    </button>
    <button
        data-win-control="WinJS.UI.AppBarCommand"
        data-win-options="{
            id:'filterTimeEntriesCommand',
            label:'Filter',
            icon:'filter',
            type: 'flyout',
            flyout: 'filterFlyout',
            section:'global',
            tooltip:'Filter'}">
    </button>
</div>
```

Think for a moment about how the Windows 8 Start screen works. When you select one or more tiles on the Start screen, an app bar appears with commands that are appropriate for your selection. Our requirements for Clok are similar. By default, the Delete button we just added is disabled, but when one or more time entries is selected, the app bar should be shown, and the Delete button should be enabled. Add the code in Listing 12-39 to list.js.

Listing 12-39. Configuring the App Bar, Based on the Current Selection

```
timeEntriesListView_selectionChanged: function (e) {
    var selectionCount = timeEntriesListView.winControl.selection.count();

    if (selectionCount <= 0) {
        deleteTimeEntriesCommand.winControl.disabled = true;
        timeEntryAppBar.winControl.hide();
    } else {
        deleteTimeEntriesCommand.winControl.disabled = false;
        timeEntryAppBar.winControl.show();
    }
},
```

Every time the user selects or deselects items in the ListView, this function will check how many items are currently selected. If one or more items are selected, the app bar will be shown with the Delete button enabled (see Figure 12-15).

Figure 12-15. *Any selections cause the app bar to display and the Delete button to be enabled*

When the user clicks the Delete button, we, of course, want to delete the time entries from the list. Before we define a `delete` function in the `Storage` class, let's look at the function that will execute when the user clicks the Delete button. Add the code from Listing 12-40 to `list.js`.

Listing 12-40. Handling the Delete Button Click

```
deleteTimeEntriesCommand_click: function (e) {
    timeEntriesListView.winControl.selection.getItems()
        .then(function complete(selectedItems) {
            var deletePromises = selectedItems.map(function (item) {
                return storage.timeEntries.delete(item.data);
            });

            return WinJS.Promise.join(deletePromises);
        })
        .then(null, function error(result) {
            new Windows.UI.Popups
                .MessageDialog("Could not delete all selected records.", "An error occurred. ")
                .showAsync();
        });
},
```

The ListView class has a selection property, which in turn has a getItems function for identifying which items in the ListView are currently selected. The getItems function doesn't actually return the items that are selected, however. Instead, it returns a Promise object. When that promise completes, its then method is called, and the selected items are passed as a parameter to the complete function—the first parameter of then. The delete function we are going to add to the Storage class will also return a Promise (we'll define that shortly), and, using the map method, the user's selection is mapped to an array of Promise objects representing delete operations. The first then call returns a new Promise created from that array with the join method. A Promise created from join is fulfilled when all of the input Promise objects are fulfilled. If all of the selected time entries are successfully deleted, the second then function doesn't do anything, because it doesn't have a complete function (the first parameter is null). However, if there are any errors, a message is displayed to the user.

Add the highlighted code in Listing 12-41 to the ready function in list.js to wire up the timeEntriesListView_selectionChanged and deleteTimeEntriesCommand_click handlers.

Listing 12-41. Wiring Up the Event Handlers

```
ready: function (element, options) {

    this.bindListOfProjects(filterProjectId);

    this.setupListViewBinding(options);

    timeEntriesListView.winControl.onselectionchanged =
        this.timeEntriesListView_selectionChanged.bind(this);
    timeEntriesListView.winControl.layout = new WinJS.UI.ListLayout();

    deleteTimeEntriesCommand.winControl.onclick =
        this.deleteTimeEntriesCommand_click.bind(this);
},
```

Now, we need to define the delete function in the Storage class. Add the code in Listing 12-42 to storage.js after the definition for storage.timeEntries.save.

Listing 12-42. A Delete Function for Time Entries

```
storage.timeEntries.delete = function (te) {
    var canceled = false;

    var delPromise = new WinJS.Promise(function (complete, error) {
        setTimeout(function () {
            try {
                if (te && te.id) {
                    var index = this.indexOf(te);
                    if (!canceled && index >= 0) {
                        this.splice(index, 1);
                    }
                }
                complete();
            } catch (e) {
                error(e);
            }
        }.bind(this), 100);
    }.bind(this),
```

```
    function oncancel(arg) {
        canceled = true;
    }.bind(this));

    return WinJS.Promise.timeout(20, delPromise);
};
```

Granted, in our simple case, where we are using in-memory data, this code is overkill. We could remove everything aside from the highlighted code and call it a day. There are two reasons, however, that I'm not going to do it that way. First, we're not always going to be using in-memory data like this. Second, and more important, I'm writing a chapter about promises, so I had to create an example to illustrate creating a Promise and canceling it.

Let's walk through the code in Listing 12-42. I've created a new Promise, which, after a 100 millisecond delay defined in setTimeout, does the work of actually deleting the data, assuming the canceled variable is still false. If this succeeds, the complete method is called, which signals success back to our code in Listing 12-40. If there are any errors, the Promise is put into an error state, ultimately causing the dialog to display to the user. In this example, I've included a second parameter to the Promise constructor. The oncancel function is called if the Promise needs to cancel any remaining work for some reason.

There are two ways to use the WinJS.Promise.timeout function. The first is when only the first parameter is supplied, and that parameter is numeric. In this case, a successfully completed Promise is returned after the specified delay. The second version of WinJS.Promise.timeout, which I have used in Listing 12-42, takes two parameters. The first is still a number, and the second is another Promise. If the Promise does not complete before the specified number of milliseconds has passed, the Promise is canceled. In this case, I am canceling the Promise, which deletes the data after 20 milliseconds. Because there is a 100 millisecond delay before that Promise begins to execute, it will be canceled every time. Run Clok and select some time entries, then click the Delete button. Because the timeout happens before the Promise executes, the Promise is canceled, which is captured as an error. Then, a message is displayed to the user (see Figure 12-16).

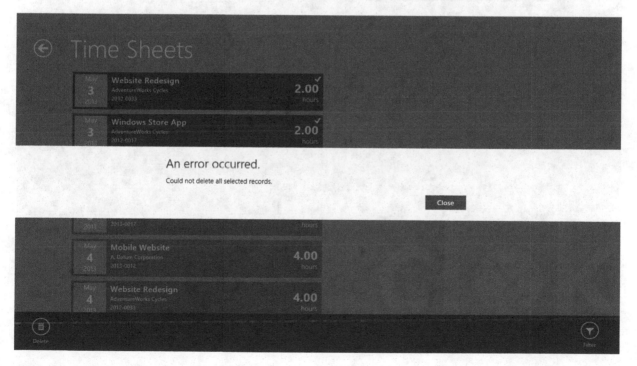

Figure 12-16. *An error message informing the user that the delete operation failed*

I hope it's clear that this forced failure is only for the purpose of showing how this works. It's good to have code in our delete function, to handle the case where the Promise needs to be canceled, and it's good to have code in our Delete button's click handler, to do something intelligent in case of an error. It might be a good practice to have a timeout on code that is dependent on external resources that might legitimately have to be canceled if it takes too long to execute. However, it's not very practical to have a WinJS.Promise.timeout cancel the delete operation before it has had a chance to execute. So, update the delete function in storage.js with the highlighted code from Listing 12-43.

Listing 12-43. The Updated Delete Function

```
storage.timeEntries.delete = function (te) {
    // SNIPPED

    return delPromise;
};
```

Now that this function returns the uncanceled Promise, you can run Clok and delete some time entries. You should be able to delete as many as you wish, either one at a time or several at once (see Figure 12-17). You can select multiple items by swiping on a touch display or right-clicking with a mouse.

Figure 12-17. All but one time entry has been deleted

■ **Note** Although it is not covered in this book, functionality to edit an existing time entry is included in the source code that accompanies the book.

Conclusion

This was another chapter that covered a lot of code. In the process of adding the ability to add, view, and delete time entries, I introduced a few different ways to take advantage of the WinJS.Promise class, to allow your application to remain responsive while waiting for asynchronous operations to complete. When saving new time entries from the Clok dashboard screen, I covered how to coordinate two different promises and execute some code, once both promises had been fulfilled, using the join function. In the process of viewing and filtering time entries, I covered how to create your own Promise object to execute some code asynchronously, return that Promise, and handle the various possible states in which the Promise might be. I also covered how to define a Promise that supports being canceled and how to use Promise.timeout to cancel a Promise that hasn't responded quickly enough. Promises can provide a nice syntax for working with the results of asynchronous code. In the next chapter, I'll introduce web workers, which will allow you to run multi-threaded asynchronous code.

CHAPTER 13

▪▪▪

Web Workers

In Chapter 12, I introduced promises as a way to handle values returned from asynchronous operations. While promises offer a lot of flexibility in how you do async work, I pointed out that *asynchronous* does not imply multiple threads. JavaScript applications execute in a single-threaded environment. *Asynchronous* does not mean "do two things at the same time." Instead, it means "do this thing later, and let me know what happened when it's done." That said, applications executing on multiple threads have several advantages, such as taking advantage of multiple processors to perform a task more quickly or to perform some work in the background, while the user can continue to use other parts of the application.

So, what are our options as we develop Windows Store applications? Well, we could write portions of our applications as WinRT components in C# or C++, which support threading. In fact, this article on MSDN discusses that option: http://msdn.microsoft.com/en-us/library/windows/apps/hh779077.aspx. I won't cover that detail in this book, although I will introduce building WinRT components with C# in Chapter 18. Not a C# or C++ developer? Fortunately, HTML5 offers Web Workers as a new option.

Web Workers

A worker (or, more officially, a Web Worker) is a JavaScript script that runs in the background. Workers are a feature of HTML5 and are not specific to building Windows Store applications with HTML and JavaScript. If you've worked with workers in a web-development project, then you can probably skip this chapter. If you aren't familiar with workers yet, then this chapter will provide a basic introduction, starting with Listing 13-1, which shows the code needed to create a worker.

Listing 13-1. Creating an Instace of a Web Worker

```
var myWorker = new Worker("/path/to/worker/script.js");
```

Workers run on a separate thread. JavaScript is a single-threaded environment, however, so each worker is executed within its own environment. As a result, a worker does not have access to any objects on the main UI thread, such as the document object. It cannot manipulate the DOM. It cannot change the value of a JavaScript variable on your page. It is completely isolated in its own environment.

This is great for thread safety. You never have to worry about conflicts because two workers changed the same variable. You don't have race conditions—two or more threads that will cause unexpected results if they don't complete in the correct order—to deal with. You don't have to lock anything. You don't have to worry about many of the concepts that make multi-threaded development challenging in other programming environments. That said, how useful is a script that can't change anything on the main thread? Sure, it could be helpful in some situations where you want to "fire and forget," but to make practical use of them, it would be nice if there were some way to affect your main thread from the worker thread.

That's where messages come in. While a worker thread cannot change anything on the main thread, and vice versa actually, messages can be passed from one thread to another. Listing 13-2 contains an example of how you might configure your main thread to communicate with the worker thread.

269

Listing 13-2. Passing Messages Between the Main Thread and the Worker Thread

```
myWorker.onmessage = function(e) {
    var messageFromWorker = e.data;
    // do something with the message
};

// send a message to the worker thread
myWorker.postMessage(messageToWorker);
```

On the other side of this process, in the worker thread, there is a similar `onmessage` event and `postMessage` method (see Listing 13-3).

Listing 13-3. Handling and Sending Messages from the Worker Thread

```
self.onmessage = function (e) {
    processTheData(e.data);
};

self.postMessage(responseMessage);
```

Although we now have two JavaScript environments, each executing its own script, each of those environments is still single-threaded. Confused? I'll use an analogy to explain what's going on.

Imagine that you and I are both working on the same team at work, except that I am working in a different building, and we never see each other or speak to each other in person. The only way we communicate in this fictional scenario is by sending notes to each other via inter-office messenger. When you need something from me, you give the messenger a note (call `worker.postMessage`). He or she leaves it on my desk, and whenever I can get to it, I take it (`self.onmessage`) and start doing the work you requested in your message. When I'm done, I ask the messenger to deliver the results back to you (`self.postMessage`). You complete the cycle when you see the results (`worker.onmessage`) and decide what you want to do with them. As long as we can agree on how to write notes in a way that the other person can understand, we can each do our own job (each in a single-threaded environment) without getting in the other's way.

Graphing Time Entries

In Chapter 12, we added features to Clok that allow users to enter the time that they worked on a project. It would be helpful if users could see a graph illustrating how much time they spent working for each client. I'm going to show you how to implement that with Web Workers in this chapter, using an open-source graphing library called Flotr2 (`www.humblesoftware.com/flotr2/`).

■ **Note** The Web Hypertext Application Technology Working Group (WHATWG), the group responsible for development of the HTML specification, including Web Workers, has offered some guidance regarding workers. It says that workers are "relatively heavy-weight" and are "expected to be long-lived." While our graphing example will illustrate how a developer can take advantage of workers, it is not the ideal-use case for workers, because the process is actually pretty quick. Read the WHATWG HTML specification online at `www.whatwg.org/specs/web-apps/current-work/multipage/workers.html`.

Before we start, let's identify a few requirements for our time-entry graph:

- A bar graph should be created to represent time entries. It should be displayed on its own page, linked from the Time Sheets page.

- Any filter applied to the Time Sheets page should be applied to the graph as well.

- Data points for the graph should be grouped by client. That is, if the user worked on multiple projects for the same client, the hours worked on those projects would be combined into a single bar on the graph.

Starting Without Web Workers

In the timeEntries folder, add a new page control named graph.html. As the name suggests, this is the page that will display the graph you will be adding. The first iteration of developing this feature will focus on getting a correctly formatted test graph to display on the page. We'll start with the graph data hard-coded directly in the JavaScript file of the page control.

The Flotr2 graphing library will generate a graph on a canvas element that it dynamically creates. We have only to supply a placeholder on our page that will contain this new canvas element. Modify the body element of graph.html with the highlighted code in Listing 13-4.

Listing 13-4. Adding a Container for the Graph

```
<body>
    <div class="graph fragment">
        <header aria-label="Header content" role="banner">
            <button class="win-backbutton" aria-label="Back" disabled type="button"></button>
            <h1 class="titlearea win-type-ellipsis">
                <span class="pagetitle">Time Entries</span>
            </h1>
        </header>
        <section aria-label="Main content" role="main">
            <div id="graphcontainer"></div>
        </section>
    </div>
</body>
```

Next, make changes to graph.css, as highlighted in Listing 13-5. These rules will cause the graph rendered by Flotr2 to display in the center of the page.

Listing 13-5. CSS Changes

```
.graph section[role=main] {
    /* remove the CSS properties that were added to this rule by default */
}

#graphcontainer {
    width: 70vw;
    height: 70vh;
    margin: 8px auto;
}
```

271

The Flotr2 project is pretty extensive, but I'll only cover as much of it as is required to accomplish our goal for this chapter. Please visit the project's web site (www.humblesoftware.com/flotr2/) to get acquainted with the functionality it provides. After scanning the documentation and reviewing some of the examples, download the JavaScript file named flotr2.js. Alternatively, because the Flotr2 creators have released it with a permissive open source license, you can find a copy in the source code that is available with this book. (See the Source Code/Downloads tab of the book's Apress product page [www.apress.com/9781430257790].) Once you have a copy of the file, place flotr2.js in the path specified in Listing 13-6, then add that JavaScript reference to graph.html.

Listing 13-6. Referencing the Graphing Library

```
<head>
    <!-- SNIPPED -->
    <script type="text/javascript" src="/js/lib/flotr2/flotr2.js"></script>
</head>
```

I mentioned earlier that we will be building the first iteration of our graphing functionality with hard-coded data. In fact, our test graph is based on the Flotr2 stacked bar chart example. Add the code from Listing 13-7 to the ready function of graph.js.

Listing 13-7. Generating Test Data and Displaying the Graph

```
var d1=[], d2=[], d3=[], graph, i;

for (i=-10; i<10; i++) {
    d1.push([i, Math.random()]);
    d2.push([i, Math.random()]);
    d3.push([i, Math.random()]);
}

var graphdata=[
    { data: d1, label: 'Series 1' },
    { data: d2, label: 'Series 2' },
    { data: d3, label: 'Series 3' }
];

var graphoptions={
    bars: {
        show: true,
        stacked: true,
        horizontal: false,
        barWidth: 0.6,
        lineWidth: 1,
        shadowSize: 0
    },
    legend: {
        position: "ne",
        backgroundColor: "#fff",
        labelBoxMargin: 10,
    },
    grid: {
        color: "#000",
        tickColor: "#eee",
```

```
        backgroundColor: {
            colors: [[0, "#ddf"], [1, "#cce"]],
            start: "top",
            end: "bottom"
        },
        verticalLines: true,
        minorVerticalLines: true,
        horizontalLines: true,
        minorHorizontalLines: true,
    },
    xaxis: {
        color: "#fff",
    },
    yaxis: {
        color: "#fff",
    },
    HtmlText: true
};
```

graph = Flotr.draw(graphcontainer, graphdata, graphoptions);

I won't go through all of this code in detail, because the Flotr2 documentation covers much of it. I do want to quickly cover the highlighted code statements. The code creates three data series: d1, d2, and d3. To each of these it adds random data points. Note, however, that this is not the data object that gets passed to the draw method. Instead, each of these series is wrapped as the data property of an object that contains a label property, which will be displayed in the graph's legend. Flotr2 supports setting additional properties on this object, but we're only taking advantage of the label property. An array of wrapper objects, named graphdata, is passed to the draw method, along with a reference to the graphcontainer div we added to graph.html in Listing 13-4. The graphoptions object sets a number of display properties for our graph, and these are documented on the Flotr2 web site.

Adding a navigation option to the Time Sheets page is the last thing needed before the graph page can be loaded. I've done this with a new button on the app bar. Following the same pattern used in Listing 12-31 and Figure 12-11, where you added a Time Sheet button to the app bar of the Project Detail screen, create a new sprite-based AppBarCommand on the Time Sheets page (see Figure 13-1).

Figure 13-1. New Graph button on the Time Sheets app bar

■ **Note** If you'd rather not create your own image, you can use the version that I created. You'll find it in the source code that accompanies this book. (See the Source Code/Downloads tab of the book's Apress product page [www.apress.com/9781430257790].)

Of course, this button needs a handler defined for its click event. Add the code from Listing 13-8 in list.js. Be sure to wire this function to the click event in the ready function as well.

Listing 13-8. Click Handler, Passing the Current Filter to the Graph Page

```
graphTimeEntriesCommand_click: function (e) {
    WinJS.Navigation.navigate("/pages/timeEntries/graph.html", {
        filter: this.filter,
    });
},
```

■ **Note** If you forget how to wire the click event to this handler, refer to Listing 12-32 for an example.

Although we won't be using it in this section, we are passing the user's current Time Sheets filter along to graph.html. This will ensure that whatever time entries the user was reviewing on the Time Sheets page will be included in the graph. I'll show you how to make this work later in this chapter. In the meantime, you should have a working test graph. Run Clok and click the Graph button on the Time Sheets app bar to see how it looks (see Figure 13-2).

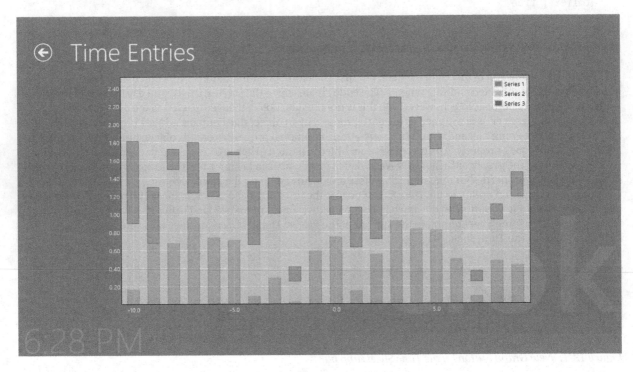

Figure 13-2. *Our first graph*

Thanks to the hard work of some open-source developers, we have a pretty slick-looking graph, without a lot of code. Next, let's see how we can introduce a Web Worker into this feature.

Returning Graph Data from a Web Worker

Our ultimate goal is to use a worker to calculate the data points the graph should display, based on the filters selected on the Time Sheets page. In this section, we'll continue to work with hard-coded data, but we'll move that logic to generate data to a worker.

Create a folder named workers in the js folder of your Visual Studio project. Select the Dedicated Worker file type and add a worker named timeGraphWorker.js to the workers folder (see Figure 13-3).

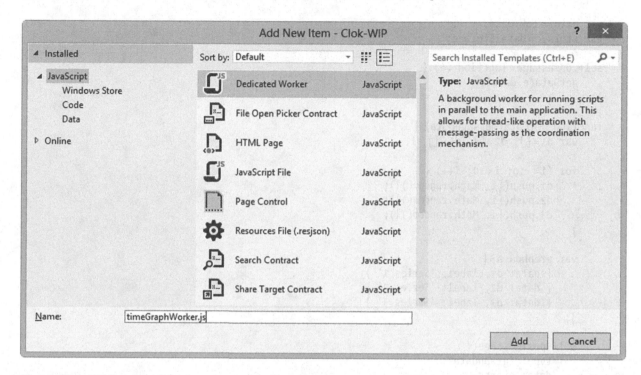

Figure 13-3. Adding a worker

■ **Note** It is worth noting that the HTML5 specification defines a Dedicated Web Worker and a Shared Web Worker. Shared workers provide a way for multiple scripts to connect to the same worker. However, shared workers are not supported in Windows Store applications. I'll only cover dedicated workers here. If you are doing web development targetting the limited set of browsers that support shared workers, you'll find more information online.

Delete the default code in your worker and replace it with the code in Listing 13-9.

Listing 13-9. First Draft of Our Worker

```
/// <reference group="Dedicated Worker" />

importScripts(
    "//Microsoft.WinJS.1.0/js/base.js",
    "/js/extensions.js",
    "/js/utilities.js",
```

```
    "/data/project.js",
    "/data/timeEntry.js",
    "/data/storage.js"
    );

(function () {
    "use strict";

    var data = Clok.Data;
    var storage = data.Storage;

    self.onmessage = function (e) {
        getData(e.data);
    };

    function getData(messageData) {
        var d1 = [], d2 = [], d3 = [], i;

        for (i = -10; i < 10; i++) {
            d1.push([i, Math.random()]);
            d2.push([i, Math.random()]);
            d3.push([i, Math.random()]);
        }

        var graphdata = [
            { data: d1, label: 'Series 1' },
            { data: d2, label: 'Series 2' },
            { data: d3, label: 'Series 3' }
        ];

        self.postMessage({
            type: "graphdata",
            data: graphdata
        });
    }
})();
```

The first thing this script does is import a number of other scripts. Because workers run in their own environment, the scripts included in the head element of the graph.html page or the default.html page are not available in the worker. You can use the importScripts function to reference the files we need. When this worker receives a message in the onmessage handler, the getData function is called. Ultimately, the messageData parameter will be the filter object from the Time Sheets page, but I won't cover that until the next section. Within getData, the same code I introduced in Listing 13-7 is used to create a graphdata object, which is then passed back to the main thread using postMessage.

But none of that happens until the worker receives a message from the main thread. Listing 13-10 contains a new definition for the ready function, as well as a helper function for formatting dates. Add both of these functions to graph.js.

Listing 13-10. Creating a Worker Thread and Communicating with It

```
ready: function (element, options) {
    var timeGraphWorker=new Worker("/js/workers/timeGraphWorker.js");

    timeGraphWorker.onmessage=function getGraphData(e) {
        var message=e.data;

        if (message && message.type === "graphdata") {
            var graphoptions={
                bars: {
                    show: true,
                    stacked: true,
                    horizontal: false,
                    barWidth: 0.6,
                    lineWidth: 1,
                    shadowSize: 0
                },
                legend: {
                    position: "ne",
                    backgroundColor: "#fff",
                    labelBoxMargin: 10,
                },
                grid: {
                    color: "#000",
                    tickColor: "#eee",
                    backgroundColor: {
                        colors: [[0, "#ddf"], [1, "#cce"]],
                        start: "top",
                        end: "bottom"
                    },
                    verticalLines: true,
                    minorVerticalLines: true,
                    horizontalLines: true,
                    minorHorizontalLines: true,
                },
                xaxis: {
                    color: "#fff",
                },
                yaxis: {
                    color: "#fff",
                },
                title: this.formatDate(options.filter.startDate)
                    + " - "+this.formatDate(options.filter.endDate),
                HtmlText: true
            };

            var graph=Flotr.draw(graphcontainer, message.data, graphoptions);
```

```
            timeGraphWorker.terminate();
            graph.destroy();
        } else if (message && message.type === "noresults") {
            graphcontainer.innerHTML = "No data found.  Try adjusting the filters.";
        }
    }.bind(this);

    timeGraphWorker.postMessage({
        startDate: options.filter.startDate,
        endDate: options.filter.endDate,
        projectId: options.filter.projectId
    });
},

formatDate: function (dt) {
    var formatting = Windows.Globalization.DateTimeFormatting;
    var formatter = new formatting.DateTimeFormatter("day month.abbreviated");
    return formatter.format(dt);
},
```

The highlighted portion of the code is the same as what we added in Listing 13-7. However, instead of executing that code directly in the ready function when the page loads, I've moved it into the onmessage event handler for a new Worker object named timeGraphWorker. This is the function that receives the message sent from the worker thread when postMessage is called in Listing 13-9. When a message is received, the message's type property is checked. If the message contains data, the main thread uses that data to render the graph. If the type is noresults, then a message is shown to the user. Because our data is still hard-coded, we won't see that message yet. After wiring up the onmessage event handler, the call to timeGraphWorker.postMessage sends the filter object from the Time Sheets page to the worker. Until that call happens, the worker isn't actually doing anything.

■ **Note** You'll find a call to timeGraphWorker.terminate near the end of Listing 13-10. There are two ways to terminate a worker thread. This, the first, is to call the terminate method from the main thread. The other is to call the close method from the worker thread itself. They are equivalent.

If you run Clok now and navigate to the graph page, you'll see a graph similar to that in Figure 13-4. It's really not any different than the one in Figure 13-2, aside from the fact that the data is random, but the data for this one was calculated in a worker thread. OK, it was actually hard-coded in a worker thread, but still, you've just created some multi-threaded JavaScript, which is impressive.

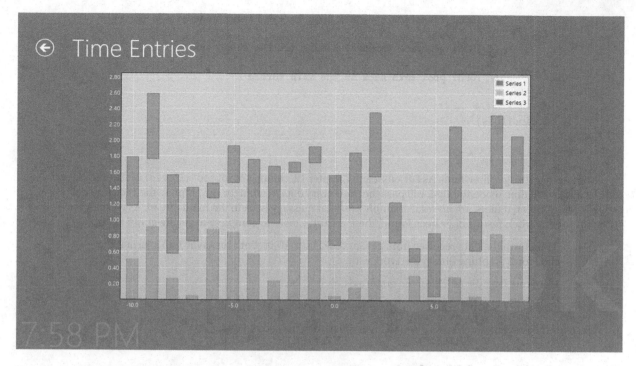

Figure 13-4. The second iteration of our graph is much like the first

Passing Time-Sheet Filter as Message

So far, we've got a nice-looking graph populated with data hard-coded in a worker thread. The last piece of the puzzle is to replace that hard-coded data with real data from our Storage class. Replace the current version of the getData function in timeGraphWorker.js with the version from Listing 13-11.

Listing 13-11. Get Real-Time Entry Data from the Storage Class

```
function getData(messageData) {
    storage.timeEntries.getSortedFilteredTimeEntriesAsync(
            messageData.startDate,
            messageData.endDate,
            messageData.projectId)
        .then(
            function complete(results) {
                if (results.length <= 0) {
                    self.postMessage({
                        type: "noresults"
                    });
                } else {
```

```
                    // TODO: transform the data into format Flotr2 understands

                    // TODO: generate friendly labels for the graph axis

                    // TODO: post data back to the main thread

                }
            }.bind(this)
        );
}
```

Now we're getting somewhere. As I discussed in Chapter 12, calling getSortedFilteredTimeEntriesAsync returns a Promise that, when fulfilled, will pass the time-entry data needed for the graph to the then function's complete parameter. If there are no results, simply post that message back to the main thread. As you can see by the TODO comments, when results have been found, there are three tasks to complete to get the graph to display.

- Transform the data received from getSortedFilteredTimeEntriesAsync into a format that the Flotr2 graphing library can work with.

- Generate friendly labels for the graph axis.

- Post data back to the main thread for Flotr2 to render.

I'll cover the first and third tasks together, then finish with the second task.

Map and Reduce and Map Again

The results of calling getSortedFilteredTimeEntriesAsync include all of the data needed to create a graph. Actually, we only need three values from each timeEntry object in results. Unfortunately, the format of a timeEntry object does not match that for a data point that Flotr2 needs.

Getting the data into the correct format can be done in a number of ways. You could create a number of for loops to iterate over the results and build step-by-step a data object for the graphing library. I've opted to use the map and reduce functions to take care of this. Replace the first TODO comment with the code in Listing 13-12.

Listing 13-12. Transforming the Data

```
var msInDay = 86400000; // to normalize dates

var graphdata = results.map(function (item) {
    // First, map to an array containing only the raw data needed
    return {
        clientName: item.project.clientName
            + ((messageData.projectId > 0)
                ? ": " + item.project.name
                : ""),
        dateWorked: item.dateWorked.removeTimePart(),
        timeWorked: Clok.Utilities.SecondsToHours(item.elapsedSeconds, false)
    };
}).reduce(function (accumulated, current) {
    // Second, reduce all hours worked on each day for the same client into a single value

    var found = false;
    for (var i = 0; i < accumulated.length; i++) {
```

```
            if (accumulated[i][0] === current.clientName) {
                found = true;
                continue;
            }
        }

        if (!found) {
            var worked = [];
            var dt = messageData.startDate;
            while (dt <= messageData.endDate) {
                worked[worked.length] = [dt / msInDay, 0];
                dt = dt.addDays(1);
            }
            accumulated[accumulated.length] = [current.clientName, worked];
        }

        for (var i = 0; i < accumulated.length; i++) {
            if (accumulated[i][0] === current.clientName) {
                for (var j = 0; j < accumulated[i][1].length; j++) {
                    if (accumulated[i][1][j][0] === current.dateWorked.getTime() / msInDay) {
                        accumulated[i][1][j][1] += current.timeWorked;
                        continue;
                    }
                }
            }
        }

        return accumulated;
}, []).map(function (item) {
    // Finally, map the reduced values into the format Flotr2 requires
    return { label: item[0], data: item[1] };
});
```

The code isn't pretty, but it does just what it needs to do. I've highlighted some comments at the various steps of this task to illustrate what is happening. The first call to map simplifies the hierarchical structure of each timeEntry object into a flattened object containing only the client, date, and time worked. The first two blocks of the reduce function ensure that each client will have a graph value for each date, which is 0 by default. After that initialization process, the reduce function then iterates over the array of those flattened objects, grouping them by client and date, summing the time worked for each group. If you are familiar with SQL, a similar task might be accomplished with a query similar to the one in Listing 13-13.

Listing 13-13. This Looks Much Clearer to Me

```sql
select clientName, dateWorked, sum(timeWorked) as timeWorked
from timeEntries
group by clientName, dateWorked
```

Unfortunately, you can't embed SQL in JavaScript. That said, the point of this chapter isn't writing ideal MapReduce code. Other people have covered this at length, and plenty of algorithms and techniques can be found online.

The graphdata object contains the result of all of your mapping and reducing. All you need to do now is replace the third TODO comment in Listing 13-11 with the code in Listing 13-14 to send this data back to the main thread.

Listing 13-14. Posting the Results of Our Intense Calculation Back to the Main Thread

```
self.postMessage({
    type: "graphdata",
    data: graphdata
});
```

When you run Clok and navigate to the graph, you will see a nice, accurate graph like that in Figure 13-5.

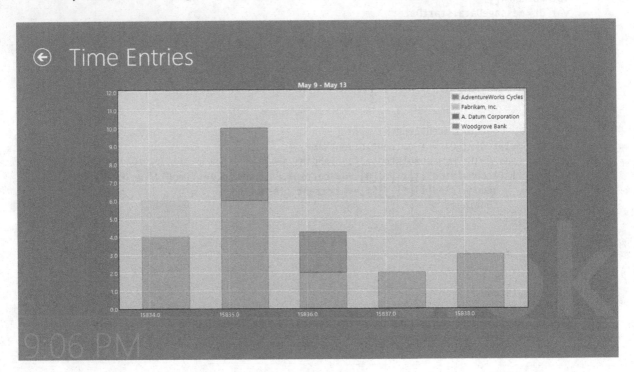

Figure 13-5. *The bars on the graph look good, but the axis labels don't*

While the bars appear to be accurate, the labels on the horizontal axis don't make any sense. Let's fix that.

Creating Axis Labels for the Graph

As it turns out, by default, Flotr2 treats dates as very large numbers—the number of milliseconds since January 1, 1970 as returned by the getTime function of a Date object. That means that each bar on our graph would be 86,400,000 (the number of milliseconds in each day) units away from the bar for the next day. That makes the bars of the graph hard to see, so I've normalized the dates in Listing 13-12 by dividing by that number. So, instead of the number of milliseconds since 1970, the values on the horizontal axis represent the number of days since 1970.

While better than 1,368,144,000,000, a label of 15,835 isn't especially helpful to a user trying to figure out what day he or she worked 10 hours. Fortunately, Flotr2 allows you to correlate a label with each value on the horizontal axis. Replace the second TODO comment in Listing 13-11 with the code in Listing 13-15.

Listing 13-15. Making User-Friendly Axis Labels

```
var tickDays = [], otherDays = [];

var dateFormatter = function (dt) {
    var formatting = Windows.Globalization.DateTimeFormatting;
    var formatter = new formatting.DateTimeFormatter("day month.abbreviated");
    return formatter.format(dt);
};

var dt = messageData.startDate;
while (dt <= messageData.endDate) {
    if ((dt.getDay() === 0)
            || (messageData.startDate.addDays(7) >= messageData.endDate)
            || (messageData.startDate.getTime() === dt.getTime())
            || (messageData.endDate.getTime() === dt.getTime())
        ) {
        tickDays.push([dt / msInDay, dateFormatter(dt)]);
    } else {
        otherDays.push([dt / msInDay, dateFormatter(dt)]);
    }

    dt = dt.addDays(1);
}
```

In this code, `tickDays` stores a friendly version of the date to be shown on the graph. If the graph requested is for seven or fewer days' worth of data, each date in the range gets added to `tickDays`. Otherwise, `tickDays` contains user-friendly labels for dates that are either Sundays or match the filter's `startDate` or `endDate` properties. Any date that doesn't meet these criteria are added to `otherDays` instead. In addition to displaying friendly labels on the graph's horizontal axis, these two arrays will determine where the vertical lines will appear on the graph. Before that is possible, we have to get those values back to the main thread. Add the highlighted code in Listing 13-16 to the `postMessage` call from Listing 13-14.

Listing 13-16. Adding More Values to Our Message

```
self.postMessage({
    type: "graphdata",
    ticks: tickDays,
    minorTicks: otherDays,
    data: graphdata
});
```

One last change is needed in the main thread to display the graph labels correctly. Modify the `graphoptions` object by adding the highlighted code in Listing 13-17 to the `xaxis` property.

Listing 13-17. Configuring Axis Labels

```
xaxis: {
    color: "#fff",
    showLabels: true,
    ticks: message.ticks,
    minorTicks: message.minorTicks,
},
```

Now Flotr2 can render the graph and labels as expected (see Figure 13-6).

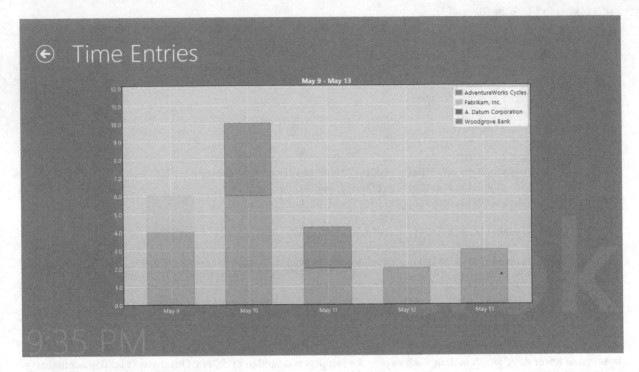

Figure 13-6. *The labels make more sense now*

A Quick Word About Promises

The graph looks great. The data points for the graph are calculated in a worker thread and passed back to the main thread in a message. Axis labels are nice and readable. You could stop now and be happy with your work. In fact, this is as far as I will take this exercise.

That said, there is an extra step you can include, if you are looking for some homework. If you like a common syntax, you could wrap this Web Worker in a `WinJS.Promise`. That would allow you to handle the message passed from the worker in a `then` or `done` method, instead of in an `onmessage` event handler. The functionality doesn't change—only the syntax. If this is something that interests you, then I recommend reading this forum message for an example of how you might accomplish this: `http://social.msdn.microsoft.com/Forums/en-US/winappswithhtml5/thread/9722d406-6de2-4705-9f00-4fdd7c2ad6b3`.

■ **Note**   The technique described in the listed forum posting has been documented by Kraig Brockschmidt, in his book *Programming Windows® 8 Apps with HTML, CSS, and JavaScript* (Microsoft Press, 2012).

While not in the context of Web Workers, I use a similar technique in Chapter 14, when I wrap the creation of a database connection in a `Promise`, which is fulfilled when the connection is successfully opened. You'll see this code in Listing 14-1 and Listing 14-2.

Conclusion

While promises allow you to handle asynchronous operations in a convenient manner, Web Workers provide the opportunity to have code execute on a different thread. Having the worker thread isolated from the main thread means that the two threads cannot reference the same variables. While that seems counter-productive at first, it actually leads to a more stable, decoupled system, where you, as the developer, don't have to worry about the common issues in multi-threaded development, such as race conditions and locking. Configuring your main thread and your worker thread to communicate by passing and receiving messages is a simple task that enables multi-threaded application development, without the potential fragility one might experience in other languages.

CHAPTER 14

■ ■ ■

Data Source Options

In Chapter 11, I introduced data binding and covered a handful of different techniques you can use to display your application's data on the screen. So far, however, all of the data in Clok has been stored in memory. Test data is loaded when the application is launched, and any modifications to that data are discarded when the application is closed. While that allows us to build an application that looks nice and to work out the details of allowing the user to interact with data, it is not enough to be a usable application.

By the end of this chapter, however, Clok will be in a state where someone could actually start to use it on a daily basis. That's not to say that it is a completed application—we will still add a number of features to improve the user experience throughout the rest of the book. That said, I started using Clok myself after finishing the exercises in this chapter.

So, what will it take to get Clok from an application that appears to function to one that is actually usable? The biggest feature missing from Clok is the ability to save data in a persistent format. In this chapter, I'll discuss working with local data, using IndexedDB, as well as integrating remote data into Clok, using the WinJS.xhr function.

Local Data Sources

The case for local data is clear. Accessing data in local data sources is faster than accessing the same data in a remote data source. It is available at all times, whether or not the user is connected to the Internet or an internal network. In the case where the user is not connected, an application that relies only on remote data is useless. For the majority of this section, I'm going to cover a technology known as the Indexed Database API, or simply IndexedDB.

IndexedDB

IndexedDB is a database engine that is built into modern web browsers, such as the Internet Explorer, Firefox, and Chrome web browsers. Because Windows Store applications built with HTML and JavaScript take advantage of Internet Explorer's rendering and scripting support, IndexedDB is also available in applications such as Clok. Using IndexedDB, you can store your user's data locally, right in your application, making that data available anytime, whether connected or not.

Unlike a relational database-management system (RDBMS), such as Microsoft SQL Server or Oracle Database, IndexedDB stores your data as objects. A single object could have a deep hierarchy, such as a customer object containing a collection of orders, each with a collection of products in the order. Or it could be a simple object, such as a Project object or TimeEntry object.

■ **Note** Before getting started with IndexedDB, be sure to comment the code in storage.js that is used to populate the in-memory lists with temporary data. Later in this chapter you will move a modified version of this code to a new file.

Populating In-Memory Lists from IndexedDB

In Chapter 7, I alluded to the fact that my preference is to work with objects and collections of objects, instead of building my user interface to be directly coupled to the data itself. This allows some flexibility in how I choose to read and write data. With that in mind, I'm going to illustrate how to support our existing in-memory data objects with IndexedDB as data storage.

The first thing you'll need to do when working with IndexedDB is create a database. Add the highlighted code from Listing 14-1 to storage.js, before the storage class definition.

Listing 14-1. Creating an IndexedDB Database

```
"use strict";

var data = Clok.Data;

var _openDb = new WinJS.Promise(function (comp, err) {
    var db;

    var request = indexedDB.open("Clok", 1);

    request.onerror = err;

    request.onupgradeneeded = function (e) {
        var upgradedDb = e.target.result;
        upgradedDb.createObjectStore("projects", { keyPath: "id", autoIncrement: false });
        upgradedDb.createObjectStore("timeEntries", { keyPath: "id", autoIncrement: false });
    };

    request.onsuccess = function () {
        db = request.result;

        // Do something with the database here
    };
});
```

```
var storage = WinJS.Class.define(
    // SNIPPED
```

Because all IndexedDB operations happen asynchronously, I've defined _openDb as a Promise representing the database. Because of the async nature, a common pattern when working with IndexedDB is to make a request of some type and examine the response of that request within a handler. That's exactly what's happening in Listing 14-1. With the call to indexedDB.open, I've made a request to open version 1 of a database named Clok. Any errors with that request are handled by the Promise object's err function. Once there is a successful connection to the database, the onsuccess event handler will do something interesting, and I'll show that in a moment.

At present, however, version 1 of the Clok database does not exist. When a new version of a database is requested, the onupgradeneeded event handler is invoked, and this is where you can create the collections, or object stores, where data will be maintained. Each object requires a key, and the id property on the Project and TimeEntry classes makes an ideal key. Because we already have logic to set the value of these id properties, I've specified that the keys are not auto-incrementing.

■ **Note** In addition to being used to create the initial database, the onupgradeneeded handler is also used to upgrade an existing database to a new version. In that case, you would add code within the handler to check e.oldVersion, to determine how outdated the user's database is, and what steps are needed to successfully upgrade it. You can see an example of this at www.w3.org/TR/IndexedDB/.

Once the database has been created and opened, the success event is raised, invoking the onsuccess handler. So far, nothing interesting is happening there. I've only set a reference to the database in a variable named db. Because I plan to continue to use in-memory lists of data throughout Clok, when the database is opened, it should populate those lists with the data currently in the database so that the existing screens continue to work as before. Add the highlighted code from Listing 14-2 to the onsuccess handler.

Listing 14-2. This Code Executes When the Database Is Successfully Opened

```
request.onsuccess = function () {
    db = request.result;

    _refreshFromDb(db).done(function () {
        comp(db);
    }, function (errorEvent) {
        err(errorEvent);
    });
};
```

Define _refreshFromDb by adding the code in Listing 14-3 immediately after the _openDb declaration.

Listing 14-3. Populating In-Memory Lists with Data in the Database

```
var _refreshFromDb = function (db) {
    return new WinJS.Promise(function (comp, err) {
        while (storage.projects.pop()) { }
        while (storage.timeEntries.pop()) { }
        var transaction = db.transaction(["projects", "timeEntries"]);

        transaction.objectStore("projects").openCursor().onsuccess = function (event) {
            var cursor = event.target.result;
            if (cursor) {
                var project = data.Project.createFromDeserialized(cursor.value);
                storage.projects.push(project);
                cursor.continue();
            };
        };

        transaction.objectStore("timeEntries").openCursor().onsuccess = function (event) {
            var cursor = event.target.result;
            if (cursor) {
                var timeEntry = data.TimeEntry.createFromDeserialized(cursor.value);
```

```
                    storage.timeEntries.push(timeEntry);
                    cursor.continue();
                };
            };

        transaction.oncomplete = comp;
        transaction.onerror = err;
    });
}
```

The `_refreshFromDb` function returns a `Promise` that first empties the in-memory lists. Within a transaction, as all IndexedDB operations are, a cursor is opened to each of the object stores in the database. As long as the cursor has a value, that value is then added into the appropriate in-memory list. The transaction's `oncomplete` handler is set to the `comp` handler of the `Promise`, which will trigger the done function in Listing 14-2. At that point, the `comp` handler of the `_openDb` `Promise` is called to provide a reference to the database that can be used in whatever code has referenced `_openDb`.

■ **Note** When saving WinJS objects into an IndexedDB database, only the properties defined in the constructor are saved. Any properties defined as instance members, such as the `project` property in the `TimeEntry` class, do not have a value when the object is retrieved from the database. To alleviate this, in both the `Project` and `TimeEntry` classes, I have added a new static function, named `createFromDeserialized`. The function takes the anonymous object returned from the cursor and creates a fully hydrated object based on those values. The definition of these functions is available in the source code that accompanies this book. You can find the code samples for this chapter on the Source Code/Downloads tab of the book's Apress product page (`www.apress.com/9781430257790`).

If you run Clok now, you'll quickly find that there is no data (see Figure 14-1). We removed our test data and are now populating those lists with data from the database. However, there is no data in the database yet. Later in this chapter, I'll show some functionality that will help us as developers, by providing a way to reset our test data and explore the data in the database. Before we get to that, let's make changes to Clok, so that our database is updated when the user saves or deletes data.

Figure 14-1. *No projects in Clok*

■ **Note**   In Clok, I've used IndexedDB to populate the in-memory lists of data that were added in prior chapters. This provides the benefit of not requiring any changes to existing screens for displaying and managing project and time-entry data. If you prefer, you can implement the `IListDataSource` interface to create your own data source that works directly with IndexedDB. This would allow you to bind `ListView` controls, for example, directly to your data, without first having to load it into a `WinJS.Binding.List` object, as I've done in Clok. See the following blog entry for an example of how to do this: http://stephenwalther.com/archive/2012/07/10/creating-an-indexeddbdatasource-for-winjs.

Updating IndexedDB When Data Changes

You wouldn't know it by running the application, but we have made all the changes needed to load data from our IndexedDB database into memory to be displayed on the screen. In this section, I'll show the changes required in order to save and delete data from the database. Fortunately, all of the changes needed are confined to `storage.js`, which is another benefit of loading data into in-memory lists and using those lists thoughout the application. Add the code from Listing 14-4 after the definition of `_refreshFromDb` in `storage.js`.

Listing 14-4. Methods to Work with the Data in the IndexedDB Database

```
var _getObjectStore = function (db, objectStoreName, mode) {
    mode = mode || "readonly";

    return new WinJS.Promise(function (comp, err) {
        var transaction = db.transaction(objectStoreName, mode);
```

```
            comp(transaction.objectStore(objectStoreName));
            transaction.onerror = err;
        });
    };

    var _saveObject = function (objectStore, object) {
        return new WinJS.Promise(function (comp, err) {
            var request = objectStore.put(object);
            request.onsuccess = comp;
            request.onerror = err;
        });
    };

    var _deleteObject = function (objectStore, id) {
        return new WinJS.Promise(function (comp, err) {
            var request = objectStore.delete(id);
            request.onsuccess = comp;
            request.onerror = err;
        });
    };
```

■ **Note** All of these functions return `Promise` objects, and you'll also be modifying the `save` and `delete` functions to return `Promise` objects as well. While I won't cover it in this chapter, you could make updates to the various places these functions are called, to take advantage of the async benefits promises provide. For example, you could provide a progress indicator when the user clicks a Save button, and then remove it when the `Promise` is fulfilled.

With these functions defined, we can now make changes to the save and delete functions. Replace the functions to save and delete projects with the new versions specified in Listing 14-5.

Listing 14-5. New Versions of Functions to Save and Delete Projects

```
storage.projects.save = function (p) {
    if (p && p.id) {
        var existing = storage.projects.getById(p.id);
        if (!existing) {
            storage.projects.push(p);
        }

        return _openDb.then(function (db) {
            return _getObjectStore(db, "projects", "readwrite");
        }).then(function (store) {
            return _saveObject(store, p);
        });
    }

    return WinJS.Promise.as();
};
```

```
storage.projects.delete = function (p, permanent) {
    permanent = permanent || false;

    if (p && p.id) {
        if (!permanent) {
            var existing = storage.projects.getById(p.id);
            if (existing) {
                // soft delete = default
                existing.status = data.ProjectStatuses.Deleted;
                return storage.projects.save(existing);
            }
        } else {
            var index = this.indexOf(p);
            if (index >= 0) {
                this.splice(index, 1);

                return _openDb.then(function (db) {
                    return _getObjectStore(db, "projects", "readwrite");
                }).then(function (store) {
                    return _deleteObject(store, p.id);
                });
            }
        }
    }
    return WinJS.Promise.as();
};
```

The changes to the save function are pretty straightforward. I've simply added code to get a connection to the database, select the correct object store, and save the project object into that store. I made a few more changes to the delete function, however. Previously, there was not a way to permanently delete a project from Clok. Projects were just assigned a Deleted status and then saved. In the course of typical Clok usage, that will still be the case. However, when we add functionality to reset temporary data in the next section, we'll need a way to permanently remove data.

In both functions, a Promise is now returned. In the case of a successful operation, the Promise defined in the corresponding _saveObject or _deleteObject function in Listing 14-4 is returned to the calling code. Otherwise, an empty Promise is returned using the WinJS.Promise.as function, without supplying any parameters to it. This last step isn't necessarily required, but it does ensure consistency in the type of object being returned by calling save or delete—it's always a Promise.

Updated versions of the functions to save and delete time entries can be seen in Listing 14-6. The changes to these functions are very similar to the changes made in Listing 14-5, although the delete function is simpler, in that it always permanently deletes time entries.

Listing 14-6. New Versions of Functions to Save and Delete Time Entries

```
storage.timeEntries.save = function (te) {
    if (te && te.id) {
        var existing = storage.timeEntries.getById(te.id);
        if (!existing) {
            storage.timeEntries.push(te);
        }
```

```
        return _openDb.then(function (db) {
            return _getObjectStore(db, "timeEntries", "readwrite");
        }).then(function (store) {
            return _saveObject(store, te);
        });
    }

    return WinJS.Promise.as();
};

storage.timeEntries.delete = function (te) {
    if (te && te.id) {
        var index = this.indexOf(te);
        if (index >= 0) {
            this.splice(index, 1);

            return _openDb.then(function (db) {
                return _getObjectStore(db, "timeEntries", "readwrite");
            }).then(function (store) {
                return _deleteObject(store, te.id);
            });
        }
    }

    return WinJS.Promise.as();
};
```

■ **Note**   In Listing 14-5 and Listing 14-6, you'll notice that when I update data, whether saving or deleting it, I am updating in both the in-memory list and the IndexedDB database. An alternative would be to update only the database and then repopulate the lists from the database, similar to how they are loaded when the database connection is first made. There's nothing wrong with that approach, but I chose this direction in order to minimize changes to the application. Reloading the lists each time would require changes to various screens to reload data after the list had been repopulated.

Now let's get some temporary data back into Clok, to make it easier to test.

IndexedDB Explorer

For the purposes of development, it would still be nice to have temporary test data in Clok. In fact, because we just implemented functionality for persisting all Clok data, it would be nice to be able to clear out any data and reset the database to a default test state. In this section, I'll show you how to add a settings flyout that not only allows you to reset test data but also provides a small database explorer you can use to view the various objects stored in your IndexedDB database.

Creating the Settings Flyout

Add an HTML file named `idbhelper.html` in the `settings` folder. Replace the default contents of `idbhelper.html` with the code from Listing 14-7.

Listing 14-7. The Shell of a New Settings Flyout

```
<!DOCTYPE html>
<html>
<head>
    <title>IndexedDB Helper</title>
</head>
<body>
    <div id="settingsDiv" data-win-control="WinJS.UI.SettingsFlyout"
        aria-label="IndexedDB Helper"
        data-win-options="{settingsCommandId:'idbhelper',width:'wide'}">

        <div class="win-ui-dark win-header" style="background-color: #000046;">
            <button type="button" class="win-backbutton"
                onclick="WinJS.UI.SettingsFlyout.show()">
            </button>
            <div class="win-label clok-logo">IndexedDB Helper</div>
        </div>
        <div class="win-content">
            <div class="win-settings-section">

            </div>
        </div>
    </div>
</body>
</html>
```

Next, modify `default.js` by adding the highlighted code in Listing 14-8. Rather than adding the new command definition to `e.detail.applicationcommands` in the same manner as the `options` and `about` settings flyouts, add it separately, so that it will be easier show or hide it based on the user's preference, a feature that will be added in Chapter 15.

Listing 14-8. Wiring Up the Settings Flyout

```
WinJS.Application.onsettings = function (e) {
    e.detail.applicationcommands = {
        "options": {
            title: "Clok Options",
            href: "/settings/options.html"
        },
        "about": {
            title: "About Clok",
            href: "/settings/about.html"
        }
    };
```

```
e.detail.applicationcommands.idbhelper = {
    title: "IndexedDB Helper",
    href: "/settings/idbhelper.html"
};

WinJS.UI.SettingsFlyout.populateSettings(e);
};
```

Now that you have a new, empty settings flyout, let's add some functionality that will help us as developers to build and test Clok.

Downloading and Configuring IDBExplorer from Microsoft

The Internet Explorer team at Microsoft has created a tool named IDBExplorer. Initially used internally, Microsoft made it available to developers, to explore their IndexedDB databases, including structure and data. You can read about this tool and download it from the following blog post: http://blogs.msdn.com/b/ie/archive/2012/01/25/debugging-indexeddb-applications.aspx. Download the ZIP file containing the tool and copy the folder named IDBExplorer from that package into the settings folder of your Visual Studio project. Figure 14-2 shows the correct folder hierarchy that you should have when complete. You can reference the completed version of this process in the source code that accompanies this book.

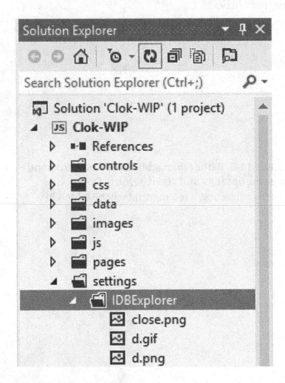

Figure 14-2. *Adding the IDBExplorer tool into the settings folder*

If we were building a web site instead of a Windows Store application, we would be done. In order to get this helpful tool working in our application, however, we have a few more steps to complete. IDBExplorer includes an older version of jQuery. A recent version of jQuery, however, works better in Windows Store applications, so I recommend downloading jQuery version 2.0 or later from www.jquery.com and adding it into the IDBExplorer you just added to the project. I chose to download the minified version, as seen in Figure 14-3, but the uncompressed version will work as well.

Figure 14-3. *Updating to a newer version of jQuery*

■ **Note**   While jQuery version 2.0 works well with Windows Store applications, you may occasionally see errors when running Clok in debug mode (pressing F5 instead of Ctrl+F5). It is safe to continue past any errors you might see in your debugger. When running Clok normally, without the debugger attached, these errors do not have any adverse effects. I suspect that some future version of jQuery will eliminate this issue.

The last change you have to make to the IDBExplorer tool itself before adding it to the settings flyout is to update the contents of IDBExplorer.html with the code from Listing 14-9.

Listing 14-9. Updating the Page to Work Better with Windows Store Applications

```
<!DOCTYPE html>
<html xmlns="http://www.w3.org/1999/xhtml">
<head>
    <!-- IDBExplorer references -->
    <script src="jquery-2.0.2.min.js"></script>
    <script src="jquery.jstree.js"></script>
    <script src="IDBExplorer.js"></script>
    <link rel="stylesheet" type="text/css" href="IDBExplorer.css" />
    <link rel="stylesheet" type="text/css" href="style.css" />
</head>
<body onload="setDBName();initIDBExplorer();">
</body>
</html>
```

With that, there are no more modifications to make to IDBExplorer, and you simply have to show this tool in the settings flyout by adding an iframe to host it. Add the highlighted code in Listing 14-10 to idbhelper.html.

Listing 14-10. Hosting IDBExplorer in an iframe

```
<div class="win-settings-section">
    <iframe style="width: 550px; height: 600px"
        src="/settings/IDBExplorer/IDBExplorer.html?name=Clok"></iframe>
</div>
```

Run Clok now and open the IndexedDB Helper settings flyout. You should see IDBExplorer displaying information about our empty database (see Figure 14-4). Once we add test data back into Clok, this tool will be much more helpful. I'll show you how to do that later in the next section.

Figure 14-4. *IDBExplorer showing an empty database*

Adding Buttons to Reset and Load Test Data

Earlier in this chapter, I had you remove the code in storage.js that loaded temporary data into Clok. In this section, I'll show you how to get that temporary data back into Clok. Start by adding a few buttons to the top of the IndexedDB Helper settings flyout. Add the highlighted code from Listing 14-11 to idbhelper.html.

Listing 14-11. Adding Buttons to Reset Our Test Data

```
<div class="win-settings-section">
    <button onclick="deleteAllData();" style="background-color:red;">Delete All Data</button>
    <button onclick="addTestData();">Add Test Data</button>
    <iframe style="width: 550px; height: 600px"
        src="/settings/IDBExplorer/IDBExplorer.html?name=Clok"></iframe>
</div>
```

Because the IndexedDB Helper settings flyout is only for developer use, and should be deleted from the project before deploying, I decided to add the JavaScript code directly in idbhelper.html. Add the script references from Listing 14-12 to the head element of idbhelper.html.

Listing 14-12. JavaScript References and Button-Click Handlers

```
<script src="//Microsoft.WinJS.1.0/js/base.js"></script>
<script src="//Microsoft.WinJS.1.0/js/ui.js"></script>

<script src="/js/extensions.js"></script>
<script src="/js/utilities.js"></script>

<script src="/data/project.js"></script>
<script src="/data/timeEntry.js"></script>
<script src="/data/storage.js"></script>

<script>

    function deleteAllData() {
        // SNIPPED
    }

    function addTestData() {
        // SNIPPED
    }

</script>
```

Resetting our temporary data is a two-step process. First, we must delete all data currently in the database, and then we must add the temporary data to the database. Replace the deleteAllData function in idbhelper.html with the code from Listing 14-13.

Listing 14-13. Delete All Data Button Handler

```
function deleteAllData() {
    var msg = new Windows.UI.Popups.MessageDialog(
        "This cannot be undone.  Do you wish to continue?",
        "You're about to remove all data from Clok.");

    msg.commands.append(new Windows.UI.Popups.UICommand(
        "Yes, Delete It", function (command) {

            var storage = Clok.Data.Storage;
            storage.projects.forEach(function (p) {
                storage.projects.delete(p, true);
            });
            storage.timeEntries.forEach(function (te) {
                storage.timeEntries.delete(te);
            });
        }));
```

```
msg.commands.append(new Windows.UI.Popups.UICommand(
    "No, Don't Delete It", function (command) { }));

msg.defaultCommandIndex = 0;
msg.cancelCommandIndex = 1;

msg.showAsync();
}
```

When the Delete All Data button is clicked, a message dialog requests confirmation before continuing. If confirmed, all projects and time entries are permanently removed from the in-memory lists, which in turn remove the data from the IndexedDB database.

The code for adding temporary data is almost identical to what we added in Chapter 11, with three notable differences:

- If any data already exists, test data cannot be added.

- Instead of calling projects.push and time.push to add objects to the lists, I now call projects.save and time.save, which will add the items to the WinJS.Binding.List objects as well as to the IndexedDB database.

- One of the projects has address detail specified, which will be helpful later in this chapter, when I discuss working with remote data.

Replace the addTestData function in idbhelper.html with the code from Listing 14-14.

Listing 14-14. Add Test Data Button Handler

```
function addTestData() {

    var projects = Clok.Data.Storage.projects;
    var time = Clok.Data.Storage.timeEntries;

    if (projects.length > 0 || time.length > 0) {
        var msg = new Windows.UI.Popups.MessageDialog(
            "You cannot add test data since Clok already contains data.",
            "Cannot add test data.");
        msg.showAsync();
        return;
    }

    var createProject = function (name, projectNumber, clientName, id, status) {
        // SNIPPED
    }

    // SNIPPED

    // one needs an address for map example
    var project = createProject(name1, "2012-0017", client3, 1368296808748);
    project.address1 = "1 Microsoft Way";
    project.city = "Redmond";
    project.region = "WA";
    project.postalCode = "98052";
    projects.save(project);
```

```
// SNIPPED

var createTime = function (id, projectId, dateWorked, elapsedSeconds, notes) {
    // SNIPPED
}

// SNIPPED

time.save(createTime(timeId++, 1368296808757, date1, 10800, "Lorem ipsum dolor sit."));

    // SNIPPED
}
```

■ **Note**   You can find a version of addTestData with more detail, in the source code that accompanies this book. You can find the code samples for this chapter on the Source Code/Downloads tab of the book's Apress product page (www.apress.com/9781430257790).

Run Clok and open the IndexedDB Helper settings flyout. Click the button to Add Test Data, then view the projects node (see Figure 14-5) and the timeEntries node. You should see all your test data listed, and you'll be able to click different items in the top pane, to see details in the lower pane. As you make changes to *projects* and *timeEntries*, those changes will be reflected in IDBExplorer in this settings flyout. Whenever you need fresh test data, just return to this settings flyout to delete the current data and add new test data.

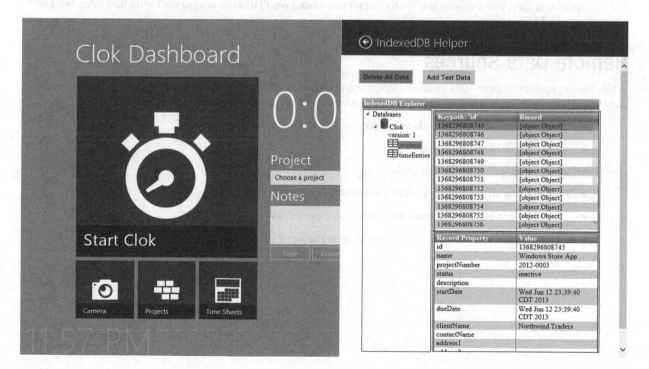

Figure 14-5. *Completed IndexedDB Helper*

■ **Note**   You may notice that when first launching Clok, the project drop-down list on the dashboard screen does not always have the complete list of active projects initially. However, if you navigate to a different page, then back, the list is complete. This is due to the async loading of data from the IndexedDB database into the `WinJS.Binding.List` that populates that control. We could fix this by using promises to populate the control after the data has loaded. Instead, we'll leave this as is for now and address it when I cover handling application-state changes in Chapter 17.

SQLite

IndexedDB is a very convenient option for local data storage, but it isn't your only option. If your background is similar to mine, you might have a fair amount of experience working with relational database systems, such as Microsoft SQL Server. Unfortunately, you cannot directly access data stored in a server-based database from your Windows Store application. You could write a service layer to support your relational database and access it as a remote data source.

You can also use something like SQLite to build local databases in your Windows Store application. While this is not directly supported out of the box, and I won't cover it in this book, you can use third-party libraries to add support for SQLite to your applications. One such library, named *SQLite3-WinRT*, can be found here: https://github.com/doo/SQLite3-WinRT.

File Storage

In addition to IndexedDB and SQLite, you can use files to store data locally. You can save JavaScript objects into a file. For that matter, in files, you can save text in any format you wish. I won't discuss how to work with files here, but I will cover that topic in Chapter 16.

Remote Data Sources

While having options to store data locally is important, that doesn't minimize the need to be able to support remote data sources as well. There are countless scenarios for working with remote data, for example:

- Getting directions to your client's office—we'll examine this scenario next
- Reading and sending e-mails
- Subscribing to news or blog feeds
- Calculating shipping fees for various shipping companies
- Viewing and editing customer data from a corporate CRM
- Getting data from another process running on the same machine

> ■ **Note**   It's important to note that the term *local data* does not refer simply to data that is on the same machine as the application. It refers to data that is stored within the application itself. Because Windows Store applications are isolated from one another, one application cannot directly access data that another application contains, even if the same developer created both applications. Even though the two applications are on the same machine, there is a wall between them, and data sharing must happen through some type of service.

Very often, data from remote services is exposed over HTTP, with either a REST API or RPC API. If you aren't familiar with those terms, plenty of detailed information about REST and RPC is available online, but the biggest distinction between them is that REST places emphasis on finding and working with some data (resources), while RPC, such as SOAP, places emphasis on performing some remote action, essentially calling a function running in a different process. To completely oversimplify it, REST focuses on nouns, and RPC focuses on verbs. The example I'm about to introduce gets data from a REST API.

WinJS.xhr

If you've been developing web applications for any length of time, you are familiar with XMLHttpRequest (XHR), which is used to submit a request to a web server somewhere and evaluate the response. The web server could be on the public Internet, a private network, or even on the same machine as the application making the request. Additionally, even though XML is part of its name, XMLHttpRequest can also receive JSON data from the server. Because requests to remote servers do not respond instantly, requests made using XMLHttpRequest will specify a handler function to execute when the response is available. Listing 14-15 shows a very simple example of using XMLHttpRequest to request someUrl and do something with the response from the server.

Listing 14-15. Requesting Something from a Remote Server with XMLHttpRequest

```
var request = new XMLHttpRequest();

request.onreadystatechange = function() {
    if (request.readyState === 4 && request.status === 200) {
        // do something with the response
    } else {
        // something bad happened
    }
}

var asyncRequest = true;
request.open("GET", someUrl, asyncRequest);
request.send();
```

This example isn't fully implemented. It only checks the case where readyState is 4 (the request has completed) and the HTTP status code is 200. It considers any other scenario to be an error. The WinJS.xhr function wraps up the functionality of XMLHttpRequest within a WinJS.Promise. Instead of specifying a handler function, the response is available in the then or done function of the Promise. Listing 14-16 performs the same task as Listing 14-15, using WinJS.xhr and promises instead.

Listing 14-16. Requesting Something from a Remote Server with WinJS.xhr

```
WinJS.xhr({ url: someUrl, type: "GET" })
    .done(function success(completeEvent) {
        // do something with the response
    }, function err(errorEvent) {
        // something bad happened
    });
```

It's arguably a little simpler to read, but because this function returns a Promise, it does fit nicely with the async programming style prevalent throughout WinJS. In addition to requesting data with a GET method, you can submit data with WinJS.xhr as well. If you are using WinJS.xhr to submit data, you will probably use the POST method instead of GET and will also have to specify a data property to the options parameter. For example, you might use code similar to Listing 14-17 to save a new user into a remote data source.

Listing 14-17. Posting Data with WinJS.xhr

```
WinJS.xhr({ url: someUrl, type: "POST", data: { name: "Scott", dob: "Dec 1" } })
```

A new requirement for Clok is to provide users with driving directions to their client's location. I'll walk you through configuring and using the Bing Maps API with WinJS.xhr to add this functionality.

Bing Maps Setup

You may be familiar with Microsoft's Bing Maps product. As with other companies providing maps and directions, Microsoft also offers an API for developers to integrate Bing Maps into their own software. At the time of this writing, Bing Maps can be added to a Windows Store application with no licensing fees for applications using fewer than 50,000 transactions per day (www.microsoft.com/maps). As much as I expect Clok to be a smashing success in the Windows Store, I don't see usage approaching that figure any time soon.

Even though the service is free, at least initially, in order to use the Bing Maps API, a key is required. Create an account and log in to the Bing Maps Portal (www.bingmapsportal.com). From there, start the process to create a new Basic key for a Windows Store application (see Figure 14-6).

Create key
* Application name
Clok Time Sheets
Application URL
http://clok.us
* Key type
Basic
What's this?
* Application type
Windows Store app
* Enter the characters you see
Try a new image
Submit

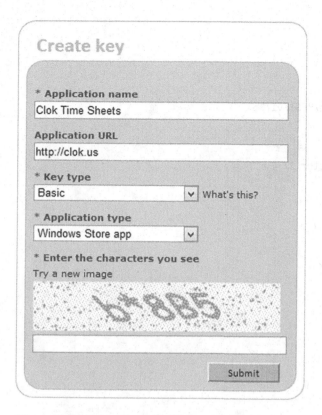

***Figure 14-6.** Requesting a Bing Maps API key*

Once you've completed the form, your key will be available. In Figure 14-7, you can see my list of keys, with the key itself blurred out. It's a long string of letters and numbers. I'll show you where to add that key to Clok in just a moment. You'll be able to retrieve it from the Bing Maps Portal at any time, if you misplace it.

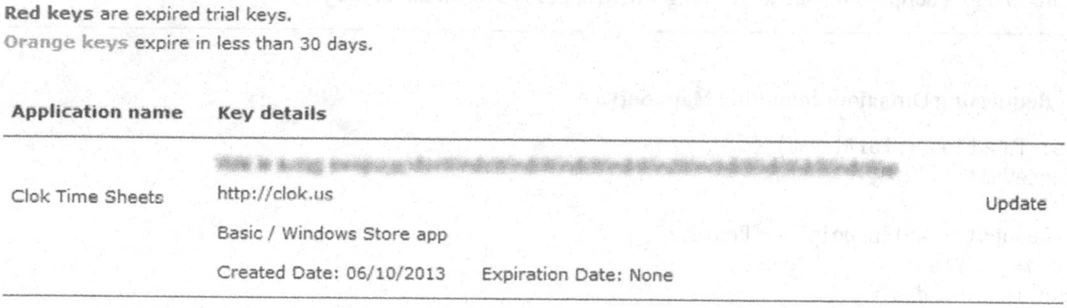

Red keys are expired trial keys.
Orange keys expire in less than 30 days.
Application name
Key details
Clok Time Sheets
http://clok.us
Basic / Windows Store app
Created Date: 06/10/2013
Expiration Date: None
Update

***Figure 14-7.** My current list of Bing Maps API keys*

Now that you have a key, you need a place to put it. Create a new JavaScript file named `bingMapsWrapper.js` in the `data` folder of your Visual Studio project. Add the code from Listing 14-18 to `bingMapsWrapper.js`. Make sure you add your Bing Maps API key in the `apikey` variable.

Listing 14-18. Defining the BingMaps Class

```
(function () {
    "use strict";

    var apikey = "PUT_YOUR_KEY_HERE";
    var apiEndpoint = "http://dev.virtualearth.net/REST/v1/";
    var xhrTimeout = 2000;

    var mapsClass = WinJS.Class.define(
        function constructor() { /* empty constructor */ },
        { /* static class, no instance members */ },
        {
            credentials: {
                get: function () { return apikey; }
            },

            getDirections: function (start, end) {
                // TODO: get the directions here
            }
        }
    );

    WinJS.Namespace.define("Clok.Data", {
        BingMaps: mapsClass,
    });
})();
```

So far, this class is pretty bare, only exposing your key in the credentials property. The getDirections function accepts a starting address (start) and a destination address (end) and will use those values to request driving directions from the Bing Maps service. Replace the definition of getDirections with the code in Listing 14-19.

■ **Note**   Be sure to add a script reference to the bingMapsWrapper.js file in default.js.

Listing 14-19. Requesting Directions from Bing Maps Service

```
getDirections: function (start, end) {
    var distanceUnit = "mi";

    var routeRequest = apiEndpoint + "Routes?"
        + "wp.0=" + start
        + "&wp.1=" + end
        + "&du=" + distanceUnit
        + "&routePathOutput=Points&output=json"
        + "&key=" + apikey;

    return WinJS.Promise.timeout(xhrTimeout, WinJS.xhr({ url: routeRequest }))
        .then(function (response) {
            var resp = JSON.parse(response.responseText);
```

```
            if (resp
                    && resp.resourceSets
                    && resp.resourceSets[0]
                    && resp.resourceSets[0].resources
                    && resp.resourceSets[0].resources[0]
                    && resp.resourceSets[0].resources[0].routeLegs
                    && resp.resourceSets[0].resources[0].routeLegs[0]
                    && resp.resourceSets[0].resources[0].routeLegs[0].itineraryItems
                    && resp.resourceSets[0].resources[0].routeLegs[0].itineraryItems.length > 0
            ) {
                var directions = {
                    copyright: resp.copyright,
                    distanceUnit: resp.resourceSets[0].resources[0].distanceUnit,
                    durationUnit: resp.resourceSets[0].resources[0].durationUnit,
                    travelDistance: resp.resourceSets[0].resources[0].travelDistance,
                    travelDuration: resp.resourceSets[0].resources[0].travelDuration,
                    bbox: resp.resourceSets[0].resources[0].bbox
                }

                var itineraryItems =
                    resp.resourceSets[0].resources[0].routeLegs[0].itineraryItems.map(
                        function (item) {
                            return {
                                compassDirection: item.compassDirection,
                                instructionText: item.instruction.text,
                                maneuverType: item.instruction.maneuverType,
                                travelDistance: item.travelDistance,
                                travelDuration: item.travelDuration,
                                warnings: item.warnings || []
                            };
                        });

                directions.itineraryItems = new WinJS.Binding.List(itineraryItems);

                return directions;
            }

            return null;
        });
}
```

■ **Note**   For now, Clok will only offer driving directions with distances specified in miles. In Chapter 15, you'll add a feature to allow the user to specify if he or she prefers miles or kilometers.

After constructing the URL to the Bing Maps service, that value is passed to the WinJS.xhr function, which we have wrapped in a call to WinJS.Promise.timeout. This technique is common to put a limit on how long your application should attempt to connect to the specified URL. In this example, xhrTimeout is set to 2000 milliseconds, so if any attempt to get directions from the service takes longer than 2 seconds, the user will be assumed to be offline, and the request will be canceled. Later in this chapter, I'll handle the error this cancellation produces, to show the user an appropriate message.

If, on the other hand, the request succeeds, the response, which will be JSON-formatted text, is parsed into a JavaScript object named resp. A valid response from Bing Maps service has a very deep hierarchy. If resp has this hierarchy defined, a directions object is constructed. This object is a flattened, simplified version of the actual response received. To make data binding simpler when the UI is built for this data, I've removed many unnecessary fields and layers of the hierarchy. The getDirections function returns a Promise, and the directions object will be available to a new Directions page via a then or done function. I'll illustrate this in a moment, but first we need to make a few changes to the Project Detail page, to allow the user to request driving directions.

Adding Button to Project Detail

The user will need a way to navigate to the new Directions page we will be creating in the next section. You'll have to add a button to the app bar on the Project Detail screen, which will navigate to the new page. By this point, you're fairly capable at adding buttons to an app bar and handling the click event, so I'll just summarize the important points. Add a Directions button to the app bar on the Project Detail screen. Set the icon property to directions and the disabled property to true (see Listing 14-20).

Listing 14-20. Adding an App Bar Button on the Project Detail Screen

```
<button
    data-win-control="WinJS.UI.AppBarCommand"
    data-win-options="{
        id:'goToDirectionsCommand',
        label:'Directions',
        icon:'directions',
        section:'selection',
        tooltip:'Directions',
        disabled: true}">
</button>
```

Next, add the code in Listing 14-21 to detail.js. Don't forget to wire up this click event handler in the ready function in detail.js as well.

Listing 14-21. Navigate to the Directions Screen

```
goToDirectionsCommand_click: function (e) {
    if (this.currProject
            && this.currProject.id
            && this.currProject.isAddressSpecified()) {
        WinJS.Navigation.navigate("/pages/projects/directions.html", {
            project: this.currProject
        });
    }
},
```

Modify the configureAppBar function in detail.js by adding the highlighted code from Listing 14-22. This will allow the Directions button to become enabled for projects that have an address. If no address has been saved to the project being viewed, or if the project hasn't been saved yet, the button will remain disabled.

Listing 14-22. Enable the Directions Button, If the Current Project Has an Address

```
configureAppBar: function (existingId) {
    var fields = WinJS.Utilities.query("#projectDetailForm input, "
        + "#projectDetailForm textarea, "
        + "#projectDetailForm select");

    fields.listen("focus", function (e) {
        projectDetailAppBar.winControl.show();
    }, false);

    if (existingId) {
        deleteProjectCommand.winControl.disabled = false;
        goToTimeEntriesCommand.winControl.disabled = false;

        if (this.currProject.isAddressSpecified()) {
            goToDirectionsCommand.winControl.disabled = false;
        }
    }
},
```

Both Listing 14-21 and Listing 14-22 reference a new function named isAddressSpecified. To define that function, add the code from Listing 14-23, as an instance member in the Project class in data\project.js.

Listing 14-23. A Function to Determine If a Project Has an Address Specified

```
isAddressSpecified: function () {
    return (!!this.address1
            || !!this.city
            || !!this.region
            || !!this.postalCode);
}
```

Run Clok and navigate to a few different projects, one with a client address and one without. If you used the test data as specified in the source code that accompanies this book, one project will have an address. If none of the projects in your test data has a client address, add an address to one. Figure 14-8 shows the Project Detail screen for a project that does not have a client address, and Figure 14-9 shows the same screen for a project with a client address.

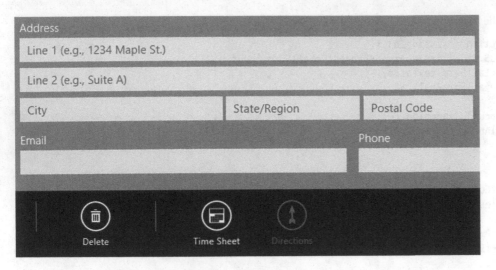

Figure 14-8. This project does not have a client address

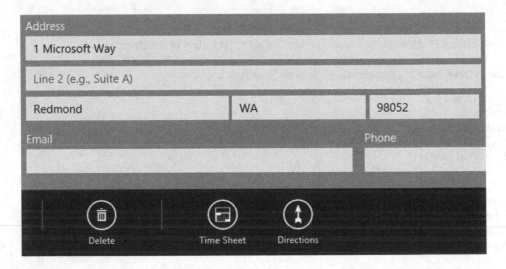

Figure 14-9. This project has a client address, and the user can request directions

With that, the user can now navigate to the new Directions page. Well, they could if we had created it yet. Right now, the application will merely crash, if you click the Directions button.

Displaying Driving Directions

The last step for completing this feature is to actually display driving directions to the user. Let's define a few simple requirements for a new Directions page.

- The user can enter his or her starting address.
- If directions cannot be retrieved for any reason, the user will see a simple error message.
- If directions are successfully retrieved from the Bing Maps service, they will be displayed in a list.

Create a new page control named `directions.html` in the `pages\projects` folder. Set the page title to Directions and replace the contents of the main section element with the code from Listing 14-24.

Listing 14-24. Directions Page

```html
<div id="directionsTemplate" data-win-control="WinJS.Binding.Template" style="display: none">
    <div class="directionsItem">
        <div class="directionsItem-instruction">
            <h3 class="directionsItem-instructionText"
                data-win-bind="textContent: instructionText"></h3>
        </div>
        <div class="directionsItem-distance">
            <h2 class="directionsItem-formattedDistance"
                data-win-bind="textContent: travelDistance
                    Clok.Data.TravelDistanceConverter"></h2>
        </div>
    </div>
</div>

<div id="directionsContainer">
    <div id="locationsPane">
        <h2>Get Directions</h2>
        <div class="formField">
            <label for="fromLocation">From</label><br />
            <input id="fromLocation">
        </div>
        <div class="formField">
            <label for="toLocation">To</label><br />
            <span id="toLocation"></span>
        </div>
        <button id="getDirectionsButton">Get Directions</button>
    </div>
    <div id="directionsPane">
        <div id="directionsSuccess" class="hidden">
            <div id="totalDistance">
                Total distance:
                <span
                    data-win-bind="textContent: travelDistance
                        Clok.Data.TravelDistanceConverter"></span>
            </div>
            <div id="totalTime">
                Est. travel time:
                <span
                    data-win-bind="textContent: travelDuration
                        Clok.Data.TravelTimeConverter"></span>
            </div>
```

```
            <div
                id="directionsListView"
                class="itemlist win-selectionstylefilled"
                data-win-control="WinJS.UI.ListView"
                data-win-options="{
                    layout: {type: WinJS.UI.ListLayout},
                    itemTemplate: select('#directionsTemplate'),
                    selectionMode: 'none',
                    swipeBehavior: 'none',
                    tapBehavior: 'none'
                }">
            </div>
            <div data-win-bind="textContent: copyright"></div>
        </div>
        <div id="directionsError" class="hidden">
            Could not get directions. Please check your
            addresses and internet connection.
        </div>
    </div>
</div>
```

The layout of the page is similar to the Time Sheets screen, so I won't explain it in detail. There is a form on one side and a ListView containing the list of directions on the other. The flexbox CSS layout is used to display them on their respective sides.

I also won't cover the full CSS file here, because there is nothing in it that you haven't already seen, and a complete version of directions.css is available in the source code that accompanies this book. The one thing that I will point out here is that I've added CSS to highlight the last step in the list of directions, using the CSS specified in Listing 14-25.

Listing 14-25. Highlighting the Final Step in the Directions

```
#directionsPane #directionsListView .win-container:last-of-type {
    background-color: limegreen;
}
```

I did this to improve the user experience, as it gives a very clear indicator that there are no more steps, which is less clear when scrolling through a long list of directions that all look the same. In addition to the last-of-type pseudo element, you can also use nth-of-type(odd) or nth-of-type(even) to alternate between two different styles.

Replace the contents of directions.js with the code in Listing 14-26.

Listing 14-26. Page Definition for the Directions Screen

```
(function () {
    "use strict";

    var maps = Clok.Data.BingMaps;

    WinJS.UI.Pages.define("/pages/projects/directions.html", {
        // This function is called whenever a user navigates to this page. It
        // populates the page elements with the app's data.
        ready: function (element, options) {
            this.populateDestination(options);
            getDirectionsButton.onclick = this.getDirectionsButton_click.bind(this);
        },
```

```javascript
populateDestination: function (options) {
    if (options && options.project) {
        var proj = options.project;

        var addressParts = [
            proj.address1,
            proj.city,
            ((proj.region || "") + " " + (proj.postalCode || "")).trim()];

        this.dest = addressParts.filter(function (part) {
            return !!part;
        }).join(", ");
        toLocation.textContent = this.dest;
    }
},

showDirectionResults: function (hasDirections) {
    if (hasDirections) {
        WinJS.Utilities.removeClass(directionsSuccess, "hidden");
        WinJS.Utilities.addClass(directionsError, "hidden");
    } else {
        WinJS.Utilities.addClass(directionsSuccess, "hidden");
        WinJS.Utilities.removeClass(directionsError, "hidden");
    }
},

getDirectionsButton_click: function (e) {

    if (fromLocation.value) {

        maps.getDirections(fromLocation.value, this.dest)
            .then(function (directions) {

                if (directions
                        && directions.itineraryItems
                        && directions.itineraryItems.length > 0) {

                    WinJS.Binding.processAll(
                        document.getElementById("directionsContainer"), directions);

                    this.showDirectionResults(true);

                    directionsListView.winControl.itemDataSource
                        = directions.itineraryItems.dataSource;

                    directionsListView.winControl.forceLayout();

                } else {
                    this.showDirectionResults(false);
                }
```

```
                    }.bind(this), function (errorEvent) {
                        this.showDirectionResults(false);
                    }.bind(this));

            } else {
                this.showDirectionResults(false);
            }
        },
    });
})();
```

When navigating to this screen from the Project Detail screen, the current project is passed to the Directions page as a property of the options parameter. The populateDestination function extracts the destination address and converts it into a standard format that will be used in the call to get directions. Then, it displays the destination address on the screen. The showDirectionResults function is used to toggle between the list of directions, when directions have been retrieved, and an error message, when directions cannot be retrieved.

The call to the Bing Maps service occurs in getDirectionsButton_click. If the user has specified a starting address, a call is made to the getDirections in the BingMaps class. If there is a successful response, the data binding for the page is wired up with a call to WinJS.Binding.processAll. Otherwise, the error message is displayed.

The final step is adding the binding converters referenced in Listing 14-24. Add the highlighted code from Listing 14-27 to bingMapsWrapper.js.

Listing 14-27. Binding Converters for the List of Directions

```
var secondsToTravelTimeConverter = WinJS.Binding.converter(function (s) {
    if (s > 3600) {
        return Clok.Utilities.SecondsToHours(s, true) + " hr";
    } else if (s > 60) {
        return (s / 60).toFixed(0) + " min";
    } else {
        return "< 1 min"
    }
});

var travelDistanceConverter = WinJS.Binding.converter(function (distance) {
    if (distance >= 5) {
        return distance.toFixed(0) + " mi";
    } else if (distance >= 0.2) {
        return distance.toFixed(2) + " mi";
    } else {
        return (distance * 5280).toFixed(0) + " ft";
    }
});

WinJS.Namespace.define("Clok.Data", {
    BingMaps: mapsClass,
    TravelTimeConverter: secondsToTravelTimeConverter,
    TravelDistanceConverter: travelDistanceConverter
});
```

The Bing Maps service is returning distances in miles and durations in seconds. I've used some simple formulas to convert to a more user-friendly value, based on the number of miles or seconds. Run Clok now and get directions from your location to one of your clients. Figure 14-10 should be similar to your screen, with a list of directions in a list on the right, including your final destination highlighted in green (or in a lighter color gray, if you're reading a black-and-white version of this book).

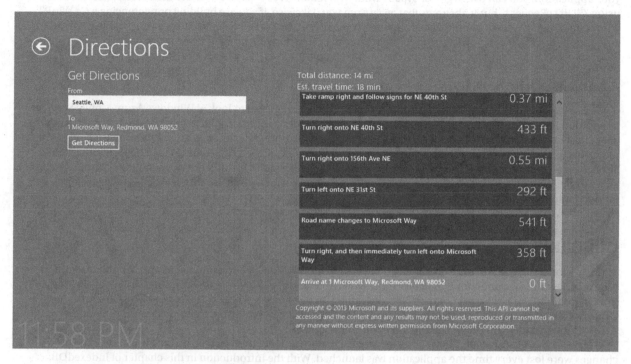

Figure 14-10. Directions from Seattle to Redmond

■ **Note**   Each value in `directions.itineraryItems` contains a `maneuverType` property and a `warnings` property. We won't be using those in this book, but the ambitious developer could use those to supply additional information to the user in the `ListView`. For example, when `maneuverType` is "TurnRight," you may wish to display an arrow pointing to the right, and when there is a "Tollbooth" warning, you may display a currency symbol. There are more than 60 maneuver types and over 30 warning types that could be returned from the Bing Maps service. More information about maneuver types and warnings is available on MSDN at `http://msdn.microsoft.com/en-us/library/gg650392.aspx` and `http://msdn.microsoft.com/en-us/library/hh441731.aspx`, respectively.

External Libraries

While most access to remote data in Windows Store applications built with HTML and JavaScript will use `WinJS.xhr` to retrieve or submit data, there are other options. Using external libraries, whether JavaScript libraries or other WinRT libraries, can implement their own method of working with remote data. For example, if you use jQuery in your application, you can use `$.get` or `$.post` work with remote HTTP services. Under the covers, jQuery is still using `XMLHttpRequest`, but it abstracts that away from you. Likewise, if you are building or referencing a C# WinRT component, it may access remote data using the `HttpClient` class. While I will introduce a very simple C# WinRT component in Chapter 18, I won't be covering remote data sources with either of these techniques.

Azure Mobile Services

If you are looking for a complete remote data solution, I'd encourage you to look at Windows Azure Mobile Services. In addition to data storage and retrieval, Mobile Services provides a number of great features, such as data validation, user authentication with single sign-on, push notifications, and more. All of these features are supported on multiple platforms, including Windows Store applications, Windows Phone, iOS, Android, and HTML applications. Mobile Services is an enormous topic, and an entire book could be dedicated to it. Rather than attempt that here, I'd suggest going to the Windows Azure Mobile Services Dev Center online at www.windowsazure.com/en-us/develop/mobile, for documentation and tutorials.

Conclusion

There is a lot of data out there. Sometimes, you need it to be available locally, within your app, for offline use, and IndexedDB is a great option for that. Other times, you need to access data from a third-party service, or save data to a custom HTTP service your company has developed. In these cases, `WinJS.xhr` is a great place to start. Other options exist, however, including SQLite, for local data storage, and using external libraries or Windows Azure Mobile Services, to provide access to remote data sources.

Clok is now an application that someone could actually use. Until this chapter, no data was saved, and any changes were lost every time the application was launched. With the introduction in this chapter of IndexedDB, all changes to projects and time entries are now saved. There are still a number of improvements we will continue to make over the next several chapters to improve the user experience, including allowing the user to save some application preferences, which I'll cover in Chapter 15.

■ ■ ■

Session State and Settings

In Chapter 14, I introduced some techniques for working with local and remote data sources. In addition to the data that the user creates and interacts with in your application, there are often other values that have to be saved and loaded as well. For example, you may wish to save the contents of a form that the user is working on, so that you can repopulate the form after your application is terminated and then resumed. Or the user may wish to specify certain preferences to use each time they run your application.

Although possible, storing these types of values in an IndexedDB database is not ideal. In practice, while IndexedDB can store a lot of information in an efficient manner, there are better ways to store these types of values. This is especially true if your application has no other reason to use IndexedDB, due to the overhead that creating and connecting to an IndexedDB database incurs.

The types of values to which I'm referring would be considered session state or settings. Session state and settings are similar concepts, in that they allow you to store simple values, usually small in size, using a simple syntax. Windows Store applications can take advantage of session state and two types of settings—local and roaming. In this chapter, I'll introduce the following topics:

- *Session state*: Store values required to maintain and restore the state of your application, if it is suspended and terminated

- *Local settings*: Store values that have to be maintained between app launches and after reboots. Local to the single machine that the user is currently using

- *Roaming settings*: Functionally the same as local settings, except that they are synchronized between multiple machines

---

■ **Note** Microsoft has published an article on MSDN titled "Storing and retrieving state efficiently." It compares the various options you might consider for storing data, session state, and settings. You can find it at http://msdn.microsoft.com/en-us/library/windows/apps/hh781225.aspx.

Session State

When using Windows 8, you can launch any number of applications from the Start screen. You can have an application running in full-screen mode, or you can have two applications visible, snapped side-by-side. You can switch between open applications at will, and when you return to an application you were previously using, you can pick up where you left off. Standard stuff, right? In reality, all of those applications may not be running all the time. In fact, when you switch away from an application, Windows suspends it. The application is kept in memory until you switch back, at which point Windows resumes the application. Because the application was in memory, this is a pretty seamless experience, and it appears that the application never stopped running.

So, why bring it up? Occasionally, after you switch away from an application, your computer will not have sufficient resources to keep the application in memory. At that point, Windows will terminate the application, releasing the resources it was using. As an example, imagine you were using the application to complete a lengthy form and switched away to look up some information you needed to complete the form. When you find the information you need, you switch back to the application and complete the form. If, while you were looking up the information, Windows terminated the application, what would happen when you switched back? Solving that problem is the purpose of session state. Session state can be used to capture the current state of the application while you are using it, and then restore it when the terminated application is restarted.

Fortunately, WinJS makes it easy to save and retrieve items from session state. I'm going to show you how to incorporate session state into Clok on the Project Detail page. If Clok is terminated while working on this screen, when it resumes, session state will be used to make the screen look just as it did before Clok was terminated.

Saving Session State

In this section, you'll add code to save the current state of the Project Detail form into session state. When a user changes the value in a field, you'll update session state. It's a pretty simple requirement, with a pretty simple implementation. First, open detail.js and add the class aliases highlighted in Listing 15-1 near the top of the file.

Listing 15-1. Adding Some Aliases to Make Things Easier on Ourselves

```
var app = WinJS.Application;
var data = Clok.Data;
var storage = Clok.Data.Storage;
```

The WinJS.Application class has an object named sessionState, which is our access point to working with session state. Because JavaScript is a dynamic language, you can simply attach new properties to sessionState, and they will be saved. Update the ready function by adding the highlighted code in Listing 15-2.

Listing 15-2. Updating Session State When Fields Change

```
ready: function (element, options) {

    // SNIPPED

    WinJS.Utilities.query("input, textarea, select")
        .listen("change", function (e) {
            this.populateProjectFromForm();
            app.sessionState.currProject = this.currProject;
        }.bind(this));

    projectStatus.addEventListener("change", function (e) {
            this.populateProjectFromForm();
            app.sessionState.currProject = this.currProject;
        }.bind(this));
},
```

This code adds an event handler for the change event on any input field, text area, or drop-down list, as well as one for the projectStatus ToggleSwitch. The code for both handlers is the same. First, the populateProjectFromForm function that you added in Chapter 11 is called. Before this point, this function was only used just prior to saving the currProject variable (see Listing 15-3).

Listing 15-3. Previous Usage of the populateProjectFromForm Function

```
this.populateProjectFromForm();
storage.projects.save(this.currProject);
```

In Listing 15-3, the populateProjectFromForm function updates the value of currProject, based on the values in the form fields. Then currProject is saved into app.sessionState, which, as the name suggests, is where session state is stored in WinJS applications.

Pretty simple so far, and this will work great at keeping session state up to date, as the user makes changes to the Project Detail form. However, the change event does not get raised as the user is typing. For text-input controls, it only gets raised after the user changes the control's value and then removes focus from the input field. In many cases, this wouldn't make much difference. However, imagine you had typed several paragraphs into the Description field before the application was terminated. If you had been typing but never triggered the change event by, for example, moving to the next field, your changes would not be added into session state.

To handle this scenario, you have to handle the checkpoint event of WinJS.Application, which is triggered when the application is about to be suspended. Add the highlighted code in Listing 15-4 to detail.js.

Listing 15-4. Handling the Checkpoint Event

```
ready: function (element, options) {

    // SNIPPED

    this.app_checkpoint_boundThis = this.checkpoint.bind(this);
    app.addEventListener("checkpoint", this.app_checkpoint_boundThis);

    WinJS.Utilities.query("input, textarea, select")
        .listen("change", function (e) {
            this.populateProjectFromForm();
            app.sessionState.currProject = this.currProject;
        }.bind(this));

    projectStatus.addEventListener("change", function (e) {
            this.populateProjectFromForm();
            app.sessionState.currProject = this.currProject;
        }.bind(this));
},

checkpoint: function () {
    this.populateProjectFromForm();
    app.sessionState.currProject = this.currProject;
},
```

Although it could be simpler for this current task, the unusual syntax when adding the event listener will come in handy in a moment. In short, I've defined app_checkpoint_boundThis as a function that is the checkpoint function with the this variable scoped to be the same as it is in the ready function. In the checkpoint function, the same code is used as in the other two event handlers defined in Listing 15-2.

Now, any change the user has made, or is in the process of making, will be saved to session state. If he or she has made the change to a field, session state will be updated immediately. If the user is in the process of making a change when the application is terminated, session state will be updated when the application's checkpoint event is triggered.

■ **Note** Windows 8 will not raise an event when it is terminating your application. It will notify the application when it is being suspended, via the `checkpoint` event. Session state should be saved as changes are made to the values being saved, as well as when your application is being suspended.

The checkpoint event is part of the `WinJS.Application` class. That means that the application itself, not just this screen, is raising the event. As a result, we want to make sure that we don't bother to handle the event when this page is not active, such as when the user has navigated away. Likewise, if the user has explicitly navigated away from this page, we can discard the value store in session state. Remember: The purpose of session state is to make your application appear as if it had never been suspended or terminated. Add the code from Listing 15-5 after the ready function in `detail.js`.

Listing 15-5. Resetting Things When the User Navigates Away from the Page

```
unload: function () {
    app.sessionState.currProject = null;
    app.removeEventListener("checkpoint", this.app_checkpoint_boundThis);
},
```

Reading Session State

It was pretty easy to save an object into session state. Now, I'll show you how to put that to use when resuming a terminated application. Currently, when this screen loads, the code in Listing 15-6 is executed to initialize the `currProject` property. If we are editing an existing project, we set `currProject` to that value; otherwise, we set it to a new, empty `Project`.

Listing 15-6. Current Initialization of currProject

```
this.currProject = storage.projects.getById(options && options.id)
    || new Clok.Data.Project();
```

Now that we are adding session state as another factor in initializing `currProject`, the logic is going to get a little more complicated. Let's move that logic into a new function, in an attempt to keep the ready function easier to understand. Replace the code in Listing 15-6, which is the first line of the ready function of `detail.js`, with the code in Listing 15-7.

Listing 15-7. Replacement Code

```
this.setCurrentProject(options);
```

You have to add the newer initialization logic, so define the `setCurrentProject` function in `detail.js` by adding the code from Listing 15-8.

Listing 15-8. New Logic for Initializing currProject

```
setCurrentProject: function (options) {
    var sessionProject = (app.sessionState.currProject)
        ? data.Project.createFromDeserialized(app.sessionState.currProject)
        : null;
```

```
    if (options && options.id && sessionProject && options.id !== sessionProject.id) {
        sessionProject = null;
    }

    this.currProject = sessionProject
        || storage.projects.getById(options && options.id)
        || new Clok.Data.Project();

    app.sessionState.currProject = this.currProject;
},
```

The first thing this function does is determine if a project is currently saved in session state. If it is, but for some reason it is not the same project currently being viewed, the value in session state is ignored. At that point, currProject is set to the Project object from session state, if it exists. If not, but we are editing a project, currProject is set to that Project object. Otherwise, when we are adding a new project, currProject is set to a new, empty Project object. Then, at the end, currProject is saved into session state.

Because the Project Detail screen already binds its form to the currProject property, that's all we have to do. The Project Detail screen will now save its state in session state and recover when the application is resumed after terminating. Let's see how we can test this.

Testing Suspend and Terminate

To test this code from Visual Studio, you have to debug the application (F5), instead of running the application without debugging (Ctrl+F5). You can also click the Debug button on the Visual Studio toolbar. Figure 15-1 shows my Debug button with the debug target set to Simulator. This will start Clok and attach the Visual Studio debugger.

Figure 15-1. *Debugging in the Windows Simulator*

Debug Clok now. I prefer using the Simulator, but you can also choose Local Machine or Remote Machine, if you prefer. Navigate to the Project Detail screen for an existing project and make changes to one or more fields (see Figure 15-2).

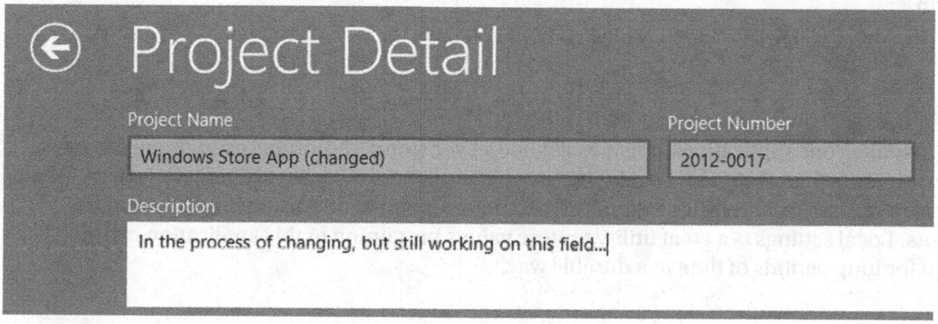

Project Detail

Project Name

Windows Store App (changed)

Project Number

2012-0017

Description

In the process of changing, but still working on this field...

Figure 15-2. *Project Detail, with a change made in one field and a change in progress in another*

While you are still on the Project Detail screen, before you save the project, switch back to Visual Studio. While Clok is running with the debugger attached, you'll see a menu similar to that shown in Figure 15-3 on the toolbar. If you only click the button, it will suspend the application. If, instead, you expand the menu, you have the option to Suspend, Resume, or Suspend and shutdown.

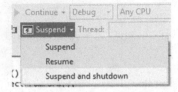

***Figure 15-3.** Simulate application termination*

Because of the way Windows handles suspending an application and resuming it, those scenarios will "just work," and Clok will behave as if it were never interrupted. The Suspend and shutdown option, however, simulates your application being terminated by Windows when resources are too low to keep it in memory while not being used. If you select that option now, Clok will close.

If you launch it again, however, it should return to the same screen, with your in-progress changes still displayed in the form. It should still look like Figure 15-2.

Quick Notes About Session State

Session state is a handy feature of WinJS that allows your application to appear as if it never stopped running. However, there are a few times when session state is discarded.

- We added code to discard it when the user navigates to another screen.

- It is discarded if the user manually closes the application, such as by pressing Alt+F4, or swiping down from the top of a touch screen and dragging the application to the bottom of the screen.

- It is discarded when the user reboots the computer.

In the code that accompanies this book (see the Source Code/Downloads tab of the book's Apress product page [www.apress.com/9781430257790]), you can find a version of the Directions screen that also takes advantage of session state. I have not added it to the Time Entry screen. In case you're feeling ambitious, it might be a good exercise to add session state to that screen. It's a little more complicated than what we've seen here, because it has to take into account which items, if any are selected in the list of time entries, in addition to keeping track of the current state of the time entry add/edit form.

Local Settings

Session state stores values to make your application appear as if it had never stopped running, even though it may have been suspended or terminated, then resumed. Local settings, on the other hand, have a different purpose. While session state eventually gets discarded, local settings are maintained between application launches, application closes, and computer reboots. Local settings is a great utility to store values pertaining to this application on this computer and to store them for long periods of time in a durable way.

Saving Local Settings

While Clok is usable now, there are a number of inconveniences. One glaring issue is that if you start the timer on the dashboard and then close the application or navigate to another screen, when you return, the timer has been stopped and reset. In this section, I'll show you how to use local settings to keep the timer state between application launches and navigation.

To accomplish this, we are going to save the current state of the timer (its startStops property), the currently selected project, and any notes that have been entered into local settings. With these values, it will be possible to show the timer in the correct state when launching Clok or navigating back to the dashboard from another screen in the application. Open home.js and add the code from Listing 15-9 near the top of the file.

Listing 15-9. Adding More Aliases

```
var appData = Windows.Storage.ApplicationData.current;
var localSettings = appData.localSettings;
```

Next, add the code in Listing 15-10 to home.js within that PageControl definition.

Listing 15-10. Functions to Update Local Settings

```
saveDashboardStateToSettings: function () {
    var state = JSON.stringify({
        startStops: elapsedTimeClock.winControl.startStops,
        projectId: Number(project.options[project.selectedIndex].value),
        timeNotes: timeNotes.value,
    });

    localSettings.values["dashboardState"] = state;
},

removeDashboardStateFromSettings: function () {
    localSettings.values.remove("dashboardState");
},
```

Many types of values can be saved to local settings, but, unfortunately, an array of objects representing the times the timer was started and stopped cannot. To get around this, I have used the stringify function in the JSON class to convert the JavaScript object to a JSON-formatted string. While not as convenient as simply saving the state variable into local settings, it's a simple step.

The functions defined in Listing 15-10 will be called from various places in home.js. The saveDashboardStateToSettings function will be called any time the user starts or stops the timer, selects a project, or enters notes. Add the highlighted code in Listing 15-11 to home.js.

Listing 15-11. Calling the Function to Save Local Settings

```
project_change: function (e) {
    this.enableOrDisableButtons();
    this.saveDashboardStateToSettings();
},

timeNotes_change: function (e) {
    this.saveDashboardStateToSettings();
},
```

```
toggleTimer: function () {
    this.timerIsRunning = !this.timerIsRunning;
    this.setupTimerRelatedControls();
    this.saveDashboardStateToSettings();
},
```

Similarly, the removeDashboardStateFromSettings function will be called at one of two different times: when a time entry is either saved or discarded. At the end of both the save and discard functions is a done function, which currently only resets the timer. Add the highlighted code in Listing 15-12 to both of those done functions, to clean up local settings when the value is no longer needed.

Listing 15-12. Cleaning Up Local Settings in Both Save and Discard Functions

```
.done(function () {
    self.resetTimer();
    self.removeDashboardStateFromSettings();
});
```

Reading Local Settings

As with session state, saving local settings is a pretty simple task. You won't be surprised to find that reading them is just as simple. In this section, I'll show you how to read previously saved local settings to cause the Clok dashboard to work as our users expect. The timer will appear as if it has been running continuously, even though the application may not be running. This is one of the reasons I refactored the Timer control from the Clock control in Chapter 12. Because we can calculate the elapsed time based on starts and stops of the timer, we can make the timer appear as if it has been running when it hasn't.

The first thing you'll have to do is add code to read the local setting we created in Listing 15-10. Because we had to save it as a JSON-formatted string, we will have to use the JSON.parse function to convert it back into an object. Add the code in Listing 15-13 to home.js.

Listing 15-13. Function to Read Local Settings and Initialize Controls

```
setDashboardStateFromSettings: function () {
    var state = localSettings.values["dashboardState"];

    if (state) {
        state = JSON.parse(state);

        elapsedTimeClock.winControl.startStops = state.startStops;
        project.selectedIndex = this.getIndexOfProjectId(state.projectId);
        timeNotes.value = state.timeNotes;

        if (elapsedTimeClock.winControl.isRunning) {
            this.startTimer();
        }
    }
},
```

```
getIndexOfProjectId: function (projectId) {
    var index = 0;

    for (var i = 0; i < project.options.length; i++) {
        if (!isNaN(project.options[i].value)
                && Number(project.options[i].value) === projectId) {

            index = i;
            break;
        }
    }

    return index;
}
```

After getting the state out of local settings, it is used to set the correct values for the timer, the selected project, and the notes field. Then, if the timer control should be running, we start it by calling the startTimer function. The startTimer function is new, but the code in it isn't. I just refactored the setupTimerRelatedControls function and pulled out the logic for starting and stopping. Update the setupTimerRelatedControls function and add the two new functions in Listing 15-14.

Listing 15-14. Refactored Function

```
setupTimerRelatedControls: function () {
    if (this.timerIsRunning) {
        this.startTimer();
    } else {
        this.stopTimer();
    }

    this.enableOrDisableButtons();
},

startTimer: function () {
    elapsedTimeClock.winControl.start();
    timerImage.src = "/images/Clock-Running.png";
    timerTitle.innerText = "Stop Clok";
    this.timerIsRunning = true;
},

stopTimer: function () {
    elapsedTimeClock.winControl.stop();
    timerImage.src = "/images/Clock-Stopped.png";
    timerTitle.innerText = "Start Clok";
    this.timerIsRunning = false;
},
```

A small change is needed to the Timer control. Currently, the only way to make the timer start counting is to call the start function. However, this function only works if the timer is not already running. In the case where we are returning to the dashboard screen where the timer should be running, we have to be able to start the interval that updates the elapsed time. Add the highlighted code in Listing 15-15 to the start function in timerControl.js.

Listing 15-15. Add Condition to Allow the Timer to Pick Up Where It Left Off

```
start: function () {
    if (!this.isRunning) {
        this._intervalId = setInterval(this._updateTimer.bind(this), 250);
        this.startStops[this.startStops.length] = { startTime: (new Date()).getTime() };
        this.dispatchEvent("start", {});
    } else if (this._intervalId <= 0) {
        // timer is running, but not updating yet
        this._intervalId = setInterval(this._updateTimer.bind(this), 250);
    }
},
```

The Timer control's isRunning property is true when there is an item in startStops that has a startTime without a stopTime. As long as we stay on the dashboard, the interval to update the UI will be started or stopped, based on the isRunning property. However, if we start the timer, then later relaunch Clok, or simply return to the dashboard screen from another screen in the application, the startStops array would cause isRunning to be true, even though the interval was not updating the UI. With this change, calling start will start the interval either way.

Now update the ready function in home.js with the code from Listing 15-16.

Listing 15-16. Modified Ready Function

```
ready: function (element, options) {

    this.initializeMenuPointerAnimations();
    this.bindListOfProjects();
    this.setDashboardStateFromSettings();
    this.setupTimerRelatedControls();

    toggleTimerMenuItem.onclick = this.toggleTimerMenuItem_click.bind(this);
    project.onchange = this.project_change.bind(this);
    timeNotes.onchange = this.timeNotes_change.bind(this);
    editProjectButton.onclick = this.editProjectButton_click.bind(this);
    saveTimeButton.onclick = this.saveTimeButton_click.bind(this);
    discardTimeButton.onclick = this.discardTimeButton_click.bind(this);

    projectsMenuItem.onclick = this.projectsMenuItem_click.bind(this);
    timesheetMenuItem.onclick = this.timesheetMenuItem_click.bind(this);

},
```

Aside from putting some of the statements in a different order to group similar code, the main difference is that I am calling the new setDashboardStateFromSettings function that we just added in Listing 15-13. Now, there is just one more issue to deal with before launching Clok and testing things out.

You may remember a note in the previous chapter describing the delay in loading the list of projects on the dashboard, due the the data being loaded asynchronously from the IndexedDB database. If you run this code now, the application may still launch, without a fully populated list of projects. Don't worry; the data is there and will be displayed if you navigate to, for example, the Projects screen and then back to the dashboard. However, we just added code to select the appropriate project in this list, based on the state saved to local settings. I mentioned that I would be discussing a way to alleviate this in Chapter 17, when I discuss splash screens and application state. That said, it's hard to show this example working as expected, without a list of projects. I'll show you how to temporarily fix this issue with promises. Add the code in Listing 15-17 as a static member in storage.js.

Listing 15-17. Creating a Function to Initialize IndexedDB

```
initialize: function () {
    return _openDb;
},
```

Wrap the contents of the ready function in home.js (see Listing 15-16) with a call to the initialize function, which returns a Promise object (see Listing 15-18).

Listing 15-18. Wrapping the Contents of the Ready Function in a Promise

```
ready: function (element, options) {
    storage.initialize().done(function () {
        // SNIPPED
    }.bind(this));
},
```

■ **Note**   This is actually a perfectly valid way to handle this issue, but we will address this in a different way in Chapter 17. This fixes the data-loading race condition when the dashboard is the first screen loaded, but it does not address the issue of the user somehow opening Clok to a different screen. That could happen if the user resumed a terminated application performed previously on a different screen, or it might happen by clicking a notification or activating Clok from the Windows Search interface, a topic I will cover in Chapter 19.

Testing Local Settings

There's not much I can demonstrate in a static screenshot that doesn't just look like an image of the dashboard. However, if you run Clok now, you can see the fruits of your labor by a small test.

1. Launch Clok.

2. Start the timer and select a project.

3. Close Clok for a few moments.

4. Relaunch Clok.

When Clok is relaunched, the dashboard will display the total time elapsed since you first started the timer. Test it out by leaving the timer running before closing the application and again by leaving it stopped before closing. You could even reboot your computer in the process.

If Clok was a usable application at the end of Chapter 14, then it is much more usable now. There are still a number of features to be added, but this was the most obvious shortcoming. Another feature that would improve the overall user experience would be to allow him or her to specify some preferences for different options in the application. I'll cover that next, when I introduce roaming settings.

Roaming Settings

Local settings and roaming settings are very similar. They both store values permanently, between application launches and even computer reboots. Because they are both instances of ApplicationDataContainer, their APIs are identical. Both are good choices for storing user preferences. The difference is that anything stored in local settings will only be available on the computer where it was stored. On the other hand, anything stored in roaming settings will be synchronized with any other computers on which the same user has your software installed.

In this section, I'll show you how to use roaming settings to store user preferences for Clok. It is recommended that any settings of this type, which affect the way the user interacts with your application, be stored in roaming settings instead of local settings. If they use the application on another computer, these settings will be synchronized between computers.

At first, it seemed counterintuitive to me to roam settings between computers, but my problem at the time was that every example I was considering was a setting that only made sense for a single computer. I was writing an application to load image files from the user's hard drive, and I wanted to store recently used paths in settings. That wouldn't actually make sense on multiple computers, because the directory containing images on one computer may not exist on the other. When I started thinking about other types of settings, however, I began to see how roaming settings should be my first choice, reverting to local settings, when appropriate. If a setting affects how a user interacts with the application in general, then the setting should roam. For example, in Clok, we're going to allow users to specify if they prefer a 12-hour clock or a 24-hour clock. If they prefer a 12-hour clock on one computer, they will most likely prefer a 12-hour clock on every computer.

One thing to remember with roaming settings is that the settings only roam if users employ a Microsoft Account to log in to their computers. If they do not log in to the computer with a Microsoft Account, roaming settings behave like local settings. Microsoft has published "Guidelines for roaming application data" on MSDN at http://msdn.microsoft.com/en-us/library/windows/apps/hh465094.aspx. If you want to test the synchronization functionality of roaming settings, you can switch your login to a Microsoft Account by going to the Start screen, typing "Users," switching the search context to Settings, and clicking the Users search result. From there, you'll be able to configure your computer so that you can log in with a Microsoft Account (see Figure 15-4).

Figure 15-4. *Switch to a Microsoft account*

Saving Roaming Settings

Clok has a few features for which our users might want to specify preferences. In this section, I'll walk you through how to implement UI to allow them to specify their preferences, as well as how to save those preferences into roaming settings. Specifically, we will allow the user to change the following:

- Whether the current time will be displayed in a 12-hour or 24-hour format

- Whether seconds will be displayed as part of the current time

- A connection timeout for making Bing Maps requests

- Whether to display distances in miles or kilometers on the Directions screen

- Whether to enable or disable the IndexedDB Helper settings flyout we added in Chapter 14

The first thing you'll have to do is add controls to the Clok Options settings flyout that allow the user to indicate his or her preferences. Replace the "win-content" div in settings\options.html with the code from Listing 15-19.

Listing 15-19. Building the Clok Options UI

```
<div class="win-content">
    <div class="win-settings-section">
        <h3>Current Time</h3>
        <div id="clockModeToggle"
            data-win-control="WinJS.UI.ToggleSwitch"
            data-win-options="{
                title:'12-hour format or 24-hour format',
                labelOn: '15:30',
                labelOff: '3:30 PM'
            }"></div>
        <div id="clockSecondsToggle"
            data-win-control="WinJS.UI.ToggleSwitch"
            data-win-options="{
                title:'Show or hide seconds',
                labelOn: 'Show',
                labelOff: 'Hide'
            }"></div>
    </div>

    <div class="win-settings-section">
        <h3>Bing Maps API</h3>
        <label>Connection Speed (timeout)</label>
        <label><input type="radio"
            name="bingMapsTimeout"
            id="bingMapsTimeout_2000"
            value="2000" />Fast connection (2 sec)</label>
        <label><input type="radio"
            name="bingMapsTimeout"
            id="bingMapsTimeout_5000"
            value="5000" />Normal connection (5 sec)</label>
        <label><input type="radio"
            name="bingMapsTimeout"
            id="bingMapsTimeout_10000"
            value="10000" />Slow connection (10 sec)</label>

        <div id="bingMapsDistanceUnitToggle"
            data-win-control="WinJS.UI.ToggleSwitch"
            data-win-options="{
                title:'Metric or Imperial System',
                labelOn: '6.4 km',
                labelOff: '4 mi'
            }"></div>
    </div>

    <div class="win-settings-section">
        <h3>Debugging</h3>
        <div id="indexedDbHelperToggle"
            data-win-control="WinJS.UI.ToggleSwitch"
```

```
            data-win-options="{
                title:'Enable IndexedDB Helper',
                labelOn: 'Enabled',
                labelOff: 'Disabled'
            }"></div>
    </div>
</div>
```

I've added a few ToggleSwitch controls for configuring the current time. Radio buttons are used to specify the Bing Maps connection timeout. Two more ToggleSwitch controls are used for specifying miles or kilometers and for enabling the IndexedDB Helper. Of course, simply showing these controls to the user doesn't update roaming settings. Create a new JavaScript file named options.js in the settings folder, and reference it in the head element of options.html (see Listing 15-20).

Listing 15-20. Referencing

```
<head>
    <title>Options</title>
    <script src="options.js"></script>
</head>
```

Next, add the code in Listing 15-21 to the new options.js file.

Listing 15-21. Saving Roaming Settings

```
(function () {
    "use strict";

    var appData = Windows.Storage.ApplicationData.current;
    var roamingSettings = appData.roamingSettings;

    var page = WinJS.UI.Pages.define("/settings/options.html", {

        ready: function (element, options) {
            clockSecondsToggle.onchange = this.clockSecondsToggle_change;
            clockModeToggle.onchange = this.clockModeToggle_change;

            bingMapsTimeout_2000.onchange = this.bingMapsTimeout_change;
            bingMapsTimeout_5000.onchange = this.bingMapsTimeout_change;
            bingMapsTimeout_10000.onchange = this.bingMapsTimeout_change;

            bingMapsDistanceUnitToggle.onchange = this.bingMapsDistanceUnitToggle_change;
            indexedDbHelperToggle.onchange = this.indexedDbHelperToggle_change;
        },

        clockSecondsToggle_change: function (e) {
            roamingSettings.values["clockSeconds"] =
                clockSecondsToggle.winControl.checked;
        },
```

```
        clockModeToggle_change: function (e) {
            roamingSettings.values["clockMode"] =
                (clockModeToggle.winControl.checked)
                ? Clok.UI.ClockModes.CurrentTime24
                : Clok.UI.ClockModes.CurrentTime12;
        },

        bingMapsTimeout_change: function (e) {
            roamingSettings.values["bingMapsTimeout"] = Number(e.currentTarget.value);
        },

        bingMapsDistanceUnitToggle_change: function (e) {
            roamingSettings.values["bingDistanceUnit"] =
                (bingMapsDistanceUnitToggle.winControl.checked) ? "km" : "mi";
        },

        indexedDbHelperToggle_change: function (e) {
            roamingSettings.values["enableIndexedDbHelper"] =
                indexedDbHelperToggle.winControl.checked;
        },
    });
})();
```

When working with user preferences in a settings flyout, the best practice is to apply any changes as soon as they are made. When a user changes the value of a `ToggleSwitch`, for example, that change should take effect immediately. For that reason, there is no Save or Submit button on the settings flyout. Instead, I've handled the change event for each control with a function that saves the preference into roaming settings as soon as the user indicates a change.

As you can see in this code, any setting that is currently being stored in local settings can be moved to roaming settings by simply changing `localSettings.values["someKey"]` to `roamingSettings.values["someKey"]`. Knowing this, an inspired developer could build a more complex preferences system that allows the user to specify which settings, if any, he or she wants to roam. Based on the user's preference, you would determine whether to use the `localSettings` container or the `roamingSettings` container.

Saving roaming settings was pretty easy. What about reading them?

Reading Roaming Settings

When a user has not specified a preference for a certain setting, your application should use reasonable default values. This actually applies to any kind of setting: local setting, roaming setting, and even session state. There are a few ways you could handle this. One option would be to use a default value when you are inspecting a setting, to get the user's preference and find that he or she hasn't specified one. In some cases, that would be fine, and that is the approach I took with session state. However, with this approach, you would have to check for a value and set a default each time you needed the user's preference. If a particular setting was used in multiple places in your application, you would have duplicate code in each.

Another option is to ensure that the setting always has a value. This is the approach I've taken in Clok. Add the function defined in Listing 15-22 to `default.js`. This function looks at each of the roaming settings and assigns them a default value, if they don't already have a value.

Listing 15-22. Ensure That Roaming Settings Have Appropriate Default Values

```
var initializeRoamingSettings = function () {
    roamingSettings.values["clockSeconds"] =
        roamingSettings.values["clockSeconds"] || false;

    roamingSettings.values["clockMode"] =
        roamingSettings.values["clockMode"] || Clok.UI.ClockModes.CurrentTime12;

    roamingSettings.values["bingMapsTimeout"] =
        roamingSettings.values["bingMapsTimeout"] || 5000;

    roamingSettings.values["bingDistanceUnit"] =
        roamingSettings.values["bingDistanceUnit"] || "mi";

    roamingSettings.values["enableIndexedDbHelper"] =
        roamingSettings.values["enableIndexedDbHelper"] || false;
};
```

Be sure to add the aliases in Listing 15-23 at the top of default.js, near the other aliases.

Listing 15-23. Aliases for Roaming Settings

```
var appData = Windows.Storage.ApplicationData.current;
var roamingSettings = appData.roamingSettings;
```

Because the code in Listing 15-22 will be executed very soon after the application starts, before we have a chance to try to read roaming settings, these settings will always have a value specified. That allows us to simply check the setting when we need it and not be concerned with what to do if the user never saved a value for a particular setting.

While we're still working in default.js, let's add the code to show or hide the IndexedDB Helper settings flyout, based on the user's preference. Update default.js with the highlighted code in Listing 15-24. This includes both a call to initializeRoamingSettings and the logic to decide if the IndexedDB Helper settings flyout should be available.

Listing 15-24. Initializing Roaming Settings and Deciding to Add a Settings Flyout

```
initializeRoamingSettings();

// add our SettingsFlyout to the list when the Settings charm is shown
WinJS.Application.onsettings = function (e) {
    e.detail.applicationcommands = {
        "options": {
            title: "Clok Options",
            href: "/settings/options.html"
        },
        "about": {
            title: "About Clok",
            href: "/settings/about.html"
        }
    };
```

```
    if (roamingSettings.values["enableIndexedDbHelper"]) {
        e.detail.applicationcommands.idbhelper = {
            title: "IndexedDB Helper",
            href: "/settings/idbhelper.html"
        };
    }

    WinJS.UI.SettingsFlyout.populateSettings(e);
};
```

Now let's revisit the Clok Options settings flyout. Right now, the user can open that settings flyout and save his or her settings. However, when the settings flyout is loaded, the controls on the settings flyout do not reflect the current values for each setting. Add the code in Listing 15-25 to options.js. Also, be sure to call the initializeSettingsControls function from the ready function in options.js.

Listing 15-25. Setting Initial State for Controls on Clok Options Settings Flyout

```
initializeSettingsControls: function() {
    clockSecondsToggle.winControl.checked =
        roamingSettings.values["clockSeconds"];

    clockModeToggle.winControl.checked =
        roamingSettings.values["clockMode"] === Clok.UI.ClockModes.CurrentTime24;

    switch (roamingSettings.values["bingMapsTimeout"]) {
        case 5000:
            bingMapsTimeout_5000.checked = true;
            break;
        case 10000:
            bingMapsTimeout_10000.checked = true;
            break;
        default:
            bingMapsTimeout_2000.checked = true;
    }

    bingMapsDistanceUnitToggle.winControl.checked =
        roamingSettings.values["bingDistanceUnit"] === "km";

    indexedDbHelperToggle.winControl.checked =
        roamingSettings.values["enableIndexedDbHelper"];
},
```

As I've shown, updating UI or setting object properties based on settings is simple. While I won't be showing the updates needed in bingMapsWrapper.js to incorporate roaming settings there, I'll briefly remind you where to look when you make these changes yourself. The xhrTimeout variable should be set based on settings, as well as the distanceUnit variable in the getDirections function. Also, remember to update the travelDistanceConverter function to indicate that distances are using the metric system, if that is what the user has specified. If you get stuck, you can see a completed version of the BingMaps class in the source code that accompanies this book. (See the Source Code/Downloads tab of the book's Apress product page [www.apress.com/9781430257790].)

Data Changed Event

In the cases above, the roaming settings are checked each time they are needed. What happens, however, if a setting has already been applied, and then it changes? For example, what if the user specifies he or she wants to use a new theme for your application, but the theme has already been applied when the application launched? Or what if a user changed a roaming setting on another machine? What should your application do when that setting is synchronized to the current machine?

WinRT defines an event that you can handle in these situations. The datachanged event is triggered automatically, whenever roaming settings are synchronized. Additionally, you can trigger it in your own code. I'll walk you through this scenario, as we add code to apply the user's preferences to the formatting of the current time. Triggering the datachanged event manually in your code requires a single line of code. Update options.js with the highlighted code in Listing 15-26.

Listing 15-26. Signaling That Roaming Settings Have Changed

```
clockSecondsToggle_change: function (e) {
    roamingSettings.values["clockSeconds"] =
        (clockSecondsToggle.winControl.checked);

    appData.signalDataChanged();
},

clockModeToggle_change: function (e) {
    roamingSettings.values["clockMode"] =
        (clockModeToggle.winControl.checked)
        ? Clok.UI.ClockModes.CurrentTime24
        : Clok.UI.ClockModes.CurrentTime12;

    appData.signalDataChanged();
},
```

You'll also have to add the code from Listing 15-27 to default.js, to handle the datachanged event.

Listing 15-27. Changing the Display of the Current Time When Roaming Settings Change

```
appData.addEventListener("datachanged", function (args) {
    configureClock();
});

var configureClock = function () {
    currentTime.winControl.showClockSeconds = roamingSettings.values["clockSeconds"];
    currentTime.winControl.mode = roamingSettings.values["clockMode"];
};
```

In addition to applying the user's preferences to the current time format when the settings are changed, you should also apply them when Clok is launched. Modify default.js with the highlighted code from Listing 15-28.

Listing 15-28. Configure the Current Time When Clok Is Launched

```
args.setPromise(WinJS.UI.processAll().then(function () {
    configureClock();

    if (nav.location) {
        nav.history.current.initialPlaceholder = true;
```

```
        return nav.navigate(nav.location, nav.state);
    } else {
        return nav.navigate(Application.navigator.home);
    }
}));
```

In the source code that accompanies this book, I've also used a similar technique on the Directions screen. If users are not viewing the Directions screen when they change their preference from miles to kilometers, or vice versa, we don't have anything to worry about. The next time they get directions, the correct units will be used. However, if they just got directions that specify distances in kilometers, and they switch their preference to miles, the list of directions should be refreshed with the new units. I've accomplished this by listening for the datachanged event in directions.js and refreshing the instructions appropriately.

Size Limitations and Composite Settings

There are limits on what you can synchronize with roaming settings. Each setting can have a name up to 255 characters in length. Additionally, each setting has a maximum size of 8KB, except composite settings, which have a maximum size of 64KB. Composite settings can be used to group a number of related settings together and synchronize them as a unit. We won't be adding any composite settings to Clok, but the code in Listing 15-29 shows an example of how you might use them in your application.

Listing 15-29. Composite Settings

```
var compositeSetting = new Windows.Storage.ApplicationDataCompositeValue();
compositeSetting["first"] = "Scott";
compositeSetting["last"] = "Isaacs";
compositeSetting["dob"] = "Dec 1";
roamingSettings.values["profile"] = compositeSetting;
```

High Priority Roaming Settings

Your user can take advantage of roaming functionality by logging in to multiple machines with the same Microsoft Account. That said, while a roaming setting will take effect immediately on the computer where it was set, it is not instantly synchronized to any other computers. You can specify a single setting to be synchronized as soon as possible by naming it "HighPriority." It can be a composite setting, as described above, but it is limited in size to 8KB. This can be a helpful feature, if you have critical settings to sync, but if you go over this limit, the priority is removed, and it will sync like a normal priority setting.

Conclusion

There is a saying that the devil is in the details. In this chapter, I discussed some techniques to ensure that the little things in your application work as expected. Using session state to set the correct state of your application when it resumes after being terminated can involve a fair amount of tedious work, but if you don't do it, users will believe your application is buggy. Giving your users an opportunity to save settings can make your application appear to run more smoothly, as well as give users the flexibility to make the app function in the way they find most helpful.

Although working with session state and settings can be tedious, it's not difficult code to write or understand. As more applications are released into the Windows Store, you will want yours to stand out for its quality and attention to detail, not for its seeming incompleteness. I encourage you to take the time to evaluate what little details you can implement to improve the experience for your users.

CHAPTER 16

Files

With options ranging from IndexedDB to session state to local settings and more, you have many options when deciding how to save something for use at a later time. In this chapter, I'll cover working with an entirely different type of data: files.

Perhaps the application you're building will work with photos, spreadsheets, documents, or any other types of files. While you may find it possible to save your files using another technique, such as in an IndexedDB database, Windows 8 applications can read, write, and delete files to the user's file system. Computers have been storing files in file systems for a very long time, and unless you have a specific requirement dictating otherwise, the file system is the most logical place to start when considering your option for working with files.

Windows.Storage Namespace

If you're going to be working with files and folders in a Windows Store application, you'll be spending a lot of time working in the Windows.Storage namespace. This namespace contains all of the classes you'll need to create, edit, delete, read, or list files or folders. Some of the most common classes, which I will demonstrate throughout this chapter, are the StorageFile, StorageFolder, and FileIO classes.

The StorageFile and StorageFolder classes represent files and folders on the user's computer. You will be using these classes any time you need to work with a file or folder. Whenever a user makes a selection in a file picker or folder picker, one of these types will be returned. Both classes offer a number of methods useful for, for example, copying, creating, deleting, and opening files and folders. While the StorageFile class provides methods for working with a file on the user's computer, the FileIO class provides a number of methods for working with the *contents* of a StorageFile object. Once you have a StorageFile object, you can use the FileIO class to read the contents of the file or change the contents of the file.

■ **Note** In addition to the FileIO class, which operates on a StorageFile object, you can use the PathIO class, if you have a file path but no StorageFile object. The same methods exist in both classes.

There's one thing to keep in mind when working with files and folders in Windows Store applications. As is the case with any potentially expensive operation in the WinRT or WinJS libraries, all of the methods in the StorageFile, StorageFolder, and FileIO classes are asynchronous. They all return Promise objects to represent the operation that has been requested.

In addition to the StorageFile, StorageFolder, and FileIO classes, the Windows.Storage namespace provides an access point to the location where application data is stored. This access is provided by the same ApplicationData class used in Chapter 15 to set and retrieve local and roaming settings. Specifically, you can use the localFolder property of the Windows.Storage.ApplicationData.current object to reference files stored within the scope of your application. Unsurprisingly, localFolder is an instance of the StorageFolder class.

337

■ **Note** Windows Store application developers have two ways to access a local storage folder for their applications. As mentioned, you can use `Windows.Storage.ApplicationData.current.localFolder`. Additionally, in WinJS applications, you can use the WinJS equivalent, `WinJS.Application.local.folder`.

In this chapter, I'll walk through the usage of these classes, to show how I've implemented two new features in Clok. The first is the ability to back up the projects and time entries stored in the Clok database. The second is a document library where users can store files related to their projects.

Backups of Clok Data

Being able to back up data is a helpful feature in any application. As such, it's a feature I've added to Clok. Clok users will access this feature in the Clok Options settings flyout. From there, they will be able to click a Save Backup button, which will save a copy of project and time-entry data they've saved in Clok.

There's not a lot involved to add this functionality, and the code is pretty short. Although it is short, this code will illustrate how to use a number of the common classes mentioned in the previous section. You'll see that I've used the `localFolder` property to access Clok's local file storage, as well as used methods from each of the `StorageFile`, `StorageFolder`, and `FileIO` classes. Before I can walk you through that code, you'll first have to make a small change to `options.html`. Add the code in Listing 16-1 to `options.html`, after the code for the Debugging section.

Listing 16-1. Adding Controls to the Clok Options Settings Flyout

```
<div class="win-settings-section">
    <h3>Backups</h3>
    <p>Backup Projects and Time Entries</p>
    <p>
        <button id="saveBackupButton">Save Backup</button>
        <span id="backupConfirmation"
            class="win-type-xx-small"
            style="display: none;">Backup saved</span>
    </p>
    <p class="win-type-xx-small">Backup location: <span id="backupPath"></span></p>
</div>
```

This code adds the button that will be used to initiate the backup process, as well as a label to indicate to users where they will find the backup files. You can configure both of those controls by adding the code in Listing 16-2 to the ready function of `options.js`.

Listing 16-2. Configuring the Backups Controls

```
saveBackupButton.onclick = this.saveBackupButton_click;
backupPath.innerText = appData.localFolder.path + "\\backups";
```

The last step to complete this process is to implement the `saveBackupButton_click` handler function. Add the code in Listing 16-3 to `options.js`.

Listing 16-3. Writing a Backup File

```javascript
saveBackupButton_click: function(e) {
    var dateFormatString = "{year.full}{month.integer(2)}{day.integer(2)}"
        + "-{hour.integer(2)}{minute.integer(2)}{second.integer(2)}";
    var clockIdentifiers = Windows.Globalization.ClockIdentifiers;

    var formatting = Windows.Globalization.DateTimeFormatting;
    var formatterTemplate = new formatting.DateTimeFormatter(dateFormatString);
    var formatter = new formatting.DateTimeFormatter(formatterTemplate.patterns[0],
                formatterTemplate.languages,
                formatterTemplate.geographicRegion,
                formatterTemplate.calendar,
                clockIdentifiers.twentyFourHour);

    var filename = formatter.format(new Date()) + ".json";

    var openIfExists = Windows.Storage.CreationCollisionOption.openIfExists;

    appData.localFolder
        .createFolderAsync("backups", openIfExists)
        .then(function (folder) {
            return folder.createFileAsync(filename, openIfExists);
        }).done(function (file) {

            var storage = Clok.Data.Storage;
            var backupData = {
                projects: storage.projects,
                timeEntries: storage.timeEntries
            };
            var contents = JSON.stringify(backupData);
            Windows.Storage.FileIO.writeTextAsync(file, contents);

            backupConfirmation.style.display = "inline";
        });
},
```

The first part of this function uses the DateTimeFormatter class to generate a name for the backup file, based on the current date. Because of a limitation in the DateTimeFormatter class preventing the Clock property, which specifies 12-hour or 24-hour clocks, from being set after an instance of this class was created, I first create a formatterTemplate object, using all the default values. Then I create the formatter object, based on formatterTemplate, specifying the Clock in the constructor. Because the constructor is the only place you can specify which Clock to use, and all of the other parameters are required, this allows the formatter object to use system defaults for all of the other constructor parameters.

The workhorse of this function is the Promise chain in the last half of the function. As I mentioned above, the appData.localFolder object is an instance of StorageFolder. The call to createFolderAsync will create a backups folder in the application's local data folder, if it doesn't already exist. This folder is passed to the then function, which creates a StorageFile object with the createFileAsync call. This file is passed to the done function, which serializes our application data into a string by calling JSON.stringify and saves that to the file using the writeTextAsync call. The last line, then, simply shows a confirmation message to the user.

To see how this works, run Clok and open the Clok Options settings flyout. After clicking the Save Backup button (see Figure 16-1), use Windows Explorer to navigate to the backup location specified to see the file (see Figure 16-2).

Backups
Backup Projects and Time Entries

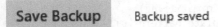

Save Backup   Backup saved

Backup location:

C:\Users\sisaacs\AppData\Local\Packages\068d38c6-

5cdc-44d8-a832-

f96ab138e866_0bzpj67fjc6np\LocalState\backups

Figure 16-1. *Saving a backup in the Clok Options settings flyout*

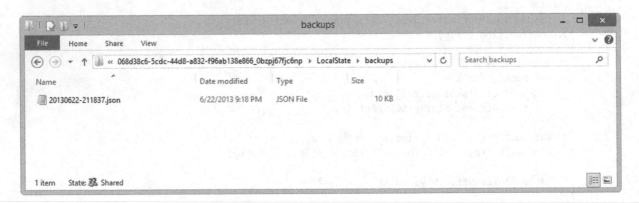

Figure 16-2. *The backup file*

This file contains a JSON representation of all of the projects and time entries in the Clok database. You can open this file in a text editor, such as Notepad (see Figure 16-3), to review its contents. While it's not the most convenient format for reviewing your data, you should be able to see that it is all there.

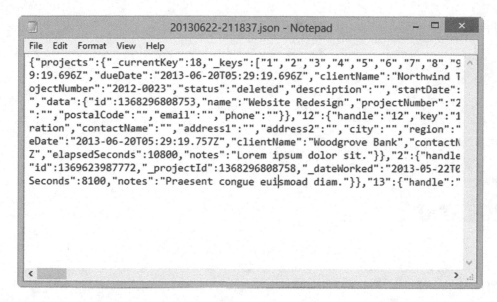

Figure 16-3. The contents of a backup file

Document Library for Clok Projects

Our initial goal for Clok was to offer users a simple way to track the time that they've worked on projects. As we accomplished that goal in Chapter 14, it's time to create some new requirements, to add some other helpful related functionality. In this section, I'll show you how to start building a document library where users can store documents associated with the projects they are working on. Ultimately, users will be able to export and delete files, but we'll start with allowing them to add documents to a project.

Creating the Document Library Page Control

The first thing to do is create a folder named documents in the pages folder of your Visual Studio project. Within the documents folder, add a new page control named library.html (see Figure 16-4).

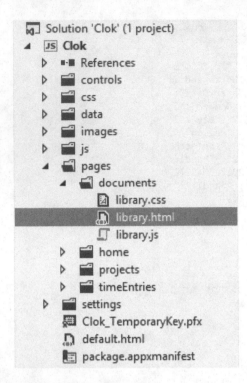

Figure 16-4. *Solution Explorer with new page control for documents*

We'll be building out the Document Library screen through the rest of this chapter, and the first change you'll make is to update the header of the screen to reflect the correct page title, as well as the name of the currently selected project. Update library.html with the highlighted code in Listing 16-4.

Listing 16-4. Showing the Name of the Current Project on the Document Library Screen

```
<div class="library fragment">
    <header aria-label="Header content" role="banner">
        <button class="win-backbutton" aria-label="Back" disabled type="button"></button>
        <h1 class="titlearea win-type-ellipsis">
            <span class="pagetitle">Document Library</span>
            <span class="win-type-x-large" id="projectName">[Project Name]</span>
        </h1>
    </header>
    <section aria-label="Main content" role="main">
        <p>Content goes here.</p>
    </section>
</div>
```

Of course, [Project Name] is just a placeholder. You have to add JavaScript code to set the correct value of the projectName span element. After you define the now familiar storage alias at the top of library.js, update the file with the highlighted code in Listing 16-5.

Listing 16-5. Setting the Project Name

```
ready: function (element, options) {
    this.projectId = options && options.projectId;
    this.setProjectName();
},

setProjectName: function () {
    if (this.projectId) {
        var project = storage.projects.getById(this.projectId);
        projectName.innerText = project.name + " (" + project.clientName + ")";
    }
},
```

Currently, there is no way for the user to navigate to the Document Library. The user should be able to reach this screen from the Project Detail screen. Make the changes needed in detail.html and detail.js to add a new button to the app bar. In the way that you added the button to navigate to the Time Sheets screen, be sure to pass the id of the current project (refer back to Listing 12-32) and enable the button only when viewing an existing project. When you're done, the app bar of the Project Detail should resemble Figure 16-5.

Figure 16-5. Project Detail app bar with new Documents button

---

■ **Note**   You can display the paper clip icon by setting the icon property of the AppBarButton to attach. A completed version of the work described in this chapter is available in the source code that accompanies this book. You can find the code samples for this chapter on the Source Code/Downloads tab of the book's Apress product page (www.apress.com/9781430257790).

Run Clok now and navigate to the Document Library screen. The screen is still empty, but the project and client name should now be displayed in the header (see Figure 16-6). Adding this information to the screen is a small feature, but things like this will go a long way to keep the user oriented as he or she uses the application.

Figure 16-6. Document Library header with project name

Adding Documents to a Project

Now that we have the Document Library page created, the next task is to allow users to add documents to a project in Clok. Adding an Add command to an app bar is the most natural choice when implementing this in the UI. Add the code in Listing 16-6 immediately after the body element.

Listing 16-6. Adding an App Bar to the Document Library Screen

```
<div id="libraryAppBar"
    class="win-ui-dark"
    data-win-control="WinJS.UI.AppBar"
    data-win-options="{ sticky: true }">

    <button
        data-win-control="WinJS.UI.AppBarCommand"
        data-win-options="{
            id:'addDocumentsCommand',
            label:'Add',
            icon:'add',
            section:'global',
            tooltip:'Add'}">
    </button>
</div>
```

In this section, I'll introduce you to the `FileOpenPicker`, which allows the user to select one or more files to be used in your application. In addition to the `FileOpenPicker`, the `Windows.Storage.Pickers` namespace also provides the `FileSavePicker` and the `FolderPicker` classes. I won't cover the `FileSavePicker` class in detail, but it allows the user to save a file with a specified name at a specified location on their computer. The `FolderPicker` class, which as the name suggests, allows the user to select a folder, will be covered later in this chapter. More information about the `Windows.Storage.Pickers` namespace, and all of its classes, is available on MSDN (http://msdn.microsoft.com/en-us/library/windows/apps/windows.storage.pickers.aspx).

Next, wire up the `click` event handler for addDocumentsCommand in the ready function of `library.js`. Also, add the aliases highlighted in Listing 16-7 to the top of `library.js`.

Listing 16-7. Adding Aliases to library.js

```
var storage = Clok.Data.Storage;
var appData = Windows.Storage.ApplicationData.current;
var createOption = Windows.Storage.CreationCollisionOption;
var pickerLocationId = Windows.Storage.Pickers.PickerLocationId;
```

The aliases used in this chapter, and throughout this book, aren't required, but they do allow us to use a shorter syntax when we use them, writing less code, which, I believe, makes it easier to read. I've previously discussed `Windows.Storage.ApplicationData`, and in this chapter we will be using it to gain access to the application's local folder. The `Windows.Storage.CreationCollisionOption` enumeration is used to specify how Windows should handle the case when a file or folder your code is trying to create already exists. Choices include having Windows generate a new file name, overwriting the existing file, using the existing file, or simply failing. The `Windows.Storage.Pickers.PickerLocationId` enumeration is used to specify the preferred location of a file or folder picker being displayed to your user. It includes a number of common locations, such as the user's Desktop folder or Pictures library. In Listing 16-8, you can see how each of these aliases is used. Add the following code to `library.js`.

Listing 16-8. Adding Documents to the Library

```javascript
getProjectFolder: function() {
    if (this.projectId) {
        var projectId = this.projectId;

        return appData.localFolder
            .createFolderAsync("projectDocs", createOption.openIfExists)
            .then(function (folder) {
                return folder.createFolderAsync(projectId.toString(), createOption.openIfExists)
            });
    } else {
        return WinJS.Promise.as();
    }
},

canOpenPicker: function () {
    var views = Windows.UI.ViewManagement;

    var currentState = views.ApplicationView.value;
    if (currentState === views.ApplicationViewState.snapped &&
            !views.ApplicationView.tryUnsnap()) {

        return false;
    }
    return true;
},

addDocumentsCommand_click: function (e) {
    if (!this.canOpenPicker()) {
        return;
    }

    var filePicker = new Windows.Storage.Pickers.FileOpenPicker();
    filePicker.commitButtonText = "Add to Document Library";
    filePicker.suggestedStartLocation = pickerLocationId.desktop;
    filePicker.fileTypeFilter.replaceAll(["*"]);

    filePicker.pickMultipleFilesAsync().then(function (files) {
        if (files && files.size > 0) {

            this.getProjectFolder().then(function (projectFolder) {
                var copyPromises = files.map(function (item) {
                    return item.copyAsync(
                        projectFolder,
                        item.name,
                        createOption.replaceExisting);
                });
```

```
                return WinJS.Promise.join(copyPromises);
            });
        } else {
            return WinJS.Promise.as();
        }
    }.bind(this));
},
```

I've defined three functions here. The first, getProjectFolder, returns a Promise representing the folder that will be used to store documents for the currently selected project. Documents will be stored in a folder named to match the id of the current project. This folder will be located in the local data folder in a folder named projectDocs. An exception will be thrown, if you try to show a FileOpenPicker, or any of the other pickers mentioned above for that matter, while your application is snapped. The second function, canOpenPicker, checks the current view state of the application, whether it is snapped or full-screen. If the application is snapped, the call to tryUnsnap attempts to unsnap it.

The third function is the addDocumentsCommand_click handler function. If the call to canOpenPicker succeeds, then the file picker is initialized before being shown to the user. I've set the commitButtonText to something appropriate, instead of the default value of "Open." I've suggested the picker start on the user's desktop, but this setting is not enforced if the user has recently selected another location. Finally, I specified that all file types should be shown. When the picker is shown, if the user selects one or more files, the selected files are copied using the copyAsync function of each StorageFile object returned from the FileOpenPicker.

Now, run Clok and navigate to the Document Library for a project. Activate the app bar (by right-clicking with your mouse or swiping from the bottom edge of a touch screen) and click the Add button. In Figure 16-7, I've selected four files from a folder on my Desktop named Import Folder. When you click the Add to Document Library button, the selected files are added to the project's document library.

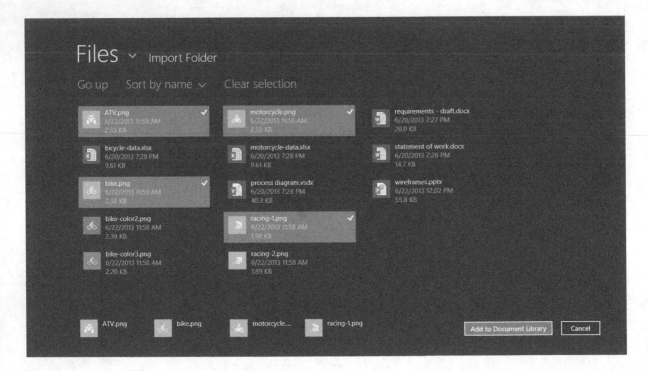

Figure 16-7. *The FileOpenPicker with four files selected*

■ **Note** In addition to specifying folders on their computer, by expanding the menu under Files, users can also specify other applications that implement a file picker contract. For example, they can choose files from their SkyDrive account or even import a picture directly from the camera on their computer.

Exploring the Project Documents

At this point, you can run Clok and add as many files as you wish to a project. Although there's not currently a way to view them in Clok, you can view them in Windows Explorer. In Figure 16-8, you can see that I've added four icons to a project.

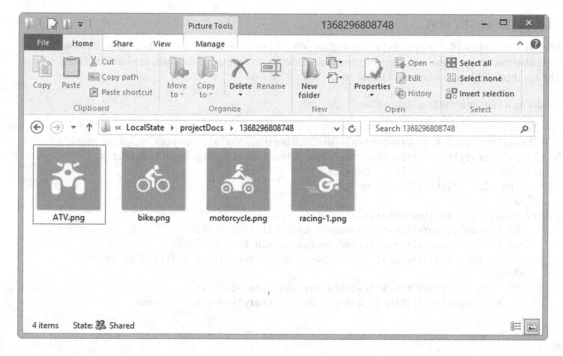

Figure 16-8. *Files added to a project*

The path to Clok's local data folder on my computer is

`C:\Users\sisaacs\AppData\Local\Packages\068d38c6-5cdc-44d8-a832-f96ab138e866_0bzpj67fjc6np\LocalState`

The path will be different on your computer, but it will be in some folder within %USERPROFILE%\AppData\ Local\Packages. You will most likely have many folders in the Packages folder, and your application's data will be in one of them. There are a few ways to find your application's local data folder: by trial and error, by examining the value of appData.localFolder.path, or by matching the "Package name" field on the Packaging tab of the package.appxmanifest file in your Visual Studio project (see Figure 16-9).

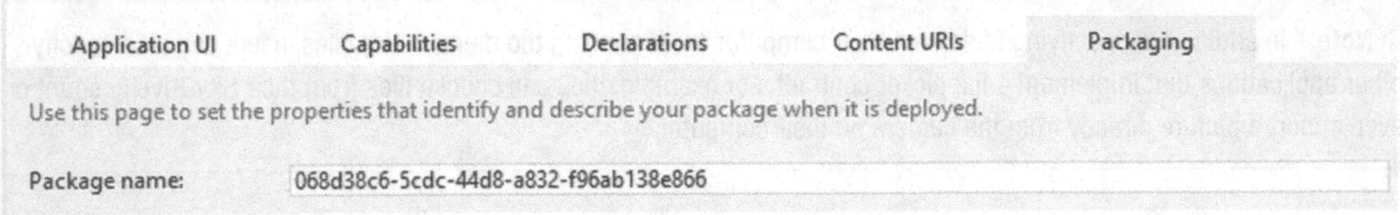

| Application UI | Capabilities | Declarations | Content URIs | Packaging |

Use this page to set the properties that identify and describe your package when it is deployed.

Package name: 068d38c6-5cdc-44d8-a832-f96ab138e866

Figure 16-9. Package name in package.appxmanifest is part of the path to the local data folder

As developers, we have tools to help us easily find this path and view the files in Windows Explorer. Of course, that's not the same for the user who doesn't have the advantage of examining variables or the package.appxmanifest file in Visual Studio. So let's take the next step in building out the Document Library: adding the ability to view files that have been added.

Configuring the ListView

The file picker shown in Figure 16-7 uses a ListView to allow select files. To be consistent with default Windows behavior, we will also use a ListView to display the files in the Document Library to the user. Replace the main section in library.html with the code from Listing 16-9.

Listing 16-9. Adding a ListView for Displaying Files

```
<section aria-label="Main content" role="main">
    <div id="libraryTemplate" data-win-control="WinJS.Binding.Template" style="display: none">
        <div class="libraryItem" data-win-bind="item: item Clok.Library.bindLibraryItem">
            <div class="libraryItem-icon-container">
                <img class="libraryItem-icon" />
            </div>
            <div class="libraryItem-details">
                <h3 class="libraryItem-filename win-type-ellipsis"></h3>
                <h6 class="libraryItem-modified-container win-type-ellipsis">
                    <strong>Modified:</strong> <span class="libraryItem-modified"></span>
                </h6>
                <h6 class="libraryItem-size-container win-type-ellipsis">
                    <strong>Size:</strong> <span class="libraryItem-size"></span>
                </h6>
            </div>
        </div>
    </div>

    <div id="libraryListView"
        class="win-selectionstylefilled"
        data-win-control="WinJS.UI.ListView"
        data-win-options="{
            itemTemplate: select('#libraryTemplate'),
            selectionMode: 'multi',
            swipeBehavior: 'select',
            tapBehavior: 'directSelect'
        }">
    </div>
    <div id="noDocuments" class="hidden">No documents found for this project.</div>
</section>
```

The `libraryListView` will allow the user to select multiple files, each displayed according to the `Template` defined by `libraryTemplate`. For each file, the `ListView` will display a file icon, the file name, the type of the file, and the date the file was last modified. You might have noticed something different about this `Template` from previous `ListView` examples. Rather than binding each value individually, this time I've only specified binding at the top level, and I've specified a binding initializer, `Clok.Library.bindLibraryItem`. This will allow us to implement more complex binding in our JavaScript code, and I'll show this in more detail in the next section.

The CSS should be pretty familiar by now, because it is very similar to what was used in the Projects, Directions, and Time Sheets screens. Add the CSS code from Listing 16-10 to `library.css`.

Listing 16-10. CSS for the Document Library

```css
.hidden {
    display: none;
}

#libraryListView {
    height: calc(100% - 88px);
}

    #libraryListView .win-container {
        background-color: #46468C;
    }

    #libraryListView .libraryItem {
        display: -ms-grid;
        -ms-grid-columns: 80px 350px;
        height: 80px;
    }

    #libraryListView .libraryItem-icon {
        -ms-grid-column: 1;
        margin: 8px;
        width: 64px;
        height: 64px;
        text-align: center;
    }

    #libraryListView .libraryItem-details {
        -ms-grid-column: 2;
        margin: 5px;
    }

    #libraryListView .libraryItem-filename {
        font-size: 1.25em;
    }
```

In all of our previous `ListView` examples, we've bound the `ListView` to a `WinJS.Binding.List` object. We could use the functions on the `StorageFile` and `StorageFolder` classes to build our own `List`, but there's a better way to show file system information in a `ListView`.

Configuring StorageDataSource

A ListView can be bound to any class that implements the IListDataSource interface. While we could populate a WinJS.Binding.List object with info about files and folders, the StorageDataSource already exists for just this purpose. Because it implements IListDataSource, we can bind directly to it. In addition to being simpler than alternatives, using StorageDataSource offers the additional benefit of being a "live view" of the files and folders. As a result, if you add a new file, or delete an existing one, the data source will immediately reflect this and update the ListView.

In this section, I'll demostrate how to create a simple StorageDataSource object to reflect the contents of a project's document library. I'll bind this data to the ListView created in the previous section, and then in the next section, I'll show you how you can allow your users to open a file directly from Clok.

Creating a StorageDataSource object to bind to our ListView requires just a few lines of code. Add the code from Listing 16-11 to library.js.

Listing 16-11. Creating a StorageDataSource Object

```
bindProjectLibraryFiles: function () {
    if (this.projectId) {
        var resizeThumbnail = thumbnailOptions.resizeThumbnail;
        var singleItem = thumbnailMode.singleItem;

        this.getProjectFolder().then(function (folder) {
            var fileQuery = folder.createFileQuery();

            var dataSourceOptions = {
                mode: singleItem,
                requestedThumbnailSize: 64,
                thumbnailOptions: resizeThumbnail
            };

            var dataSource = new WinJS.UI.StorageDataSource(fileQuery, dataSourceOptions);

            dataSource.getCount().then(function (count) {
                if (count >= 1) {
                    libraryListView.winControl.itemDataSource = dataSource;
                    WinJS.Utilities.addClass(noDocuments, "hidden");
                    WinJS.Utilities.removeClass(libraryListView, "hidden");
                } else {
                    WinJS.Utilities.removeClass(noDocuments, "hidden");
                    WinJS.Utilities.addClass(libraryListView, "hidden");
                }
            });
        });
    }
},
```

The StorageDataSource constructor takes a query object and an options object. The query parameter can either be a string from a list of common Windows libraries on the user's computer ("Music," "Pictures," "Videos," or "Documents"), or it can be an object that implements IStorageQueryResultBase. If you are working specifically with the user's Pictures or Music libraries, for example, it's very simple to just pass one of those strings as the first parameter to the StorageDataSource constructor. If you are working with another location on the user's computer, you must create a query object.

In Listing 16-11, because I already have a reference to a StorageFolder object—the current project's document library—I can call the createFileQuery function to get a valid query object. The second parameter of the StorageDataSource constructor defines some additional options, primarily related to thumbnail information that will be included in the results of the query. More information about the StorageDataSource class and these two constructor parameters is available on MSDN web site (http://msdn.microsoft.com/en-us/library/windows/apps/br212651.aspx).

■ **Note** The createFileQuery function builds a query that allows you to work with all files in the top level of the StorageFolder object. In addition to createFileQuery, the StorageFolder class defines five other functions that return different types of file or folder queries, as well as two that can be used to query both files and folders together. More information about these other StorageFolder functions is available on MSDN web site (http://msdn.microsoft.com/en-us/library/windows/apps/windows.storage.storagefolder.aspx).

After creating the data source, I've called the getCount function, to check if there are any files in the current project's document library. If there are, then I set the itemDataSource property of the ListView to this data source and make the results visible. If no files exist, then I instead show a message to the user.

I pointed out in the previous section how I only bound data to the top level of the WinJS.Binding.Template being used to format file information. Instead of binding each element individually, I've chosen to use a binding initializer function named bindLibraryItem to handle some more complex binding requirements. Add the highlighted code in Listing 16-12 after the page definition in library.js.

Listing 16-12. The Binding Initializer Function

```
(function () {
    "use strict";

    // SNIPPED

    WinJS.UI.Pages.define("/pages/documents/library.html", {
        // SNIPPED
    });

    function bindLibraryItem(source, sourceProperty, destination, destinationProperty) {
        var filenameElement = destination.querySelector(".libraryItem-filename");
        var modifiedElement = destination.querySelector(".libraryItem-modified");
        var sizeElement = destination.querySelector(".libraryItem-size");
        var iconElement = destination.querySelector(".libraryItem-icon");

        filenameElement.innerText = source.name;

        modifiedElement.innerText = source.basicProperties
            && source.basicProperties.dateModified
            && formatDateTime(source.basicProperties.dateModified);

        var size = source.basicProperties && source.basicProperties.size;
        if (size > (Math.pow(1024, 3))) {
            sizeElement.innerText = (size / Math.pow(1024, 3)).toFixed(1) + " GB";
        }
```

```
        else if (size > (Math.pow(1024, 2))) {
            sizeElement.innerText = (size / Math.pow(1024, 2)).toFixed(1) + " MB";
        }
        else if (size > 1024) {
            sizeElement.innerText = (size / 1024).toFixed(1) + " KB";
        }
        else {
            sizeElement.innerText = size + " B";
        }

        var url;

        if (source.thumbnail && isImageType(source.fileType)) {
            url = URL.createObjectURL(source.thumbnail, { oneTimeOnly: true });
        } else {
            url = getIcon(source.fileType);
        }

        iconElement.src = url;
        iconElement.title = source.displayType;
    }

    WinJS.Utilities.markSupportedForProcessing(bindLibraryItem);

    WinJS.Namespace.define("Clok.Library", {
        bindLibraryItem: bindLibraryItem,
    });

})();
```

When WinJS calls our binding initializer for each item in the ListView, it passes the data source object—the file—as the source parameter to this function and the HTML element as the destination parameter. A different initializer could have been specified for each data-bound value, and if that were the case, we would take advantage of the sourceProperty and destinationProperty parameters as well. However, in this case, I've ignored those. Instead, I use query selectors to find the elements that should display data-bound information to the user, and I set the innerText properties of those elements based on my custom logic. For example, depending on the size of the file, the file size is either displayed in gigabytes, megabytes, kilobytes, or simply bytes.

The file icon is a little different. The StorageDataSource provides the icons that would be used in Windows Explorer, and I could have chosen to display those in the ListView. Instead, I show the provided icons only when the file in the library is an image. This will cause thumbnail versions of the images to be displayed in the ListView. In all other cases, I prefer to display custom file type icons that match Clok's modern style, and I use the getIcon function, which I'll include in a moment, to determine what that icon should be.

▪ **Note** The images I've used for file type icons are available in the source code that accompanies this book. You can find the code samples for this chapter on the Source Code/Downloads tab of the book's Apress product page (www.apress.com/9781430257790).

After defining the binding initializer, I've made it available to be used from library.html, by calling markSupportedForProcessing and exposing it publicly as Clok.Library.bindLibraryItem. Additionally, a few other functions are required to make this binding initializer work. Add the code in Listing 16-13 after the bindLibraryItem definition in library.js.

Listing 16-13. Functions to Support the Binding Initializer

```
function formatDateTime(dt) {
    var formatting = Windows.Globalization.DateTimeFormatting;
    var dateFormatter = new formatting.DateTimeFormatter("shortdate");
    var timeFormatter = new formatting.DateTimeFormatter("shorttime");
    return dateFormatter.format(dt) + " " + timeFormatter.format(dt);
}

function isImageType(fileType) {
    fileType = (fileType || "").toLocaleUpperCase();

    return fileType === ".PNG"
        || fileType === ".GIF"
        || fileType === ".JPG"
        || fileType === ".JPEG"
        || fileType === ".BMP";
}

function getIcon(fileType) {
    fileType = (fileType || "").replace(".", "");

    var knownTypes = ["WAV", "XLS", "XLSX", "ZIP",
        "AI", "BMP", "DOC", "DOCX", "EPS", "GIF",
        "ICO", "JPEG", "JPG", "MP3", "PDF", "PNG",
        "PPT", "PPTX", "PSD", "TIFF", "VSD", "VSDX"];

    if (knownTypes.indexOf(fileType.toLocaleUpperCase()) >= 0) {
        return "/images/fileTypes/" + fileType + ".png";
    }

    return "/images/fileTypes/default.png";
}
```

An ambitious developer might replace the definition of getIcon with one that dynamically examines the contents of the images/fileTypes folder, to determine which icons are available. Because these icons are included in the package that is installed when the user downloads Clok, those icons will not be found in the local data folder. Instead, you should look for these files in Windows.ApplicationModel.Package.current.installedLocation, which is also a StorageFolder object.

Two more simple steps are required to display the files in the current project's document library. You'll have to add two more aliases at the top of library.js (see Listing 16-14) and add a call to this.bindProjectLibraryFiles in the ready function.

Listing 16-14. Adding Two More Aliases

```
var storage = Clok.Data.Storage;
var appData = Windows.Storage.ApplicationData.current;
var createOption = Windows.Storage.CreationCollisionOption;
var pickerLocationId = Windows.Storage.Pickers.PickerLocationId;
var thumbnailOptions = Windows.Storage.FileProperties.ThumbnailOptions;
var thumbnailMode = Windows.Storage.FileProperties.ThumbnailMode;
```

Run Clok now and navigate to the Document Library. You'll see the documents you added previously, and if you add more documents now, the `StorageDataSource` will automatically update the `ListView` with the new documents (see Figure 16-10).

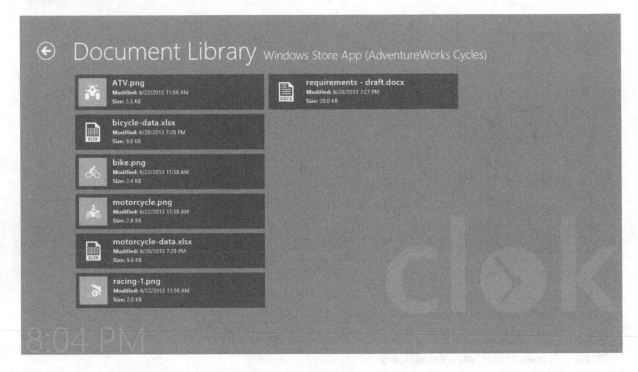

Figure 16-10. *Document Library with various images and documents*

Launching Files

Now that files are displayed in the Document Library, a helpful feature would be to allow the user to open documents directly from Clok. In this section, I'll demonstrate adding a new app bar button that does just that. Add the code from Listing 16-15 to the `AppBar` definition in `library.html`.

Listing 16-15. Adding an Open Button to the App Bar

```
<button
    data-win-control="WinJS.UI.AppBarCommand"
    data-win-options="{
        id:'openDocumentCommand',
        label:'Open',
```

```
                icon:'openfile',
                section:'selection',
                tooltip:'Open',
                disabled: true}">
</button>
```

To prevent accidental launches of multiple files at once, I've added the requirement that only one file be opened at a time. To enforce this, I've handled the onselectionchanged event of the ListView, and the Open button is only enabled when a single item is selected in the ListView. Add the code in Listing 16-16 to library.js to implement this.

Listing 16-16. Enable or Disable the Open Button, Based on the Number of Items Selected in the ListView

```
libraryListView_selectionChanged: function (e) {
    // Get the number of currently selected items
    var selectionCount = libraryListView.winControl.selection.count();

    if (selectionCount <= 0) {
        openDocumentCommand.winControl.disabled = true;
        libraryAppBar.winControl.hide();
    } else if (selectionCount > 1) {
        openDocumentCommand.winControl.disabled = true;
        libraryAppBar.winControl.show();
    } else { // if (selectionCount === 1) {
        openDocumentCommand.winControl.disabled = false;
        libraryAppBar.winControl.show();
    }
},
```

When the user clicks this button, a call to Windows.System.Launcher.launchFileAsync will open the file in the default file viewer. Add the click event handler in Listing 16-17 to library.js.

Listing 16-17. The Click Event Handler for the Open Button

```
openDocumentCommand_click: function (e) {
    libraryListView.winControl.selection.getItems()
        .then(function (selectedItems) {
            if (selectedItems && selectedItems[0] && selectedItems[0].data) {
                return Windows.System.Launcher.launchFileAsync(selectedItems[0].data);
            }
        })
        .then(null, function error(result) {
            new Windows.UI.Popups
                .MessageDialog("Could not open file.", "An error occurred. ")
                .showAsync();
        });
},
```

The code will only open the first of the selected files, but because you added the code in Listing 16-16, there should never be more than one item selected anyway. If the file can be opened, the default application for this file type is launched; otherwise, an error message is displayed. An overloaded version of launchFileAsync allows you to specify additional options to use when launching. For example, you could also add an Open With... app bar button and specify that the user should be given a choice of applications to launch for the selected file. This could be especially useful for images, because the default application may be an application that doesn't allow the user to edit the image. By allowing users to specify the application they wish to launch, they could choose to edit the file instead. Because the code is nearly identical to what I've just covered, I won't demonstrate that in this book, but I have implemented this functionality in the source code that accompanies this book. (See the Source Code/Downloads tab of the book's Apress product page [www.apress.com/9781430257790].)

The last step to allow the user to launch a document in its default application is to wire up the event handlers in the ready function. Add the highlighted code in Listing 16-18 to library.js.

Listing 16-18. Wiring Up the New Event Handlers

```
ready: function (element, options) {
    this.projectId = options && options.projectId;

    this.setProjectName();
    this.bindProjectLibraryFiles();

    libraryListView.winControl.onselectionchanged =
        this.libraryListView_selectionChanged.bind(this);

    openDocumentCommand.winControl.onclick = this.openDocumentCommand_click.bind(this);
    addDocumentsCommand.winControl.onclick = this.addDocumentsCommand_click.bind(this);
},
```

Run Clok now and navigate to the Document Library. When you select a single file, you will be able to open it with the default application for that file type (see Figure 16-11).

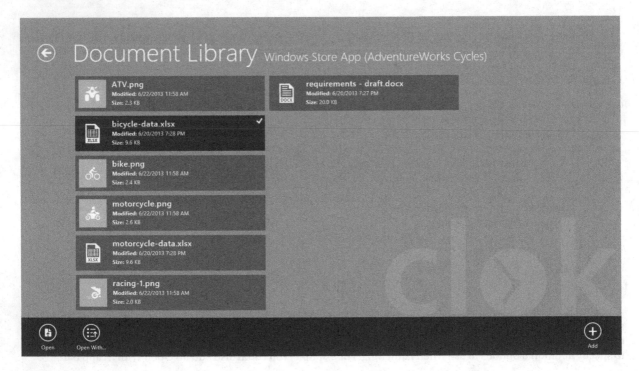

Figure 16-11. Clicking the Open button will launch the selected spreadsheet with Microsoft Excel

Managing Project Documents

Our Document Library is coming together and is already a useful addition to Clok. Before I conclude this chapter, I want to add two more features. To illustrate copying files out of Clok's local data folder, I'll implement an Export feature, and to illustrate how to delete files from a StorageFolder, I'll add a Delete feature.

■ **Note**   Your users who consider themselves power users will be happy to discover that the same keyboard shortcuts that they use in Windows Explorer also apply to items in a ListView control. If a ListView is currently in focus, you can use Ctrl+A to select all items in a ListView, the ESC key to deselect everything, and the arrow keys to navigate through the items in the ListView. Additionally, you can Shift-click or Ctrl-click items in a ListView to select multiple items.

Exporting Files with Folder Picker

How useful is it to allow the user to add to Clok as many documents as he or she wishes but not provide any way to get documents out? In this section, I'll show you how to add Export functionality to the Document Library. First, let's add a new button to the app bar. Add the code in Listing 16-19 to library.html.

Listing 16-19. Adding an Export Button to the App Bar

```
<button
    data-win-control="WinJS.UI.AppBarCommand"
    data-win-options="{
        id:'exportDocumentsCommand',
        label:'Export',
        icon:'savelocal',
        section:'selection',
        tooltip:'Export',
        disabled: true}">
</button>
```

Not surprisingly, exporting files from the Document Library is similar to adding files to it. The copyAsync method of a StorageFile object performs the actual file copy operation. The biggest difference is that instead of picking files to add to the Document Library with the FileOpenPicker and determining the StorageFolder to use with the getProjectFolder function, you will get a reference to a collection of StorageFile objects from the ListView objects selection property and will allow the user to specify a StorageFolder with a FolderPicker. Once you have a StorageFolder and collection of StorageFile objects, the basic process is the same. Add the code from Listing 16-20 to library.js.

Listing 16-20. The Click Handler for the Export Button

```
exportDocumentsCommand_click: function (e) {
    if (!this.canOpenPicker()) {
        return;
    }

    var folderPicker = new Windows.Storage.Pickers.FolderPicker;
    folderPicker.suggestedStartLocation = pickerLocationId.desktop;
    folderPicker.fileTypeFilter.replaceAll(["*"]);
```

```
folderPicker.pickSingleFolderAsync().then(function (folder) {
    if (folder) {
        return libraryListView.winControl.selection.getItems()
            .then(function (selectedItems) {
                var copyPromises = selectedItems.map(function (item) {
                    return item.data.copyAsync(
                        folder,
                        item.data.name,
                        createOption.generateUniqueName);
                });

                return WinJS.Promise.join(copyPromises);
            });
    } else {
        return WinJS.Promise.as();
    }
}).then(function error(result) {
    new Windows.UI.Popups
        .MessageDialog("All files successfully exported.", "File export is complete.")
        .showAsync();
}, function error(result) {
    new Windows.UI.Popups
        .MessageDialog("Could not export all selected files.", "An error occurred. ")
        .showAsync();
});
},
```

■ **Note**   Remember to wire up this `click` event handler in the `ready` function and to modify `libraryListView_selectionChanged`, to enable the Export button when one or more documents in the list have been selected.

While the process is the same as adding documents, I have made one change here. Instead of replacing a file that already exists, the copyAsync function will generate a new name for the copied file, if there is a naming conflict. A useful feature that you might implement yourself is to allow the user to specify if he or she wants to replace existing files, keep both copies of the file, or cancel the Export operation.

After you add code to enable the Export button when one or more items are selected in the ListView, and wire up this click event handler in the ready function of library.js, the document Export functionality will be complete. Before you test this, however, let's go ahead and add the Delete functionality as well.

Deleting Files from Local Application Folder

"Whoops! I didn't mean to add that file." "This mockup is out of date." "My hard drive is getting full."

There are many reasons a user may wish to delete a file from the Document Library, and these are only a few. Fortunately, deleting files is just as simple as exporting them. First, let's add a new button to the app bar. Add the code in Listing 16-21 to library.html.

Listing 16-21. Adding a Delete Button to the App Bar

```
<button
    data-win-control="WinJS.UI.AppBarCommand"
    data-win-options="{
        id:'deleteDocumentsCommand',
        label:'Delete',
        icon:'delete',
        section:'selection',
        tooltip:'Delete',
        disabled: true}">
</button>
```

Before deleting a file, which is a permanent operation, you'll prompt the user to make sure he or she meant to click the Delete button. Add the code from Listing 16-22 to library.js.

Listing 16-22. The Click Handler for the Delete Button

```
deleteDocumentsCommand_click: function (e) {
    var msg = new Windows.UI.Popups.MessageDialog(
        "This cannot be undone.  Do you wish to continue?",
        "You're about to permanently delete files.");

    var buttonText = (libraryListView.winControl.selection.count() <= 1)
        ? "Yes, Delete It"
        : "Yes, Delete Them";

    msg.commands.append(new Windows.UI.Popups.UICommand(buttonText, function (command) {
        libraryListView.winControl.selection.getItems()
            .then(function (selectedItems) {
                var deletePromises = selectedItems.map(function (item) {
                    return item.data.deleteAsync();
                });

                return WinJS.Promise.join(deletePromises);
            })
            .then(null, function error(result) {
                new Windows.UI.Popups
                    .MessageDialog("Could not delete selected files.", "An error occurred.")
                    .showAsync();
            });
    }));

    msg.commands.append(new Windows.UI.Popups.UICommand(
        "No, Don't Delete Anything",
        function (command) { }
    ));

    msg.defaultCommandIndex = 0;
    msg.cancelCommandIndex = 1;

    msg.showAsync();
},
```

If the user confirms that he or she does wish to continue, it's a simple matter of calling the deleteAsync for each StorageFile in the selection. Don't forget to enable the Delete button when one or more items are selected in the ListView, and be sure to wire up this click event handler in the ready function of library.js.

Now it's time to see the results of your work. You now have a completely functioning Document Library. Run Clok now and navigate to the Document Library (see Figure 16-12). Run through all of the functions to see how they work. Add some files, open them, export them, and delete them. You should find that the experience is pretty natural, and it should be familiar to anyone who has used Windows 8 for a short amount of time.

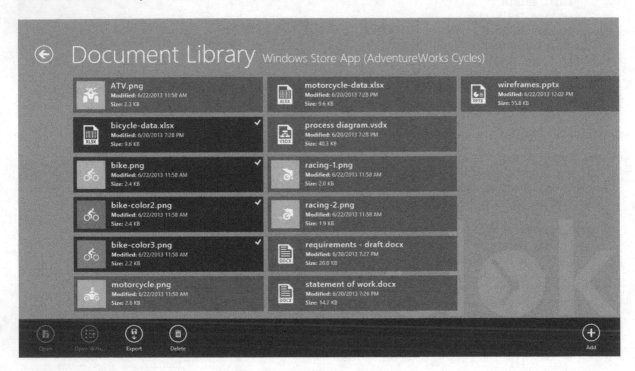

Figure 16-12. *The completed Document Library*

Conclusion

Working with files is inevitable. While the async nature of StorageFile and StorageFolder functions changes the way you interact with files and folders, if you have done any other development in other programming languages involving the file system of the user's computer, these differences are easily understood. There is a lot of advanced functionality available in the Windows.Storage namespace. If you find that this introductory chapter doesn't meet all your needs, be sure to read the MSDN documentation online (http://msdn.microsoft.com/en-us/library/windows/apps/windows.storage.aspx).

We'll revisit the Document Library in Chapter 19, when I introduce the Share contract, and again in Chapter 22, when I discuss working with the user's camera.

CHAPTER 17

∎ ∎ ∎

Handling State Changes

Arguably the most important requirement of any application is that it work as the user expects it to in every situation. Clearly it's important for your application to perform its core tasks correctly, but that's not what I'm talking about here.

The details, or little touches, that you add to your application to make it appear to "just work" will keep users coming back to it again and again. Similar to the subtle animations I described in Chapter 10, this attention to detail might never be apparent to most users, but if you left it out, they would surely notice. In this chapter, I'll discuss two areas where you can do a little work that will make your application seem more polished.

The first thing is to consider the activation state of your application. How was your application started? How was the user previously interacting with your application? Does the user think your application is still running in the background, even though Windows has terminated it, due to resource constraints? The second area is to consider the view state of your application. Are users viewing your application in landscape orientation or portrait orientation? Have they snapped your application in a narrow pane, while they look at another application beside it? Have they snapped another application in a narrow pane, while they look at your application beside it?

Considering these types of questions while building your application will allow you to make decisions that will help you meet the expectations of your users. Fortunately, the code required is usually pretty simple to implement. So, for a relatively small effort, you can address what is, again, arguably, the most important requirement of any application.

Application Activation State

There are several ways that you can allow users to activate your application. The simplest, and most common, way is to launch it by clicking a tile on their Start screen. However, your application could also be launched in one of the following ways:

- When a user uses the Windows Search charm to find something within your application

- When a user uses the Windows Share charm to share something with your application

- When a user specifies your application in a `FileOpenPicker` or `FileSavePicker` when opening or saving a file from another application

Those are just a few of the many ways your application can be activated. There are more than a dozen ways to activate a Windows Store application. The `Windows.ApplicationModel.Activation.ActivationKind` enumeration defines all of the different types of ways your application can be activated. As I mentioned, launching your application from a tile on the Start screen is the most common kind of activation, and it is the only kind I will cover in this chapter. In Chapter 19, I'll demonstrate how to search within your application, as well as how to share documents with your application.

■ **Note** Documentation of the Windows.ApplicationModel.Activation.ActivationKind enumeration is available on MSDN (http://msdn.microsoft.com/en-us/library/windows/apps/windows.applicationmodel.activation. activationkind).

When you first created the Clok Visual Studio project from the Navigation App template in Chapter 9, default.js was added to your project with a lot of boilerplate code included. That code included handling the application's activated event. It's easy to overlook what was added, but let's take a closer look now. If you open default.js, you will see the activated event handler (see Listing 17-1).

Listing 17-1. The Application's Activated Event Handler

```
var app = WinJS.Application;
var activation = Windows.ApplicationModel.Activation;

// SNIPPED

app.addEventListener("activated", function (args) {
    if (args.detail.kind === activation.ActivationKind.launch) {
        // SNIPPED
    }
});
```

The first line of this handler checks to see how the application was activated. In this generated code, the event handler only does something when the application is launched, most likely from the Start screen.

Extending the Splash Screen

Every Windows Store application has a splash screen. When you create a new project in Visual Studio using one of the project templates discussed in Chapter 4, Visual Studio adds a placeholder image on a gray background. This is the default Clok splash screen, which can be seen in Figure 17-1. In Chapter 23, I'll show you how to brand your application with a customized splash screen.

Figure 17-1. *Default Clok splash screen*

Windows automatically displays this splash screen for a short time before the first screen of your application is made visible. Sometimes, however, you might have the need to perform some tasks before the user can interact with your application. For example, you may need to load data into memory, request data from a web service, or open a large document. In these cases, your application may appear to be broken, if these tasks do not complete before your first screen is visible. This is exactly the issue we ran into in Chapter 14.

When Clok launches, data is loaded from our IndexedDB database into the WinJS.Binding.List that is used to populate the drop-down list of projects on the Clok dashboard. Because this data is loaded asynchronously, the dashboard screen often loads before the necessary data is in the List. In Chapter 15, I changed home.js to initialize the List first, and then wrapped the contents of the ready function in the done function of the Promise (see Listing 17-2).

Listing 17-2. Current Ready Function in home.js

```
ready: function (element, options) {
    storage.initialize().done(function () {
        // SNIPPED
    }.bind(this));
},
```

In this section, I'll show you how you can use an extended splash screen to load this data during Clok's activation process. An extended splash screen is not exactly what the name might initially suggest. It is not a change to the splash screen that Windows shows by default. Neither is it necessarily a separate screen, although you could theoretically implement it on a separate screen. The most common way to implement an extended splash screen is by defining it within a div element in default.html. The div is configured to look exactly like the default splash screen, optionally showing additional controls, such as a progress bar to indicate to the user that the application is still loading.

This is the technique we'll use in Clok. Start by removing the highlighted lines of code in Listing 17-2 from home.js. Then add the code from Listing 17-3 to default.html, immediately after the opening body tag.

Listing 17-3. Markup for the Extended Splash Screen

```
<div id="extendedSplash" class="hidden">
    <img id="splashImage" src="/images/splashscreen.png" />
    <progress id="splashProgress" style="color: white;"></progress>
</div>
```

The image referenced, `splashscreen.png`, is the same image used on the default splash screen seen in Figure 17-1. This file can be configured in `package.appxmanifest`, and I will cover that in Chapter 23. Beneath the image, I've added an indeterminate progress bar that will continue to animate while the extended splash screen is visible. To make the extended splash screen match the appearance of the default splash screen, add the CSS in Listing 17-4 to `default.css`.

Listing 17-4. CSS for the Extended Splash Screen

```
.hidden {
    display: none;
}

#extendedSplash {
    background-color: #3399aa;
    height: 100%;
    width: 100%;
    position: absolute;
    top: 0px;
    left: 0px;
    text-align: center;
}

    #extendedSplash #splashImage {
        position: absolute;
    }
```

We'll take advantage of the absolute positioning to ensure that `splashscreen.png` is displayed at the same location in the extended splash screen as it is in the default splash screen. I'll show this in a few moments. Additionally, I've set the background color of the extended splash screen to match the background color of Clok. If you don't have a good reason to do otherwise, the recommendation from Microsoft is to have the background color of the extended splash screen match the background color of the default splash screen, which is specified in `package.appxmanifest`. Currently, Clok's default splash screen has a gray background, but I'll show you how to change this in Chapter 23. So, while the background color does not currently match that of the default splash screen, it ultimately will before Clok is ready for the Windows Store.

■ **Note** Microsoft's guidance for splash screens is available on MSDN (http://msdn.microsoft.com/en-us/library/windows/apps/hh465338.aspx).

I will show you how to create a class that will manage the extended splash screen. This new class will take care of showing and hiding the splash screen, when needed, as well as making sure that your long-running initialization code functions at the correct point in the process. To prepare for this, a little bit of refactoring is needed in `default.js`. To help ensure that our code is still readable and understandable at the end of this section, the code that was snipped from Listing 17-1 has to be moved into its own function. In `default.js`, modify the `activated` event handler and create a new function, as illustrated in Listing 17-5.

Listing 17-5. Refactored Activated Event Handler

```
app.addEventListener("activated", function (args) {
    if (args.detail.kind === activation.ActivationKind.launch) {
        launchActivation(args);
    }
});

var launchActivation = function (args) {
    if (args.detail.previousExecutionState
            !== activation.ApplicationExecutionState.terminated) {
        // TODO: This application has been newly launched. Initialize
        // your application here.
    } else {
        // TODO: This application has been reactivated from suspension.
        // Restore application state here.
    }

    if (app.sessionState.history) {
        nav.history = app.sessionState.history;
    }

    initializeRoamingSettings();

    // add our SettingsFlyout to the list when the Settings charm is shown
    WinJS.Application.onsettings = function (e) {
        e.detail.applicationcommands = {
            "options": {
                title: "Clok Options",
                href: "/settings/options.html"
            },
            "about": {
                title: "About Clok",
                href: "/settings/about.html"
            }
        };

        if (roamingSettings.values["enableIndexedDbHelper"]) {
            e.detail.applicationcommands.idbhelper = {
                title: "IndexedDB Helper",
                href: "/settings/idbhelper.html"
            };
        }

        WinJS.UI.SettingsFlyout.populateSettings(e);
    };

    args.setPromise(WinJS.UI.processAll().then(function () {
        configureClock();
```

365

```
        if (nav.location) {
            nav.history.current.initialPlaceholder = true;
            return nav.navigate(nav.location, nav.state);
        } else {
            return nav.navigate(Application.navigator.home);
        }
    }));
}
```

So far, this is functionally equivalent to the code you just replaced. Now, we're going to change the activated event handler to instantiate a new class, Clok.SplashScreen.Extender, which will manage the extended splash screen. Update default.js with the highlighted code from Listing 17-6.

Listing 17-6. Modified Activated Event Handler

```
app.addEventListener("activated", function (args) {
    if (args.detail.kind === activation.ActivationKind.launch) {

        var extender = new Clok.SplashScreen.Extender(
            extendedSplash,
            args.detail.splashScreen,
            function (e) {
                args.setPromise(Clok.Data.Storage.initialize());
                simulateDelay(2000);
                launchActivation(args);
            });
    }
});
```

The constructor for this new class takes three parameters. The first is a reference to the div, representing the extended splash screen in default.html. The second is a reference to the default splash screen, which is available from the activated event's arguments. The third parameter is a function to initialize the application. The extended splash screen will be displayed until this function completes.

■ **Note** The code in Listing 17-6 references a function named simulateDelay. In reality, Clok's initialization is pretty quick. This function is used to simulate a longer initialization process and should be removed after the extended splash screen has been thoroughly tested. The definition of the simulatedDelay function is available in the source code that accompanies this book. You can find the code samples for this chapter on the Source Code/Downloads tab of the book's Apress product page (www.apress.com/9781430257790).

Of course, the Clok.SplashScreen.Extender class doesn't exist yet. Add a JavaScript file named extendedSplash.js to the js folder in Visual Studio. Add the code from Listing 17-7 to extendedSplash.js.

Listing 17-7. Defining the Splash Screen Extender Class

```javascript
(function () {
    "use strict";

    var util = WinJS.Utilities;

    var extenderClass = WinJS.Class.define(
        function constructor(extendedSplash, defaultSplash, loadingFunctionAsync) {
            this._extendedSplash = extendedSplash;
            this._defaultSplash = defaultSplash;
            this._loadingFunctionAsync = loadingFunctionAsync;

            this._defaultSplash.ondismissed = this._splash_dismissed.bind(this);

            this._show();
        },
        {
            _splash_dismissed: function (e) {
                WinJS.Promise.as(this._loadingFunctionAsync(e))
                    .done(function () {
                        this._hide();
                    }.bind(this));
            },

            _show: function () {
                this._updatePosition();
                util.removeClass(this._extendedSplash, "hidden");
            },

            _hide: function () {
                if (this._isVisible()) {
                    util.addClass(this._extendedSplash, "hidden");
                }
            },

            _isVisible: function () {
                return !util.hasClass(this._extendedSplash, "hidden");
            },

            _updatePosition: function () {
                var imgLoc = this._defaultSplash.imageLocation;

                var splashImage = this._extendedSplash.querySelector("#splashImage");
                splashImage.style.top = imgLoc.y + "px";
                splashImage.style.left = imgLoc.x + "px";
                splashImage.style.height = imgLoc.height + "px";
                splashImage.style.width = imgLoc.width + "px";
```

```
                    var splashProgress = this._extendedSplash.querySelector("#splashProgress");
                    splashProgress.style.marginTop = (imgLoc.y + imgLoc.height) + "px";
                },
            },
            { /* no static members */ }
    );

    WinJS.Namespace.define("Clok.SplashScreen", {
        Extender: extenderClass,
    });
})();
```

When the default splash screen is dismissed, the initialization function, _loadingFunctionAsync, specified in Listing 17-6, is executed, and when that has completed, the extended splash screen is hidden. Wrapping the call to _loadingFunctionAsync with WinJS.Promise.as allows the Extender class to treat the initialization function as if it has returned a Promise, even if it hasn't. The _updatePosition function is used to determine where the image and progress bar in the extended splash screen should be positioned on the screen, based on the position of the image on the default splash screen.

The last step to complete the extended splash screen is to add a reference to extendedSplash.js to default.html. Additionally, the order of the other script references may need to be modified, to ensure that classes and data are defined before attempting to use them. Update the head element of default.html with the code from Listing 17-8.

Listing 17-8. Script References in default.html

```
<head>
    <meta charset="utf-8" />
    <title>Clok</title>

    <!-- WinJS references -->
    <link href="//Microsoft.WinJS.1.0/css/ui-dark.css" rel="stylesheet" />
    <script src="//Microsoft.WinJS.1.0/js/base.js"></script>
    <script src="//Microsoft.WinJS.1.0/js/ui.js"></script>

    <!-- Clok references -->
    <link href="/css/default.css" rel="stylesheet" />
    <link href="/css/themeroller.css" rel="stylesheet" />

    <!-- Clok generic scripts -->
    <script src="/js/extensions.js"></script>
    <script src="/js/utilities.js"></script>
    <script src="/js/navigator.js"></script>

    <!-- Clok data and extended splash screen -->
    <script src="/data/project.js"></script>
    <script src="/data/timeEntry.js"></script>
    <script src="/data/storage.js"></script>
    <script src="/data/bingMapsWrapper.js"></script>
    <script src="/js/extendedSplash.js"></script>
```

```
<!-- Clok controls -->
<script src="/controls/js/timerControl.js"></script>
<script src="/controls/js/clockControl.js"></script>

<script src="/js/default.js"></script>
</head>
```

Now, when you launch Clok, after the initial splash screen is dismissed, the extended splash screen with progress bar is displayed (see Figure 17-2).

Figure 17-2. *The extended splash screen with progress bar*

Once the Clok.Data.Storage class is initialized, the previous activation code, now in the launchActivation function, is executed, and then the splash screen is hidden.

Previous Execution State

When users launch your application, it's important that they are greeted with the experience they expect. Most likely, their expectations are based on the last time they saw your application. In Chapter 15, I introduced session state and showed how to save the current state of the application to session state, so that it could be restored when the user returns to your application. Restoring a terminated session will go a long way toward providing the expected experience, especially because users may not realize the session was terminated in the first place.

There may be other things that users expect when your application is activated. If they manually closed the application by swiping down on a touch screen or pressing Alt+F4 on the keyboard, they probably expect to see the main screen the next time they launch your application. If the activation is the result of clicking a secondary tile (a topic I will discuss in Chapter 21) or the Windows Search charm, they probably do not expect to see the main screen. Additionally, the most sensible behavior could be different, depending on whether or not they were already using the application.

The first block of code in the launchActivation function illustrates how you can determine how the user last interacted with your application. I've copied that block to Listing 17-9.

Listing 17-9. Checking the Previous Execution State

```
if (args.detail.previousExecutionState
        !== activation.ApplicationExecutionState.terminated) {
    // TODO: This application has been newly launched. Initialize
    // your application here.
} else {
    // TODO: This application has been reactivated from suspension.
    // Restore application state here.
}
```

You can use the value of previousExecutionState to determine how to handle the application's activation. While we haven't implemented any custom logic based on previousExecutionState in Clok, this code shows how we might initialize Clok differently, if its previousExecutionState were terminated. Five options are defined in the Windows.ApplicationModel.Activation.ApplicationExecutionState enumeration. Aside from terminated, other possible values of previousExecutionState are as follows:

- notRunning: The application has not been run, because the user logged in to Windows, or it has never been run at all (a new installation).

- closedByUser: The last time the application was run, the user closed it by swiping down or pressing Alt+F4.

- running: The application is currently running when the user activates it by, for example, searching from the Windows Search charm, or other types of activation, such as clicking a secondary tile or notification.

- suspended: The application is currently suspended when the user activates it by, for example, searching from the Windows Search charm, or other types of activation, such as clicking a secondary tile or notification.

A complete definition of the Windows.ApplicationModel.Activation.ApplicationExecutionState enumeration is available on MSDN (http://msdn.microsoft.com/en-us/library/windows/apps/windows. applicationmodel.activation.applicationexecutionstate.aspx). Looking at the code in Listing 17-9, you'll notice that projects created from the Visual Studio project templates, by default, treat all of these the same, except for terminated. That's a reasonable default, but keep this property in mind, as you develop applications. You'll improve the user's experience when your application behaves as expected. In particular, I'll cover some cases in Chapter 19 where your application should behave differently for different values of previousExecutionState.

Handling Application Suspension

When a user switches away from your application, Windows suspends it. When he or she switches back, Windows will resume your application, and it will appear seamless to the user. Sometimes, however, if your application is suspended, and additional resources are needed for currently used applications, Windows will terminate your application. When the user switches back to your terminated application, it is your responsibility to make it appear seamless, taking advantage of session state, as discussed in Chapter 15.

As I mentioned in Chapter 15, the WinJS.Application.oncheckpoint event is raised when Windows suspends your application. However, no events are raised when your application is terminated. Ideally, you should keep session state up to date, as the user makes changes in your application. The oncheckpoint event, however, is called when the application is being suspended, allowing you to save any unsaved changes to session state.

To be clear, when saving session state and handling the oncheckpoint event when your application is suspended, the purpose is not for restoring a *suspended* application. Windows takes care of that for you automatically. Because your application is not informed when it is terminated, saving session state and handling the oncheckpoint event enable you to restore a *terminated* application.

When Visual Studio first created the Clok project, it included a handler for the oncheckpoint event in default.js, which can be used to store application-level settings to session state when suspending. For example, the user's navigation history is saved to session state in default.js. Additionally, as illustrated in Chapter 15, you can handle the oncheckpoint event in a page control and address page-level session state concerns there. More information about the oncheckpoint event is available on MSDN (http://msdn.microsoft.com/en-us/library/windows/apps/br229839.aspx).

Application View State

Another type of state your application has is the state of the view. Your application can be in one of a few different view states: landscape (Figure 17-3), portrait (Figure 17-4), snapped, or filled (Figure 17-5).

Figure 17-3. Weather application in landscape view

Figure 17-4. Weather application in16 portrait view

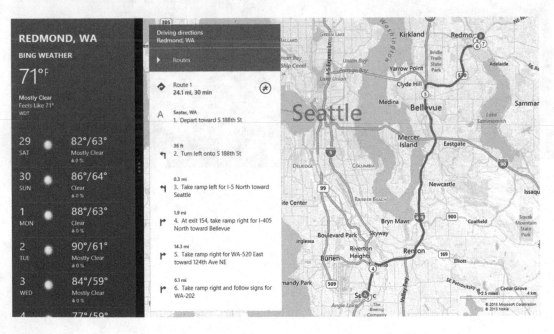

Figure 17-5. Weather application in snapped view, and Maps application in filled view

Looking at the Weather application in Figure 17-3, Figure 17-4, and Figure 17-5, you'll see that the layout of the application changes as the view changes. In landscape view, the weather forecast is displayed from left to right. In portrait view, it is displayed from top to bottom. It is also displayed from top to bottom when in snapped view, but with less detail. While those changes are rules that must be followed, it is important to consider the different ways that a user might interact with your application and to change it accordingly.

So far in Clok, we have only considered the option that the user is running Clok in landscape view. If you run Clok in the Windows Simulator, you can simulate running Clok in portrait view (Figure 17-6).

Figure 17-6. Clok Dashboard screen in portrait view

That doesn't look so good, does it? Unfortunately, it looks even worse in snapped view (see Figure 17-7).

Figure 17-7. *Clok Dashboard screen in snapped view*

Core functionality is inaccessible in both portrait and snapped views. As you might imagine, the other screens in Clok look equally bad in views other than landscape.

Updating the Layout with CSS Media Queries

Updating the Clok Dashboard screen to work in other view states can be done purely in CSS, with the use of CSS media queries. I briefly covered CSS media queries in Chapter 9, when I described how to show the Clok logo in the background in different sizes, depending on the width of the user's screen. In short, media queries allow you to specify CSS rules that only take effect if certain conditions are met. In Chapter 9, you added CSS rules that are only applied when the screen width is 1400 pixels or smaller (see Listing 17-10).

Listing 17-10. CSS Media Query Example from Chapter 9

```
@media screen and (max-width: 1400px) {
    #contenthost {
        background-size: 40%;
    }
}
```

In addition to using screen width as a condition, we can also use the current view state. The CSS rules in Listing 17-11 will only be applied when Clok is running in portrait view. Add this CSS to the end of home.css.

Listing 17-11. CSS Media Query for Clok Dashboard Screen in Portrait View

```
@media screen and (-ms-view-state: fullscreen-portrait) {

    .homepage section[role=main] {
        margin-left: 100px;
        display: block;
    }


        .homepage section[role=main] #rightPane {
            display: none;
        }

    .homepage #mainMenu {
        height: 424px;
        -ms-flex-direction: column;
    }

    .homepage #elapsedTime #elapsedTimeClock {
        font-size: 6em;
        font-weight: 200;
    }
}
```

Because most of the style of the Clok Dashboard screen is still valid in portrait view, you only need to specify the rules that are changing. For example, when Visual Studio creates a new page control, it includes media queries in the CSS file to change the margin for the main section. Any other CSS changes we might have made to the CSS for the main section before this media query still apply, even when the screen is in portrait view. So, in Listing 17-11, I didn't have to specify all of the CSS to configure the mainMenu element to use flexbox layout. Instead, I only needed to change the height and direction of the flexbox.

Run Clok now in the Windows Simulator, and rotate it so that it is in portrait view (see Figure 17-8).

Figure 17-8. *Modified Clok Dashboard screen in portrait view*

With one simple change to the flexbox definition, the Camera, Projects, and Time Sheets menu options are now displayed next to the Start/Stop Clok menu option, instead of beneath it.

Other options for `-ms-view-state` in your CSS media query include `fullscreen-portrait`, `snapped`, `filled`, `fullscreen-landscape`. Additionally, a number of other media queries, such as aspect ratio, can be used. A list of possible media queries is available on MSDN (`http://msdn.microsoft.com/en-us/library/windows/apps/hh453556.aspx`).

In the source code that accompanies this book, I've made similar changes to the Clok Dashboard screen in snapped and filled views, as well as changes to the Projects, Project Detail, and Document Library screens. I won't cover those changes in this book, because the technique of using CSS media queries is the same, and the CSS overrides are themselves pretty straightforward.

Updating the Layout in JavaScript

Some changes to accommodate different view states can easily be accomplished completely with CSS changes. Other changes, however, require changes to JavaScript code as well. Back in Chapter 7, when I first introduced the `ListView` control, I showed an example of setting the `layout` property to both `GridLayout` and `ListLayout`. In `GridLayout`, which is the default if the `layout` property is not specified, the items fill the `ListView` in a grid format from top to bottom, then from left to right. When using the `ListLayout`, items in the `ListView` are displayed from top to bottom in a single column. The Weather application displays the forecast using `ListLayout` in portrait view (see Figure 17-4) and snapped view (see Figure 17-5), and in this section, I'll show you how to update Clok's Projects screen to use `ListLayout` in snapped view, although it will continue to use `GridLayout` in portrait view.

To implement this change, no updates are needed in `list.html`. A few CSS rules are needed in a media query in `list.css`, but I won't cover those here. They are similar to the CSS changes made in the previous section and are included in the source code that accompanies this book. The bulk of the work required to add support for portrait and snapped views to the Projects screen will be done in `list.js`. Add the highlighted code in Listing 17-12 to `list.js`.

Listing 17-12. Modifying the ListView Binding, Based on View State

```
filter_value_changed: function (e) {
    this.filteredProjects = storage.projects.getGroupedProjectsByStatus(this.filter.value);

    listView.winControl.itemDataSource = this.filteredProjects.dataSource;
    listView.winControl.groupDataSource = this.filteredProjects.groups.dataSource;
    zoomedOutListView.winControl.itemDataSource = this.filteredProjects.groups.dataSource;

    this.configureListViewLayout();
},

configureListViewLayout: function () {
    var viewState = Windows.UI.ViewManagement.ApplicationView.value;

    if (viewState === Windows.UI.ViewManagement.ApplicationViewState.snapped) {
        listView.winControl.layout = new WinJS.UI.ListLayout();
        semanticZoom.winControl.enableButton = false;
    } else {
        listView.winControl.layout = new WinJS.UI.GridLayout();
        zoomedOutListView.winControl.layout = new WinJS.UI.GridLayout();
        semanticZoom.winControl.enableButton = true;
    }
},
```

After setting the data sources for the ListView controls, a new function, configureListViewLayout, is called to determine how the ListView should be displayed. The current view state is available in Windows.UI.ViewManagement. ApplicationView.value. If Clok is snapped, then the SemanticZoom control is disabled, and the ListView object's layout property is set to ListLayout. Otherwise, the ListView controls will continue to use GridLayout, and the SemanticZoom is enabled.

The last step you'll need to take is to handle the case when the view state changes. If you add a function named updateLayout to your page control definition, that method will be called when the screen size changes. Add the code from Listing 17-13 to list.js

Listing 17-13. Handling the View State Change

```
updateLayout: function (element, viewState, lastViewState) {
    this.configureListViewLayout();
},
```

Now, when the screen size changes, such as when Clok is snapped or unsnapped, the configureListViewLayout function will be called to determine whether the ListView should be rendered with ListLayout or GridLayout.

Run Clok now and navigate to the Projects screen. The ListView will now show all projects in a single column list (see Figure 17-9).

Figure 17-9. *Projects screen now uses ListLayout when snapped*

In the source code that accompanies this book, you'll find similar changes to the Document Library screen. Because the techniques used to update that screen are the same as those I've just covered, I won't cover that again in the book.

When Snapped View Is Not Supported

There may be times when some screens in your application, or your entire application, for that matter, cannot be implemented in snapped view, for some reason. A common example of this is a game that must be played in landscape view. Even the Store application is disabled in snapped view (see Figure 17-10).

Figure 17-10. *The Store application is disabled in snapped view*

In the case of Clok, there are a few screens that will not be supported in snapped view: the Directions screen, the Time Sheets screen, and the Time Sheets graph screen. Similar to the Store application shown in Figure 17-10, when you are not going to enable snapped view for a particular screen, you should instead show something that indicates to the user that the screen is not available. You should not leave the default behavior as seen in Figure 17-7, if it is not going to be usable. Additionally, you should not redirect users to another screen. When they unsnap your application, they expect to still be on the same screen they were before they snapped it.

We could implement this "unavailable screen" functionality separately for each screen that is not supported in snapped view. This would give some flexibility to show something different in each case. In Clok, however, we'll build this functionality, so that it can be reused easily. The first step is to define what the user should actually see when he or she snaps a screen that isn't supported in snapped view. Add the code from Listing 17-14 to `default.html`, after the extended splash screen you added earlier in this chapter.

Listing 17-14. *The "Unavailable Screen" Message*

```
<div id="snappedNotSupported" class="hidden">
    <img id="notSupportedImage" src="/images/logo.png" />
    <div>This screen is not available while Clok is snapped.</div>
</div>
```

Similar to the Store application pictured in Figure 17-10, Clok will display its logo with our message centered beneath the logo. Add the code in Listing 17-15 to `default.css` to style the message.

Listing 17-15. Styling the Message

```
#snappedNotSupported {
    background-color: #3399aa;
    height: 100%;
    width: 100%;
    padding-top: 200px;
    text-align: center;
}
```

The message is now defined, but I've hidden it with CSS by default. We need a way to easily show this message when it is needed. Add the function from Listing 17-16 to utilities.js.

Listing 17-16. Function to Show the "Unavailable Screen" Message When in Snapped View

```
DisableInSnappedView: function () {
    var viewState = Windows.UI.ViewManagement.ApplicationView.value;
    var appViewState = Windows.UI.ViewManagement.ApplicationViewState;

    var snappedNotSupported = document.getElementById("snappedNotSupported");

    if (snappedNotSupported) {
        if (viewState === appViewState.snapped) {
            WinJS.Utilities.removeClass(snappedNotSupported, "hidden");
        } else {
            WinJS.Utilities.addClass(snappedNotSupported, "hidden");
        }
    }
},
```

This new function, DisableInSnappedView, will determine the current view state of Clok. If Clok is in snapped view when it is called, the "unavailable screen" message will be displayed. At this point, it's a simple matter of calling DisableInSnappedView on screens that don't support snapped view. Add the highlighted code from Listing 17-17 to directions.js.

Listing 17-17. Calling the New Function on a Screen Where Snapped View Is Not Supported

```
ready: function (element, options) {

    // SNIPPED

    Clok.Utilities.DisableInSnappedView();
},

updateLayout: function (element, viewState, lastViewState) {
    Clok.Utilities.DisableInSnappedView();
},
```

The DisableInSnappedView function is called twice for this screen. It is called in the ready function when the screen first loads, and it is called again any time the view state changes in the updateLayout function. Calling it in both places will ensure that the message is shown, whether the user tries to navigate to this screen when already in snapped view, or if he or she navigates to this screen first and then tries to snap Clok.

Because the Time Sheets screen and the Time Sheets graph screen are not supported in snapped view, the code from Listing 17-17 should also be added to the JavaScript files for those screens as well. Once you've done that, run Clok and navigate to the Time Sheets screen and snap the application (see Figure 17-11).

Figure 17-11. *The Time Sheets screen is unavailable in snapped view*

■ **Note** The `logo.png` file that is currently being displayed will be replaced when I cover the steps to prepare your application for sharing in the Windows Store in Chapter 23.

Future Versions of Windows

At the time of this writing, a preview of the next version of Windows is available. In Windows 8, two Windows Store applications can be viewed simultaneously, with one in snapped view at a pre-defined width. Beginning with Windows 8.1, more than two applications can be viewed at one time, and the width of each view can be set by the user. As a result, the named view states, such as snapped, will be deprecated and may be removed in a future version of Windows.

With Windows 8.1, Microsoft recommends changing your CSS media queries (see Listing 17-18) and JavaScript (see Listing 17-19) to check for specific widths and updating the interface based on these values instead.

Listing 17-18. Sample CSS Media Query Changes

```
/* replace media queries that check for named view states like this ... */
@media screen and (-ms-view-state: snapped) {
    /* SNIPPED */
}

/* ... with media queries that check for specific widths like this */
@media (max-width: 500px) {
    /* SNIPPED */
}
```

Listing 17-19. Sample JavaScript Changes

```
// replace JavaScript that checks for named view states like this ...
var viewState = Windows.UI.ViewManagement.ApplicationView.value;
if (viewState === Windows.UI.ViewManagement.ApplicationViewState.snapped) {
    // SNIPPED
}

// ... with JavaScript that checks for specific widths like this
var windowWidth = document.documentElement.offsetWidth;
if (windowWidth <= 500) {
    // SNIPPED
}
```

These and other changes that will be made in the next version of Windows are described on MSDN (http://msdn.microsoft.com/en-us/library/windows/apps/dn263112.aspx).

Conclusion

The topics covered in this chapter—being aware of the activation state and view state of your application—can be summarized as "do what the user expects." Being aware of how the user last interacted with your application will allow you to initialize the application appropriately. Paying attention to the view state of your application, and to how the view state might change while the application is running, will allow you to format the screen to fit the appropriate space. These little touches are the kinds of things that your users might overlook, but they would notice if you hadn't made them.

CHAPTER 18

■ ■ ■

External Libraries

As you are aware by now (I hope), the purpose of this book is to introduce building Windows Store applications with HTML and JavaScript. Each chapter in this book is focused on teaching you a concept that allows you to use your existing HTML and JavaScript knowledge for building native Windows applications. This chapter will have a slightly different focus, however: working with external libraries.

External libraries provide functionality in a reusable package, whether they are JavaScript libraries or WinRT components. If your background is in web development, you might have thought first of the ubiquitous jQuery library. If your background is on development with the .NET Framework, you might have thought of something such as log4net, a popular library for performing logging operations.

When I was first writing the outline for this book, I was originally going to title this chapter *Third Party Libraries*, but I quickly realized that wouldn't offer a complete picture. While it is common to incorporate into your application libraries that others have written, it's also common to build your own reusable components and add those to your application.

In this chapter, I'll walk through some things you'll have to consider when evaluating third-party JavaScript libraries. I'll also provide a simple example of creating a WinRT component in C# for use in Clok, at the same time allowing you to reuse the functionality in other Windows Store applications or even Windows Phone applications.

JavaScript Libraries

There is no shortage of JavaScript libraries. If you are a web developer, you can find a JavaScript library to accomplish almost any task you could want, from general-purpose libraries, such as jQuery, to special purpose libraries, such as the Flotr2 graphing library I discussed in Chapter 13. In addition to third-party libraries such as these, you can also build your own custom JavaScript library, and use it in multiple Windows Store applications, as well as on your web site.

Many JavaScript libraries can be used in Windows Store applications. If you have a favorite JavaScript library, you'll be happy to know that it will probably work. That said, there are a few caveats to keep in mind.

Security Concerns

You might be thinking that it could be dangerous to let an external library have access to the user's computer, and you're right. Of course, this should always be a concern when writing software, whether you're building a web site, a desktop application, or a Windows Store application. Care should be taken when deciding to incorporate a third-party library into your application, perhaps even more in a Windows Store application than on a web site, because the user may have granted your Windows Store application access to the file system or the camera.

To limit risk, pages in your application are running in one of two contexts: the local context or the web context. Pages running in the web context, such as web pages hosted in an `iframe`, have limited access to the user's computer and can't access WinRT. Pages that are included in the application, such as every page we've added to Clok, run in the local context. These pages have much greater access to the user's computer. As a result, any scripts that run in local context have some restrictions on the content it can add to the page.

If a script in the local context adds HTML to the page, that HTML is processed by the `window.toStaticHTML` function, to determine if it is allowed to be dynamically added. If it includes code that could be malicious, such as a script or an `iframe`, an exception is thrown. This happens when content is added using certain properties or functions. Attempting to set the `innerHTML` or `outerHTML` properties, for example, will only succeed after the contents are successfully processed by `toStaticHTML`. A list of HTML elements and attributes that are not permitted is available on MSDN (`http://msdn.microsoft.com/en-us/library/windows/apps/hh465388.aspx`).

If the JavaScript library you are adding to your application uses any of these restricted properties or functions, you should be sure to do thorough testing, to make sure your application works as expected. More information about which properties and functions are restricted is available on MSDN (`http://msdn.microsoft.com/en-us/library/windows/apps/hh465380.aspx`).

■ **Note** Keep in mind that the JavaScript libraries you might include are not necessarily doing anything malicious on their own. The restrictions are to prevent these libraries from dynamically adding malicious code to the page that was obtained from the Internet through `XmlHttpRequest`, or even from user input.

Working Around Security Restrictions

There are legitimate cases where you could have some content that you trust and know to be safe, yet it is not allowed through the security enforced by the `toStaticHTML` function. If you are writing your own JavaScript library, or can modify a third-party library, there are ways around these restrictions, although they should be used cautiously. The restrictions are in place for a reason—to protect your users. You should only use these methods when you can be certain that there are no potentially dangerous effects, because the methods described in this section are not subject to the filtering described in the previous section.

In the previous section, I mentioned the `innerHTML` and `outerHTML` properties. While setting those properties is subject to filtering by `toStaticHTML`, the `WinJS.Utilities.setInnerHTMLUnsafe` and `WinJS.Utilities. setOuterHTMLUnsafe` functions are not. You can use these methods to set those properties, if you are positive that the contents are safe. More information about the `setInnerHTMLUnsafe` function and `setOuterHTMLUnsafe` function is available on MSDN (`http://msdn.microsoft.com/en-us/library/windows/apps/br211696.aspx` and `http://msdn.microsoft.com/en-us/library/windows/apps/br211698.aspx`).

Additionally, if you have a function that you have to call that would typically be considered unsafe, such as dynamically adding JavaScript references to the DOM, you can wrap it in a call to `MSApp.execUnsafeLocalFunction` (see Listing 18-1).

Listing 18-1. Executing an Unsafe Function

```
MSApp.execUnsafeLocalFunction(function() {
    // something typically considered unsafe
});
```

Other differences and similarities in HTML and JavaScript for Windows Store applications compared to HTML and JavaScript for web sites is available on MSDN (`http://msdn.microsoft.com/en-us/library/windows/apps/hh465380.aspx`).

Again, these methods should be used with extreme caution and only when you control the changes that will be made to the page.

WinRT Components

In addition to JavaScript libraries, you can also incorporate Windows Runtime components, or WinRT components, into your application. A WinRT component is a DLL that can be used from a Windows Store application. The component can be written in C#, VB, or C++ and can be used from a Windows Store application written in any of these languages, as well as your Windows Store application written with HTML and JavaScript.

Many third-party WinRT components are available. For example, if you want to use the SQLite database instead of IndexedDB, you can download a component at www.sqlite.org/download.html. Want to add phone call support to your application? Twilio has source for a WinRT component to facilitate that, available at www.github.com/twilio/twilio-csharp. If your application will take advantage of Windows Azure Mobile Services, you can get the bits you need from www.windowsazure.com/en-us/develop/mobile.

Of course, many other WinRT components are available, but in the remainder of this chapter, I'm going to cover how to build a very simple WinRT component of your own, and then incorporate it into Clok.

Reasons for Building WinRT Components

There are a few reasons you might decide to build a WinRT component. It could be that some functionality you need is not available in the JavaScript language itself and is not provided by the WinJS or WinRT libraries. Another common reason for building WinRT components is code reuse. You can build a component and reuse it in multiple Windows Store applications, or even Windows Phone applications. Additionally, you might already have an extensive code base that was written for another platform, such as code for an iOS application written in C++.

For this chapter, I've created a new requirement to add some functionality not available in JavaScript. In Chapter 11, when defining the Project class, I set the default value of the id property to a value based on the current time. For Clok, that is probably fine, but, as I mentioned at that time, it is not guaranteed to be unique. I could have changed this behavior when I introduced IndexedDB in Chapter 14 since IndexedDB allows you to specify an automatically incrementing identifier, but I didn't want the Project and TimeEntry classes to be dependent on the choice of data source. In addition, while not covered in this book, I may decide at some point that Clok needs to share its data across multiple devices. While the chances of having two objects created at the same millisecond, therefore having the same id, are very slim, it's not impossible. Short of moving all storage and id generation to a centralized server somewhere, requiring Clok to always be connected to the Internet, using a globally unique identifier, a GUID, as the id is the best option. Unfortunately, JavaScript doesn't have a way to create GUIDs. Fortunately, C# does, and it is very easy.

■ **Note** As I mentioned, WinRT components can be created in C#, VB, or C++. I'll be using C# in this example, but feel free to use one of these other languages, if you're more comfortable with them.

Creating a C# WinRT Component

If you've done any .NET development before, then you're probably familiar with how to create a new class library project in Visual Studio. You'll find the process of creating a WinRT component to be nearly identical. The following steps will walk you through the process.

1. Right-click the Clok solution in Visual Studio's Solution Explorer. Select Add ➤ New Project (see Figure 18-1).

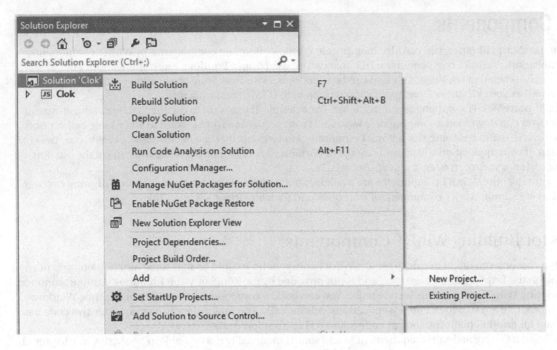

Figure 18-1. *Adding a new project to the Clok Visual Studio solution*

2. In the left pane of the New Project dialog (see Figure 18-2), select Visual C# ➤ Windows Store.

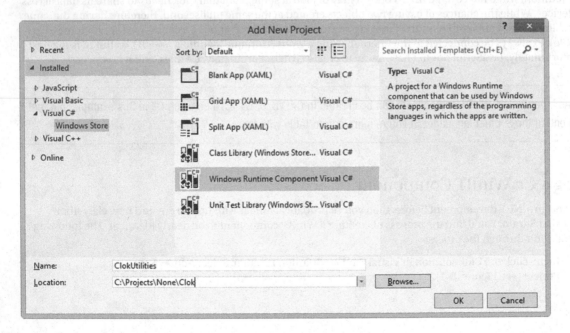

Figure 18-2. *Visual Studio's C# Windows Store project templates*

3. Select the Windows Runtime Component project template.

4. Give the project a name: ClokUtilities.

5. Click "OK" to create your project.

When Visual Studio creates the project for you, it also adds a C# class file named Class1.cs to the project (see Figure 18-3). Right-click the Class1.cs file in Solution Explorer and rename it to Guid.cs.

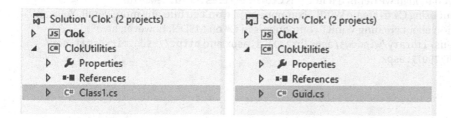

Figure 18-3. *The class file that is created automatically (left), renamed to Guid.cs (right))*

This class file, Guid.cs, is the only file in the ClokUtilities project that we're going to modify in this book. You could use this project to add any other functionality you'd like to build in C#, however. The component is not limited to a single class. Our requirements for now are simple, however. I'll show you some C# code that performs two simple tasks. First, it provides a way to create a GUID and use it in our JavaScript. Second, it provides a way for us to check a string to determine if it is a valid GUID. Replace the contents of Guid.cs with the code in Listing 18-2.

Listing 18-2. The Guid Class

```csharp
public sealed class Guid
{
    public static string NewGuid()
    {
        return System.Guid.NewGuid().ToString();
    }

    public static bool IsGuid(string guidToTest)
    {
        if (string.IsNullOrEmpty(guidToTest))
        {
            return false;
        }

        System.Guid guid;
        return System.Guid.TryParse(guidToTest, out guid);
    }
}
```

Now, from the Build menu in Visual Studio, select the Build Solution option. That's it. You've just created a WinRT component, albeit a very simple one. Before moving on to the next section, I want to point out a few things about this class and about WinRT components in general. First, notice that the Guid class is public and sealed. This is required to use a WinRT class in JavaScript.

Second, while it is fine to use .NET classes internally within the component, the types that are exposed publicly must be WinRT types. This includes the return types of any public functions, the types of any parameters to public functions, and the types of any public properties. Because of this requirement, I cannot return a value of type System.Guid from the NewGuid function. Instead, I must first convert it to a string and return that value instead. A list of WinRT types is available on MSDN (http://msdn.microsoft.com/en-us/library/br205768(v=vs.85).aspx).

Third, when using WinRT classes from JavaScript, property and function names are in camel case—that is, the first character is lowercase and each subsequent word in the name begins with an uppercase character. Namespaces and classes, on the other hand, are in Pascal case—each word, including the first character of the name, begins with an uppercase character. So, when you use the Guid class from JavaScript later in this chapter, you'll call ClokUtilities.Guid.newGuid, even though we defined it in C# as ClokUtilities.Guid.NewGuid.

Because this isn't a book about using C# to create WinRT components, I won't go into any more detail. You can find plenty of additional information about creating WinRT components in C# on MSDN, however, at http://msdn.microsoft.com/en-us/library/windows/apps/br230301.aspx and http://msdn.microsoft.com/en-us/library/windows/apps/hh779077.aspx.

Updating Clok

In this section, I'll walk you through the changes needed to take advantage of the Guid class you just created. I'll cover updating the id properties of the Project and TimeEntry classes to use the newGuid function, as well as testing for valid GUIDs with the isGuid function.

Referencing the ClokUtilities Project in Clok

Before you can use the new WinRT component, you must first reference the ClokUtilities project from Clok.

In Solution Explorer, expand the Clok project. Then right-click References and choose Add Reference… from the context menu (see Figure 18-4).

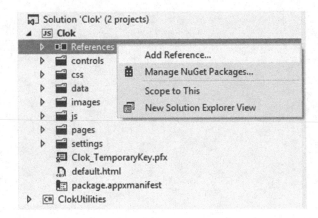

Figure 18-4. *Opening the Reference Manager*

In the Reference Manager window that opens, select Solution ➤ Projects from the left pane and check the box next to ClokUtilities (see Figure 18-5). Then click the OK button to add the reference and close the Reference Manager window.

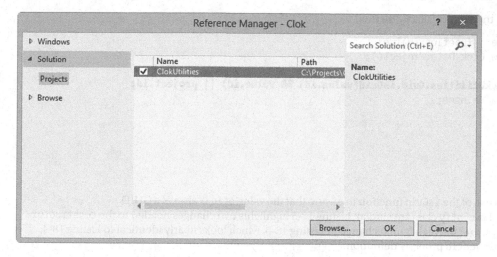

Figure 18-5. Adding a reference in the Reference Manager

With the reference to your component added, you can now access the Guid class created in the previous section from your JavaScript code. Completing the conversion from using numbers to GUIDs for the id property requires a number of small changes to existing files.

Changes to the Data Classes

The bulk of the changes needed are to the classes in the data folder: the Project, TimeEntry, and Storage classes. Let's start with the Project class. In the data folder, open project.js and update the constructor function with the highlighted code from Listing 18-3.

Listing 18-3. Changing the Project Constructor

```
function constructor() {
    this.id = ClokUtilities.Guid.newGuid();
    this.name = "";
    // SNIPPED
},
```

This changes the default value of the id property from a number based on the current time to a string representation of a GUID generated from the ClokUtilities WinRT component. A similar change is needed in the createFromDeserialized function in project.js. Update the createFromDeserialized function with the highlighted code from Listing 18-4.

Listing 18-4. Changing the Project Factory Method

```
createFromDeserialized: function (value) {
    var project = new Clok.Data.Project();

    project.id = (ClokUtilities.Guid.isGuid(value.id) && value.id) || project.id;
    project.name = value.name;

    // SNIPPED

    return project;
},
```

This change makes use of the isGuid function to ensure that the value of id is always a GUID.

The changes to the TimeEntry class are similar. Listing 18-5 highlights two changes needed to the constructor function in timeEntry.js, and the highlighted change in Listing 18-6, which looks nearly identical to Listing 18-4, should be made in the projectId property definition.

Listing 18-5. Changing the TimeEntry Constructor

```
function constructor() {
    this.id = ClokUtilities.Guid.newGuid();
    this._projectId = "";
    this._dateWorked = (new Date()).removeTimePart();
    this.elapsedSeconds = 0;
    this.notes = "";
},
```

Listing 18-6. Changing the projectId Property in the TimeEntry Class

```
projectId: {
    get: function () {
        return this._projectId;
    },
    set: function (value) {
        this._projectId = (ClokUtilities.Guid.isGuid(value) && value) || this._projectId;
    }
},
```

The only change needed in the Storage class is to the getSortedFilteredTimeEntriesAsync function, which is used to determine which time entries are displayed on the Time Sheets page. Update storage.js with the highlighted line of code in Listing 18-7.

Listing 18-7. The Only Change in the Storage Class

```
storage.timeEntries.getSortedFilteredTimeEntriesAsync = function (begin, end, projectId) {
    return new WinJS.Promise(function (complete, error) {
        setTimeout(function () {
            try {

                var filtered = this
                    .createFiltered(function (te) {
```

```
                    if (begin) {
                        if (te.dateWorked < begin) return false;
                    }

                    if (end) {
                        if (te.dateWorked >= end.addDays(1)) return false;
                    }

                    if (projectId && ClokUtilities.Guid.isGuid(projectId)) {
                        if (te.projectId !== projectId) return false;
                    }

                    if (!te.project || te.project.status !== data.ProjectStatuses.Active)
                        return false;

                    return true;
                });

                var sorted = filtered.createSorted(storage.compareTimeEntries);

                complete(sorted);
            } catch (e) {
                error(e);
            }
        }.bind(this), 10);
    }.bind(this));
};}
```

Changes to the Clok Dashboard Screen

You'll have to make four changes to the Clok Dashboard screen to support GUIDs. Three of the changes are exactly the same, so I'll just show it once. Update the editProjectButton_click function in home.js with the highlighted code from Listing 18-8.

Listing 18-8. Remove the Conversion to a Number

```
editProjectButton_click: function (e) {
    var id = project.options[project.selectedIndex].value;
    nav.navigate("/pages/projects/detail.html", { id: id });
},
```

Because we treat GUIDs as strings in JavaScript, this change is to remove the conversion of the id property to a number. In addition to editProjectButton_click, the same change is also needed in the save function and in the saveDashboardStateToSettings function, also in home.js. Actually, the same change is also needed in the getIndexOfProjectId function, in addition to a change to verify a value is a GUID, instead of verifying it is a number. Update the getIndexOfProjectId function in home.js with the highlighted code from Listing 18-9.

Listing 18-9. Finding the Specified Project in the Drop-Down List

```
getIndexOfProjectId: function (projectId) {
    var index = 0;

    for (var i = 0; i < project.options.length; i++) {
        if (ClokUtilities.Guid.isGuid(project.options[i].value)
                && project.options[i].value === projectId) {

            index = i;
            break;
        }
    }

    return index;
}
```

Changes to IndexedDB Helper Settings Flyout

In addition to the changes described above, you'll also have to make changes to the addTestData function in idbhelper.html. This is necessary before you can use the Add Test Data button on the IndexedDB Helper settings flyout. The necessary changes simply replace hard-coded numbers with hard-coded GUIDs, so I won't illustrate the changes here. You can find the updated file in the source code samples for this chapter on the Source Code/ Downloads tab of the book's Apress product page (www.apress.com/9781430257790).

Debugging WinRT Components

When debugging your application that uses a WinRT component that you've created, Visual Studio does not allow you to debug both the C# code and the JavaScript code at the same time. You'll have to choose one or the other, unfortunately. Fortunately, switching between the two requires only a few clicks. First, right-click the Clok project in Solution Explorer and select the Properties menu item (see Figure 18-6).

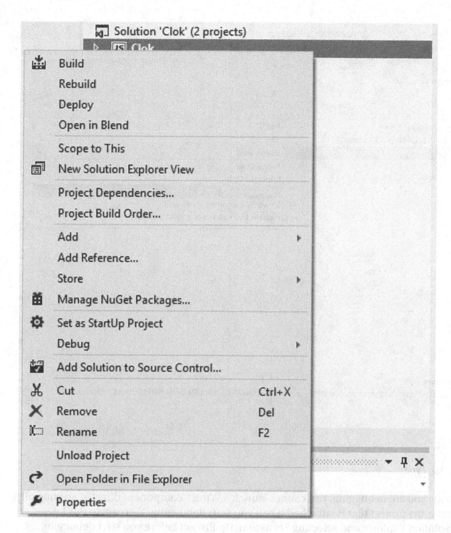

Figure 18-6. *Selecting the Properties menu item in Solution Explorer*

This will open the Clok Property Pages window. Select Debugging in the left pane and then change the Debugger Type to the type you wish to debug (see Figure 18-7). Select "Script Only," for debugging an HTML/JavaScript project such as Clok, or select "Managed Only," for debugging a WinRT component written in C#, such as ClokUtilities.

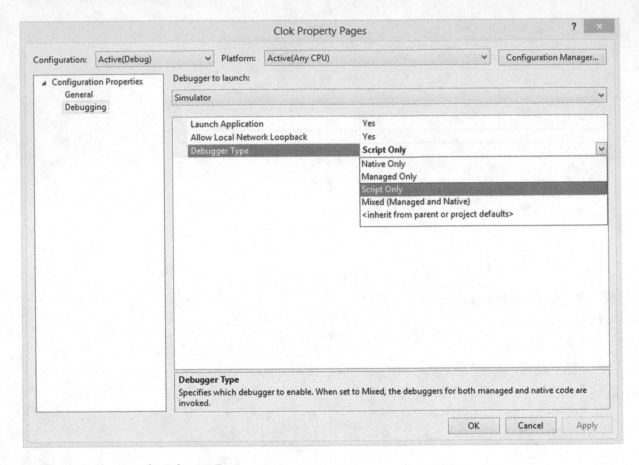

Figure 18-7. *Changing the Debugger Type*

Regardless of which type of code you are debugging, you cannot launch a WinRT component directly. So you will have to ensure that the Clok project is the project that is launched when you start debugging. You can do this by right-clicking the Clok project in Solution Explorer and selecting Set as StartUp Project before you start debugging.

Preserving User Data During Upgrades

If you run Clok now, you won't see any of your projects in the drop-down list on the Clok Dashboard screen. You won't see any of your previous time entries on the Time Sheets page either. This change was pretty low-risk, because Clok has not yet been released. If users were already using Clok, however, and had project and time-entry data stored, they would be pretty disappointed if that data were all lost.

Of course, if you had users, you should be concerned with preserving the user's data during a change such as this. When making similar changes in the future, you should be sure to include code to modify all the existing data in your application to the new format. There are a number of ways to accomplish this, but the most appropriate place is in the IndexedDB initialization code. In `storage.js`, instead of calling `indexedDB.open("Clok", 1)`, you would call `indexedDB.open("Clok", 2)`, to indicate that you want to open a connection to version 2 of the database. Because version 2 of the database won't exist the first time you try to open it, you would then have to update the `onupgradeneeded` function to migrate the data from version 1 of the database to version 2 (see Listing 18-10).

Listing 18-10. Incomplete Example of Migrating Data to New Format

```
request.onupgradeneeded = function (e) {
    var upgradedDb = e.target.result;
    if (e.oldVersion < 1) {
        // Version 1: the initial version of the database
        upgradedDb.createObjectStore("projects", { keyPath: "id", autoIncrement: false });
        upgradedDb.createObjectStore("timeEntries", { keyPath: "id", autoIncrement: false });
    }
    if (e.oldVersion < 2) {
        // Version 2: data updated to use GUIDs for id values
        // TODO - modify all projects and time entries
    }
};
```

But we don't have any users yet, so for now, just run Clok and use the IndexedDB Helper to remove all current data and add new test data. Once you've done that, you shouldn't notice anything different from the version at the end of Chapter 17. All the changes are behind the scenes.

Conclusion

External libraries are a great way to reuse functionality, whether created by someone else or by you. Multitudes of JavaScript libraries are available for nearly any purpose, or you could reuse a JavaScript library you've created for your web site. If you require functionality that is not available in JavaScript, or if you have existing code originally written for another platform, WinRT components are a great way to supplement your project. While the WinRT component you created in this chapter was very simple, the same techniques can be applied to build more complex functionality, which can be used in all your Windows Store applications, as well as in Windows Phone applications.

■ ■ ■

CHAPTER 19

Search and Share Contracts

With Windows 8, users can interact with your application in new and different ways. Of course, they can launch your application and take advantage of the user interface you've built. In addition to that, your application can implement certain functionality that will allow tighter integration with the operating system itself. By taking advantage of contracts, you can ensure that your application supports common features of Windows in a consistent manner.

When you sign an agreement to do some work in exchange for payment, that document describes the responsibilities and expectations of both you and your client. Similarly, a Windows 8 contract describes the interaction between your application and another, or between your application and Windows itself. Windows 8 includes a number of contracts that you can implement in your application. For example, by implementing the File Save Picker contract (refer to the section titled File Pickers later in this chapter), when users save a file from another application, they can choose to save the file in your application, or you could implement the Contact picker extension to provide users with contact details stored in your application. The contracts that Windows Store applications can implement are listed on MSDN (`http://msdn.microsoft.com/en-us/library/windows/apps/hh464906.aspx`).

You already have implemented the Settings contract, to allow Clok to add a few settings flyouts to the Settings pane. In this chapter, I'll walk you through implementing the Search contract, to add support to Clok for searching projects from the Windows Search charm, as well as implementing the Share contract to add support for sharing documents to and from the Document Library.

Search

With Windows 8, users expect to employ a common interface for searching. Regardless of what they are searching for, they will use the Windows Search charm. The Windows charms, including the Search charm, are always available in Windows 8. There are a few ways to open them.

- Windows Logo Key+C on a keyboard

- Swiping from the right edge of a touch screen

- Moving the mouse to the top right corner of the screen

With the charms visible, a system-wide search interface is available, by selecting the Search charm shown in Figure 19-1.

Figure 19-1. *The Windows Search charm*

■ **Note** Users can also activate the Windows Search interface directly, by typing Windows Logo Key+Q on a keyboard. Additionally, you can write code to activate this interface from within your application.

With the Windows Search interface open, the user can enter a search term. By default, search is scoped to the currently active application, but the user can select any other application that supports search, as well as switching to search files or settings. In Figure 19-2, you can see a recent search of mine for "WinJS" within the Channel 9 application. With a simple click of the mouse, I could decide to choose to search within Clok instead.

Figure 19-2. *Common search interface in Windows 8*

In the rest of this section, I'll show you how to add support to Clok to allow users to search for projects from the Windows Search interface. Conveniently, much of the tedious work is done automatically when you add a Search contract to your application.

Adding the Search Contract

In order to implement the Search contract and have Clok appear in the list of applications that a user can search, a few steps have to be completed.

- The Search contract must be declared in the package manifest (`package.appxmanifest`).

- An `activated` event handler must handle the case when the `kind` of application activation is `search`.

- A search results screen must be created.

- Functionality must be implemented to search your application's data, so that it can be displayed on the search results screen.

These steps, which can be done in any order, can all be done manually. For certain applications, that may actually be the easiest or best way to add search to your application. The first three steps, however, can all be done by adding a new item to your project. In this section, I'll walk you through how to add the Search contract item to Clok, so that it appears in the list of applications that a user can search. In subsequent sections, I'll walk through some steps of customizing the default Search contract implementation, to fit better into Clok.

Search contracts are added from the same Add New Item dialog that you've used for adding page controls. In fact, as you'll see in a moment, just like with new page controls, when adding a Search contract, three files—an HTML file, a CSS file, and a JavaScript file—get created. You'll need to make a home for these new files. Create a folder named `searchResults` in the pages folder. Right-click the new `searchResults` folder and choose the option to add a new item. In the Add New Item dialog that opens, select the Search Contract item type and create a new one named `searchResults.html` (see Figure 19-3).

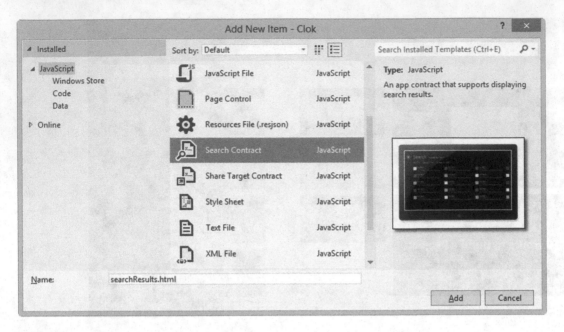

Figure 19-3. Adding a Search Contract

Although this process adds the HTML, CSS, and JavaScript files that will be used to display search results, the JavaScript file is not actually referenced in the HTML file. This is different from when creating a page control. Instead, you'll have to manually add a reference to searchResults.js to default.html. Add the highlighted code from Listing 19-1 to default.html.

Listing 19-1. Referencing Search Contract Script in default.html

```
<script src="/pages/searchResults/searchResults.js"></script>
<script src="/js/default.js"></script>
```

We'll make some changes to both searchResults.js and default.js in an upcoming section. Before that, it's important to see the changes that were made for you in the project manifest. Open package.appxmanifest and switch to the Declarations tab (see Figure 19-4).

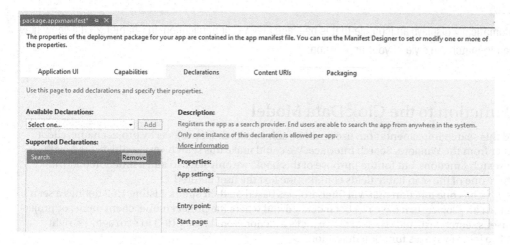

Figure 19-4. *The package.appxmanifest file is automatically updated*

When you added the Search contract item to the project, Visual Studio declared that Clok supports Search by adding the correct elements to package.appxmanifest. This file is actually an XML file, and Visual Studio offers a nice interface for updating the file. Listing 19-2 shows the XML that Visual Studio added to the manifest, to allow Clok to support search.

Listing 19-2. Changes Automatically Made to package.appxmanifest

```
<Extensions>
    <Extension Category="windows.search" />
</Extensions>
```

While no searches would actually work at this point, this change to the manifest is what causes Clok to appear in the list of applications that the user can search (see Figure 19-5).

Figure 19-5. *Clok is now available to search*

■ **Note** Windows automatically displays an icon file that is packaged with your application. In Chapter 23, I'll show how you can update that icon to match the style of your application.

Add a Search Function to the Clok Data Model

Once we've completed this search implementation, users will be able to search for projects by project name, client name, or project number from the Windows Search interface. We could make this search very sophisticated, with some more intelligent search functions, but for the purpose of this book, we only have to add a function that will return any projects where one of the searchable fields contains the text the user entered.

Currently, storage.js has one function that will filter projects based on their status. Listing 19-3 defines a search function, which will return all projects that have not been deleted and where the project name, client name, or project number contains the user's search text. Add the searchProjects function from Listing 19-3 to storage.js, right before the getGroupedProjectsByStatus function definition.

Listing 19-3. Adding a Search Function to storage.js

```
storage.projects.searchProjects = function (queryText) {
    var filtered = this
        .createFiltered(function (p) {
            if (p.status == data.ProjectStatuses.Deleted) return false;

            if (!queryText) return false;

            if ((p.name.toUpperCase().indexOf(queryText.toUpperCase()) >= 0)
                    || (p.clientName.toUpperCase().indexOf(queryText.toUpperCase()) >= 0)
                    || (p.projectNumber.toUpperCase().indexOf(queryText.toUpperCase()) >= 0)) {

                return true;
            }

            return false;

        });

    return filtered.createSorted(storage.compareProjects);
};
```

In addition to this function, you'll also need to add a function for comparing and sorting projects. You've already defined a function to compare and sort project groups, so add the compareProjects function from Listing 19-4 to storage.js, right before the compareProjectGroups function definition. This function will sort projects by client and then by project name.

Listing 19-4. Sort Function for Projects

```
compareProjects: function (left, right) {
    // first sort by client name...
    if (left.clientName !== right.clientName) {
        return (left.clientName > right.clientName) ? 1 : -1;
    }
```

```
// then sort by project name...
if (left.name !== right.name) {
    return (left.name > right.name) ? 1 : -1;
}

return 0;
},
```

Changes to the Generated Search Results Screen

Visual Studio added HTML and CSS files for the search results screen when you added the Search contract to Clok. They are very close to what is needed for showing project search results in Clok. The only changes needed are to the WinJS.Binding.Template used to format each result. Because the default Template doesn't specify the fields that belong to a Project object, update searchResults.html with the code from Listing 19-5.

Listing 19-5. Modified Template

```html
<div class="itemtemplate" data-win-control="WinJS.Binding.Template">
    <div data-class="listViewItem" data-win-bind="className: status">
        <h4 data-win-bind="innerHTML: name searchResults.markText"></h4>
        <h6>
            <span data-win-bind="innerHTML: projectNumber searchResults.markText"></span>
                (<span data-win-bind="innerText: status"></span>)
        </h6>
        <h6 data-win-bind="innerHTML: clientName searchResults.markText"></h6>
    </div>
</div>
```

In addition to making some small changes to the Template, some corresponding CSS changes are also needed. This CSS is very similar to what you added when creating the Projects screen that lists all projects. Update searchResults.css with the highlighted code from Listing 19-6.

Listing 19-6. Updated CSS Rules

```css
/* SNIPPED */
    .searchResults section[role=main] .resultslist .win-container {
        margin-bottom: 10px;
        margin-left: 23px;
        margin-right: 23px;
    }

    .searchResults section[role=main] .resultslist [data-class=listViewItem] {
        min-width: 250px;
        height: 75px;
        padding: 5px;
        overflow: hidden;
    }

        .searchResults section[role=main] .resultslist [data-class=listViewItem].active {
            background-color: #000046;
        }
```

```css
.searchResults section[role=main] .resultslist [data-class=listViewItem].inactive {
    background-color: #464646;
    color: #cccccc;
}

/* Define a style for both selected filters and text matching the query. */
.searchResults section[role=main] .resultslist [data-class=listViewItem] mark {
    background: transparent;
    color: limegreen;
}
```

```css
@media screen and (-ms-view-state: snapped) {
/* SNIPPED */
```

Changes to the Generated JavaScript File

When you added the Search contract from the Add New Item dialog earlier in this chapter, Visual Studio added a lot of code on your behalf. There is some code that you will still need to add on your own, however. For example, searchResults.js has placeholders for you to define what filters will be available for the user to take advantage of, to handle the event when a user clicks an item, and, of course, to determine what results should be displayed on the screen.

In this section, I'll walk through these and a few other changes you have to make to searchResults.js. Let's first define the options a user has for filtering his or her search results. In Chapter 11, we added filters to the Projects screen for viewing all projects, only active projects, or only inactive projects. We'll add the same options to the search results screen. The code that Visual Studio generated in searchResults.js includes a function named _generateFilters. The screen is already configured to use that function to display any filters we add, as well as implement the filtering behavior. Update _generateFilters in searchResults.js with the highlighted code from Listing 19-7, to add an Active filter and an Inactive filter.

Listing 19-7. Adding Filters for Active and Inactive Projects

```javascript
_generateFilters: function () {
    this._filters = [];
    this._filters.push({
        results: null,
        text: "All",
        predicate: function (item) { return true; }
    });

    var statuses = Clok.Data.ProjectStatuses;
    this._filters.push({
        results: null,
        text: "Active",
        predicate: function (item) { return item.status === statuses.Active; }
    });
    this._filters.push({
        results: null,
        text: "Inactive",
        predicate: function (item) { return item.status === statuses.Inactive; }
    });
},
```

Because we defined the searchProjects function in Listing 19-3, finding projects that match the user's query is as simple as calling that function. Update the _searchData function in searchResults.js with the highlighted code from Listing 19-8.

Listing 19-8. Retrieving Search Results

```
_searchData: function (queryText) {
    var storage = Clok.Data.Storage;
    return storage.projects.searchProjects(queryText);
}
```

Once the user sees the list of results that this function returns, he or she, presumably, would like to click on one to view the Project Detail screen for that project. Listing 19-9 contains a new definition for the _itemInvoked function for you to update in searchResults.js.

Listing 19-9. Navigating to the Project Detail Screen

```
_itemInvoked: function (args) {
    args.detail.itemPromise.done(function itemInvoked(item) {
        WinJS.Navigation.navigate("/pages/projects/detail.html", { id: item.data.id });
    });
},
```

One useful feature provided in the searchResults.js file that Visual Studio added is the WinJS.Binding.converter function _markText. This function will highlight any occurences of the user's search term in the results. By default, _markText uses a case-sensitive match to determine what to highlight. For example, if I search for "win," projects for Northwind Traders and any projects named Windows Store App will be returned in the results. However, only the "win" in "Northwind" would be highlighted with the default _markText function, because Windows Store App begins with an uppercase *W*, and I searched for "win," with a lowercase *w*. Replace the definition of that function in searchResults.js with the one in Listing 19-10, so that all matches will be highlighted, regardless of case.

Listing 19-10. Highlighting Matching Terms

```
_markText: function (text) {
    return text.replace(new RegExp(this._lastSearch, "i"), function (match, capture) {
        return "<mark>" + match + "</mark>";
    });
},
```

The last modification needed in this file is to change the page title. Update the _initializeLayout function in searchResults.js with the highlighted line of code in Listing 19-11.

Listing 19-11. Changing the Page Title

```
_initializeLayout: function (listView, viewState) {
    /// <param name="listView" value="WinJS.UI.ListView.prototype" />

    if (viewState === appViewState.snapped) {
        listView.layout = new ui.ListLayout();
        document.querySelector(".titlearea .pagetitle").textContent
            = '"' + this._lastSearch + '"';
```

```
        document.querySelector(".titlearea .pagesubtitle").textContent = "";
    } else {
        listView.layout = new ui.GridLayout();

        document.querySelector(".titlearea .pagetitle").textContent = "Clok";
        document.querySelector(".titlearea .pagesubtitle").textContent
            = "Results for "" + this._lastSearch + '"';
    }
},
```

Changes to Application Activation

Depending on the needs of your application, you may be able to use that generated code with very little modification, such as I showed in the previous section. In the case of Clok, however, deviating from the generated code a little will provide a better experience. In Chapter 17, we defined what should happen when the user launches Clok by clicking on the tile on the Start screen. Most of that same activation logic is also needed when he or she activates Clok from the Windows Search interface.

We still have to hydrate our data model classes from IndexedDB, initialize the roaming settings, and add settings flyouts to the Settings pane, regardless of how the user activates Clok. The generated code in searchResults.js includes an event handler for the WinJS.Application.onactivated event. Because the activation process is nearly the same either way, we'll consolidate this into the event handler that already exists in default.js. First, let's get rid of the redundant event handler in searchResults.js. Find the code from Listing 19-12 in searchResults.js and delete it.

Listing 19-12. Remove the Activated Handler from searchResults.js

```
WinJS.Application.addEventListener("activated", function (args) {
    // SNIPPED
});
```

Modify the handler for the onactivated event in default.js with the highlighted code from Listing 19-13. This will allow all of our existing logic to execute, whether the user launches Clok from the Start screen or by performing a search.

Listing 19-13. Checking for Activation by Search

```
app.addEventListener("activated", function (args) {
    if ((args.detail.kind === activation.ActivationKind.launch)
            || (args.detail.kind === activation.ActivationKind.search)) {

        var extender = new Clok.SplashScreen.Extender(
            extendedSplash,
            args.detail.splashScreen,
            function (e) {
                args.setPromise(Clok.Data.Storage.initialize());
                simulateDelay(500);
                launchActivation(args);
            });
    }
});
```

While all of the activation code we've added throughout the book applies to either type of activation, there is one difference between a launch activation and a search activation. Clok should navigate to a different screen, depending on how it was activated. In the case of a launch activation, the user should see the screen he or she was previously on, if applicable, or the Clok Dashboard screen. In the case of a search activation, however, there are a few possibilities. Add the highlighted code from Listing 19-14 to default.js.

Listing 19-14. Navigating to the Correct Screen After Activation

```
args.setPromise(WinJS.UI.processAll().then(function () {
    configureClock();

    if (args.detail.kind === activation.ActivationKind.search) {
        var searchPageURI = "/pages/searchResults/searchResults.html";
        var execState = activation.ApplicationExecutionState;

        if (args.detail.queryText === "") {
            if ((args.detail.previousExecutionState === execState.closedByUser)
                    || (args.detail.previousExecutionState === execState.notRunning)) {
                return nav.navigate(Application.navigator.home);
            } else if ((args.detail.previousExecutionState === execState.suspended)
                    || (args.detail.previousExecutionState === execState.terminated)) {
                return nav.navigate(nav.location, nav.state);
            }
            else {
                return nav.navigate(searchPageURI, { queryText: args.detail.queryText });
            }
        } else {
            if (!nav.location) {
                nav.history.current = {
                    location: Application.navigator.home,
                    initialState: {}
                };
            }

            return nav.navigate(searchPageURI, { queryText: args.detail.queryText });
        }
    } else if (nav.location) {
        nav.history.current.initialPlaceholder = true;
        return nav.navigate(nav.location, nav.state);
    } else {
        return nav.navigate(Application.navigator.home);
    }
}));
```

There are two ways to activate Clok from the Windows Search interface.

- The user can enter a search term and then click Clok in the list of applications.

- The user can click Clok in the list of applications and then enter a search term.

If users enter search terms and then select Clok, the code in Listing 19-14 will pass their search term—the queryText property—to the search results screen, which will display any results. However, if users have the Windows Search interface active and click on Clok before entering any search terms, to "pre-scope" their search to Clok, the value of queryText will be empty. In this case, users likely have a different expectation of what they will see while they are searching. So, we follow a pattern similar to when a user launches Clok. If the application was suspended or terminated, return users to the screen that they believe is still active. If the application was not running previously, show the Clok Dashboard screen. If it was running, navigate to the search results screen, even though there are no results to display yet. You may decide to handle these cases differently in your application. The important thing is to consider what users expect to happen in various situations.

Run Clok now and perform a search in Clok. Figure 19-6 shows the results of my search for "cycles," with any matches for that term highlighted in the results.

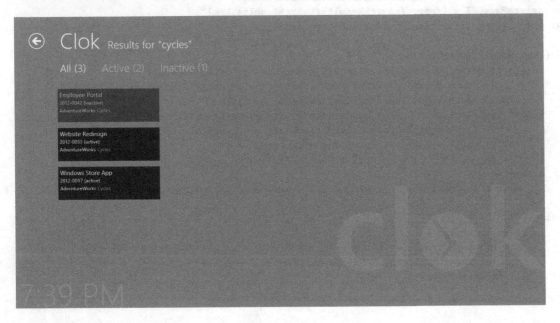

Figure 19-6. *Search results*

You probably realized how similar this screen is to the Projects screen, which lists all projects. You could go through the process of combining the two into a single screen. This would eliminate some code that is redundant, such as the CSS and markup, to display results and functionality to filter the results. The biggest difference currently is that, by default, the Projects screen shows all projects in Clok, while the search results screen won't show any results until a search is performed. There is one reason in particular to consider leaving them as separate screens, however. With a dedicated search results screen, you could modify the logic to also include searches for time entries or even documents within a consolidated list of results. This behavior wouldn't make sense if you combined the Projects screen with the search results screen. Again, do what you think is best for your user. Be mindful.

As you complete this section, you'll notice that adding the Search contract item from the Add New Item dialog to your Visual Studio project wasn't actually a required step. There isn't anything special about what Visual Studio added when you completed that step. You could have done each step manually. In fact, if we needed many more modifications to the generated code, or if we did want to combine the Projects screen with the search results screen, it might have been simpler to do it all manually. To reiterate what I stated earlier in this chapter, implementing the Search contract involves a handful of steps.

- The Search contract must be declared in the package manifest (`package.appxmanifest`).

- An `activated` event handler must handle the case when the `kind` of application activation is `search`.

- A search results screen must be created.

- Functionality must be implemented to search your application's data, so that it can be displayed on the search results screen.

Visual Studio can generate some, or most, of this code for you, or you can do it manually.

Debugging Search Activation

I should point out a helpful debugging tip when testing alternate activations of your application. Most of the time I start Clok without attaching the Visual Studio debugger. You do this by typing Ctrl+F5, or you can go to Debug ➤ Start Without Debugging. When I have to step through code to figure out an issue or see the value of different variables as Clok is running, I start Clok with the Visual Studio debugger. You do this by typing F5, going to Debug ➤ Start Debugging (see Figure 19-7), or clicking the button in the toolbar.

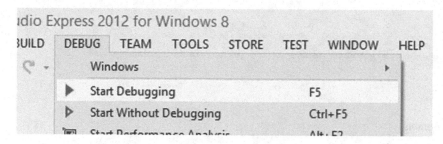

Figure 19-7. *Start Debugging or Start Without Debugging*

By default, when debugging, Visual Studio will launch Clok. Most of the time, this is desired. However, in the case of debugging alternate kinds of activation, you don't actually want Clok to be running initially, so that you can debug the various code branches added to the `onactivated` event handler. Fortunately, there is a simple way to change that.

Right-click the Clok project in Solution Explorer and select Properties from the context menu. Make sure to select the Clok project, not the Clok solution at the top level, which has the same name. In the left pane of the Clok Property Pages window, select Debugging. Then change the value of Launch Application to No (see Figure 19-8).

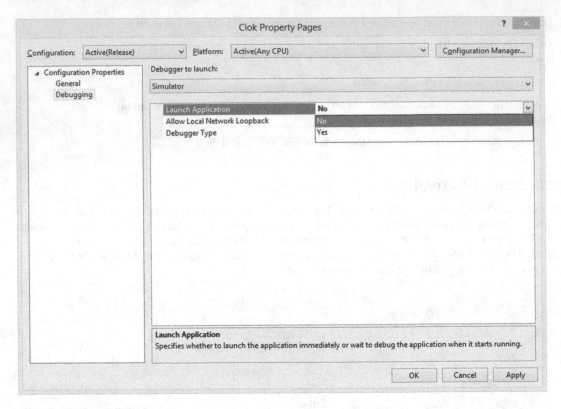

Figure 19-8. *Changing debugging options*

If you debug now (press F5), Visual Studio switches to its debug mode and waits for Clok to be activated, before doing anything else. If you use the Windows Search interface to search for a project now, you'll be able to step through the activation handler. Just remember to set this property back to Yes before debugging other Clok features not related to activation of the application.

Share

Another new feature in Windows 8 is the ability to share data between applications. When an application supports sharing, the user can use the Share charm shown in Figure 19-9 to open the Windows Share interface and make data available to another application.

Figure 19-9. *The Windows Share charm*

■ **Note**   Users can also activate the sharing interface directly, bypassing the Share charm, by typing Windows Logo Key+H on a keyboard. Additionally, I'll show later in this chapter how you can activate the sharing interface programmatically.

Out of the box, you can add support to your applications for sharing text, HTML, URIs, images, and files. Additionally, you can create custom data types and share those as well. In this section, I'll walk through the steps to configure Clok as both a share target and share source.

Share Target

Your application will identify itself to Windows as a share target after you implement the Share Target contract. A share target is an application that is capable of receiving shared data from another application, which is the share source. When implementing the Share Target contract, you specify what types of data your application is capable of receiving, and when a user shares that type of data, your application will be in the list of target applications he or she can choose. In this section, I'll show you how to add support for sharing documents with Clok and adding them to a project's Document Library.

Before we start implementing the Share Target contract in Clok, you will need an application on your computer that can share files. You probably already have one or more applications that can do this, but instead of trying to determine which applications are capable of sharing documents, I suggest that you look at the sample project named "Sharing content source app sample." You can download this sample project individually (http://code.msdn.microsoft.com/windowsapps/Sharing-Content-Source-App-d9bffd84), but I suggest downloading the entire sample app pack from MSDN (http://msdn.microsoft.com/en-US/windows/apps/br229516). When you build this application in Visual Studio, it will show on your Start screen as Share Source JS.

Adding the Share Target Contract

Similar to the Search contract, implementing the Share Target contract is most easily done by adding a particular type of item to your project in Visual Studio. Create a new folder named shareTarget in the pages folder in your Visual Studio project. Then add a new Share Target Contract item named shareTarget.html to the shareTarget folder (see Figure 19-10).

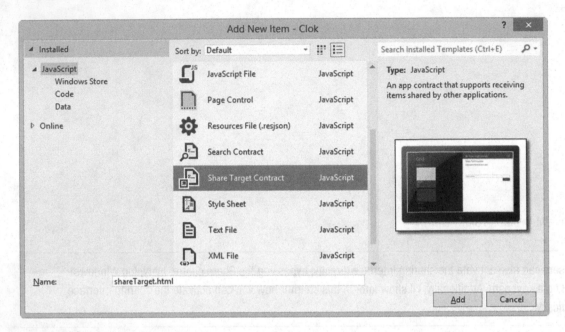

Figure 19-10. *Adding a Share Target contract*

When you add an item of this type, Visual Studio makes modifications to package.appxmanifest. It adds the required Share Target declaration, so Clok will show in the list of targets in the Windows Share interface. By default, it specifies that your project can receive shared text and URIs (see Figure 19-11).

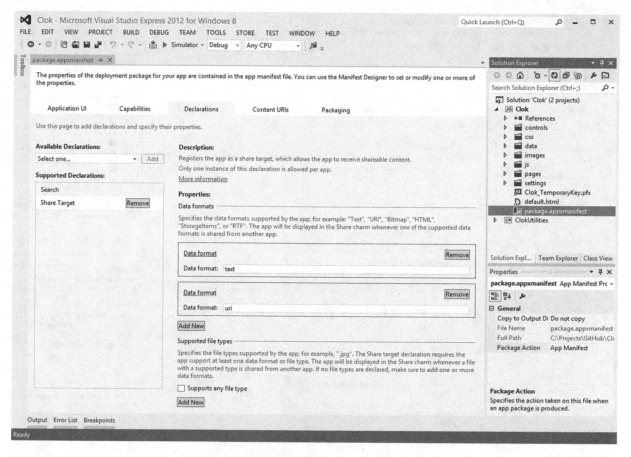

Figure 19-11. *The Share Target declaration added by Visual Studio*

We won't be supporting those formats in Clok, so remove both of them. Because we want users to be able to share documents into the Document Library, we have to specify which file types are supported. If we only wanted to accept Microsoft Word documents, we could add a new supported file type and specify ".docx" as the file type. In the case of Clok, however, the user may wish to share a Microsoft Word document, a spreadsheet, some mock-ups, or any number of other types of files. To support this, simply check the box for "Supports any file type" (see Figure 19-12).

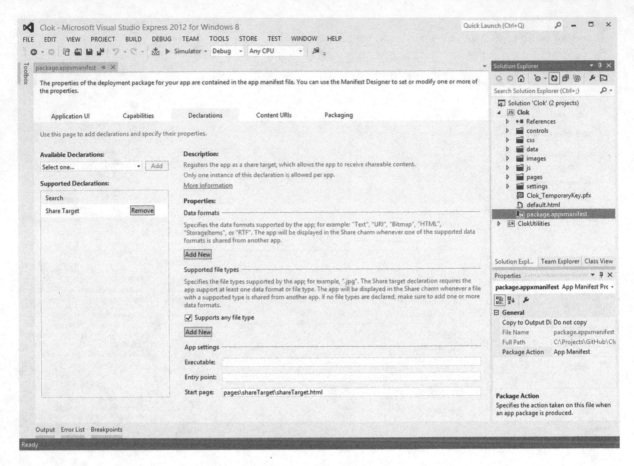

Figure 19-12. *Updating the package.appxmanifest file*

In Clok, shared files are simply saved into the Document Library, without ever looking at the contents of the files. If your application will be working with the contents of the shared files, you should limit the file types to those that your application can understand. Also, as is the case any time your application accepts data from the user, you should carefully analyze the contents to make sure they are in the appropriate format, before doing anything else with the file. It's easy to change the name and extension of a file from, for example, `badThing.exe` to `niceThing.xml`.

Changes to the Generated Share Target Screen

In addition to the changes to `package.appxmanifest`, when you added the Share Target contract, Visual Studio created a page that will be displayed to the user when he or she selects Clok as the share target. Windows will load `shareTarget.html` into a sliding window that resembles a settings flyout. This page must be customized to process the shared data in a manner that makes sense to your application.

In the case of adding documents to a project's Document Library in Clok, we will show some details about the files being shared and provide the user with a list of projects to choose from. Unlike a settings flyout, this page is not loaded as part of `default.html`, so you must include any script references needed to complete the sharing operation. Update `shareTarget.html` with the code from Listing 19-15.

Listing 19-15. Updated Contents of searchTarget.html

```html
<!DOCTYPE html>
<html>
<head>
    <meta charset="utf-8" />
    <meta name="ms-design-extensionType" content="ShareTarget" />
    <title>Share Target Contract</title>

    <link href="//Microsoft.WinJS.1.0/css/ui-light.css" rel="stylesheet" />
    <script src="//Microsoft.WinJS.1.0/js/base.js"></script>
    <script src="//Microsoft.WinJS.1.0/js/ui.js"></script>

    <link href="/css/default.css" rel="stylesheet" />
    <link href="/css/themeroller.css" rel="stylesheet" />

    <script src="/js/extensions.js"></script>
    <script src="/js/utilities.js"></script>
    <script src="/js/navigator.js"></script>

    <script src="/data/project.js"></script>
    <script src="/data/timeEntry.js"></script>
    <script src="/data/storage.js"></script>

    <link href="shareTarget.css" rel="stylesheet" />
    <script src="shareTarget.js"></script>
</head>
<body>
    <!-- The content that will be loaded and displayed. -->
    <section aria-label="Main content" role="main">
        <header>
            <div>
                <img class="shared-thumbnail" src="#" alt="share metadata image" />
            </div>
            <div class="shared-metadata">
                <h2 class="shared-title win-type-ellipsis"></h2>
                <h4 class="shared-description"></h4>
                <ul id="fileNames"></ul>
            </div>
        </header>

        <div id="projectContainer">
            <label for="project">Select a project to add these documents to:</label><br />
            <select id="project">
                <option value="">Choose a project</option>
            </select>
        </div>

        <div class="sharecontrols">
            <div class="progressindicators">
                <progress></progress>
                <span>Sharing...</span>
```

```
            </div>
            <input class="submitbutton" type="button" value="Share" />
        </div>
    </section>
</body>
</html>
```

A few CSS changes are needed as well. First, because in Listing 19-15 you replaced a commentbox element with the projectContainer div, in shareTarget.css, update the CSS selector in Listing 19-16 with the selector in Listing 19-17.

Listing 19-16. Find This CSS Rule

```
section[role=main] .commentbox {
    -ms-grid-column-align: stretch;
    -ms-grid-column: 2;
    -ms-grid-row: 2;
    height: 25px;
    margin-top: 0px;
    width: calc(100% - 4px);
}
```

Listing 19-17. Change the Selector

```
section[role=main] #projectContainer {
    -ms-grid-column-align: stretch;
    -ms-grid-column: 2;
    -ms-grid-row: 2;
    height: 25px;
    margin-top: 0px;
    width: calc(100% - 4px);
}
```

In Listing 19-15, you added an unordered list that will contain a list of file names that the user is sharing with Clok. Add the CSS rule from Listing 19-18 to shareTarget.css.

Listing 19-18. CSS Rule for File List

```
section[role=main] header .shared-metadata #fileNames {
    overflow-y: scroll;
    height: 80px;
}
```

Receiving Shared Files

The JavaScript that Visual Studio generated when you added the Share Target contract to Clok is pretty simple. It's a good starting point, but it's not sufficient. In this section, I will walk you through the changes needed in shareTarget.js. Add the highlighted aliases from Listing 19-19 to the top of shareTarget.js.

Listing 19-19. Adding Some Aliases

```
var app = WinJS.Application;
var appData = Windows.Storage.ApplicationData.current;
var storage = Clok.Data.Storage;

var createOption = Windows.Storage.CreationCollisionOption;
var standardDataFormats = Windows.ApplicationModel.DataTransfer.StandardDataFormats;

var share;
```

When the user selects Clok from the list of targets in the Windows Share interface, Clok will be activated with the shareTarget ActivationKind. Because the sharing screen we are building is not hosted as part of default.html, you will have to handle the onactivated event in searchTarget.js. The code that Visual Studio generated defines a handler for that purpose, and it includes a substantial amount of code. In many cases it may be perfectly acceptable to include that code directly in the onactivated event handler. However, it is recommended that this event handler complete as quickly as possible. We'll follow the guidance suggested on MSDN (http://msdn.microsoft.com/en-us/library/windows/apps/hh758302.aspx) in this example and move the bulk of that logic into a new function and raise a custom event to execute that function. In shareTarget.js, replace the onactivated event handler with the code from Listing 19-20.

Listing 19-20. Handling Activation from Windows Search Interface

```
app.onactivated = function (args) {
    if (args.detail.kind === Windows.ApplicationModel.Activation.ActivationKind.shareTarget) {
        WinJS.Application.addEventListener("shareactivated", shareActivated, false);
        WinJS.Application.queueEvent({ type: "shareactivated", detail: args.detail });
    }
};

var shareActivated = function (args) {
    var thumbnail;

    document.querySelector(".submitbutton").disabled = true;
    document.querySelector(".submitbutton").onclick = onShareSubmit;

    bindListOfProjects();
    project.onchange = project_change;

    share = args.detail.shareOperation;

    document.querySelector(".shared-title").textContent = share.data.properties.title;
    document.querySelector(".shared-description").textContent
        = share.data.properties.description;

    thumbnail = share.data.properties.thumbnail;
    if (thumbnail) {
        // If the share data includes a thumbnail, display it.
        args.setPromise(thumbnail.openReadAsync().done(function displayThumbnail(stream) {
            document.querySelector(".shared-thumbnail").src
                = window.URL.createObjectURL(stream);
        }));
```

```
    } else {
        // If no thumbnail is present, expand the description  and
        // title elements to fill the unused space.
        document
            .querySelector("section[role=main] header")
            .style
            .setProperty("-ms-grid-columns", "0px 0px 1fr");

        document
            .querySelector(".shared-thumbnail")
            .style
            .visibility = "hidden";
    }

    if (share.data.contains(standardDataFormats.storageItems)) {
        share.data.getStorageItemsAsync().done(function (files) {
            if (files && files.length > 0) {
                var names = files.map(function (file) {
                    return "<li>" + file.name + "</li>";
                }).join("");
                fileNames.innerHTML = names;
            }
        });
    }
};
```

In this code, the sharing screen is configured similarly to how you have initialized previous pages in their ready function. The global share variable is set to represent the shareOperation that Windows will include in the activation. This variable is how you will access the data—files, in this case—being shared with your application. If the share variable has a thumbnail image specified, it is displayed; otherwise, the title and description are allowed to expand to the full width of the sharing screen. Finally, all files included in this sharing operation are listed, to ensure the user understands which files will be copied to his or her selected project's Document Library.

Similar to the Clok Dashboard screen, the sharing screen will include a list of active projects. The user will use this list to select which project's Document Library will receive the files he or she is sharing. Add the functions from Listing 19-21 to shareTarget.js, to populate the project list and to enable the Share button only when a project has been selected.

Listing 19-21. Binding List of Projects

```
var bindListOfProjects = function () {
    storage.initialize().then(function () {
        project.options.length = 1; // remove all except first project

        var activeProjects = storage.projects.filter(function (p) {
            return p.status === Clok.Data.ProjectStatuses.Active;
        });

        activeProjects.forEach(function (item) {
            var option = document.createElement("option");
            option.text = item.name + " (" + item.projectNumber + ")";
            option.title = item.clientName;
```

```
            option.value = item.id;
            project.appendChild(option);
        });
    });
};

function project_change() {
    document.querySelector(".submitbutton").disabled
        = (project.options[project.selectedIndex].value === "");
}
```

To get you started down the right path, the generated code includes a handler function for the Share button's click event. It will show progress indicators, so the user understands that something is happening, although in the case of Clok, the share operation will usually complete pretty quickly, so the user may never see them. Update the onShareSubmit function in shareTarget.js with the highlighted code from Listing 19-22.

Listing 19-22. Modified Button Click Handler

```
function onShareSubmit() {
    document.querySelector(".progressindicators").style.visibility = "visible";
    document.querySelector("#project").disabled = true;
    document.querySelector(".submitbutton").disabled = true;

    share.reportStarted();
    addDocuments();
    share.reportCompleted();
}
```

In addition to showing progress indicators, the generated code has been modified to disable the project list. It also disables the Share button, to prevent accidental double submissions. It ultimately calls the reportCompleted function, which will close Clok and return the user to the application he or she was previously using. In addition to calling addDocuments, the function you will define in a moment, to copy the files to the Document Library, I've also called reportStarted. I haven't used it here, but you might consider calling the reportError function as well, if your application encounters any errors while receiving shared data. These, and other, functions of the ShareOperation class are documented on MSDN (http://msdn.microsoft.com/en-us/library/windows/apps/windows. applicationmodel.datatransfer.sharetarget.shareoperation.aspx).

The last step to complete the task of making Clok a sharing target for files is to implement the addDocuments function. This function will determine which storageFolder corresponds to the selected project and copy all of the storageItem objects from the share variable, effectively adding them to that project's Document Library. Add the functions from Listing 19-23 to shareTarget.js.

Listing 19-23. Adding Documents to the Library

```
var addDocuments = function () {
    var projectId = project.options[project.selectedIndex].value;
    getProjectFolder(projectId).then(function (projFolder) {
        if (share.data.contains(standardDataFormats.storageItems)) {
            share.data.getStorageItemsAsync().done(function (files) {
                var copyPromises = files.map(function (item) {
                    return item.copyAsync(projFolder, item.name, createOption.replaceExisting);
                });
```

```
                WinJS.Promise.join(copyPromises);
            });
        }
    });
};

var getProjectFolder = function (projectId) {
    return appData.localFolder
        .createFolderAsync("projectDocs", createOption.openIfExists)
        .then(function (folder) {
            return folder.createFolderAsync(projectId.toString(), createOption.openIfExists)
        });
};
```

Seeing It in Action

With that, you have successfully configured Clok as a sharing target for files. Typically, I wouldn't devote an entire section to trying out a new feature, but there are enough points to cover in this case. Before you can debug this feature, make sure that Clok will not launch when you start the debugger (refer back to Figure 19-8).

■ **Note**   If you're not going to test this feature with the debugger attached, then you can skip that step, but you must build and run Clok once, to get it registered as a sharing target.

Earlier in this chapter, I mentioned the Share Source JS sample project. Build and run that project now. This project is an example of building an application that can be the source of a sharing operation, the topic I will cover in the next section. As such, it includes a number of features that you won't need for testing Clok. Go ahead and get familiar with the application, by trying out the different scenarios, such as sharing text with another application. For testing Clok, you should specifically look at the scenario titled "Share files" (see Figure 19-13).

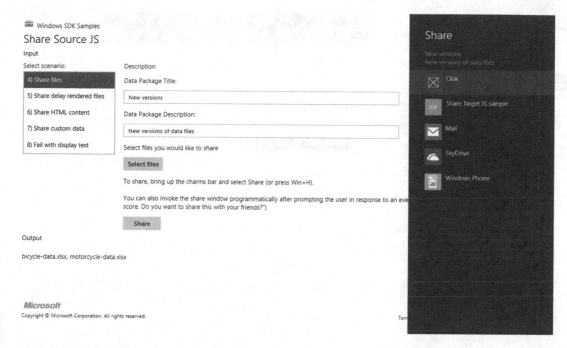

Figure 19-13. *Select a target application*

In Figure 19-13, you can see that I've used the Select files button to specify two files that should be shared: `bicycle-data.xlsx` and `motorcycle-data.xlsx`. Use the Select files button to choose a few files from your own computer to share with Clok. Once the files have been selected, activate the Windows Share interface by one of the following methods:

- Click the Share button in the Share Source JS application to programmatically open the Windows Share interface.

- Click the Share charm shown previously in Figure 19-9 to open the Windows Share interface.

- Use the keyboard shortcut Windows Logo Key+H to open the Windows Share interface directly, bypassing the Windows charms.

With the Windows Share interface active, you should see Clok listed as an optional sharing target. You won't see Clok as an option for other scenarios, such as those that share text or HTML content. Once you select Clok, the application is activated. Because `searchTarget.html` was specified as the start page for the Search Target contract, the page you've been building over the last several pages will open, and the activation code in `shareTarget.js` will be executed. You should see the list of the files you selected, as well as the list of active projects that can receive these files into their Document Library (see Figure 19-14).

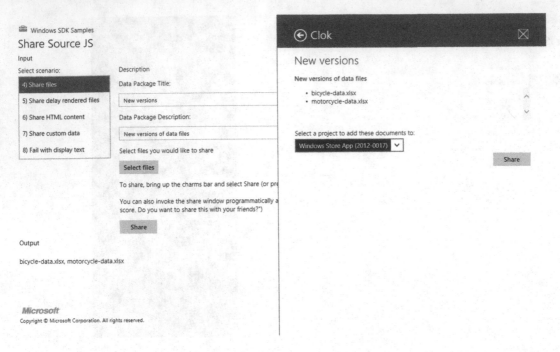

Figure 19-14. Sharing files with Clok

Select a project from the list and click the Share button. The sharing screen will close and you'll be returned to the Share Source JS application. If you launch Clok now and navigate to the Document Library for the project you selected, your files will be listed as if you had added them directly from within Clok.

When using the "Share files" scenario of the Share Source JS application, files are added to the global share variable I covered in the previous section. This scenario treats all files equally and doesn't distinguish between documents, spreadsheets, images, or any other file type. The "Share an image" scenario of the Share Source JS application, on the other hand, specifically shares images. Because the shared data is an image, that scenario specifies a thumbnail of the shared image with the sharing operation. Although Clok doesn't support the Share Target contract for images, the "Share an image" scenario of the Share Source JS sample shares an image in the bitmap data format as well as sharing it as a file. In Listing 19-20, we specified that if a thumbnail existed, it would be displayed. Test with this scenario to see how the thumbnails are displayed when are available (see Figure 19-15).

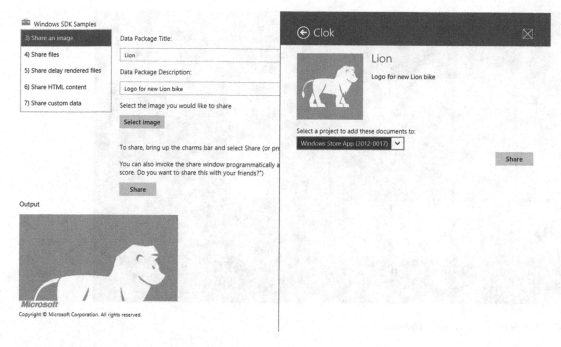

Figure 19-15. *Sharing an image with a thumbnail*

Share Source

In the previous section, you added support to Clok for receiving shared files from other applications. In this section, you will implement the opposite side of that operation, making Clok a sharing source, by adding support to the Document Library for sharing files from Clok to other applications.

In the previous section, you used the Share Source JS application to share files with Clok. The developers of that application added a button to each screen to initiate the sharing process. This is an optional step, because the user can always employ the Windows charms to accomplish this, but it is a nice step for two reasons. First, it is often a simpler user experience to click a button that is already visible than to open the Windows Share interface using one of the other methods. Second, and more important, in my opinion, is that seeing a Share button on the screen makes it completely obvious to the user that items on the current screen can be shared. More than once, I've used a Windows Store application I thought would allow me to share something. However, when I clicked on the Windows Share charm, a message appeared telling me that I couldn't (see Figure 19-16).

Figure 19-16. *There's nothing to share right now*

Adding a Share Button to the Document Library

So, before getting into the details of sharing files, let's make an addition to the user interface on the Document Library screen, by adding a Share button to the app bar. Because we configured the app bar to automatically appear whenever the user selects files in the Document Library, the ability to share documents will be obvious, and initiating the sharing process will be just a click away. Add the code from Listing 19-24 to library.html.

Listing 19-24. Add New App Bar Command

```
<button
    data-win-control="WinJS.UI.AppBarCommand"
    data-win-options="{
        id:'shareDocumentsCommand',
        label:'Share',
        icon:'url(/images/Share-small-sprites.png)',
        section:'selection',
        tooltip:'Share',
        disabled: true}">
</button>
```

■ **Note**　As always, the source code that accompanies this book includes a completed project containing all source code used in this chapter, including the Share-small-sprites.png image used for the Share AppBarCommand icon. You can find the code samples for this chapter on the Source Code/Downloads tab of the product-detail page for this book (www.apress.com/9781430257790).

When the user clicks this button, the showShareUI function will cause the Windows Share interface to open. Add the code from Listing 19-25 to library.js.

Listing 19-25. Programmatically Opening the Windows Share Interface

```
shareDocumentsCommand_click: function (e) {
    dataTransferManager.showShareUI();
},
```

Before you continue, be sure to configure this event handler in the ready function and update libraryListView_selectionChanged, to enable the Share app bar button when files are selected, similar to the Delete app bar button. Also, add the dataTransferManager alias shown in Listing 19-26 to the top of library.js.

Listing 19-26. Adding an Alias

```
var dataTransferManager = Windows.ApplicationModel.DataTransfer.DataTransferManager;
```

Working with the DataTransferManager Class

The call to showShareUI in Listing 19-25 will cause the Windows Share interface to open. When it opens, the next thing that happens is that Windows will request from Clok the data that should be shared. It does this by raising the datarequested event of a DataTransferManager object. You have to handle this event in library.js. You also have to be sure to stop handling this event when the user navigates away from this page. Because your application could share different types of data from different screens, you must ensure that the event is only handled when the data that should be shared is in scope. Add and remove an event handler for the datarequested event by adding the highlighted code from Listing 19-27 to library.js.

Listing 19-27. Adding and Removing an Event Handler

```
ready: function (element, options) {
    // SNIPPED

    var transferMgr = dataTransferManager.getForCurrentView();
    this.transferMgr_dataRequested_boundThis = this.transferMgr_dataRequested.bind(this);
    transferMgr.addEventListener("datarequested", this.transferMgr_dataRequested_boundThis);
},

unload: function () {
    var transferMgr = dataTransferManager.getForCurrentView();
    transferMgr.removeEventListener("datarequested", this.transferMgr_dataRequested_boundThis);
},
```

■ **Note**   You may be wondering why I've created the function named `transferMgr_dataRequested_boundThis`.
In general, I prefer to use the `bind` function to indicate that the `this` keyword within a function refers to the same value
of `this` where that function is declared. To ensure that the same event handler is removed in the `unload` function, I define
`transferMgr_dataRequested_boundThis` as a function with the `this` keyword already bound. Another popular technique
is to define a global variable, often named `that` or `$this`, and use it throughout your code in place of the `this` keyword.
You've probably seen that technique in many other places, and if you've been developing JavaScript for any length of
time, you are probably familiar with it. If so, you should continue to write your code that way. As with anything else you'll
encounter when building Windows Store applications with HTML and JavaScript, aside from having the WinJS and WinRT
libraries available, the code you write is just "plain old HTML and JavaScript." If you have development practices you are
comfortable with, you can still use them.

The `transferMgr_dataRequested` function, which is ultimately called when Windows requests the shared data
from Clok, is the workhorse of this feature. Add the code from Listing 19-28 to `library.js`.

Listing 19-28. Providing the Shared Data to Windows

```
transferMgr_dataRequested: function (e) {
    var request = e.request;
    var selectionCount = libraryListView.winControl.selection.count();

    if (selectionCount <= 0) {
        request.failWithDisplayText("Please select one or more documents and try again.");
        return;
    }

    libraryListView.winControl.selection.getItems()
        .then(function (selectedItems) {
            var project = storage.projects.getById(this.projectId);

            if (selectionCount === 1 && isImageType(selectedItems[0].data.fileType)) {
                // handle single image
                request.data.properties.title = "Image shared from Clok project";
                request.data.properties.description
                    = "From " + project.name + " (" + project.clientName + ")";

                var streamRef = Windows.Storage.Streams.RandomAccessStreamReference;
                var stream = streamRef.createFromFile(selectedItems[0].data);
                request.data.properties.thumbnail = stream;
                request.data.setBitmap(stream);
            } else {
                // handle non-images or multiple files
                request.data.properties.title = "File(s) shared from Clok project";
                request.data.properties.description
                    = selectionCount.toString() + " file(s) from "
                        + project.name + " (" + project.clientName + ")";
            }
```

```
        // share as files whether single image, non-images or multiple files
        var files = selectedItems.map(function (item) {
            return item.data;
        });

        request.data.setStorageItems(files);
    }.bind(this));
},
```

If the user has not selected any files to share, the failWithDisplayText function can be used to show him or her a message or instructions (see Figure 19-17).

Figure 19-17. *There's (still) nothing to share right now*

Document libraries in Clok can contain any type of file, including image files, such as JPG or PNG files. The sharing functionality in Windows supports sharing files of any type, but it also supports sharing images as a stream of data. This is useful if the image you want to share is not on disk, perhaps because you retrieved it from a database, for example. Some applications might support receiving shared image streams, and others might support receiving files; Clok only supports receiving images as files.

Knowing that some applications may not support one format or the other, when sharing a single image from the Document Library screen, the code in Listing 19-28 shares the image in both formats. This will increase the number of applications that the user can specify as sharing targets, consequently improving their experience. If the user is sharing more than one file, or a file that is not an image, then we only share data as files. Additionally, if only a single image is being shared, we specify that image should be used as the thumbnail for the sharing operation.

Seeing It in Action

Much less effort is involved to allow Clok to be a sharing source. The only thing that's left to do is to try it out. Run Clok and navigate to a Document Library that has some files in it. Select one or more files and share them by one of the following methods (see Figure 19-18):

- Click the Share button in the app bar.

- Click the Share charm shown in Figure 19-9.

- Use the keyboard shortcut Windows Logo Key+H, bypassing the Windows charms.

Figure 19-18. *Sharing files from the Document Library*

■ **Note**   If you're debugging with Visual Studio, don't forget to change the project properties again, so that Clok is automatically launched when you start debugging.

Select a target application. In my testing, I selected the Mail application, which, as you can see in Figure 19-19, has a more extensive sharing screen, allowing the user to send the files as attachments to a client.

Figure 19-19. *Sharing files to the Mail application*

Other Concepts Similar to Sharing

In addition to configuring your application as a sharing target or a sharing source, there are other ways to allow the users to put data into and get data out of your application. Two common ways to support this type of sharing (here I refer to the general definition of "sharing," not the Windows 8–specific definition) are File Pickers and Copy and Paste.

File Pickers

The File Open Picker contract and the File Save Picker contract are similar to being a sharing source and a sharing target, respectively. These contracts allow your application to be selected when the user is employing a file picker to open or save files. For example, when adding files to the Document Library, you can choose other applications that have declared the File Open Picker contract and import files directly from those applications, such as SkyDrive or the Photos application (see Figure 19-20), even if they don't currently exist in the file system of your computer.

Figure 19-20. *File Open Pickers*

Likewise, if you added the File Save Picker contract to Clok, you could save attachments directly from e-mails in the Mail application into a Document Library. I won't be implementing any file pickers in this book, but you might consider adding them to Clok yourself, as homework. More information about the File Picker contracts is available on MSDN (http://msdn.microsoft.com/en-us/library/windows/apps/hh465174.aspx).

Copy and Paste

Copying and pasting has been a part of our lives for a long time now. I remember using copy and paste on my first Apple Macintosh computer almost 30 years ago. Windows 8 supports copy and paste in the most expected way, right out of the box: your users will be able to copy from, and paste into, text-input controls automatically. Additionally, you can programmatically manipulate the clipboard.

A useful example of this would be to add support for copying time entries from the Time Sheets screen into a tab-separated format that can be easily pasted into Microsoft Excel. In fact, while I won't cover it in this book, that feature has been implemented in the source code that accompanies this book. (You can find the code samples for this chapter on the Source Code/Downloads tab of the product page for this book [www.apress.com/9781430257790].) Another case for copy-and-paste support in Clok would be to add it to the Document Library, to allow the user to copy a document from the Document Library of one project to the Document Library of another project. More information about copying and pasting data in your applications is available on MSDN (http://msdn.microsoft.com/en-us/library/windows/apps/hh758298.aspx).

Conclusion

Windows 8 has done a lot to promote consistency for completing common tasks in your applications. With a common interface for searching and sharing data between applications, users will quickly become familiar with the way that Windows Store applications should support these features. Although it's perfectly acceptable, even recommended, to deviate from the common Windows Search interface if search is a substantial feature of your application, following established conventions is better, in most cases—better for the user, because it's consistent, and better for you as a developer, because much of the plumbing code has been written for you.

In addition to Search and Share contracts, Windows 8 provides a number of contracts and extensions to help you build applications that are automatically familiar to your users. I encourage you to review them on MSDN (http://msdn.microsoft.com/en-us/library/windows/apps/hh464906.aspx).

Conclusion

■ ■ ■

CHAPTER 20

Printing

I've been writing software for many years now. Whenever the topic of adding printing features was discussed, I had one of two reactions internally. If I was working on a web-development project, I'd think, "OK, no big deal. Printer-friendly web pages are usually simple." If I was working on a WinForms or WPF desktop application, I'd think, "Ugh." It wasn't rocket science to add printing support to a desktop application, but it was usually more challenging than other features that had similar value.

Fortunately, if you are using HTML and JavaScript to build Windows Store applications, adding printing support to installed applications is simple again. As you'll see in this chapter, printing can be done using the same techniques you currently use for printing web pages. However, Windows Store applications also have additional printing functionality available to them that, for just a little more work, offer some extra benefit that you can't get otherwise.

The beauty of this is that you get to choose. If the additional benefit, which I'll discuss in the coming pages, isn't worth adding an extra 50 or so lines of code to your application, then you don't have to. Of course, I'm about to give you those 50 lines of code, so maybe it will be worthwhile.

Web Development–Style Printing

If your background is in web development, the first technique for printing from your Windows Store application that I will discuss in this chapter will be familiar. In this section, I'll demonstrate printing the Project Detail screen in Clok, using CSS and `window.print`, a function built into HTML browsers such as Internet Explorer, which shares the same HTML rendering engine as Windows Store applications. I'll cover the following in this section:

- Adding a Print button to the app bar of the Project Detail screen

- Using media queries to specify CSS rules that should be applied only when printing

- Implementing the code to send the content to the printer

Adding a Print Button to the Project Detail Screen

The first step we'll take is to add a Print button to the app bar of the Project Detail screen. Add the code from Listing 20-1 to the end of the AppBar definition in `pages\projects\detail.html`.

Listing 20-1. Adding a Print Button to the App Bar

```
<button
    data-win-control="WinJS.UI.AppBarCommand"
    data-win-options="{
        id:'printCommand',
        label:'Print',
```

```
        icon:'url(/images/Print-small-sprites.png)',
        section:'global',
        tooltip:'Print',
        disabled: true}">
</button>
```

■ **Note** The source code that accompanies this book includes a completed project containing all source code and image files used in this chapter. You can find the code samples for this chapter on the Source Code/Downloads tab of the product detail page for this book (www.apress.com/9781430257790).

Similar to the Directions and Time Sheet app bar buttons, this Print button should also be hidden when the application is in snapped view. Add the highlighted code from Listing 20-2 to detail.css within the media query that specifies rules for when Clok is in snapped view.

Listing 20-2. Hiding the Print Button in Snapped View

```
#projectDetailAppBar #goToDirectionsCommand,
#projectDetailAppBar #goToTimeEntriesCommand,
#projectDetailAppBar #printCommand {
    display: none;
}
```

Additionally, this button should only be enabled when the user is viewing details for an existing project. Add the code from Listing 20-3 to the configureAppBar function in detail.js.

Listing 20-3. Enable the Print Button

```
printCommand.winControl.disabled = false;
```

CSS Media Query for Printing

The next step is to specify alternate CSS rules that will be applied when printing. Compared to the current layout of the Project Detail screen (see Figure 20-1), the printed version of this screen does not require the Back button or such a wide margin along the left edge. Additionally, the app bar and current time should be hidden. Finally, the Description field should be expanded to show longer text, and just for good measure, we'll move it to the end of the page when printing.

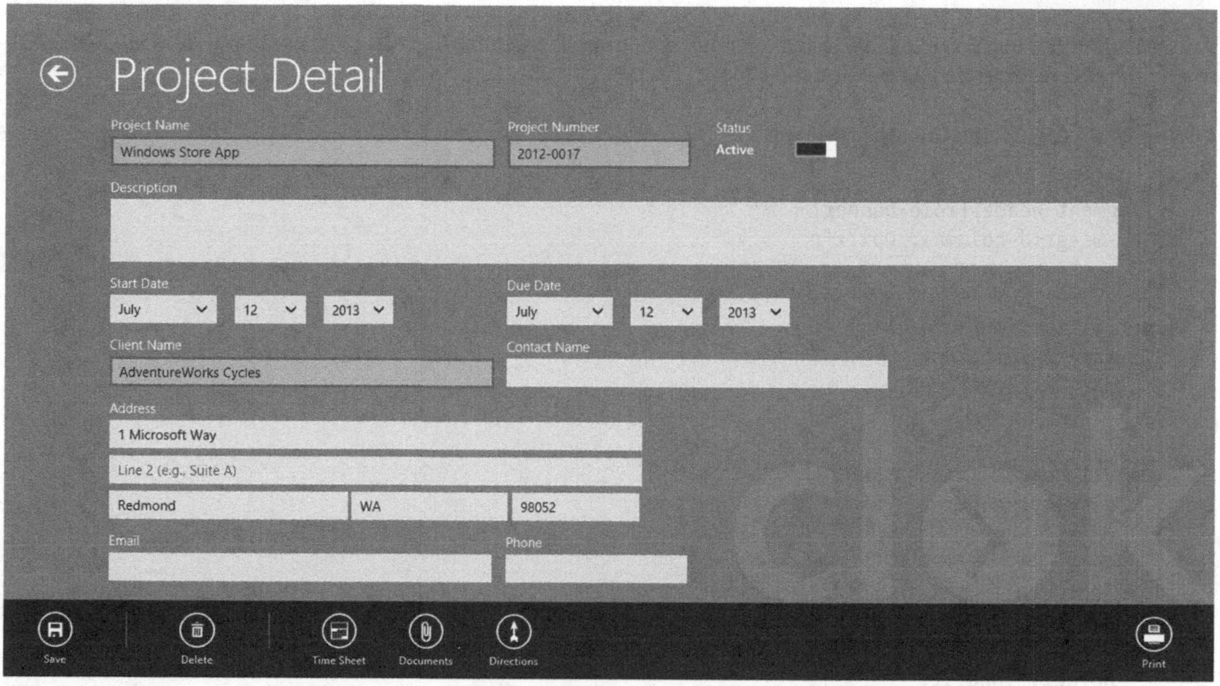

Figure 20-1. *Project Detail screen*

The form is using the CSS grid layout to position the various elements on the screen. In Chapter 11, where the Project Detail screen was added, we specified the `-ms-grid-row` and `-ms-grid-column` CSS properties with inline styles in `detail.html`. Because you will use CSS to reposition the Description field while printing, you'll have to make a small change to the HTML that defines it. Update `detail.html` with the highlighted code from Listing 20-4.

Listing 20-4. Updates to the Description Form Field

```html
<div class="formField" id="descriptionLabelAndField"
        style="-ms-grid-column: 1; -ms-grid-column-span: 3;">
    <label for="projectDescription">Description</label><br />
    <textarea id="projectDescription" data-win-bind="value: description"></textarea>
</div>
```

The `-ms-grid-row` CSS property has been removed, and it now has to be added to `detail.css` in a new rule. Add the highlighted code from Listing 20-5 to `detail.css`.

Listing 20-5. Position the Description Field in the Second Row of the Grid When Viewing Onscreen

```css
#descriptionLabelAndField {
    -ms-grid-row: 2;
}

#projectDescription {
    height: 60px;
    width: calc(90vw - 120px);
}
```

Now you have to define the CSS rules that will be applied when the screen is printed. If you have many rules, you can add them in a second CSS file and reference that from `detail.html`. In this case, not many rules are needed, so add the CSS from Listing 20-6 to the end of `detail.css`.

Listing 20-6. CSS Media Query for Printing

```css
@media print {
    .fragment header[role=banner] {
        -ms-grid-columns: 0px 1fr;
    }

    .detail section[role=main] {
        margin-left: 0px;
        margin-right: 0px;
    }

    .detail header .win-backbutton {
        display: none;
    }

    #projectDetailForm .formField.required input,
    #projectDetailForm .formField.required textarea,
    #projectDetailForm .formField.required select {
        border: inherit;
        background-color: inherit;
    }

    #descriptionLabelAndField {
        -ms-grid-row: 7;
    }

    #projectDescription {
        height: 350px;
        width: 90vw;
    }

    #currentTime,
    #projectDetailAppBar {
        display: none;
    }
}
```

Because these rules are enclosed within a print media query (@media print), they will only be applied when printing this screen. These rules accomplish the various requirements I described at the beginning of this section, such as removing the Back button and moving the Description field to the end of the page by placing it in the seventh row of the CSS grid layout.

Sending to the Printer

The final step is to send the page to the printer. Add the code from Listing 20-7 to `detail.js`. Also be sure to wire up this `click` event handler in the ready function of `detail.js`.

Listing 20-7. Printing the Screen

```
printCommand_click: function (e) {
    window.print();
},
```

Run Clok now and navigate to the Project Detail screen for an existing project. If you click the Print button, the Print pane will open, allowing you to select a printer from a list of printers installed on your computer (see Figure 20-2).

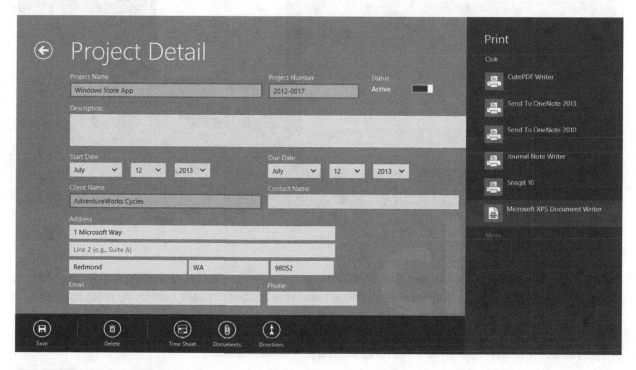

Figure 20-2. *Printer selection*

After selecting a printer—the Microsoft XPS Document Writer in this example—the Print Preview pane is shown (see Figure 20-3). This view allows you to see a thumbnail version of what will be printed, as well as some printing options supported by the selected printer. In Figure 20-3, the only option visible is the option to change the Orientation from Portrait to Landscape.

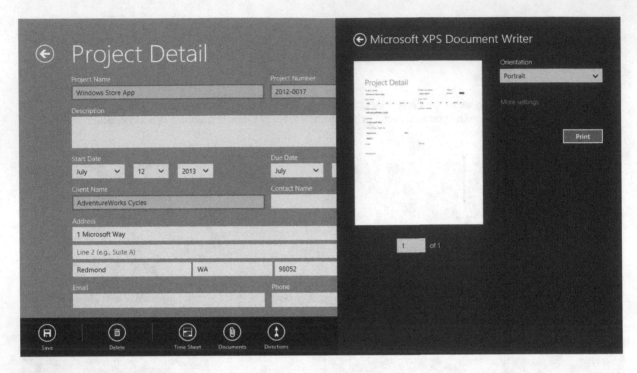

Figure 20-3. *Print preview*

■ **Note** The Microsoft XPS Document Writer is a virtual printer that allows you to convert anything that can be printed into an XPS file. If I had instead selected a physical printer, I would see additional options, such as the option to change the number of copies being printed or change the color mode from color to black-and-white. Additional options can be configured for the Print Preview pane. More information about these other options is available on MSDN (http://msdn.microsoft.com/en-us/library/windows/apps/hh761453.aspx).

From the Print Preview pane, clicking the Print button will submit the document to the selected printer. In the example in Figure 20-2 and Figure 20-3, an XPS file will be created on my computer.

WinRT Printing

In the previous section, I described the typical method used for printing web pages: define print-friendly CSS rules and initiate the printing process. When building web applications, you can trigger printing by calling window.print, similar to what you saw in Listing 20-7. Additionally, the web browser itself offers a Print function to perform the same task. Windows Store applications do not have a Print function by default, but Windows does allow applications to print, using the Devices charm (see Figure 20-4).

Figure 20-4. *The Windows Devices charm*

As with the Windows Share charm, nothing can be sent to other devices by default (see Figure 20-5). However, by adding a relatively small amount of code, you can enable your application to send to other devices, such as printers.

Figure 20-5. *This app can't send to other devices right now*

Creating the Printer Class

This integration with Windows is one of the benefits of using the WinRT printing classes in your application. You can always include a Print button in your application to print something, but adding the necessary hooks into your application to support the Windows Print interface is an easy step that makes your application seem more polished.

Declaring a print contract in your application is simpler than adding a search contract or share target contract. You don't have to make any modifications to `package.appxmanifest`. At the simplest level, three steps are required.

1. Get an instance of the `Windows.Graphics.Printing.PrintManager` class and handle its `printtaskrequested` event.

2. Create an instance of the `Windows.Graphics.Printing.PrintTask` class.

3. Specify the source document to be printed.

While these three steps, which I will cover in a moment, are the only requirements for printing, there are a few other steps you can take to make your application more robust and polished when it comes to printing. For example, each screen of your application that supports printing must handle the `PrintManager` object's `printtaskrequested` event. However, only one handler of this event can be active at any given time. So, if you have multiple screens that have to support printing, you must unregister handlers of this event that are not associated with the currently visible screen.

Additionally, the `PrintTask` object has a `completed` event, which you can optionally handle to notify your application of the success or failure of the printing process. This communication about the status of your printing job back to your application from Windows is the other major advantage to using the WinRT printing classes. When using `window.print`, your application does not receive any feedback about the status of the print job. In many cases, this isn't a requirement, but if successful printing is a vital step for users of your application, the additional information you can obtain using WinRT printing classes will be helpful.

In this section, I'll discuss a class that I've added to Clok to encapsulate some of these details and make it easier to reliably add printing support to any number of screens in your application. Create a new JavaScript file named printing.js in the js folder of your Visual Studio project. Be sure to add a reference to this file in default.html. Add the code from Listing 20-8 to printing.js.

Listing 20-8. Adding a Printing Utility Class

```javascript
(function () {
    "use strict";

    var printingClass = WinJS.Class.define(
        function ctor() {
            this.printManager = Windows.Graphics.Printing.PrintManager.getForCurrentView();
            this.printManager_printtaskrequested_boundThis
                = this.printManager_printtaskrequested.bind(this);
            this._document = null;
            this._title = "Clok";
            this._completed = null;
        },
        {
            register: function (title, completed) {
                this._title = title || this._title;
                this._completed = completed || this._completed;
                this.printManager.addEventListener("printtaskrequested",
                    this.printManager_printtaskrequested_boundThis);
            },

            unregister: function () {
                this.printManager.removeEventListener("printtaskrequested",
                    this.printManager_printtaskrequested_boundThis);
            },

            setDocument: function (doc) {
                this._document = doc;
            },

            print: function () {
                Windows.Graphics.Printing.PrintManager.showPrintUIAsync();
            },

            printManager_printtaskrequested: function (e) {
                if (this._document) {
                    var printTask = e.request.createPrintTask(this._title, function (args) {
                        args.setSource(MSApp.getHtmlPrintDocumentSource(this._document));
                        printTask.oncompleted = this._completed;
                    }.bind(this));
                }
            },
        }
    );
```

```
    WinJS.Namespace.define("Clok", {
        Printer: printingClass,
    });
})();
```

In the constructor of the Clok.Printer class that this code defines, the PrintManager for the current view is obtained. In the register function, its printtaskrequested event is handled, and in the unregister function, that handler is removed. The print function simply opens the Windows Print interface—the same that is available by clicking the Devices charm. The printManager_printtaskrequested handler function creates the required PrintTask object, indicating that the source to be printed is the value specified in the setDocument function. If a completed event handler is specified in the register function, it will be called when the PrintTask object's completed event is raised.

Sending to the Printer

The Printer class created in the previous section encapsulates all of the logic needed to support most common printing scenarios in your application. In this section, I'll show you how to use the Printer class on a screen that should support printing. We'll update the printing logic added to the Project Detail screen earlier in this chapter to use the new Printer class instead.

■ **Note**   The print-friendly CSS that was added to the Project Detail screen earlier in this chapter will still be needed for this section. Using the WinRT printing classes does not affect how the document gets rendered for printing. It only affects how the rendered document is sent to the printer.

Earlier in this chapter, I specified that printing should only be enabled when viewing an existing project. When using the window.print technique, the user will never be able to initiate the printing process using the Devices charm. In that case, it was sufficient to simply disable the Print button for new projects. After updating Clok to use the WinRT printing classes, the user will be able to print from the Devices charm, so disabling the Print button in Clok is not sufficient. Instead, you must specify the document that should be printed. Add the function in Listing 20-9 to detail.js.

Listing 20-9. Specifying the Document to Be Printed

```
configurePrintDocument: function (existingId) {
    if (existingId) {
        this.printer.setDocument(document);
    } else {
        this.printer.setDocument(null);
    }
},
```

In this case, when viewing an existing project, the current document object—the same document object you are familiar with if you're a web developer—will be sent to the printer. If the user is not viewing an existing project, null is specified, to disable printing for the current screen. Later in this chapter, I'll discuss some options you have to print alternate content, that is, how you can print content that is not only styled differently from the current screen but is actually different content altogether.

The configurePrintDocument definition references this.printer, which you haven't defined yet. Add the highlighted code from Listing 20-10 to the ready function and unload function in detail.js.

Listing 20-10. Registering and Unregistering an Instance of the Printer Class

```
ready: function (element, options) {
    this.printer = new Clok.Printer();
    this.printer.register("Project Detail", function (e) {
        if (e.completion === Windows.Graphics.Printing.PrintTaskCompletion.failed) {
            // printing failed
        }
    });

    this.setCurrentProject(options);

    this.configureAppBar(options && options.id);
    this.configurePrintDocument(options && options.id);
    var form = document.getElementById("projectDetailForm");
    WinJS.Binding.processAll(form, this.currProject);

    // SNIPPED
},

unload: function () {
    app.sessionState.currProject = null;
    app.removeEventListener("checkpoint", this.app_checkpoint_boundThis);
    this.printer.unregister();
},
```

In ready, this.printer is defined, and its register function gets called. In this example, I've specified a handler for the completed event, but I've left the implementation to you, as an exercise. Currently, I've only added a condition for when the printing task has failed. Additionally, you can test for when e.completion is submitted, canceled, or abandoned. Documentation for the Windows.Graphics.Printing.PrintTaskCompletion enumeration is available on MSDN (http://msdn.microsoft.com/en-us/library/windows/apps/windows.graphics.printing.printtaskcompletion).

In addition to specifying a handler for the completed event, I've also specified a title for the underlying PrintTask object. In many cases, the user will never see this title, but there are two instances in particular where having a friendly, relevant title will be helpful to users.

- They will see this title when they view the printer's queued jobs (see Figure 20-6).

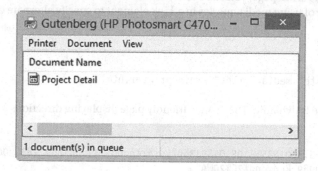

Figure 20-6. Printer queue for Gutenberg, my printer at home

- It will be the default file name when using the XPS Document Writer, or other virtual printer drivers that create files instead of sending the document to a physical printer.

443

There is one more step to change the Project Detail screen to use the WinRT printing classes instead of `window.print`. The call to `window.print` has to be replaced with a call to the `print` function in our new `Printer` class. Update the definition of the `printCommand_click` handler function in `detail.js` with the code in Listing 20-11.

Listing 20-11. Printing with the New Printer Class

```
printCommand_click: function (e) {
    this.printer.print();
},
```

For the simplest of printing tasks, `window.print` may be sufficient. However, as you've seen in this section, integrating with Windows for printing requires a small development investment. In many applications, the `Clok.Printer` class defined in Listing 20-8 can be used with little or no modification, so I encourage you to add this functionality to your applications that have to print.

Printing Alternate Content

The two previous sections demonstrated printing a printer-friendly version of the current screen. Sometimes, however, you have to print different, but related, content. Sometimes, the HTML that is generated by WinJS controls is not appropriate for printing, even though it contains the content you wish to print. In this section, I'll show two techniques you can use to address the issue of printing alternate content:

- Specifying an alternate document for printing in the head element
- Printing a document from an `iframe`

To demonstrate these techniques, we'll give the user the ability to print driving directions and invoices. In both cases, we will use the `Clok.Printer` class created in the previous section.

Printing Driving Directions

Printing driving directions from the Directions screen was the first possible printing example that came to my mind when planning the content for this chapter. As it turns out, printing from a `ListView` doesn't always give the desired results. Rather than try to come up with print-friendly CSS rules for the complicated HTML generated by the `ListView` control on the Directions screen, I decided to print the directions directly from the Bing Maps website.

Using a `link` element within the head of an HTML page, you can specify alternate content that should be used when printing. Listing 20-12 shows an example of using media queries in a `link` element to specify alternate content for printing.

Listing 20-12. Using the Link Element

```
<link id="alternateContent" rel="alternate" media="print" href="printer.html" />
```

The link to Bing Maps printer-friendly page is dynamic. The printer-friendly page displaying directions from Milwaukee to Redmond, Washington, is

```
http://www.bing.com/maps/print.aspx?cp=45.3601835,-105.018913&pt=pf&rtp=pos.43.041809_-87.906837_
Milwaukee%2C%20WI~pos.47.678558_-122.130989_Redmond%2C%20WA
```

Because it is dynamic, you can't add the `link` element to `directions.html`, as in Listing 20-12. Instead, you'll construct this `link` element and add it to the page dynamically in `directions.js`. In the rest of this section, I'll walk you through the changes needed in Clok to allow the user to print driving directions from the Bing Maps website.

Adding a Print Button to the Directions Screen

The first step we'll take is to add an app bar with a Print button to the Directions screen. Add the code from Listing 20-13 to pages\projects\directions.html.

Listing 20-13. Adding an App Bar to the Directions Screen

```
<div id="directionsAppBar"
    class="win-ui-dark"
    data-win-control="WinJS.UI.AppBar"
    data-win-options="{ sticky: true }">

    <button
        data-win-control="WinJS.UI.AppBarCommand"
        data-win-options="{
            id:'printCommand',
            label:'Print',
            icon:'url(/images/Print-small-sprites.png)',
            section:'global',
            tooltip:'Print',
            disabled: true}">
    </button>
</div>
```

Although the Directions screen will not be printing the document that the user is viewing, you can still use the Clok.Printer class you added earlier in this chapter to print the driving directions from Bing Maps. We'll make a few small modifications to the Printer class in the next section, to more easily support specifying alternate content for printing. In the meantime, update directions.js with the highlighted code from Listing 20-14.

Listing 20-14. Registering, Unregistering, and Handling the Click Event for an Instance of the Printer Class

```
ready: function (element, options) {
    this.printer = new Clok.Printer();
    this.printer.register("Directions");

    printCommand.onclick = this.printCommand_click.bind(this);

    // SNIPPED
},

unload: function () {
    // SNIPPED

    this.printer.unregister();
},

printCommand_click: function (e) {
    this.printer.print();
},
```

■ **Note**   Admittedly, the Clok Directions screen is not as comprehensive as the Bing Maps website, without a map or means to change the destination. To give the user these options, you will find, in the source code that accompanies this book, that I've added an additional button to the app bar that launches the Bing Maps website with the user's current search. You can find the code samples for this chapter on the Source Code/Downloads tab of the product detail page for this book (www.apress.com/9781430257790).

Changes to the Printer Class

The task of printing alternate content could be completed without making any changes to the Printer class you added earlier in this chapter. The link element that must be added to the head element of the page could easily be created within directions.js. In fact, that is how I originally developed this feature. However, in the spirit of making the Printer class more easily reusable, in this section, I'll walk you through a few small changes to add that logic to the Printer class. Update printing.js with the highlighted code from Listing 20-15.

Listing 20-15. Supporting Alternate Content Within the Printer Class

```
unregister: function () {
    this.printManager.removeEventListener("printtaskrequested",
        this.printManager_printtaskrequested_boundThis);
    this._removeAlternateContent();
},

setAlternateContent: function (href) {
    this._removeAlternateContent();

    var alternateContent = document.createElement("link");
    alternateContent.setAttribute("id", "alternateContent");
    alternateContent.setAttribute("rel", "alternate");
    alternateContent.setAttribute("href", href);
    alternateContent.setAttribute("media", "print");
    document.getElementsByTagName("head")[0].appendChild(alternateContent);

    this.setDocument(document);
},

_removeAlternateContent: function () {
    var alternateContent = document.getElementById("alternateContent");
    if (alternateContent) {
        document.getElementsByTagName("head")[0].removeChild(alternateContent);
    }
},
```

The creation of the link element occurs in the setAlternateContent function. After it is created and added to the document object, setDocument is called with the current document object, which contains the necessary link element, as the parameter. The _removeAlternateContent function, which is used to remove any previously specified alternate content, is called before defining the link element and when the Printer class is unregistered. This safeguard ensures that there is never more than one such element specified.

Changes to the BingMaps Class

The URI of the printer-friendly Bing Maps page includes latitude and longitude coordinates, as follows:

```
http://www.bing.com/maps/print.aspx?cp=45.3601835,-105.018913&pt=pf&rtp=pos.43.041809_-87.906837_
Milwaukee%2C%20WI~pos.47.678558_-122.130989_Redmond%2C%20WA
```

Coordinates for the starting point and the destination are required, as well as the coordinates of the center point between them. Currently, the Clok.Data.BingMaps class does not include any coordinates, but because the Bing Maps API includes the needed coordinates, it will be easy to add these values. Update the getDirections function in bingMapsWrapper.js in the data folder with the highlighted code from Listing 20-16.

Listing 20-16. Including Coordinates of the Starting Point and Destination

```
var directions = {
    copyright: resp.copyright,
    distanceUnit: resp.resourceSets[0].resources[0].distanceUnit,
    durationUnit: resp.resourceSets[0].resources[0].durationUnit,
    travelDistance: resp.resourceSets[0].resources[0].travelDistance,
    travelDuration: resp.resourceSets[0].resources[0].travelDuration,
    bbox: resp.resourceSets[0].resources[0].bbox,
    startCoords: resp.resourceSets[0].resources[0].routeLegs[0].actualStart.coordinates,
    endCoords: resp.resourceSets[0].resources[0].routeLegs[0].actualEnd.coordinates
}
```

■ **Note**   If you are working from the source code that accompanies this book, you will have to add your Bing Maps API key in bingMapsWrapper.js before you run these samples.

Setting Alternate Content

The final step to enabling the user to print driving directions is to specify the alternate content that should be printed. Because the alternate content is specified by a URI, that URI must be constructed when the user requests directions. Update the getDirectionsButton_click handler function in directions.js with the highlighted code from Listing 20-17.

Listing 20-17. Constructing the URI to the Print-Friendly Page and Setting It As the Alternate Content to Be Printed

```
getDirectionsButton_click: function (e) {
    printCommand.winControl.disabled = true;
    this.printer.setDocument(null);

    if (fromLocation && fromLocation.value && this.dest) {

        maps.getDirections(fromLocation.value, this.dest)
            .then(function (directions) {

                if (directions
                        && directions.itineraryItems
                        && directions.itineraryItems.length > 0) {
```

```
                    WinJS.Binding.processAll(
                        document.getElementById("directionsContainer"), directions);

                    this.showDirectionResults(true);

                    directionsListView.winControl.itemDataSource
                        = directions.itineraryItems.dataSource;

                    directionsListView.winControl.forceLayout();

                    var printPage = "http://www.bing.com/maps/print.aspx?cp="
                        + ((directions.startCoords[0] + directions.endCoords[0]) / 2) + ","
                        + ((directions.startCoords[1] + directions.endCoords[1]) / 2)
                        + "&pt=pf&rtp=pos." + directions.startCoords[0] + "_"
                        + directions.startCoords[1] + "_" + fromLocation.value
                        + "~pos." + directions.endCoords[0] + "_" + directions.endCoords[1]
                        + "_" + this.dest

                    this.printer.setAlternateContent(printPage);

                    printCommand.winControl.disabled = false;
                } else {
                    this.showDirectionResults(false);
                }
            }.bind(this), function (errorEvent) {
                this.showDirectionResults(false);
            }.bind(this));
        } else {
            this.showDirectionResults(false);
        }
    },
```

The first change in this function is to disable printing functionality when the user initiates a new request for driving directions. Calling the setDocument function is called with null, as the parameter will disable printing for the current screen, even if the user attempts to print using the Devices charm. If driving directions are available for the user's request, the URI is created and passed to the setAlternateContent function. This will enable printing from the Devices charm but will not automatically enable the Print app bar button, so we explicitly enable it.

Run Clok now and navigate to the Directions screen for a project that has a client address specified, then enter a starting location and click Get Directions. After the directions load, use the Print button or Devices charm to print the driving directions (see Figure 20-7).

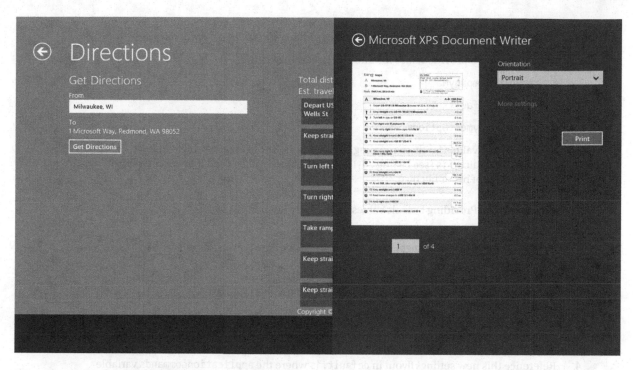

Figure 20-7. *Preview of print-friendly driving directions*

■ **Note** If you use the Microsoft XPS Document Writer to test your printing functionality, it will save an XPS document in your Documents folder.

Printing Invoices for Project Time Sheets

In the previous section, you used a link element to specify alternate content for printing. The URI to that content could reference a file within your application or a page on the Internet, but in either case, the printed content is retrieved by requesting the contents of the specified URI. In this section, I'll discuss hosting content within an iframe element and specifying that the contents of the iframe should be used as the alternate content for printing, and I'll show you how to use this technique to build a printable invoice from the Time Sheets screen.

Adding an Invoice Options Settings Flyout

So far in Clok, the users have not had a way to specify the name of their own company or their billing rate—two things that are required to create an invoice. In this section, you'll add a new Invoice Options settings flyout, to allow users to specify these two values, as well as provide a paragraph describing their billing terms. These values could be added to a new section of the existing Clok Options settings flyout you created in Chapter 15, but, in my opinion, they are unrelated to the other settings available on that settings flyout, so I recommend adding a new one. Because the steps are nearly identical to those taken to build the Clok Options settings flyout, I won't discuss the details here, but I will highlight the steps you need to take.

1. Create a new settings flyout named `invoiceOptions.html` and a corresponding JavaScript file named `invoiceOptions.js` in the `settings` folder of your Visual Studio project.

2. Allow the user to provide values for three new roaming settings:

   a. `invoiceCompanyName`

   b. `invoiceDefaultRate`

   c. `invoicePaymentOptions`

3. Specify default values for these roaming settings in the `intializeRoamingSettings` function in `default.js` (see Listing 20-18). These values will be used if the user does not specify values of his or her own.

Listing 20-18. Providing Default Values for the New Roaming Settings

```
roamingSettings.values["invoiceCompanyName"] =
    roamingSettings.values["invoiceCompanyName"] || "Your Company Name";

roamingSettings.values["invoiceDefaultRate"] =
    roamingSettings.values["invoiceDefaultRate"] || 50.00;

roamingSettings.values["invoicePaymentOptions"] =
    roamingSettings.values["invoicePaymentOptions"] || "Payment is due within 30 days.";
```

4. Reference this new settings flyout in `default.js` where the `applicationcommands` variable is set, so that it is included in the Settings pane.

This process is the same that you followed in Chapter 15 when adding the Clok Options settings flyout. A completed version of the Invoice Options settings flyout, and all of other source code from this chapter, is available in the source code that accompanies this book.

■ **Note** These changes will allow the user to specify a single billing rate to be used for all projects. A helpful feature you may wish to add would be to allow the user to specify in addition a billing rate for each project. If a project rate is specified, that rate would be used in invoice calculations; otherwise, this default rate would be used.

Updates to the Time Sheets Screen

A number of changes are needed to the Time Sheets screen, in the HTML (`pages\timeSheets\list.html`) and the JavaScript code (`pages\timeSheets\list.js`). Following the same pattern used in the previous sections of this chapter, add a Print Invoice button to the app bar of the Time Sheets screen. Don't forget to register an instance of `Clok.Printer` and to handle the Print Invoice button's `click` event, by calling the `print` function of the `Printer` instance.

In this section, you will use the contents of an `iframe` element as the alternate content for printing. Add that `iframe` element now to `list.html` (see Listing 20-19).

Listing 20-19. The iframe Element That Will Contain the Invoice

```
<iframe height="0" width="0" id="invoiceFrame" src="/templates/invoice.html"></iframe>
```

The iframe can be placed pretty much anywhere on the screen, because it has no height or width. However, I recommend placing it right before the timeEntriesContainerdiv and temporarily setting the height and width attributes to positive numbers, so you can see the contents of the iframe during testing. The invoice.html file referenced in the src attribute doesn't exist yet. I'll cover the details of that file in the next section, but in the meantime, create a new folder in the root of your Visual Studio project named templates, then add a placeholder HTML file named invoice.html in that folder (see Figure 20-8).

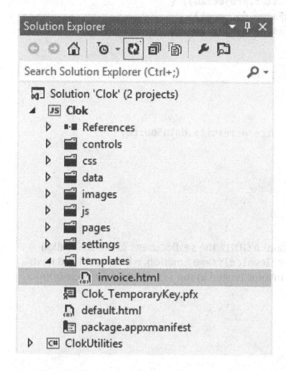

Figure 20-8. *Adding an invoice template to the Visual Studio project*

Invoices can only be printed when a single project is selected using the Filter button in the app bar. When the user updates the filter, you'll have to add code to determine if a project is selected. Update the filter_changed function in list.js with the highlighted code from Listing 20-20.

Listing 20-20. Regenerating the Invoice When the Filter Changes

```
filter_changed: function (e) {
    this.updateResultsArea(searchInProgress);
    this.printer.setDocument(null);
    printInvoiceCommand.winControl.disabled = true;

    storage.timeEntries.getSortedFilteredTimeEntriesAsync(
            this.filter.startDate,
            this.filter.endDate,
            this.filter.projectId)
```

451

```
        .then(
            function complete(results) {
                if (results.length <= 0) {
                    timeEntryAppBar.winControl.show();
                    this.updateResultsArea(noMatchesFound);
                } else {
                    if (ClokUtilities.Guid.isGuid(this.filter.projectId)) {
                        this.printer.setDocument(invoiceFrame.document);
                        printInvoiceCommand.winControl.disabled = false;
                    }
                    this.updateInvoiceIframe(results);
                    this.updateResultsArea(timeEntriesListView);
                }
                this.showAddForm();
                this.filteredResults = results;
                timeEntriesListView.winControl.itemDataSource = results.dataSource;
            }.bind(this),
            function error(results) {
                this.updateResultsArea(searchError);
            }.bind(this)
        );
},
```

When a project is selected, and this.filter.projectId contains a GUID, the setDocument function is called with the document object of the iframe as the parameter. The updateInvoiceIframe function, which you'll add next, is used to pass time sheet data from the Time Sheets screen to the invoice hosted in the iframe. Add the code from Listing 20-21 to list.js.

Listing 20-21. Sending Time Sheet Data to the Invoice

```
updateInvoiceIframe: function (results) {
    var invoiceLines = results.map(function (item) {
        return {
            elapsedSeconds: item.elapsedSeconds,
            dateWorked: item.dateWorked,
            notes: item.notes
        };
    });

    var invoiceProject = results.getAt(0).project;

    var invoiceData = {
        project: invoiceProject,
        lines: invoiceLines
    }
    invoiceFrame.postMessage(invoiceData, "ms-appx://" + document.location.host);
},
```

Communication with the iframe is accomplished using postMessage, in much the same way that communication with Web Workers was accomplished in Chapter 13. An invoiceData object is created and contains details of each of the time entries to be included on the invoice, as well as a reference to the project being invoiced. For security reasons, the call to postMessage includes the current domain as the second parameter. In invoice.html, we will verify that the posted message originated from this same domain.

Generating the Invoice

In this section, I'll show the contents of invoice.html, the file that will be printed when the user prints from the Time Sheets screen. The iframe can contain any contents you wish for your application. For Clok, I've built invoice.html as a single file that includes the necessary CSS and JavaScript within the file, as opposed to referencing external page-specific CSS and JavaScript files, as we've done in the rest of the application. In the previous section, you created a placeholder invoice.html file. Update that file with the code from Listing 20-22. If you'd rather not type all of this code, you will find a completed version of this file in the source code that accompanies this book.

Listing 20-22. The Contents of the Invoice Template in invoice.html

```
<!DOCTYPE html>
<html>
<head>
    <title></title>
    <style type="text/css">
        body {
            font-family: sans-serif;
        }

        h4.sectionHead {
            margin-bottom: 0px;
        }

        .invoiceLines {
            border-collapse: collapse;
            border-spacing: 0px;
        }

            .invoiceLines th,
            .invoiceLines td {
                border: 1px solid black;
                margin: 0px;
                padding: 2px;
            }

            .invoiceLines .totals {
                font-weight: bold;
            }

            .invoiceLines #totalDesc {
                background: black;
            }
    </style>

    <script src="//Microsoft.WinJS.1.0/js/base.js"></script>
    <script src="//Microsoft.WinJS.1.0/js/ui.js"></script>

    <script src="/data/timeEntry.js"></script>
    <script src="/data/project.js"></script>
```

```
<script>
    var appData = Windows.Storage.ApplicationData.current;
    var roamingSettings = appData.roamingSettings;

    var formatDate = function (dt) {
        var formatting = Windows.Globalization.DateTimeFormatting;
        var formatter = new formatting.DateTimeFormatter("shortdate");
        return formatter.format(dt);
    }

    window.onmessage = function (message) {
        if (message.origin !== "ms-appx://" + document.location.host) {
            return;
        }

        WinJS.UI.processAll().then(function () {
            var compName = roamingSettings.values["invoiceCompanyName"];
            var rate = Number(roamingSettings.values["invoiceDefaultRate"]);
            var pmtOptions = roamingSettings.values["invoicePaymentOptions"];
            if (pmtOptions.indexOf("<br") < 0) {
                pmtOptions = pmtOptions.replace(/\r\n/g, "<br />").replace(/\n/g, "<br />");
            }

            var invoiceLines = document.getElementById("invoiceLines");
            var template = document.getElementById("invoiceLineTemplate").winControl;

            var sumHour = 0;
            var sumCost = 0;

            invoiceLines.innerText = "";
            message.data.lines.forEach(function (item) {
                var hrs = item.elapsedSeconds / 3600;

                item.dateWorked = formatDate(item.dateWorked);
                item.hours = hrs.toFixed(2);
                item.lineCost = (rate * hrs).toFixed(2);

                sumHour += hrs;
                sumCost += rate * hrs;

                template.render(item, invoiceLines);
            });

            invoiceDate.innerText = formatDate(new Date());
            projectName.innerText = message.data.project.name;
            projectNumber.innerText = message.data.project.projectNumber;

            companyName.innerText = compName;
            clientName.innerHTML = message.data.project.clientName;
            contactName.innerHTML = message.data.project.contactName;
```

```
                address1.innerHTML = message.data.project.address1;
                address2.innerHTML = message.data.project.address2;
                city.innerHTML = message.data.project.city;
                region.innerHTML = message.data.project.region;
                postalCode.innerHTML = message.data.project.postalCode;

                totalHours.innerText = sumHour.toFixed(2);
                totalCost.innerText = sumCost.toFixed(2);

                paymentOptions.innerHTML = pmtOptions;
            });
        }

    </script>
</head>
<body>
    <h1>Invoice</h1>
    <h2 id="companyName"></h2>

    <h4 class="sectionHead">To:</h4>
    <div>
        <div id="clientName"></div>
        <div id="contactName"></div>
        <div id="address1"></div>
        <div id="address2"></div>
        <div>
            <span id="city"></span>,
            <span id="region"></span>
            <span id="postalCode"></span>
        </div>
    </div>

    <h4 class="sectionHead">For:</h4>
    <div>
        <div>
            Invoice Date: <span id="invoiceDate"></span>
            <br />
            Project:  <span id="projectName"></span>
            <br />
            Ref #:  <span id="projectNumber"></span>
            <br />
        </div>
    </div>

    <h4 class="sectionHead">Invoice Details</h4>
    <table style="display: none;">
        <tbody data-win-control="WinJS.Binding.Template" id="invoiceLineTemplate">
            <tr>
                <td data-win-bind="textContent: dateWorked"></td>
                <td data-win-bind="textContent: notes"></td>
```

455

```
                    <td data-win-bind="textContent: hours"></td>
                    <td data-win-bind="textContent: lineCost"></td>
                </tr>
            </tbody>
        </table>

        <table class="invoiceLines">
            <thead>
                <tr>
                    <th>Date</th>
                    <th>Note</th>
                    <th>Hours</th>
                    <th></th>
                </tr>
            </thead>
            <tbody id="invoiceLines"></tbody>
            <tfoot>
                <tr class="totals">
                    <td id="totalDesc" colspan="2"></td>
                    <td id="totalHours"></td>
                    <td id="totalCost"></td>
                </tr>
            </tfoot>
        </table>

        <p id="paymentOptions"></p>
    </body>
</html>
```

Most of invoice.html is standard, uninteresting HTML, CSS, and JavaScript. There are a few things that I've highlighted in Listing 20-22 that I'd like point out, however.

- Because invoice.html is loaded with the ms-appx protocol, it has full access to the WinRT and WinJS libraries, as well as any classes we've added to Clok. You can see above that I've added script references to the WinJS JavaScript files as well as to Clok's Project and TimeEntry class definitions.

- As a result of referencing the WinJS library, I was able to take advantage of the WinJS.Binding.Template class to create a template named invoiceLineTemplate that defines how the line items in the invoice will be displayed.

- In the onmessage handler function, the invoiceData that was sent via postMessage in Listing 20-21 is available as message.data. Individual placeholders are populated, based on properties of this object, and the line items of the invoice are rendered by the invoiceLineTemplatetemplate.

- The values of the three roaming settings you created earlier in this chapter are used to display the user's company name and billing terms, as well as to calculate the amount due.

Run Clok now and navigate to the Time Sheets screen. After filtering the list for a single project, you can print an invoice, either using the Print Invoice button in the app bar or using the Devices charm (see Figure 20-9).

Invoice

Scott Isaacs, Inc.

To:
AdventureWorks Cycles
1 Microsoft Way
Redmond, WA 98052

For:
Invoice Date: 7/20/2013
Project: Windows Store App
Ref #: 2012-0017

Invoice Details

Date	Note	Hours	
6/7/2013	Donec sit amet porttitor.	2.00	100.00
6/10/2013	Curabitur euismod mollis.	2.00	100.00
6/14/2013	Praesent congue euismod diam. Another line	2.00	100.00
		6.00	**300.00**

Payment is due within 30 days. Please send payment to:
1234 Some St.
Milwaukee, WI 55555

Thank you for your business.

Figure 20-9. *A sample invoice printed from the Time Sheets screen*

Advanced Printing Topics

In this chapter, I've only covered the basics of printing from Windows Store applications. Of course, printing follows the 80/20 rule, where 80% of what you need to accomplish is done with 20% of the possible features. It may even be a 90/10 rule. However, there are a number of other classes in the Windows.Graphics.Printing namespace that you may find useful for some more niche printing requirements. For example, there are classes to facilitate tasks such as communicating the progress of a print task or allowing the user to specify more or fewer options, such as print quality or paper size, in the print preview pane.

More information about the Windows.Graphics.Printing namespace is available on MSDN (http://msdn.microsoft.com/en-us/library/windows/apps/windows.graphics.printing.aspx).

Conclusion

The basics of printing from Windows Store applications are very similar to printing from a web site. In this chapter, I covered some different ways you can define what content is printed, as well as a few different ways of initiating the printing process. Content can be specified by applying print-only CSS rules to onscreen content, by linking to the URI of alternate content that should be printed instead of the current screen, or by printing the contents of an `iframe` element. You can use the native `window.print` function to initiate the printing process, but with a small amount of work, you can take advantage of the WinRT printing classes, to provide a more integrated experience to your users. With little or no modification, the `Clok.Printer` class created in this chapter should be able to handle a large number of printing tasks you may face.

■ ■ ■

CHAPTER 21

Notifications and Tiles

One of the best features of Windows 8, in my opinion, is that so much information is available simply by glancing at the screen.

With the introduction of Live Tiles, applications can provide up-to-date information to the user in bite-sized pieces. In many cases, the summary information is all I need ("your next meeting is tomorrow morning in John's office" or "it's 78 degrees and sunny right now"), and other times, it prompts me to launch the application to get more detail ("John just e-mailed me an agenda for our meeting" or "four of the applications I've installed have updates available"). Additionally, toast notifications, a small rectangle with a short message displayed in the upper corner of the screen, are a great way to get updates from applications as things occur, whether you're on the Start screen or using another application.

In this chapter I'll cover a few different ways to give your users easy access to the information in your application. I'll introduce toast notifications and Live Tiles for displaying small updates, and I'll cover secondary tiles for giving the user quick access to frequently used screens within your application.

Toast Notifications

Toast notifications, sometimes referred to as simply *toasts* or *notifications*, are a great way to provide short, timely information from your application to your user. Displayed as a small rectangle in the upper corner of the screen, these notifications can appear regardless of what the user is doing on the computer, whether using your application, using a different Windows Store application, on the Start screen or on the desktop (see Figure 21-1). Users can click the notification to activate your application; they can dismiss the notification; or they can simply ignore it, and it will go away.

Figure 21-1. Toast notification, while using the Store application, reminding me to write this chapter

There are a few types of notifications available:

- *Local*: A notification created and displayed while the user is using your application

- *Scheduled*: A notification created while the user is using your application, but not displayed until some specified time in the future, when the user may or may not be using your application

- *Push*: A notification created and sent from a remote server, such as Windows Azure Mobile Services, displayed whether or not the user is using your application

Local Notifications

In this section, I'll show you how to add a simple toast notification to Clok. When the user resumes Clok with the timer already running, the notification will be displayed to inform the user how long the timer has been running.

Changes to Application Manifest

Before your application can display any toast notifications, you'll have to make a small configuration change in the application manifest. This is a simple step that is very easy to overlook. No errors occur if this step is overlooked; the code to create notifications is just silently ignored. I once wasted about ten minutes trying to figure out why notifications were not being displayed, before I realized my mistake.

Fortunately, it's a simple change. Open `package.appxmanifest` and scroll down to the Visual Assets section of the Application UI tab. Select All Image Assets from the list on the left and set Toast capable to Yes (see Figure 21-2).

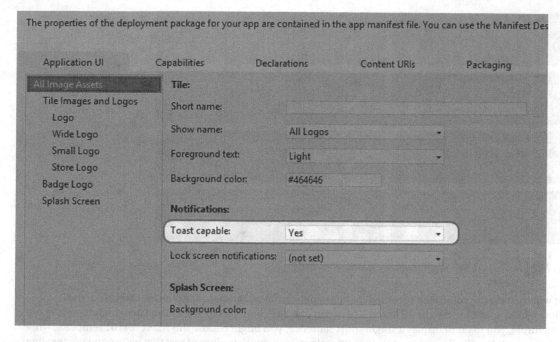

The properties of the deployment package for your app are contained in the app manifest file. You can use the Manifest Des

Figure 21-2. Enabling toast notifications

Additionally, a limitation of the Windows Simulator is that it does not display toast notifications. Be sure your debug target is set to either Local Machine or Remote Machine before testing this functionality (see Figure 21-3).

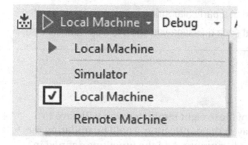

Figure 21-3. Changing the debug target

Toast Notification Templates

When deciding to show a notification to your users, you will have to carefully consider what information must be included. Depending on your needs, you will choose from one of eight templates that exist in the WinRT library (see Figure 21-4).

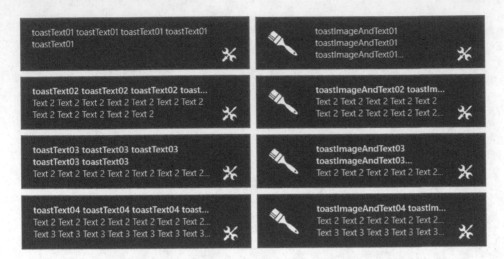

Figure 21-4. *The toast notification templates available in WinRT*

All eight will include the small icon specified for your application in `package.appxmanifest`. Four of the templates allow you to specify text to be included—between one and three pieces, depending on which template you select. If, for example, you need to display a single short sentence, you might choose the `toastText01` template, while the `toastText02` template will allow you to specify a title, along with another piece of text that will wrap over two lines. Additionally, the other four templates provide the same choices but also allow you to specify an image to accompany the text of your notification. The various templates are documented on MSDN (`http://msdn.microsoft.com/en-us/library/windows/apps/hh761494.aspx`).

■ **Note**   Although there is not a specific character limit for each piece of text, if a particular string is too long for its allotted space, it is truncated, and ellipses are added. With that in mind, make sure that each message you show is clear and concise.

Creating the Notification

Let's see how this works, by adding a notification to Clok. To display one of these eight templates, you will have to create XML that defines which template to use and which values to display in the notification. You'll be updating the Clok Dashboard to show a notification Clok is started, with the timer already running. Add the functions defined in Listing 21-1 to `home.js`.

Listing 21-1. Creating a Notification

```
getStillRunningToastContent: function () {
    var seconds = elapsedTimeClock.winControl.timerValue;

    if (elapsedTimeClock.winControl.isRunning && seconds > 0) {
        var hours = Math.floor(Clok.Utilities.SecondsToHours(seconds, false));

        var template = notifications.ToastTemplateType.toastImageAndText02;
        var toastContent = notificationManager.getTemplateContent(template);
```

```
            // image
            var imageNodes = toastContent.getElementsByTagName("image");
            imageNodes[0].setAttribute("src", "ms-appx:///images/Clock-Running.png");

            // text
            var textNodes = toastContent.getElementsByTagName("text");
            textNodes[0].appendChild(toastContent.createTextNode("Clok is running"));
            textNodes[1].appendChild(toastContent.createTextNode(
"Clok has been running for more than " + hours + " hours."));

            return toastContent;
        }
    },

showLocalToast: function () {
    var toastContent = this.getStillRunningToastContent();

    if (toastContent) {
        var toast = new notifications.ToastNotification(toastContent);
        notificationManager.createToastNotifier().show(toast);
    }
},
```

The getStillRunningToastContent function first determines if the timer is running and how much time has passed. If the user has just launched Clok, and the timer is still running from a previous use, then a notification is created. In this case, I have selected the toastImageAndText02 template, which allows me to specify an image, a title, and a slightly longer piece of text in the notification.

In Listing 21-1, I've used the getTemplateContent function to retrieve a Windows.Data.Xml.Dom.XmlDocument object representing the XML needed to create a notification. Then I manipulate the nodes of that XmlDocument object to specify the image and text that should be displayed. In addition to manipulating an XmlDocument object, you can alternatively build a string containing the necessary XML and create a notification from that. The process of creating Live Tiles follows the same steps, and I will demonstrate the string manipulation technique in the section "Creating Live Tiles" later in this chapter.

The getStillRunningToastContent function returns a notification, and the showLocalToast function passes that to the show function of a ToastNotifier object, which will display the notification. Now add the highlighted code from Listing 21-2 to the setDashboardStateFromSettings function in home.js.

Listing 21-2. Displaying the Notification

```
setDashboardStateFromSettings: function () {
    var state = localSettings.values["dashboardState"];

    if (state) {
        state = JSON.parse(state);

        elapsedTimeClock.winControl.startStops = state.startStops;
        project.selectedIndex = this.getIndexOfProjectId(state.projectId);
        timeNotes.value = state.timeNotes;
```

```
        if (elapsedTimeClock.winControl.isRunning) {
            this.startTimer();
            this.showLocalToast();
        }
    }
},
```

Additionally, add the highlighted aliases in Listing 21-3 to home.js.

Listing 21-3. Adding Aliases to Notification Classes

```
var appData = Windows.Storage.ApplicationData.current;
var localSettings = appData.localSettings;
var notifications = Windows.UI.Notifications;
var notificationManager = notifications.ToastNotificationManager;

var nav = WinJS.Navigation;
var storage = Clok.Data.Storage;
```

Now run Clok and start the timer, then close Clok. After a moment, launch Clok again. At this point, Clok will display a notification to remind you that the timer is running (see Figure 21-5).

Figure 21-5. Displaying a notification to the Clok user

464

While I won't be covering it here, the source code that accompanies this book includes a simple feature to improve the user experience, by allowing users to specify in the Clok Options settings flyout if they'd like to see this reminder when Clok is launched. You can find the code samples for this chapter on the Source Code/Downloads tab of this book's product detail page (www.apress.com/9781430257790).

Scheduled Notifications

In the previous section, you added functionality to make it clear to the user if the timer is already running when he or she launches Clok. As a user, I might find that useful if, for example, when I launch Clok to get driving directions to my client's location, I am reminded that I started the timer yesterday. If I already completed this work, this reminder might prompt me to quickly stop the timer and correct the time entry while it is fresh in my mind.

What about the situation, however, when I am not using Clok? What if I am writing an e-mail or playing a game? In this section, I'll show you how to schedule a notification to appear when the timer has been running for eight hours.

Scheduling a Notification

In the previous section, you created a `ToastNotification` object and used the `show` function to display it to the user immediately. Scheduling a notification is very similar. In this section, you will create a `ScheduledToastNotification` object and use the `addToSchedule` function to display it to the user at some point in the future. Add the code from Listing 21-4 to home.js.

Listing 21-4. Scheduling a Future Notification

```
scheduleToast: function () {
    var reminderThreshold = 8; // hours
    var toastContent = this.getStillRunningToastContent();

    if (toastContent) {
        var seconds = elapsedTimeClock.winControl.timerValue;
        var notifyTime = (new Date()).addSeconds(-seconds).addHours(reminderThreshold);
        if (notifyTime.getTime() > (new Date()).getTime()) {
            var snoozeTime = 30 * 60 * 1000; // 30 min
            var snoozeCount = 5;
            var toast = new notifications.ScheduledToastNotification(
                toastContent,
                notifyTime,
                snoozeTime,
                snoozeCount);
            toast.id = "IsRunningToast";
            notificationManager.createToastNotifier().addToSchedule(toast);
        }
    }
},
```

■ **Note** In the source code that accompanies this book, I've added a few new functions to the `Date` prototype: `addSeconds`, `addMinutes`, and `addHours`.

This code uses the same getStillRunningToastContent function to define the notification. After doing some date and time math to determine when the timer will reach eight hours, the toastContent object, returned from the getStillRunningToastContent function, is used to create a ScheduledToastNotification object. Additionally, I've added optional code that will allow the user to "snooze" the notification for 30 minutes, up to five times. A notification can be snoozed by ignoring it, swiping it away on a touch screen, or clicking the × button that appears when you hover your mouse over the notification.

If the user clicks the notification, the snoozing will be canceled; Clok will be launched; and the Clok Dashboard screen will be displayed. If you specify a value for the launch attribute of the toast node in the XmlDocument that defines the notification, you can examine the args.detail.arguments property to retrieve that value in your application's activation process and navigate to a different screen, instead of the Clok Dashboard screen. For example, if you were creating a calendar application, clicking a meeting reminder notification should open that meeting in the application. More information about the launch attribute is available on MSDN (http://msdn.microsoft.com/en-us/library/windows/apps/br230846.aspx). I will cover a different, but similar, topic later in the chapter, when I introduce secondary tiles.

Before calling addToSchedule, I assigned a value to the id property of the toast object. This id property can be up to 16 characters in length and can be used to reference scheduled notifications that have not yet been displayed. Additionally, if you create another scheduled notification using the same value for the id property, the new notification will replace the previously defined one. Multiple different notifications can be scheduled by providing a different value of the id property for each. If, for example, you were building a calendar application, you could schedule reminder notifications to appear for each meeting in the user's calendar by specifying a different value for id for each notification. Because there is only one timer in Clok, I've hard-coded the id property to IsRunningToast. You'll use this in the next section to cancel scheduled notifications. Before a notification can be canceled, it must be scheduled in the first place. Update the setupTimerRelatedControls function in home.js with the highlighted code from Listing 21-5, to call the new scheduleToast function.

Listing 21-5. Schedule the Notification When the Timer Is Started

```
setupTimerRelatedControls: function () {
    if (this.timerIsRunning) {
        this.startTimer();
        this.scheduleToast();
    } else {
        this.stopTimer();
    }
    this.enableOrDisableButtons();
},
```

Now, when the timer is started, a notification is scheduled to appear when the timer has been running for eight hours. The notification users see, if the timer is already running when they launch Clok, will be the same as the notification they see if they've left the timer running for eight hours. That behavior allows you to reuse the existing getStillRunningToastContent function when creating a scheduled notification. However, if you run Clok now and start the timer, when the notification finally appears at the scheduled time, it's not quite right (see Figure 21-6).

Figure 21-6. *The notification that appears when the timer has been running for eight hours*

■ **Note** For quicker testing, I suggest temporarily changing the `notifyTime` variable to `(new Date()).addSeconds(20)`. Be sure to change this value back to the value specified in Listing 21-4 when you are done testing in this section, to prevent an endless cycle of scheduled notifications.

So what's happening? When scheduling a notification to be displayed in the future, you must create the content of the notification when it is scheduled. If we leave the `getStillRunningToastContent` function unchanged, even though the notification will be displayed correctly after the timer has been running for eight hours, the message will indicate incorrectly that it has been running less time. The exact value displayed will depend on whether the user stopped and resumed the timer. For example, if he or she stopped the timer in the middle of the day to take lunch, and then resumed it after lunch, the message might indicate that the timer had been running for more than four hours. To fix this, a change is needed, to determine what the message should be when it is finally displayed. We have to add the ability to specify the `seconds` variable as a parameter to the `getStillRunningToastContent` function. Update the `getStillRunningToastContent` function in `home.js` with the highlighted code from Listing 21-6.

Listing 21-6. Specifying Seconds As a Parameter

```
getStillRunningToastContent: function (seconds) {
    seconds = seconds || elapsedTimeClock.winControl.timerValue;

    // SNIPPED
},
```

If no value is provided for the `seconds` parameter, it will follow the logic you added previously in Listing 21-1, using the current value of the timer. So, you won't have to make any changes to the `showLocalToast` function. However, the `scheduleToast` function must be updated to pass this value to the `getStillRunningToastContent` function. Update the `scheduleToast` function in `home.js` with the highlighted code from Listing 21-7.

Listing 21-7. Update to the scheduleToast Function

```
scheduleToast: function () {
    var reminderThreshold = 8; // hours
    var toastContent = this.getStillRunningToastContent(reminderThreshold * 60 * 60);

    // SNIPPED
},
```

Now, when the scheduled notification is displayed, it shows the correct message (see Figure 21-7).

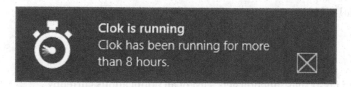

Figure 21-7. *The corrected notification that appears when the timer has been running for eight hours*

■ **Note** A nice feature you might wish to add to improve the user experience would be to include a setting on the Clok Options settings flyout that would allow the user to provide a value for the reminderThreshold variable.

Canceling a Scheduled Notification

The changes you made in the previous section will schedule a notification to appear when the timer has been running for eight hours. Right? Well, technically, it schedules a notification to be displayed when it *would be running* for eight hours. There's a slight difference in the way I've worded it, but it's an important difference. What would happen right now if the user stopped the timer at seven hours? What would happen if he or she saved the time entry? What would happen if he or she discarded it?

In case the title of this section hasn't already given away the answer, it is that, as it stands now, the notification would still be displayed when the timer would have reached eight hours. Fortunately, the solution is simple. Whenever the user timer stops, any scheduled notification should be canceled. Add the highlighted code in Listing 21-8 to the setupTimerRelatedControls function in home.js.

Listing 21-8. Cancel the Scheduled Notification When the Timer Is Stopped

```
setupTimerRelatedControls: function () {
    if (this.timerIsRunning) {
        this.startTimer();
        this.scheduleToast();
    } else {
        this.stopTimer();
        this.unscheduleToast();
    }
    this.enableOrDisableButtons();
},
```

Next, add the unscheduleToast function defined in Listing 21-9 to home.js.

Listing 21-9. Removing the Notification from the Schedule

```
unscheduleToast: function () {
    var notifier = notificationManager.createToastNotifier();
    var scheduled = notifier.getScheduledToastNotifications();

    for (var i = 0, len = scheduled.length; i < len; i++) {
        if (scheduled[i].id === "IsRunningToast") {
            notifier.removeFromSchedule(scheduled[i]);
        }
    }
},
```

As you would expect, the getScheduledToastNotifications function gets a list of all notifications currently scheduled for your application. Looping through them, I've identified the one that has the same id value that we set in Listing 21-4 and pass it to the removeFromSchedule function to cancel it. Now, any time the timer is stopped, any future notifications are canceled.

Adding Sound

There are some situations for which a notification might be important enough to really try to grab the user's attention. Suppose you were building an alarm clock application. If the user was asleep, simply showing a notification would not be sufficient to get his or her attention. Or perhaps the notification is for something the user has indicated is very important and timely. What could you do to improve the likelihood of the user seeing the notification if, for example, he or she were talking on the phone and not actively using the computer?

In situations such as these, you might consider adding sound to your notifications. Add the highlighted code from Listing 21-10 to the getStillRunningToastContent function in home.js.

Listing 21-10. Including Audio with the Notification

```
getStillRunningToastContent: function (seconds) {
    seconds = seconds || elapsedTimeClock.winControl.timerValue;

    if (elapsedTimeClock.winControl.isRunning && seconds > 0) {

    // SNIPPED

        // audio
        var toastNode = toastContent.selectSingleNode("/toast");
        toastNode.setAttribute("duration", "long");

        var audio = toastContent.createElement("audio");
        audio.setAttribute("src", "ms-winsoundevent:Notification.Looping.Call");
        audio.setAttribute("loop", "true");

        toastNode.appendChild(audio);

        return toastContent;
    }
},
```

These changes cause the notification to be displayed for a longer duration and play a particular sound repeatedly (looping) while it is displayed. It's a simple change that will take effect for all timer-related notifications we've created within Clok. There are some limitations to this feature to keep in mind, however.

You can only reference sounds from a short list. There are five non-looping sounds that are appropriate for simple notifications. In fact, depending on the settings you've made in the Sound control panel (see Figure 21-8) on your computer, you may have already been hearing the default sound with each notification. I'll come back to this point in a moment.

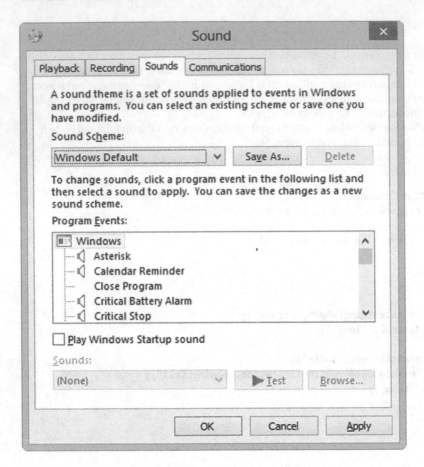

Figure 21-8. *Sounds tab of the Sound control panel*

Additionally, there are 20 longer sounds suitable for looping. These sounds are intended for situations such as receiving incoming calls in a chat application, similar to how your phone will ring several times to give you a chance to answer an incoming phone call. These looping sounds, one of which I used in Listing 21-10, will be played regardless of the settings made in the Sound control panel, even if the No Sounds sound scheme is selected.

The first five non-looping sounds map to specific items in the Program Events list pictured in Figure 21-8. For example, the Notification.Default sound corresponds to the Notification program event in the Sound control panel. If the user has changed his or her sound scheme to one that does not have a sound specified for the Notification event, he or she will not hear anything if you have specified Notification.Default as the sound to play. This caused a moment of confusion for me initially, because I usually have the No Sounds sound scheme selected. So, I would hear the sound when I specified one of the looping sounds, but not when I specified one of the non-looping sounds.

This leads to another point. I mentioned a moment ago that you may have been hearing sounds with each notification all along. By default, unless specified otherwise, all notifications will play the Notification.Default sound when they are displayed. If you have a sound scheme selected on your computer that has a sound specified for the Notification program event, that sound would have been played with every notification displayed in this chapter. If necessary, you can display a notification with no sound at all, regardless of the user's selected sound scheme. To do this, instead of setting the src attribute of the audio node of the toast's XML definition, you have to set its silent attribute to true. More information about the various sounds that can be specified is available on MSDN (http://msdn.microsoft.com/en-us/library/windows/apps/hh761492.aspx).

Take care when setting sounds for notifications, however, and for using notifications in general as well. A user may get frustrated with your application if he or she feels that the application is too noisy. If you feel you should include sounds with notifications, especially the longer looping sounds, it might be a good idea to allow the user to specify which, if any, sound he or she would like to hear.

Push Notifications

So far, I've covered local and scheduled notifications. In both cases, the notification is created while your application is running. Push notifications, on the other hand, are created and sent from another server. For example, if you were to extend Clok to support multiple users with a centralized storage system in the cloud, you might send a push notification to one user when another user adds a document to a project's document library.

As I mentioned in Chapter 14, Microsoft's Windows Azure Mobile Services offers push notification functionality, in addition to a host of other features, all of which are supported on multiple platforms. In addition to the Windows Azure Mobile Services Dev Center I mentioned in Chapter 14 (`www.windowsazure.com/en-us/develop/mobile`), a sample application integrating push notifications from Azure Mobile Services into a Windows Store application is available as well (`http://code.msdn.microsoft.com/windowsapps/Tile-Toast-and-Badge-Push-90ee6ff1`). Unlike many of the other sample applications I've mentioned throughout the book, this sample project is not available in the Windows SDK sample application pack and must be downloaded separately.

Tiles

Every Windows Store application has a tile that is added to the Start screen when the application is installed. It's a requirement of building an application. In fact, when you create a project from any of the Visual Studio project templates discussed in Chapter 4, Visual Studio automatically adds some default images to your project, including a file named `logo.png`, which is displayed on your application's tile (see Figure 21-9).

Figure 21-9. *Default tile logo included with every Visual Studio project*

In Chapter 23, I'll show you how to update your application's tile image and color to complement what we've been building within the application itself. In this chapter, however, I'll cover adding wide tiles, Live Tiles, and secondary tiles for your application.

Wide Tiles

As the name suggests, a wide tile is wider than a standard square tile. In Windows 8, a standard tile size is 150×150 and a wide tile is 310×150 (see Figure 21-10).

Figure 21-10. *The wide tile of the Weather application*

Adding a wide tile is a simple process. The first step is to create an image. For Clok, I made a copy of the logo.png file, named it widelogo.png, and added it to the Clok Visual Studio project in the images folder. Then I used an image-editing program to increase the width of the image file to 310 pixels. The second, and final, step is to reference this file in package.appxmanifest (see Figure 21-11).

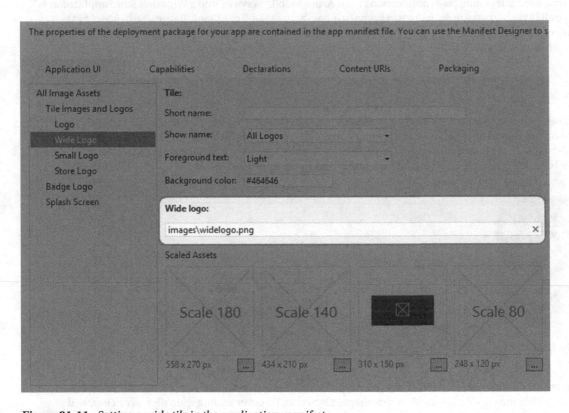

Figure 21-11. *Setting a wide tile in the application manifest*

If you specify a wide tile in the application manifest, when your application is installed, the default tile displayed on the Start screen will be the wide tile (see Figure 21-12). The user will be able to switch between the standard tile and the wide tile by right-clicking it on the Start screen and choosing his or her desired option from the app bar that appears.

Figure 21-12. *Wide tile for Clok*

Live Tiles

Anyone who has used Windows 8 for more than five minutes is familiar with Live Tiles, even if they aren't familiar with the term. The technique to update tiles on the Start screen to show relevant pieces of information is a popular feature of the operating system. In this section, I'll show you how to create a Live Tile for Clok on the Start screen. Similar to the notifications added earlier in this chapter, the Live Tile will indicate at a glance to the user if the Clok timer is running.

Tile Templates

Before I show you how to create a Live Tile, I want to quickly discuss the available templates you can use to create them. As with the toast notifications I introduced earlier in this chapter, there are a number of predefined templates you can use to create a Live Tile. While there were eight templates available for notifications, there are forty-six available for Live Tiles—ten for standard square tiles, and thirty-six for wide tiles. That's too many to cover in detail in this book. In general, they can be categorized into a few types of Live Tiles, as follows:

- *Text-only templates*: Similar to notifications, these have several formats, each supporting a different number of text elements, such as the example in Figure 21-13. These are available for both standard and wide Live Tiles.

Figure 21-13. *Wide text-only template*

- *Image-only templates*: As the name suggests, no text elements are specified as part of the template (see Figure 21-14). However, if you have a particular tile layout that cannot be achieved using any of the other templates, one option is to use an image-only template and specify an application-generated image as the content. These are available for both standard and wide Live Tiles.

Figure 21-14. *Wide image-only template*

- *Text-and-image templates*: These combine images and text into a single Live Tile, as shown in Figure 21-15, and are available only for wide Live Tiles.

Figure 21-15. *Wide text-and-image template*

- *Peek tile templates*: These are the Live Tiles that "flip" back and forth between an image-only view and a view similar to one of the other tile templates. Figure 21-16 shows the progression of a peek tile's change.

Figure 21-16. *Progression of a wide peek template as it changes*

One thing to remember is that a square Live Tile template will only be used when the tile on the user's Start screen is set to the standard square size. Likewise, a wide Live Tile template will only be used when the tile on the user's Start screen is set to the wide size. For this reason, it is a good practice to specify templates for each tile size your application supports. I'll show you how to do this in the next section. A full listing of all of the templates available in each of these categories is available on MSDN (http://msdn.microsoft.com/en-us/library/windows/apps/hh761491.aspx).

Creating Live Tiles

Creating a Live Tile is very similar to creating a notification. A Live Tile template is used to create an XML document specifying the various properties. From the list of templates mentioned in the previous section, I have selected a standard square template (TileSquarePeekImageAndText04) and a wide template (TileWidePeekImage06). Before I show you how to implement these, add the alias highlighted in Listing 21-11 to home.js.

Listing 21-11. Adding Another Alias

```
var appData = Windows.Storage.ApplicationData.current;
var localSettings = appData.localSettings;
var notifications = Windows.UI.Notifications;
var notificationManager = notifications.ToastNotificationManager;
var tileUpdateManager = notifications.TileUpdateManager;

var nav = WinJS.Navigation;
var storage = Clok.Data.Storage;
```

Next, add the two functions defined in Listing 21-12 to home.js.

Listing 21-12. Functions to Enable and Disable the Live Tile

```
enableLiveTile: function () {
    var tileContentString = "<tile>"
        + "<visual>"
        + "<binding template=\"TileSquarePeekImageAndText04\" branding=\"logo\">"
        + "<image id=\"1\" src=\"ms-appx:///images/Clock-Running.png\"/>"
        + "<text id=\"1\">Clok is running</text>"
        + "</binding>  "
        + "<binding template=\"TileWidePeekImage06\" branding=\"none\">"
        + "<image id=\"1\" src=\"ms-appx:///images/widelogo.png\"/>"
        + "<image id=\"2\" src=\"ms-appx:///images/Clock-Running.png\"/>"
        + "<text id=\"1\">Clok is running</text>"
        + "</binding>"
        + "</visual>"
        + "</tile>";

    var tileContentXml = new Windows.Data.Xml.Dom.XmlDocument();
    tileContentXml.loadXml(tileContentString);

    var tile = new notifications.TileNotification(tileContentXml);
    tileUpdateManager.createTileUpdaterForApplication().update(tile);
},

disableLiveTile: function () {
    tileUpdateManager.createTileUpdaterForApplication().clear();
},
```

■ **Note**   Earlier in this chapter, I showed how you can create a notification by manipulating an XmlDocument object. While that is an option for Live Tiles as well, in this case, I'm building a string containing the necessary XML. Either technique is allowed, whether creating notifications or Live Tiles.

You'll notice, in the enableLiveTile function, that I have specified both the standard square Live Tile and the wide Live Tile in the same XML, each within a different binding element contained in the same visual element. When the update function is called at the end of the enableLiveTile function, having both specified will update both versions of the tile. If the user has pinned either size tile to his or her Start screen, the static logo image will be replaced with the appropriate Live Tile. The only remaining step is to enable the Live Tile when the timer is running and disable it when the timer is not running. Update the `setupTimerRelatedControls` function in `home.js` with the highlighted code from Listing 21-13.

Listing 21-13. Enabling the Live Tile When the Timer Is Started and Disabling It When the Timer Is Stopped

```
setupTimerRelatedControls: function () {
    if (this.timerIsRunning) {
        this.startTimer();
        this.scheduleToast();
        this.enableLiveTile();
    } else {
        this.stopTimer();
        this.unscheduleToast();
        this.disableLiveTile();
    }
    this.enableOrDisableButtons();
},
```

Now run Clok and start the timer. Leave the timer running and switch to the Start screen. Depending on which size tile you have pinned, you'll see the tile get replaced with either the standard square Live Tile (see Figure 21-17) or the wide Live Tile (see Figure 21-18).

Figure 21-17. *Clok's standard size Live Tile "peeking"*

Figure 21-18. *Clok's wide size Live Tile "peeking"*

■ **Note**　Live Tiles are not displayed in the Windows Simulator. To test this functionality, you will have to set your debug target either to Local Machine or Remote Machine, before testing this functionality (refer back to Figure 21-3).

Secondary Tiles

Every Windows Store application automatically has a tile that can be pinned to the Start screen. When clicked, it will launch the application and display the default screen of the application. In the previous section, I showed you how to change your application's default tile into a Live Tile, which can provide useful information to the user at a glance. Like the default tile, it will also display the application's default screen.

Secondary tiles, the topic of this section, are similar in that they can be displayed on the user's Start screen. They are different, however, in that they can cause your application to load a different page when it is launched. You can use this functionality to automatically load a top-level section of your application when launched, such as the Time Sheets screen in Clok. You can also use it to display a more detailed screen, such as the Project Detail screen, for a specific project. In this section, we'll implement the latter feature in Clok, by allowing users to add or remove a secondary tile—often referred to as pinning and unpinning—to their Start screen that will allow them to view details for a specific project within Clok with a single click.

Adding a Button to the Project Detail Screen

Adding, or pinning, secondary tiles to the Start screen will require the user's permission. You cannot programmatically add secondary tiles to the user's Start screen as the direct result of the user clicking a button. Instead, Windows provides an interface to request permission from the user (see Figure 21-19), and you must show this interface, displayed in a flyout control, when you'd like to add the tile.

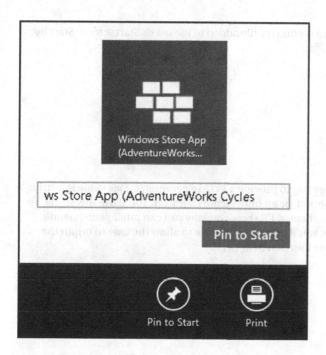

Figure 21-19. *Requesting the user's permission to pin a tile to the Start screen*

In the next section, I'll show you how to display the flyout control to request the user's permission to add the tile. In this section, you'll add a new button to the app bar on the Project Detail screen. Add the code from Listing 21-14 right before the Print button in the detail.html file in the pages\projects folder.

Listing 21-14. Adding the Pin Button

```
<button
    data-win-control="WinJS.UI.AppBarCommand"
    data-win-options="{
        id:'pinUnpinCommand',
        label:'Pin to Start',
        icon:'pin',
        section:'global',
        tooltip:'Pin to Start',
        disabled: true}">
</button>
```

The user will click this button to pin a project to his or her Start screen. If the project is already pinned, this button can be used to remove it, or unpin it, from the Start screen. In the following sections, I'll show you how to repurpose this button to handle both the pinning and unpinning tasks. Before that, there are a couple remaining tasks to complete that should be pretty familiar by this point in the book. In the ready function in detail.js, add a click event handler for this button to a function named pinUnpinCommand_click, which you'll add in the next section. Also, don't forget to update the configureAppBar function, to enable this button when viewing details for an existing project.

Pinning a Secondary Tile

In this section, I'll walk through the few steps needed to get a secondary tile added to the user's Start screen. Start by adding the highlighted aliases from Listing 21-15 to detail.js.

Listing 21-15. Adding Aliases

```
var app = WinJS.Application;
var startScreen = Windows.UI.StartScreen;
var secondaryTile = startScreen.SecondaryTile;
var data = Clok.Data;
var storage = Clok.Data.Storage;
```

When creating a secondary tile, the constructor requires you to provide a tileId parameter. This value is a string of up to 64 characters and can include letters, numbers, a period, or an underscore character. You'll use this string to identify the tile throughout your application. Later in this chapter, I'll show you how you can intelligently handle application activation from secondary tiles using this value. You'll also use this value to allow the user to unpin the tile. Add the highlighted code from Listing 21-16 to the ready function in detail.js.

Listing 21-16. Setting an id for the Tile

```
ready: function (element, options) {
// SNIPPED

    this.setCurrentProject(options);
    this.secondaryTileId = "Tile.Project." + this.currProject.id.replace(/-/g, ".");

    // SNIPPED
},
```

Another situation where you'll use this value is when using the WinRT library to determine if the tile already exists on the user's Start screen. Add the app bar button click event handler from Listing 21-17 to detail.js.

Listing 21-17. Handling the Click Event

```
pinUnpinCommand_click: function (e) {
    if (!secondaryTile.exists(this.secondaryTileId)) {
        this.pinToStart();
    }
},
```

If the tile does not already exist, the pinToStart function is called to request the user's permission to add the tile. Add the pinToStart function from Listing 21-18 to detail.js.

Listing 21-18. Requesting Permission to Add the Tile to the Start Screen

```
pinToStart: function () {
    // build the tile that will be added to the Start screen
    var uriLogo = new Windows.Foundation.Uri("ms-appx:///images/Projects.png");
    var displayName = this.currProject.name + " (" + this.currProject.clientName + ")";

    var tile = new secondaryTile(
        this.secondaryTileId,
        displayName,
        displayName,
        this.currProject.id,
        startScreen.TileOptions.showNameOnLogo,
        uriLogo);

    tile.foregroundText = startScreen.ForegroundText.light;

    // determine where to display the request to the user
    var buttonRect = pinUnpinCommand.getBoundingClientRect();
    var buttonCoordinates = {
        x: buttonRect.left,
        y: buttonRect.top,
        width: buttonRect.width,
        height: buttonRect.height
    };
    var placement = Windows.UI.Popups.Placement.above;

    // make the request and update the app bar
    tile.requestCreateForSelectionAsync(buttonCoordinates, placement)
        .done(function (isCreated) {
            // TODO
        }.bind(this));
},
```

The first several lines in the pinToStart function create the tile that the user will be asked to add to his or her Start screen. I've specified the same Projects icon that is displayed on the Clok Dashboard screen as the icon on this tile. The name, which the user can change, will have a default value consisting of the project and client names, and specifying showNameOnLogo will cause this name to be displayed beneath the icon. In addition to providing secondaryTileId for the tileId parameter, I've also provided the id property of the current project as the arguments parameter. In the next section, I'll show you how to use the arguments parameter in Clok's activation process.

The next few lines of the pinToStart function are used to determine where the flyout that requests the user's permission will be displayed. The recommended practice is to base the position of the flyout on the position of the app bar button that opened the flyout. This prevents unnecessary mouse movements and makes the process more natural for the user. The last block of code in the pinToStart function requests the user's permission and adds the tile. This happens asynchronously, and we'll add a bit more code to the done function to update the app bar when the process is complete.

Run Clok and navigate to the Project Detail screen for an existing project. Click the Pin to Start app bar button and then click the Pin to Start button in the flyout that opens (refer to preceding Figure 21-19). A few seconds later, a new tile will appear on your Start screen (see Figure 21-20). New tiles get added at the end of the Start screen, so you may have to scroll to see the tile.

Figure 21-20. *The secondary tile the user is adding to his or her Start screen*

You are not limited to a single secondary tile. Your users can add tiles for all of their frequent projects. Also, in addition to making static secondary tiles, as we've done in this section, you can also create Live Tiles for your secondary tiles. The process of creating Live Tiles for secondary tiles is nearly identical to creating Live Tiles for the application itself. Instead of calling the createTileUpdaterForApplication function, as you did in Listing 21-12, you call the createTileUpdaterForSecondaryTile function, passing secondaryTileId as a parameter, similar to the code in Listing 21-19.

Listing 21-19. Creating a Live Tile for a Secondary Tile

```
var secondaryTile = new notifications.TileNotification(secondaryTileXml);
tileUpdateManager.createTileUpdaterForApplication(secondaryTileId).update(secondaryTile);
```

Activating Clok from a Secondary Tile

At this point, you can add secondary tiles to your Start screen, but if you click this tile, you'll find yourself back on the Clok Dashboard instead of viewing the Project Detail screen for a particular project. Adding a few lines to the launchActivation in default.js will correct this. Add the highlighted code from Listing 21-20 to default.js.

Listing 21-20. Updates to the launchActivation Function

```
if (args.detail.kind === activation.ActivationKind.search) {
    // SNIPPED
} else if ((args.detail.tileId.indexOf("Tile.Project.") >= 0)
        && (ClokUtilities.Guid.isGuid(args.detail.arguments))) {
    nav.navigate("/pages/projects/detail.html", { id: args.detail.arguments });
} else if (nav.location) {
    nav.history.current.initialPlaceholder = true;
    return nav.navigate(nav.location, nav.state);
} else {
    return nav.navigate(Application.navigator.home);
}
```

The tileId property of the secondary tile that was clicked is available in the args.detail.tileId property. Although in Clok, we've only added one type of secondary tile, I've decided to use the tileId property to determine how to handle activation from the secondary tile. If the value of the tileId property is in the correct format, and if the value of the arguments property is a GUID, then the application navigates to the Project Detail screen for the selected project.

■ **Note**   You can also use the arguments property when your application is launched, by clicking on a toast notification. In this case, the value of the arguments property is set in the launch attribute of the notification's XML definition.

Unpinning a Secondary Tile

Suppose a user pins a secondary tile for a project to his or her Start screen. When the project is complete, he or she will probably want to remove the tile from the Start screen. This can, of course, be done from the Start screen directly, by right-clicking the tile and selecting Unpin from Start from the app bar that appears. In this section, I'll show you the steps to allow a user to remove the tile from within Clok.

The first step to take to complete this task is to update the Pin to Start button in the app bar. Add the function defined in Listing 21-21 to detail.js.

Listing 21-21. Changing the App Bar Button

```
updatePinUnpinCommand: function () {
    if (secondaryTile.exists(this.secondaryTileId)) {
        pinUnpinCommand.winControl.icon = "unpin";
        pinUnpinCommand.winControl.label = "Unpin from Start";
        pinUnpinCommand.winControl.tooltip = "Unpin from Start";
    } else {
        pinUnpinCommand.winControl.icon = "pin";
        pinUnpinCommand.winControl.label = "Pin to Start";
        pinUnpinCommand.winControl.tooltip = "Pin to Start";
    }
},
```

This function, when called, will update the pinUnpinCommand button in the app bar. If the tile already exists, the button will be changed to indicate that it will unpin the tile when clicked. If the tile does not already exist, the button will be updated to indicate that clicking it will add the tile to the Start screen. Now, we have to call this function from a few different locations. First, update the ready function in detail.js with the highlighted code from Listing 21-22.

Listing 21-22. Calling the Function to Update the App Bar Button

```
ready: function (element, options) {
    // SNIPPED

    this.setCurrentProject(options);
    this.secondaryTileId = "Tile.Project." + this.currProject.id.replace(/-/g, ".");
    this.updatePinUnpinCommand();

    // SNIPPED
},
```

The updatePinUnpinCommand function also has to be called from within the done function you added in the pinToStart function back in Listing 21-18. Add the highlighted code from Listing 21-23 to the pinToStart function in detail.js.

Listing 21-23. Calling the Function to Update the App Bar Button After the Tile Has Been Added

```
// make the request and update the app bar
tile.requestCreateForSelectionAsync(buttonCoordinates, placement)
    .done(function (isCreated) {
        this.updatePinUnpinCommand();
    }.bind(this));
```

Now, when a project has a secondary tile pinned to the Start screen, the app bar icon will change to say Unpin from Start. Clicking that button now won't actually do anything, because the click event handler only does something if the tile doesn't exist. Change that by adding the highlighted code from Listing 21-24 to the pinUnpinCommand_click handler function.

Listing 21-24. Do Something Different If the Tile Already Exists

```
pinUnpinCommand_click: function (e) {
    if (!secondaryTile.exists(this.secondaryTileId)) {
        this.pinToStart();
    } else {
        this.unpinFromStart();
    }
},
```

As with requesting permission to add a new tile to the Start screen, you must also request permission to remove an existing secondary tile from the Start screen. The unpinFromStart function handles this for you (see Listing 21-25). This function will have similarities with the pinToStart function. It determines where to display the request, and then it asynchronously requests the user to delete the selected tile. If successful, the updatePinUnpinCommand function is called to switch the Unpin from Start app bar button back to a Pin to Start button.

Listing 21-25. Request the User's Permission to Remove the Secondary Tile from the Start Screen

```
unpinFromStart: function () {
    var buttonRect = pinUnpinCommand.getBoundingClientRect();
    var buttonCoordinates = {
        x: buttonRect.left,
        y: buttonRect.top,
        width: buttonRect.width,
        height: buttonRect.height
    };
    var placement = Windows.UI.Popups.Placement.above;

    var tile = new secondaryTile(this.secondaryTileId);

    tile.requestDeleteForSelectionAsync(buttonCoordinates, placement)
        .done(function (success) {
            this.updatePinUnpinCommand();
        }.bind(this));
},
```

Now run Clok and navigate to the Project Detail screen for a project that has a secondary tile pinned to the Start screen. The button in the app bar will be changed to say Unpin from Start. Clicking this button will display the request to delete the tile in a flyout control (see Figure 21-21). Clicking the Unpin from Start button in the flyout will remove the tile from the Start screen and switch the app bar button back to its default state.

Figure 21-21. *Requesting the user's permission to remove a tile from the Start screen*

Future Versions of Windows

At the time of this writing, a preview of the next version of Windows is available. Windows 8.1 will introduce two new tile sizes, large (310×310) and small (70×70). Additionally, new Live Tile templates will be added to support the new large tile size (the small tile will not support Live Tiles). As a result, the names of the templates will be changing. The names used in this chapter, such as `TileSquarePeekImageAndText04`, are still required for Windows 8 applications and will be supported in Windows 8.1 applications but may be removed in a future version of Windows.

As an example of the coming change, the tile template currently named `TileSquarePeekImageAndText04` should be referred to as `TileSquare150x150PeekImageAndText04` in any new development after Windows 8.1 has been released. These and other coming changes are described on MSDN (`http://msdn.microsoft.com/en-us/library/windows/apps/bg182890.aspx`).

Conclusion

As they become more familiar with Windows 8, users will come to expect quick and easy access to information. With the simple steps described in this chapter, you can provide instant information in notifications and Live Tiles, as well as quick access to frequently used information within your application, using secondary tiles. Not every application is the perfect candidate for each of these techniques, and adding these features unnecessarily could make your application seem noisy or busy. With careful consideration, however, you can build an application that not only meets the user's basic needs but also improves his or her experience.

■ ■ ■

CHAPTER 22

Camera and Location

Nearly every tablet and laptop available at the time of this writing has a webcam built in. I looked at each of the first 15 laptops listed on a popular retail web site today, and every single one included a webcam. My own laptop has one built into the lid, and my Surface tablet has two—a front-facing camera and a rear-facing camera. For the user whose computer does not have a built-in webcam, USB webcams are a fairly cheap investment, with some basic models available for less than US$20.

In previous versions of Windows, integrating cameras into your application did not always have a trivial solution. With Windows 8, however, Microsoft has created a simple, straightforward way to add photo functionality to your applications.

In addition to integrating cameras, by taking advantage of data from a Windows Location Provider, you can make your applications location-aware. WinRT exposes location data with simple APIs that allow your application to request the current location of a computer or handle events to receive updates when the computer moves.

In this chapter, I'll show you how to integrate both a camera and location data into Clok. Clok users will be able to deploy the camera to add photos to a project's Document Library. They will also be able to get driving directions from their current location to a client's office.

Camera

Have you ever been in a meeting where someone was writing on a whiteboard? Maybe they were diagramming the user interface of an application, or drawing flowcharts for a process, or simply taking notes. Whatever the case, when the meeting was over, before another group of people came into the room for a meeting of their own, one of a few things probably occurred.

- Someone hurriedly tried to capture all of the notes onto paper or into a document on his or her computer.

- Someone wrote SAVE THIS in big letters on the whiteboard, intending to revisit the notes or diagrams at some point in the future.

- Someone pulled out his or her phone and took a picture of the whiteboard.

Personally, I have taken many photos of whiteboards with my phone. In this section, you'll add a feature to Clok that will allow the user to use the camera on his or her tablet to capture photos such as this and add them to a project's Document Library.

■ **Note**   In this chapter, I will use the terms *webcam*, *camera*, *photo* and *video*. In each of these instances, I am referring to images or video captured by a webcam attached to the user's computer. The features you will add to Clok in this chapter will only be available to users who have either a built-in webcam or a USB webcam. Additionally, your computer must have a webcam in order to test the functionality you will be adding in this section. In this book, I will not cover working with digital cameras, such as point-and-shoot or DSLR-type cameras.

While it is already possible to use the Camera application to take a picture and then use the Share charm to add it to a Document Library, the changes you make in this section will allow you to capture a photo from within the Clok application without having to launch the Camera application separately. There are two techniques for working with a webcam in your applications. You can use the CameraCaptureUI class or the MediaCapture class.

The CameraCaptureUI Class

The CameraCaptureUI class allows you, with relatively few lines of code, to quickly add camera functionality to your application. The camera-capture functionality is handled by a built-in Windows interface in a manner very similar in concept to a File Open Picker. In this section, I'll explain how to show this interface to your users and how to get the photos they take into a Document Library.

Application Manifest Changes

Having access to the webam attached to the user's computer is a potential security concern. Because of this, you must indicate in your project's application manifest that it may make use of the user's webcam. This fact is made known when a potential user is reading about your application in the Windows Store (see Figure 22-1).

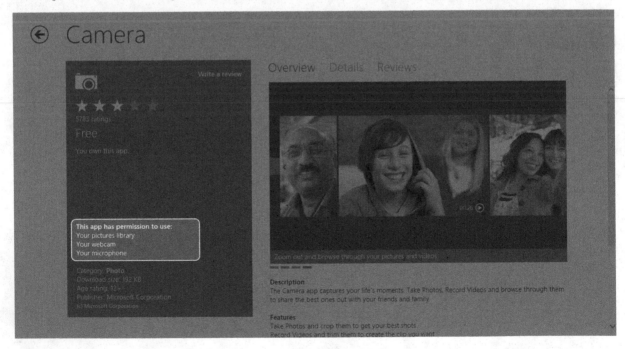

Figure 22-1. *The Camera application listing in the Windows Store*

The change to the manifest is a simple check box. Open package.appxmanifest and switch to the Capabilities tab. In the Capabilities list, check the Webcam item (see Figure 22-2).

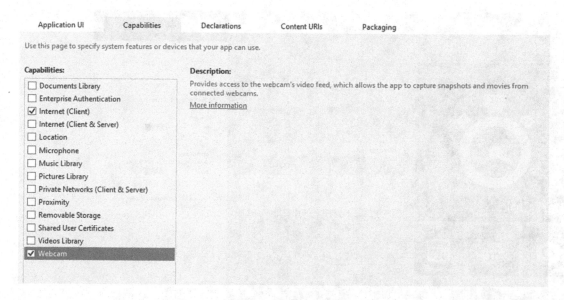

Figure 22-2. Specifying the Webcam capability

Even with this declaration in the application manifest, however, your application doesn't have wide-open access to the camera. The first time your application attempts to access the camera—you'll add code to do this in the coming sections—the user is prompted to confirm that he or she will allow it (see Figure 22-3).

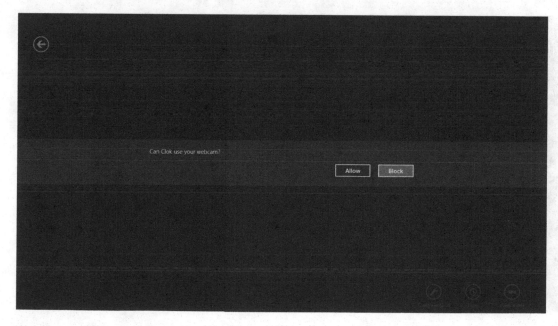

Figure 22-3. Prompting the user for permission

Additionally, the user can change this setting at any time, by opening the Permissions settings flyout and toggling the value of the Webcam setting (see Figure 22-4).

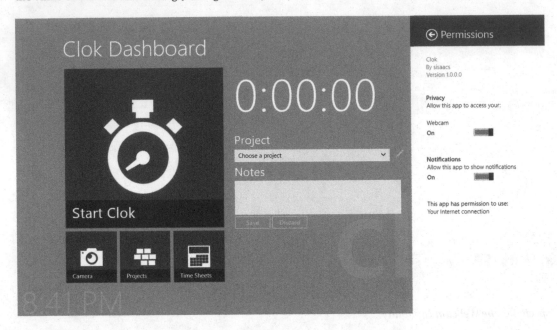

Figure 22-4. *The user can revoke this permission anytime*

The interface the Windows will display when you use the `CameraCaptureUI` class will prompt the user to change permissions if he or she has previously blocked access to the camera (see Figure 22-5).

Figure 22-5. *The CameraCaptureUI interface instructs the user to enable permission to use the camera*

Updating the Camera Button on the Clok Dashboard Screen

With the Webcam capability specified, the next step is to give the user a way to access the Camera screen that we will be building in the next section. The Camera menu option on the Clok Dashboard screen already exists, but it isn't currently implemented. Remove the notImplemented CSS class highlighted in Listing 22-1 from home.html.

Listing 22-1. Remove the Highlighted CSS Class

```
<div id="cameraMenuItem" class="mainMenuItem secondaryMenuItem notImplemented">
```

You must also define a click event handler for this menu option in home.js. Add the code from Listing 22-2 to home.js and also wire up this click event handler in the ready function.

Listing 22-2. Click Event Handler for the Camera Menu Option

```
cameraMenuItem_click: function (e) {
    nav.navigate("/pages/documents/cameraCapture.html");
},
```

In the source code that accompanies this book, I've also added the ability for a user to right-click the Camera menu option and pin that to the Start screen (see Figure 22-6). Because I just covered this in Chapter 21, I won't go into detail here. You can find the code samples for this chapter on the Source Code/Downloads tab of the product-detail page for this book (www.apress.com/9781430257790).

Figure 22-6. Pin the Clok Camera to the Start screen

Adding the Camera Page Control

Although the user interface that the CameraCaptureUI class displays is provided by Windows itself, and we have no control over the layout and functionality it offers, a page is still required to allow the user to preview the captured image and select a Document Library to add it to. In the pages\documents folder, create a new page control named cameraCapture.html. Update the title in cameraCapture.html, changing it to Camera (see Listing 22-3).

Listing 22-3. Changing the Screen's Title

```
<span class="pagetitle">Camera</span>
```

When you're done building this screen, it will display a preview of the captured photo on the left side of the screen, and, on the right, a drop-down list to select which project's Document Library the photo will be added to. Update the main section in cameraCapture.html with the code from Listing 22-4. In the event the user's computer does not have a camera, a message will be displayed instead.

Listing 22-4. The Layout of the Camera Screen

```
<section aria-label="Main content" role="main">
    <div id="cameraContainer">
        <div id="cameraPane">
            <img id="capturedImage" src="/images/camera-placeholder.png" />
        </div>
        <div id="controlsPane">
            <select id="projects">
                <option value="">Choose a project</option>
            </select>
            <button id="goToDocumentsButton" disabled="disabled">&#xe16c;</button>
            <br />
            <button id="saveCameraCaptureButton">Save</button>
            <button id="discardCameraCaptureButton">Discard</button>
        </div>
    </div>
    <div id="noCamera" class="hidden">No camera is available on this computer.</div>
</section>
```

As always, the referenced image is available as part of the source code that accompanies this book. Update cameraCapture.css with the CSS from Listing 22-5.

Listing 22-5. Styling the Camera Screen

```
.cameraCapture section[role=main] {
    margin-left: 120px;
    margin-right: 120px;
}

.hidden {
    display: none;
}
```

```css
.cameraCapture #cameraPane {
    float: left;
    width: 720px;
    height: 540px;
}

    .cameraCapture #cameraPane #capturedImage {
        max-width: 720px;
        max-height: 540px;
    }

.cameraCapture #controlsPane {
    float: left;
    margin-left: 10px;
}

    .cameraCapture #controlsPane #goToDocumentsButton {
        border: 0px;
        min-width: inherit;
        font-size: 1.5em;
    }

@media screen and (-ms-view-state: fullscreen-portrait) {
    .cameraCapture section[role=main] {
        margin-left: 20px;
        margin-right: 20px;
    }
}
```

Over the course of the next few sections, you'll be taking advantage of a handful of aliases in cameraCapture.js. Rather than adding them one at a time, add them all now. Add the code from Listing 22-6 to cameraCapture.js.

Listing 22-6. Adding Some Aliases

```js
var appData = Windows.Storage.ApplicationData.current;
var createOption = Windows.Storage.CreationCollisionOption;
var capture = Windows.Media.Capture;
var devices = Windows.Devices.Enumeration;
var nav = WinJS.Navigation;
var storage = Clok.Data.Storage;
```

Clok's Camera screen won't be enabled when the application is in the snapped state. In Chapter 17, you added a function named DisableInSnappedView, and it should be called from the ready and updateLayout functions. Add the code from Listing 22-7 to cameraCapture.js.

Listing 22-7. Disabling the Camera Screen in Snapped View

```js
ready: function (element, options) {
    Clok.Utilities.DisableInSnappedView();
},

updateLayout: function (element, viewState, lastViewState) {
    Clok.Utilities.DisableInSnappedView();
},
```

Determining If a Camera Is Present

Although, it's increasingly common for laptops and tablets to have a camera built in, it's quite possible that some of your users may have a computer without a camera. In this section, you'll determine whether a camera is available and initialize Clok's Camera screen, based on the presence of a camera.

The Windows.Devices.Enumeration namespace defines a number of classes you can utilize to add support for various types of devices to your application. This includes external storage devices, audio input and output devices, and video input devices. Video devices are instruments that can capture photos or video, such as a webcam. More information about this namespace and all of the classes it contains is available on MSDN (http://msdn.microsoft.com/en-us/library/windows/apps/windows.devices.enumeration.aspx). In this section, we'll make use of the Windows.Devices.Enumeration.DeviceInformation class to determine whether the computer has a camera. Add the highlighted code from Listing 22-8 to the ready function in cameraCapture.js.

Listing 22-8. Determining If a Camera Exists and Initializing the Screen

```
ready: function (element, options) {
    this.file = null;

    var deviceInfo = devices.DeviceInformation;
    return deviceInfo.findAllAsync(devices.DeviceClass.videoCapture)
        .then(function (found) {
            return found && found.length && found.length > 0;
        }, function error() {
            return false;
        }).then(function (exists) {
            this.showCameraControls(exists);
            if (exists) {
                this.bindProjects();
                capturedImage.addEventListener("click", this.capturedImage_click.bind(this));
                saveCameraCaptureButton.addEventListener("click",
                    this.saveCameraCaptureButton_click.bind(this));
                discardCameraCaptureButton.addEventListener("click",
                    this.discardCameraCaptureButton_click.bind(this));
                goToDocumentsButton.onclick = this.goToDocumentsButton_click.bind(this);
                projects.addEventListener("change", this.projects_change.bind(this));

                this.resetScreen();

                // TODO: automatically initiate capture

            }
        }.bind(this));

    Clok.Utilities.DisableInSnappedView();
},
```

Here, I've used the findAllAsync function to enumerate all of the video capture devices (webcams) on the user's computer. If there are any errors, or none is found, the showCameraControls function, which I'll show in a moment, will display a message to the user. If a webcam is found, however, the showCameraControls function will display the UI defined in Listing 22-4, a drop-down list of active projects will be populated, and various event handlers will be wired up to their respective controls. These steps are all typical steps you would normally include directly within the ready function. Because this screen is only available when a camera exists, I've simply nested them within a condition.

The file variable at the top of the ready function will be used to hold a reference to a StorageFile object that will eventually be returned from the CameraCaptureUI interface. I'll come back to that later.

■ **Note**   In Clok, we've already provided other techniques for the user to add documents, including images, into a Document Library. In other applications, you may want to consider offering alternative methods of working with images, such as a File Open Picker, if a webcam is not available.

The code in Listing 22-8 references a handful of functions and event handlers. Define these by adding the code from Listing 22-9 to cameraCapture.js.

Listing 22-9. Functions and Event Handlers for the Camera Screen

```
showCameraControls: function (show) {
    if (show) {
        WinJS.Utilities.removeClass(cameraContainer, "hidden");
        WinJS.Utilities.addClass(noCamera, "hidden");
    } else {
        WinJS.Utilities.addClass(cameraContainer, "hidden");
        WinJS.Utilities.removeClass(noCamera, "hidden");
    }
},

bindProjects: function () {
    projects.options.length = 1; // remove all except first project

    var activeProjects = storage.projects.filter(function (p) {
        return p.status === Clok.Data.ProjectStatuses.Active;
    });

    activeProjects.forEach(function (item) {
        var option = document.createElement("option");
        option.text = item.name + " (" + item.projectNumber + ")";
        option.title = item.clientName;
        option.value = item.id;
        projects.appendChild(option);
    });
},

projects_change: function (e) {
    if (!this.file) {
        saveCameraCaptureButton.disabled = true;
    } else {
        saveCameraCaptureButton.disabled = !projects.options[projects.selectedIndex].value;
    }

    var id = projects.options[projects.selectedIndex].value;
    goToDocumentsButton.disabled = !ClokUtilities.Guid.isGuid(id);
},
```

493

```
goToDocumentsButton_click: function (e) {
    var id = projects.options[projects.selectedIndex].value;
    if (ClokUtilities.Guid.isGuid(id)) {
        nav.navigate("/pages/documents/library.html", { projectId: id });
    }
},

discardCameraCaptureButton_click: function (e) {
    this.resetScreen();
},

resetScreen: function () {
    capturedImage.src = "/images/camera-placeholder.png";
    this.file = null;
    saveCameraCaptureButton.disabled = true;
    discardCameraCaptureButton.disabled = true;
},
```

Most of the code in Listing 22-9 is similar to code you have already added to Clok. I've highlighted one block in particular within the projects_change event handler that might not be immediately clear. This block enables the Save button only if a project has been selected from the drop-down list and an image has been captured by the CameraCaptureUI interface.

Additionally, I've highlighted the resetScreen function. As the name suggests, this function will put the Camera screen in a state that is ready to capture an image. In addition to it being called when the screen is first loaded and when the user discards a photo, in the next section, you'll see how the function can also be called after the user has captured and saved a photo.

Capturing a Photo with the CameraCaptureUI Interface

A few steps remain to complete this functionality. You still have to show the CameraCaptureUI interface to the user, retrieve the captured image and display it so the user can preview it, and implement the functionality to save the image into a project's Document Library. The first two of these three remaining steps can be completed by adding the code from Listing 22-10 to cameraCapture.js.

Listing 22-10. Showing the CameraCaptureUI Interface

```
capturedImage_click: function (e) {
    this.showCameraCaptureUI();
},

showCameraCaptureUI: function () {
    var dialog = new capture.CameraCaptureUI();
    dialog.photoSettings.maxResolution =
        capture.CameraCaptureUIMaxPhotoResolution.highestAvailable;

    dialog.captureFileAsync(capture.CameraCaptureUIMode.photo)
        .done(function complete(file) {
            if (file) {
                var photoBlobUrl = URL.createObjectURL(file, { oneTimeOnly: true });
                capturedImage.src = photoBlobUrl;
```

```
        saveCameraCaptureButton.disabled =
            !projects.options[projects.selectedIndex].value;
        discardCameraCaptureButton.disabled = false;
        this.file = file;
    } else {
        this.resetScreen();
    }
}.bind(this), function error(err) {
    this.resetScreen();
}.bind(this));
},
```

When the user clicks on the preview image, the `CameraCaptureUI` interface will be displayed. Similar to to the `FileOpenPicker`, the `CameraCaptureUI` interface is a dialog created and managed by Windows. Using promises, the selected `StorageFile`, this time containing the photo just captured by the camera, is available as a parameter of the done function's `complete` parameter. In Listing 22-10, I've created an object URL from that file and set the source of the preview image to that URL. The Save button is enabled if a project has already been selected from the drop-down list, and a reference to the file is stored in the `file` variable defined in Listing 22-8. If there are any errors, or no photo was taken, the `resetScreen` function is called to reset each control on the screen to its original state.

It's easy enough for users to click the preview image placeholder to initiate the photo-capture process. However, if they just clicked the Camera menu option on the Clok Dashboard, or a secondary tile they may have pinned to their Start screen, we can show the `CameraCaptureUI` interface to them immediately, without requiring them to click again. Listing 22-8 contains a TODO comment. Replace that comment in the ready function of `cameraCapture.js` with the highlighted code from Listing 22-11.

Listing 22-11. Automatically Showing the CameraCaptureUI Interface

```
if (exists) {
    // SNIPPED
    // only if navigated, not if back arrow
    if (!nav.canGoForward) {
        this.showCameraCaptureUI();
    }
}
```

■ **Note**   When I originally wrote this functionality, I did not include this call to `showCameraCapture` within a condition. However, after clicking the `goToDocumentsButton` added in Listing 22-4, and then clicking the Back arrow included on every page control, it seemed awkward to me to load the `CameraCaptureUI` interface in that situation. By checking the value of the `WinJS.Navigation.canGoForward` property, you can determine if the Camera screen is loaded, as the result of clicking the Back arrow.

The final piece of this puzzle is to implement the functionality to save the photo to the selected project's Document Library. Add the code from Listing 22-12 to `cameraCapture.js`.

Listing 22-12. Saving a Photo to the Document Library

```
getProjectFolder: function (projectId) {
    return appData.localFolder
        .createFolderAsync("projectDocs", createOption.openIfExists)
        .then(function (folder) {
            return folder.createFolderAsync(projectId.toString(), createOption.openIfExists)
        });
},

saveCameraCaptureButton_click: function (e) {
    var dateFormatString = "{year.full}{month.integer(2)}{day.integer(2)}"
        + "-{hour.integer(2)}{minute.integer(2)}{second.integer(2)}";
    var clockIdentifiers = Windows.Globalization.ClockIdentifiers;

    var formatting = Windows.Globalization.DateTimeFormatting;
    var formatterTemplate = new formatting.DateTimeFormatter(dateFormatString);
    var formatter = new formatting.DateTimeFormatter(formatterTemplate.patterns[0],
                formatterTemplate.languages,
                formatterTemplate.geographicRegion,
                formatterTemplate.calendar,
                clockIdentifiers.twentyFourHour);

    var filename = formatter.format(new Date()) + ".png";

    var projectId = projects.options[projects.selectedIndex].value;

    this.getProjectFolder(projectId)
        .then(function (projectFolder) {
            return this.file.copyAsync(projectFolder,
                filename,
                createOption.generateUniqueName);
        }.bind(this)).then(function (file) {
            this.resetScreen();
        }.bind(this));
},
```

The getProjectFolder function should be familiar from the work you did to create the Document Library in Chapter 16, as well as from the code you added to make Clok a Share target in Chapter 19. After generating a value for the filename variable based on the current date and time, the photo, referenced by the file variable, is copied to the project's Document Library using the copyAsync function introduced in Chapter 16. Then the resetScreen function is called, to allow the user to quickly take another photo.

Run Clok now and click the Camera menu option on the Clok Dashboard screen. If you have a camera and have authorized Clok to use it, you'll see the CameraCaptureUI interface (see Figure 22-7).

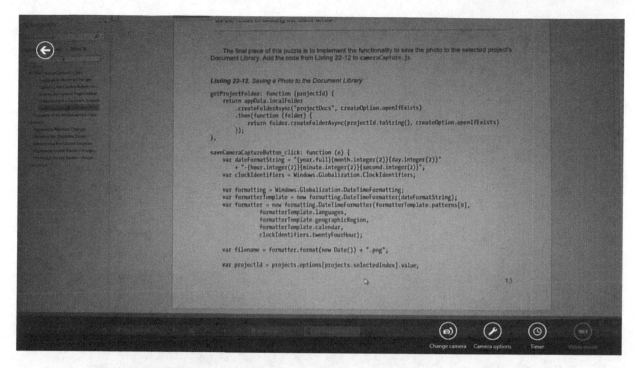

Figure 22-7. *About to capture a photo of some work in progress*

After taking a photo, you'll see a preview of that photo and will be able to select which project's Document Library it will be saved to (see Figure 22-8).

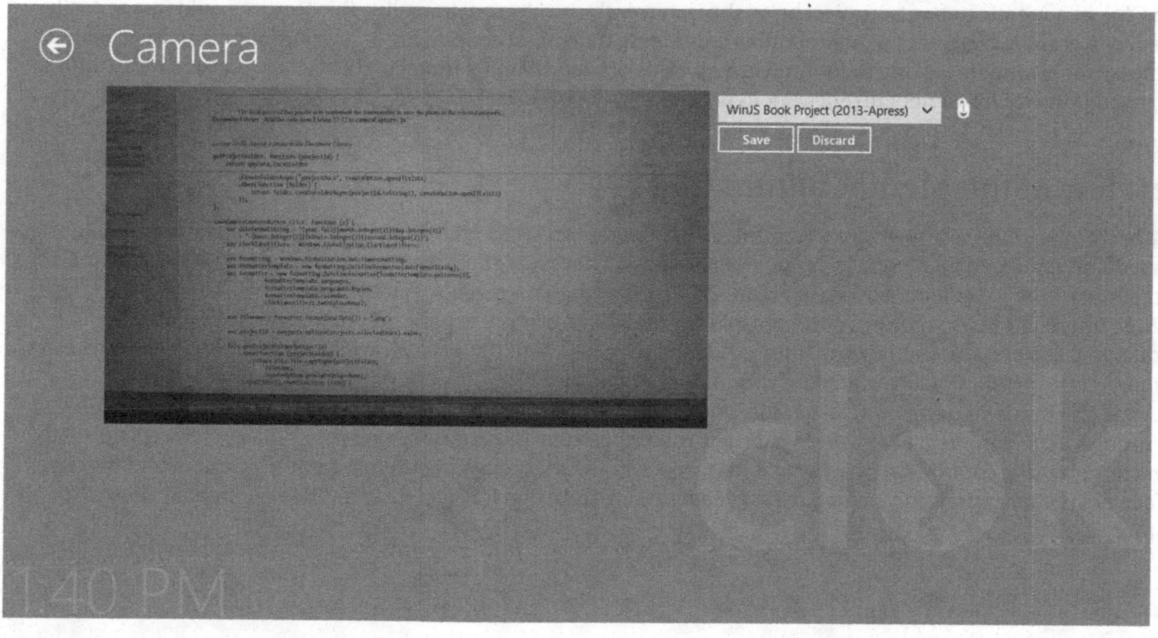

Figure 22-8. *Previewing a captured photo*

Finally, just to verify that everything worked as expected, navigate to that Document Library. You have the option to use the paper clip icon on the Camera screen as a shortcut. You should see your photo in the Document Library (see Figure 22-9).

Figure 22-9. *The captured photo, saved into the Document Library*

For most of this example, I've assumed that the user is another software developer who is using his or her tablet to run Clok in a meeting about a project he or she is currently working on. In reality, this feature could just as easily be used by a graphic designer taking a photo of something that might inspire his or her design for a project, or even by a landscape contractor taking before and after photos of a landscaping project. The user could even be an author capturing a photo of his or her current work in progress.

Overview of the MediaCapture Class

The CameraCaptureUI class provides a simple way to integrate an attached camera into your application. The interface is created and managed by Windows, however, so you don't have any control over it. If you're not happy with the full-screen-capture experience shown in Figure 22-7 (preceding), then you're out of luck.

Well, not really. If you require more control over the photo-capture experience, then instead of using the CameraCaptureUI class, you should use the MediaCapture class. With this class, you can embed the live video preview and image capture functionality right into your own user interface.

I won't be implementing this class in this book, but I will briefly discuss it here. Among the samples included in the Windows SDK sample pack (http://msdn.microsoft.com/en-US/windows/apps/br229516) is one called *Media capture using capture device sample*. This project shows a few examples of integrating a camera into the user interface of an application. Take a look at BasicCapture.html. In that file, you'll see a video element as shown in Listing 22-13.

Listing 22-13. A Video Element from the MediaCapture Sample Project

```
<video width="320" height="240" id="previewVideo1" style="border: 1px solid black"> </video>
```

This is a standard HTML5 video element. In the associated JavaScript file, BasicCapture.js, a MediaCapture object named mediaCaptureMgr is created, and a number of properties are set on that object. Once it has been configured, the src property of the video element from Listing 22-13 is set, referencing the mediaCaptureMgr object (see Listing 22-14).

Listing 22-14. Setting the Video Source

```
video.src = URL.createObjectURL(mediaCaptureMgr, { oneTimeOnly: true });
```

To capture an image from this mediaCaptureMgr object, the capturePhotoToStorageFileAsync function is called. Similar to the captureFileAsync function from Listing 22-10, a StorageFile object representing the captured image is made available as a parameter of the done function's complete parameter.

I've excluded many details from this section, but the referenced sample is fairly straightforward. If the ability to integrate camera capture functionality into the UI of your own application is important, then I encourage you to look closely at the sample project. Additionally, more information about the MediaCapture class is available on MSDN (http://msdn.microsoft.com/library/windows/apps/Windows.Media.Capture.MediaCapture.aspx).

Location

In Windows 8, the location of the user's computer is made available by a Windows Location Provider. A location provider can use a number of different methods to determine the location of the computer, indicated by a latitude and longitude measurement, along with an indicator of the accuracy of these measurements. The provider in Windows 8 uses the following techniques to attempt to determine the location, from least accurate to most accurate:

- IP address data

- WiFi triangulation

- Global Position System (GPS)

The most accurate measurements available will be reported by the provider. For example, if a GPS device is present in the computer, those results would be returned instead of the results of an IP address lookup. More information about Windows Location Providers is available on MSDN (http://msdn.microsoft.com/en-us/library/windows/apps/hh464919.aspx).

In this section, I'll show how to give the user an easy way to get driving directions from their current location.

Application Manifest Changes

As it was with the camera, having access to the user's location is a potential security concern. You must indicate in your project's application manifest that you intend to access the user's location. As it was with the camera, too, the change to the manifest is a simple check box. Open package.appxmanifest and switch to the Capabilities tab. In the Capabilities list, check the Location item (see Figure 22-10).

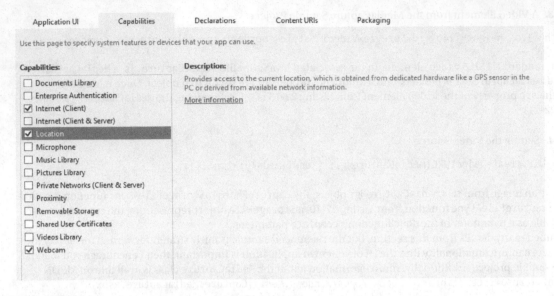

Figure 22-10. Specifying the Location capability

Updating the Directions Screen

Very few changes are required to implement this functionality. The first step is to add a button on the Directions screen that will be used to determine the user's current location. Add the highlighted code from Listing 22-15 to directions.html.

Listing 22-15. Adding a Button to Get the Current Location

```
<div class="formField">
    <label for="fromLocation">From</label><br />
    <input id="fromLocation">
    <button id="getLocationButton">&#xe1d2;</button>
</div>
```

Then add the new CSS rule from Listing 22-16 to directions.css.

Listing 22-16. Styling the Button

```
#locationsPane #getLocationButton {
    border: 0px;
    min-width: inherit;
}
```

While this button doesn't do anything yet, you can run Clok and navigate to the Directions screen to see how it looks (see Figure 22-11).

Figure 22-11. Button to get current location

In the next section, I'll show you how to get the user's current location when he or she clicks this button.

Determining the Current Location

It doesn't make sense to let the user click the button if his or her location cannot be determined. In this section, you'll add some code to enable the button only if the user's location is available, as well as some code to populate the From field with his or her location when the button is clicked. Add the highlighted code from Listing 22-17 to the ready function of directions.js.

Listing 22-17. Changes to the Ready Function

```
printCommand.onclick = this.printCommand_click.bind(this);

this.currentCoords = null;
getLocationButton.disabled = true;
this.checkForGeoposition();
getLocationButton.onclick = this.getLocationButton_click.bind(this);

fromLocation.value = app.sessionState.directionsFromLocation || "";
```

The checkForGeoposition function is the workhorse of this feature. Add the function from Listing 22-18 to directions.js.

Listing 22-18. Requesting the User's Current Location

```
checkForGeoposition: function () {
    var locator = new Windows.Devices.Geolocation.Geolocator();
    var positionStatus = Windows.Devices.Geolocation.PositionStatus;
```

```
    if (locator != null) {
        locator.getGeopositionAsync()
            .then(function (position) {
                this.currentCoords = position.coordinate;
                getLocationButton.disabled = (locator.locationStatus !== positionStatus.ready);
            }.bind(this));
    }
},
```

This function gets an instance of the `Windows.Devices.Geolocation.Geolocator` class named `locator`. If `locator` doesn't exist, the new button added in the previous section is never enabled. If, however, the `getGeopositionAsync` function returns a valid position, the button is enabled, and the coordinates are stored in the `currentCoords` variable.

Fortunately for us, the Bing Maps API is perfectly capable of using coordinates, instead of an address, for a starting point or destination. So, the last step required is to populate the From field with the user's latitude and longitude when the button is clicked. Add the code from Listing 22-19 to `directions.js`.

Listing 22-19. Populating the From Field

```
getLocationButton_click: function (e) {
    fromLocation.value = this.currentCoords.latitude.toString()
        + ", " + this.currentCoords.longitude.toString();
},
```

Now, when you run Clok and click the button, your latitude and longitude will be displayed in the From field. The Get Directions button will pass these coordinates to the Bing Maps API and retrieve driving directions from your current location to the client's office (see Figure 22-12).

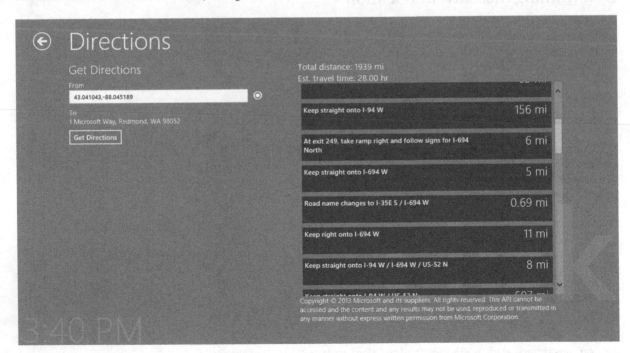

Figure 22-12. *Getting directions from the current location to the client's office*

502

Homework for the Reader—Assignment #1

As you can see, with very little code, you can integrate data from the Windows Location Provider into your application. One thing to keep in mind, though, is the accuracy of the location data. As I mentioned above, the location provider can retrieve location data from a number of sources. You will always receive the most accurate data available, but if IP address data is all that is available, that might only be accurate to within a few miles. Depending on your situation, you may expect your user to be OK with that level of possible inaccuracy, but in the case of driving directions, having the starting location off by as much as ten miles is not a good experience.

When coordinates are retrieved using the getGeopositionAsync function, an indicator of the accuracy of those coordinates, measured in meters, is included. In the source code that accompanies this book, I have added a condition to only enable the getLocationButton when the value of this.currentCoords.accuracy is within 200 meters.

Additional information about using the Geolocator class and other location-related classes is available on MSDN (http://msdn.microsoft.com/en-us/library/windows/apps/windows.devices.geolocation.aspx).

Homework for the Reader—Assignment #2

In this chapter, I showed you how to request the user's current location using the checkForGeoposition function of the Geolocator class. The Geolocator class also has an event named positionchanged, which is raised when a change in the user's location is detected. Although I haven't built any features into Clok that make use of this event, a few possibilities exist that you can choose to add to Clok. For example:

- You can update the Directions screen, such that the current step in the route is highlighted, based on the user's current position as he or she drives to his or her destination.

- You can add a toast notification that is displayed when the user arrives at the location of one of his or her clients. Clicking this notification might launch the Clok Dashboard screen with that project preselected.

Additional information about the positionchanged event is available on MSDN (http://msdn.microsoft.com/en-us/library/windows/apps/windows.devices.geolocation.geolocator.positionchanged.aspx).

Conclusion

With Windows 8, Microsoft has made it easy to integrate your application with various hardware that might be attached to your user's computer. Cameras and location data are readily available in many modern computers, and with a small amount of code, you can use these in your application. In this chapter, I scratched the surface of this functionality. In many cases, these simple implementations are more than enough to improve the user's experience with your application. Keep in mind, however, that more advanced functionality is available, if required.

CHAPTER 23

■■■

Sharing Apps in the Windows Store

Most craftsmen finishing a work don't want to tuck it away in a place where only they can see it—they want to share it with others who can appreciate it or get some value from it. This is as true of a software application as it is of a work of art. Prior to Windows 8, if you were to have asked "How do I share my applications with other people?" the answer would have invariably focused on the logistics of creating an installer package or the benefits of XCOPY deployment. The answer, however, would most likely have lacked any indication of how to make sure people know about the application's availability or how to monetize the application, if that was the goal. In this chapter, you will learn about the Windows Store, which is the primary method for distributing applications built for Windows 8. You will learn about giving your application a unique brand, packaging the application for distribution, and navigating the submission process. This chapter will not cover establishing a developer account or making use of in-app payment features enabled by the Windows Store APIs.

Branding Your Application

Throughout this book, you may have noticed that the sample application, Clok, showed the same, rather nondescript splash screen that is pictured in Figure 23-1. This is because the splash screen image is one of several components required for all Windows applications, and Microsoft includes a default for each of the required components with each new project, in order to ensure that the project can build and run immediately.

Figure 23-1. *Default application splash screen*

Replacing these generic elements with alternatives that add to the identity of your application through color, style, or imagery creates a better experience for the end user and does not leave him or her with the first impression that the developer of the application couldn't be bothered to change from the default. In this section, you will learn about the branding options in the Application UI and Packaging tabs of the package.appxmanifest file (see Figure 23-2). You'll find this file in Solution Explorer in the root of your Visual Studio project.

Figure 23-2. The Application UI tab of the package.appxmanifest file

Display Name

The display name, which is visible in Figure 23-2, is used to identify your application. It is a string of up to 256 characters and displays in the Windows Store search results and app listings, as well as search listings in Windows 8 and on application tiles, when a short name has not been defined. Because this value is displayed publically to people who may be searching for an application, care should be taken to make it unique, descriptive, and enticing.

Default Language

The default language specifies the primary language for your application in the form of a two-digit language code, followed by a hyphen and then a two-letter culture code. An application intended for English-speaking users in the United Kingdom would have a default language of en-UK, while English-speaking users in the United States would have a default language of en-US. Windows Store requirements demand that the primary language be selected from a finite set of choices, so it may be a good idea to search MSDN for *Building the app package* and review the available language selection.

Supported Rotations

Applications in Windows 8 by default are expected to handle the user rotating the display, however it suits them, and still present an effective interface. Some applications will be ill-suited to possible rotations, and the developer can select from a list of the following rotations (illustrated in Figure 23-3), to indicate what is supported by their application:

- Landscape
- Portrait
- Landscape-flipped
- Portrait-flipped

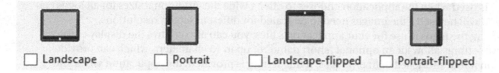

Figure 23-3. *Rotation options*

Tile

Tile settings are configured in the Visual Assets section of the Application UI tab, and they control how Windows displays various tiles shown for your application. These settings primarily revolve around various-sized logos but additionally include settings focused on the application's name display and colors. Figure 23-4 shows the Visual Assets section for editing the primary tile logo's settings.

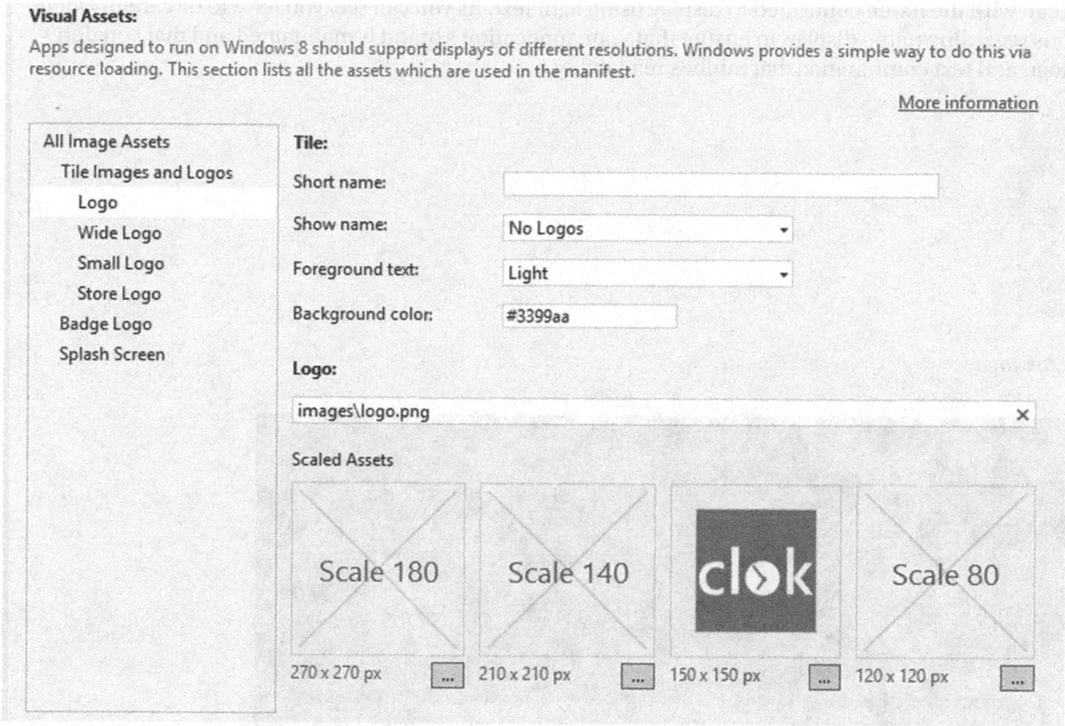

Figure 23-4. *Visual Assets section for the primary tile logo*

The logo image is displayed on the square tile for your application in the Windows Start screen. This image is required because, even if you intend to default to the wide tile on the Start screen, users can choose to display a square tile instead. As with the splash screen image, the logo must be in either PNG or JPG format. It also has specific size requirements, in that it must be 150×150 pixels. In addition to the square tile logo, a 30×30 pixel logo is required for Windows in the following places:

- In the search results on the Start screen

- In the full list of apps in the zoomed-out Start screen

- In the list of searchable apps

A 310×150 pixel logo is used when the application chooses to offer a wide tile. Additional sizes for all logos can optionally be provided and will be used if the images need to be scaled for different screen resolutions.

In addition to specifying the logos to use for your application's tiles, you can also control the display of the application's name. These settings allow for an optional "short name" of up to 13 characters, which can provide a version of the application name shortened to fit onto tiles. If this setting is provided, the application's tiles and notifications will display using this value instead of the application's full name. Additionally, you can control under what circumstances the application's name (or short name, if configured) should be displayed on the application tile. Choices include the following:

- All Logos
- Standard (square) Logo Only
- Wide Logo Only

When the application name is shown, you can additionally choose whether the text should be dark or light. Figure 23-5 shows the primary tile logo for the Clok sample application, and Figure 23-6 demonstrates the Clok tile on the Start screen with the name configured to display using light text. As you can see, you have to be careful when making decisions regarding name display, to ensure that your application's brand is maintained and that you don't end up with a logo and text combination that inhibits readability.

Figure 23-5. *Clok logo*

Figure 23-6. *Clok square tile*

Because the Clok name is actually part of the logo, it is not necessary to show the application name on the tile; however, the News application benefits from having the name included beneath the logo. A good rule of thumb is to make it clear to users what application your tile will launch when they select it, without being unnecessarily redundant. Taking that advice, I will remove the application name from the tile, because the name is part of the logo.

Splash Screen

The first thing a user sees when launching your application is the splash screen that displays as the application performs any necessary initialization. Applications must specify a splash screen image and may additionally specify a background color against which to display the image. As with tile images, this is done in the Visual Assets section of the Application UI tab. Size and format requirements are very specific in that the image must be 620×300 pixels and must be in either PNG or JPG format. Figure 23-7 illustrates a splash screen that is more appropriate for Clok.

Figure 23-7. *Clok splash screen*

■ **Note**   The source code that accompanies this book includes a completed project containing all source code and image files used in this chapter. You can find the code samples for this chapter on the Source Code/Downloads tab of the book's Apress product page (http://www.apress.com/9781430257790).

Notifications

As you learned in Chapter 21, notification mechanisms such as live tiles and toast provide an opportunity for your application to connect with users while they are using other applications. When branding your application, you can indicate whether the application will make use of toast notification. Additionally, you can configure your application to present notifications when the lock screen is active. These notifications can be displayed either with a 24×24 monochrome badge image or as a wide-tile toast notification. If the application is configured to show tile and text in the lock screen notification, then the wide-tile logo must be specified in the tile-branding options.

Publisher Display Name

When you create your developer account to publish applications in the Windows Store, one of the fields you will be required to complete is the publisher display name. This name will be visible to your customers in the store. Additionally, your project must be configured to use the same value. You can set the publisher display name for your project on the Packaging tab of the `package.appxmanifest` file (see Figure 23-8).

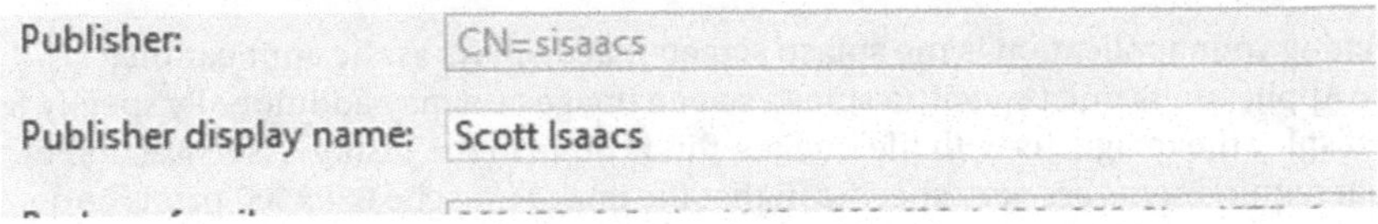

Publisher:	CN=sisaacs
Publisher display name:	Scott Isaacs

Figure 23-8. *Setting the publisher display name*

In addition to being displayed in the Windows Store, this value is also visible in the Settings pane for your application. Compare Figure 23-9, the Settings pane we created in Chapter 9, to the version in Figure 23-10, after updating the Publisher display name field.

Settings

Clok
By sisaacs

Clok Options

Figure 23-9. *Original Settings pane, from Chapter 9*

Settings

Clok
By Scott Isaacs

Clok Options

Figure 23-10. *Updated Settings pane*

Settings Flyouts

One other nice touch you might choose to add to your application is a small icon to the header for each of our `SettingsFlyout` controls. You could add the same icon to each flyout, but, instead, we will add a different, contextual icon to each. Add the highlight code in Listing 23-1 to the `about.html` `SettingsFlyout` control we created in Chapter 9.

Listing 23-1. Adding a Header Icon to Settings Flyouts

```
<div class="win-ui-dark win-header" style="background-color: #000046;">
    <button type="button" class="win-backbutton"
        onclick="WinJS.UI.SettingsFlyout.show()">
    </button>
    <div class="win-label clok-logo">About Clok</div>
    <img src="/images/about-icon.png" style="position: absolute; right: 40px;" />
</div>
```

Run the application and activate the About Clok option in the Settings pane. You'll see that the header now shows an icon to the right of the title (see Figure 23-11).

About Clok
Clok is a sample application being
developed in conjunction with
*Beginning Windows Store Application
Development: HTML and JavaScript
Edition,* an upcoming title about

Figure 23-11. *Updated settings flyout*

To complete this step, add a similar line to options.html, changing the image file name from about-icon.png to options-icon.png.

Navigating the Submission Process

It may seem a little bit out of order to discuss the process for submitting an application before I have described how to create the package that you will submit, but the submission process typically begins by reserving an application name before you even start writing your application code. It resumes when the completed application package is ready for submission. In this section, I will discuss the different steps in the submission process.

The first step to submitting your application is to create a Windows developer account at the Windows Dev Center (http://dev.windows.com) by clicking on the Dashboard menu item (see Figure 23-12). If you already have a developer account, you'll be able to log in to see the dashboard. If you don't have a developer account yet, you'll be able to walk through the steps of creating one before continuing to the dashboard.

Figure 23-12. *Windows Dev Center*

Once you have your profile set up, the process of submitting your application can begin. Figure 23-13 shows the dashboard with my applications that are currently in progress, as well as a link to submit an app. As the name suggests, you should click that link to get started.

My apps

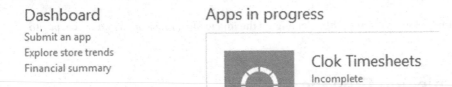

Figure 23-13. *My current apps in progress*

From this point forward, you simply have to work your way through the steps of the submission wizard. Figure 23-14 shows an in-progress submission for Clok.

Clok Timesheets: Release 1

App name
Selling details
Services
Age rating
Cryptography
Packages
Description
Notes to testers

News

Usage/quality data alert
New Windows Dev Center
Get your app noticed
Age ratings
Latest Windows ACK

App name — Complete
You reserved an app name.
You can also reserve another name for your app to use in another language or to change your app's name.
Learn more

Selling details — Complete
Your free app is scheduled for release after it passes certification.
Learn more

Services — 5 minutes
Add push notifications, authenticate users, enable cloud storage, and define in-app offers.
Learn more

Age rating and rating certificates
Windows Store age rating: 12+ Suitable for ages 12 and older
Learn more

Figure 23-14. Clok submission in progress

After each step, which I'll briefly cover next, the checklist in Figure 23-14 will update to indicate which steps are remaining. Note that, although all steps must be completed to submit an application to the Windows Store, it is not required that all steps be completed in order. Case in point, I completed the Age rating step before the Services step.

App Name

The App name portion of the registration is one of the two most important reasons to begin the submission process prior to writing the application. In this step, you are able to specify the name that will identify your application in the Windows Store. Completing the step ensures that the name you have chosen is not already used or reserved and provides you with a one-year reservation on the name, during which time you can complete the application and submit it without worrying about whether somebody used your chosen name.

Selling Details

In the Selling details step, you make selections regarding whether and how you want to make money from your application. This can include such options as making your application freely available, providing the availability of time- or feature-limited trial versions, or making money through advertising or in-app purchases. If you choose to sell your application, you must select a pricing tier for the application, which typically ranges from US$1.49 to US$4.99. For the first US$25,000 in sales, Microsoft keeps a 30 percent store fee, and then the store fee reduces to 20 percent, leaving the developer with 80 percent of the net receipts.

Services

In the Services feature step, you define whether the application should receive push notifications from a server and generate the identity information that will be used by the server to send notifications to your app. In addition to the benefit of reserving a name, obtaining the values generated during this step to include in your application code is the second-biggest reason to start the submission process prior to writing application code.

Age Rating

This step is used to specify the intended or appropriate age of your application's users. The Windows Store does not accept applications containing adult content. Applications that are assigned, or are unrated but merit, PEGI 16 or ESRB MATURE ratings are not allowed. You can upload third-party rating certificates or self-rate by assigning a Windows Store age rating.

Cryptography

In this step, you indicate whether your application makes use of cryptography. This is important, because many nations have import/export restrictions around cryptographic software or software that makes use of cryptographic components, and your selection here will affect the geographic areas in which your application can be made available.

Depending on the cryptography needs of your application—if you use cryptography for purposes other than a few specific things, such as password encryption—you may have to supply an Export Commodity Classification Number (ECCN). If you don't have one, you will be directed to the Bureau of Industry and Security web site for more information on how to find one.

■ **Note**   The cryptography step is as far as you can go in the submission process before packaging your completed application for submission.

Packages

In this step, you upload the completed application package created in Visual Studio. The submission page allows you either to use a Browse button to navigate to the package on your computer or drag and drop the package from a Windows Explorer window to the browser page.

Description

In this step, you will enter a description for your application for each supported language. The description is required and will be used in the marketing of your application, so it is important that it describe what your application does in a way that encourages the prospective user to pick your application over others that may do the same or similar jobs. In this step, you will also be required to submit at least one screenshot for use in promoting your application, copyright information, and support contact information. In addition to these required elements, you may also choose to include the following:

- Descriptive bullet points
- Keywords
- Additional license terms
- Additional screenshots and promotional images
- Links to application web site and privacy policy

Notes to Testers

Each application submitted to the Windows Store will be run through a series of automated tests to ensure conformance to Microsoft's guidelines and will also be manually reviewed for quality and content by Microsoft testers. If these testers need information, such as log-in credentials, in order to successfully exercise the application, you can provide notes for them here. The number of characters in this space is limited, so if your notes require more space than allotted, you could provide a URL to additional instruction. It's important to realize that the testers will likely have a lot of applications to test, so the easier you make the job for them, the better mood they will be in as they test your application.

Final Submission

After entering notes for the testers, you are given the opportunity to review and then finalize your submission. From this point forward, the process is out of your hands. The application will be run through automated tests and reviewed manually before a decision is made as to whether your application is accepted into the store. A dashboard within the developer portal can be used to view the current status of any submission that you have in progress.

■ **Note**   This chapter discusses the submission process but does not provide an in-depth look at the requirements against which your submission will be evaluated. To view the current requirements, search MSDN for the topic *Windows 8 app certification requirements.* This topic covers both technical and content-related requirements for Windows 8 applications.

Packaging Your Application

As described in the previous section, the first step of packaging your application for submission to the Windows Store is to reserve the application name in the store. Once the application name has been created, you can use the Associate App with the Store item in Visual Studio's Store menu (illustrated in Figure 23-15) to associate the current project with the Windows Store metadata for your reservation. This metadata includes the package display name, package name, publisher ID, and publisher display name.

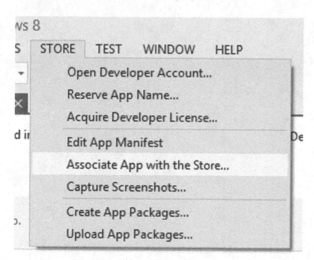

Figure 23-15. *Associating the app with Windows Store*

In addition to associating the project to a reserved application name in the Windows Store, the Store menu also provides a Capture Screenshots option, which launches your application in the simulator I discussed in Chapter 9 and includes its own screen capture tool. This is invoked using the camera icon shown in Figure 23-16. At least one screenshot must be captured for submission, and the images will be used in the Windows Store as well as any additional material Microsoft uses to promote your application.

Figure 23-16. *Camera icon*

Once you've completed the application and are ready to submit it to the Windows Store, the Create App Packages menu item initiates a short wizard that will create the necessary package files for you. Selecting Upload App Packages opens a web browser window to the developer portal and allows you to continue the application submission process at the Packages step, at which point you will upload the package you have created.

Conclusion

In this chapter, you learned how to communicate your application's unique brand and about the process for reserving names and submitting applications to be made available on the Windows Store. If you have an application to share with the world, you should open a developer account, reserve your name, and start using your skills to create the next great app.

Index